BLACK ACCESS

BLACK ACCESS
A Bibliography of Afro-American Bibliographies

Compiled by RICHARD NEWMAN

GREENWOOD PRESS
Westport, Connecticut · London, England

Library of Congress Cataloging in Publication Data

Newman, Richard.
  Black access.

  Bibliography: p.
  Includes indexes.
  1. Bibliography—Bibliography—Afro-Americans.
2. Afro-Americans—Bibliography.   I. Title.
Z1361.N39N578   1984   016.016973′0496073   83-8537
[E185]
ISBN 0-313-23282-2 (lib. bdg.)

Library of Congress Catalog Card Number: 83-8537
ISBN: 0-313-23282-2

First published in 1984

Greenwood Press
A division of Congressional Information Service, Inc.
88 Post Road West
Westport, Connecticut 06881

Printed in the United States of America

10 9 8 7 6 5 4 3 2 1

For Betty K. Gubert

CONTENTS

PREFACE

The first bibliography of black bibliographies was compiled by W.E.B. Du Bois as part of *A Selected Bibliography of the Negro American: a compilation made under the direction of Atlanta University; together with the proceedings of the Tenth Conference for the Study of the Negro Problem, held at Atlanta University, on May 30, 1905.* This bibliography of bibliographies consisted of twenty-six items and served as an introduction to a major Afro-American biliography, a booklet of seventy-one pages, the largest ever compiled up to that time.[1] Five of the bibliographies listed had appeared in previous Atlanta University conference publications, four were bibliographies in the Johns Hopkins University series of studies of slavery in the various states; in fact, all but four were appendices to monographs.

Given the recent proliferation of bibliographies on Afro-American subjects, I thought a compilation of them would be useful. I was unsure, however, if enough existed to constitute a book; I said if I could locate five hundred, that would be an acceptable minimum for a book-length manuscript. I have now collected over three thousand Afro-American bibliographies. New ones continue to be published and—it happens so regularly I am no longer surprised—I keep coming across older ones I have missed.

At the beginning I had several decisions to make. I decided to include slavery and Reconstruction, but to exclude the Civil War. I also decided to exclude bibliographies on the Caribbean, Latin America, and Africa. Too many of these deal with subjects peripheral to the Afro-American experience: exploration and natural history, for example. There are problems of language and access. Also, good bibliographic control of African material already exists, better in fact than of Afro-Americana.[2] I decided to include Canadian material. A bibliography is included only if it is in some sense "separately published," that is, it has an independent existence as a book, pamphlet, article, or chapter in a book. The effect has been to exclude all bibliographies that are appendices to monographs.

In an earlier version, this chapter was read at the Association for the Study of Afro-American Life and History national meeting held in Philadelphia, Pa., Oct. 30, 1981.

This was a difficult decision since a monograph's bibliography may be the only one on the subject or it may be the best on the subject, better than some that are separately published and thus included. But I felt that for reasons of space it would be impossible to include every bibliography in every monograph. Further, for purposes of my own research it would be impossible to look at every Afro-American book ever written and if a researcher is interested in a subject, he or she can locate relevant monographs easily in a library card catalog and so their bibliographies are therefore readily available.

I decided to include bibliographic articles and essays, but not book reviews of multiple titles, even though the line between these two literary forms is not always clear. I have tried to include every bibliography on black subjects as well as bibliographies on some non-black persons whose life and work has been significant in Afro-American history: Harriet Beecher Stowe, Carl Van Vechten, and Melville Herskovits, for example.

Not only books and articles are included, but other "source" guides of various kinds: indexes, book exhibition catalogs, calendars, checklists, and guides to papers, manuscripts, and archives. I decided to include material on historiography and selected material on Afro-American libraries, bibliophiles, and book collecting. Finally, I decided to exercise my prerogative and include a number of entries simply because I found them interesting.

Since the entries are essentially title-indicative I decided not to annotate them but I have included the number of pages as an indication of their comprehensiveness. The bibliography is arranged as a single alphabetical list by author. To include a chronological index and a detailed subject index with the names of sponsoring organizations and originating libraries were my final decisions. These are all, admittedly, arbitrary decisions, but I believe they are essentially correct.

So I set out to compile *Black Access: A Bibliography of Afro-American Bibliographies.*

Where did I search? First, the standard general reference works like Theodore Besterman's *A World Bibliography of Bibliographies,* and the H. W. Wilson Company's *Readers Guide* and *Library Literature.* Then those general reference sources that deal specifically with Afro-Americana: Monroe Work's 1928 classic *A Bibliography of the Negro in Africa and America*, and what is undoubtedly the most important single resource for the study of black history and culture, the photographic reproduction and publication in book form by G. K. Hall and Co. of the card catalogs of the major black library collections—the Schomburg, Howard, Fisk, and Chicago Union. Then the publishers' catalogs of those firms which over the past few years have issued an impressive list of book-length bibliographies: Gale Research, Garland, Greenwood Press, G. K. Hall, and Scarecrow Press.

I must say a special word about the H. W. Wilson Company's *Bibliographic Index*, since this is a work I consulted in some detail. Issued annually since

1937, the *Index* now examines some 2,600 periodicals and an unspecified number of books for bibliographic material; it is thus the major annual publication devoted to listing bibliography. One learns from hard experience, however, that unless one is willing to come to terms with the idiosyncrasies of the Library of Congress classification system, the *Index* is less than useful. Despite a system of cross-references and see-alsos so elaborate that there are often more of them than actual citations, I read through each volume in order not to miss the Afro-American references that were filed not under Afro-Americans, or blacks, or even Negroes, but under Discrimination in Housing, or perhaps Minorities—Housing, or perhaps even Segregation in Housing, all referring to similar information.

Several earlier bibliographies of black bibliographies were, of course, specially useful to me. One was Charles Henry Rowell's unpublished 1972 Ohio State University doctoral dissertation, *Afro-American Literary Bibliographies: an annotated list of bibliographic guides for the study of Afro-American literature, folklore, and related areas.* While this includes general works of reference which list Afro-Americana, a category I chose not to include, it is an extremely important bibliography. Clara O. Jackson compiled *A Bibliography of Afro-American and Other American Minorities Represented in Library and Library-Related Listings,* published by the American Institute of Marxist Studies in New York in 1970, with a substantial supplement published in 1972. This is especially strong in public library and children's literature. Gail Juris, Margaret Krash, and Ronald Krash compiled an undated *Survey of Bibliographic Activities of U.S. Colleges and Universities* published by the Pius XII Library of St. Louis University in St. Louis, Mo. This is particularly useful for its inclusion of those college libraries that issued lists of their Afro-American holdings in the later 1960s.

The work of a number of bibliographers came into focus as I collected entries: Augusta Baker, who pioneered in creating lists of Afro-American books for children; Robert A. Corrigan who compiled bibliographies on black fiction; Robert F. Ernst on geography; Benjamin F. Smith and Ambrose Caliver on education; Ora Williams on women; William French on poetry; Charlemae Rollins on children's literature; and Lenwood Davis, Casper LeRoy Jordan, Louise Roundtree, Delores Leffall, Alain Locke, Lawrence Reddick, Ann Allen Shockley, Jessie Carney Smith, Daniel T. Williams, and many more. Only Ernest Kaiser through his occasional articles and regular annotated list of recent books in *Freedomways* has the courage to attempt to be comprehensive both in covering all subjects and in resolutely keeping up to date; it is no small accomplishment.

One cannot spend very much time with black bibliographies before coming to appreciate the work of Dorothy Porter, librarian emerita at Howard University, who has contributed more to this field than any other person. Not only because of her impeccable intellectual standards and her passion to preserve the record of the Afro-American past (while others were—and are—indifferent or de-accessioning), but also because she was in touch with the great bibliophiles and collectors—Schomburg, Du Bois, Moorland, Spingarn—her equal will not be seen again. At last count there were thirty Dorothy Porter entries in *Black Access,* each one an important contribution to scholarship. One thinks especially of her *Early American Negro Writings: a bibliographical study with a preliminary checklist of the published writings of American Negroes, 1760–1835,* published in the *Papers* of the Bibliographic Society of America, which is, I would suggest, the most important Afro-American bibliography ever compiled. I am particularly pleased that Dr. Porter agreed to contribute her unpublished essay, "Fifty Years of Collecting," as the introduction to this book.

One of the more pleasant and rewarding parts of this project has been the occasional discovery of an extraordinary piece of research which I had not previously known. One example is Lorenzo Dow Turner's brilliant "Anti-Slavery Sentiment in American Literature" from the *Journal of Negro History* of October 1929. Another is Lowell J. Ragatz's *A Guide for the Study of British Caribbean History, 1763–1834, including the Abolition and Emancipation Movements* published by the United States government in 1932.

One early decision I now regret is the exclusion of dealers' catalogs. Beginning as something of a purist, I did not include them since they are not "true" bibliographies. As I kept coming across these catalogs, however, I increasingly saw how useful and important they are. Several come to mind: Francis P. Harper's *Catalogue of an Unusual Collection of Books and Pamphlets relating to the Rebellion and Slavery* issued in New York in 1894; Maggs Brothers' Catalogue no. 677, *Slavery: The History of the Slave Trade and Its Abolition,* issued in London in 1939; Charles F. Heartman's undated (1947?) *Americana Printed and in Manuscript*; and of course the more contemporary offerings of the University Place Book Shop of New York, Lambeth Books of New York, and McBlain Books of Des Moines, Iowa. Someone should undertake a bibliographic study of dealers' catalogs in Afro-Americana.

In my search for bibliographies I placed a query in *The New York Times Book Review* (July 20, 1980), and while the response was less than expected, a number of people did send entries, particularly Colin Cameron of the University of Wisconsin, an expert on poverty studies.

I found that those black poets and novelists whose books are generally included among modern first editions—Countee Cullen, Langston Hughes, Richard Wright, for example—are well documented in all the literature of book collecting. My suspicion was confirmed, however, that while there is serious bibliographic work in literature, there is not a corresponding interest or sophistication in history or the social sciences. Two exceptions are worth noting. Dwight Smith of Miami University has published two volumes of *Afro-American History: a bibliography*. These bibliographies are in fact abstracts of thousands of Afro-American articles in American and European historical journals that cannot be located in any other way. Also, Randall K. Burkett's *Newsletter of the*

Afro-American Religious History Group of the American Academy of Religion regularly carries bibliographies and bibliographic articles on black religion.

Despite some early reservations, I decided to include discographies of black music and musicians. My initial reservation was that I know nothing about music of any kind, and there is very little communication and exchange between students of music and students of the other academic disciplines that comprise black studies. I read Eileen Southern's *The Music of Black America: a history* not only as an introduction to the field, but because her index solves a real problem: it identifies musicians as black by printing their names in boldface. I thought including discographies would be an interesting experiment, as well as a contribution toward overcoming the separation between those who are knowledgeable about black music and the historians, social scientists, and literature professors who are not. The connection is too seldom made, given music's centrality to the black experience and its place as perhaps the most significant Afro-American cultural contribution. So far as I know, the only person who has combined discographies with more traditional bibliographies is Janet Sims of Howard University in her *Marion Anderson*.

I gathered discographical citations from dealers' catalogs, standard music reference sources, and primarily, the resources of the Music Division of the Performing Arts Research Center of The New York Public Library at Lincoln Center.[3] The archives staff maintains a card file of discographies in periodicals, an extraordinary asset. I was fascinated to discover the fanaticism of jazz and blues devotees, an enthusiasm which, fortunately, manifests itself in discographical compilation and journal publishing as well as record collecting and the exchange of esoteric data. I was especially surprised to discover how many of the great jazz and blues discographers are Europeans: Brian Rust in England, Willem Van Eyle in Holland, and Jorgen Grunnet Jepsen in Denmark, for example. Some European discographical research is now beginning to be available in this country. *Brian Rust's Guide to Discography* is a fine introduction to a field too little known to nonspecialists.

In tracing the early bibliographies of Afro-Americana, it occurred to me that these old, rare, and out-of-print bibliographies are of considerable historic significance and might well be made available again by being reprinted in a single volume. I therefore asked Betty K. Gubert, Head of Reference and Co-operative Services at the Schomburg Center, if she would be interested in identifying, locating, and compiling these bibliographies, and introducing them by writing explanatory notes. She agreed, and *Early Black Bibliographies, 1863–1918* was published in 1982.

The earliest of the nineteen bibliographies she collected is Samuel May, Jr.'s *Catalogue of Anti-Slavery Publications in America* published in the *Proceedings* of the American Anti-Slavery Society, Dec. 3–4, 1863, Philadelphia. Others of special interest are Daniel Murray, *Preliminary List of Books and Pamphlets by Negro Authors for the Paris Exhibition and Library of Congress*, Washington, D.C., 1900; Robert Adger, *A Portion of a Catalogue of Rare Books and Pamphlets . . . upon subjects relating to the past condition of the Colored race and the history of slavery agitation in this country*, Philadelphia, 1894; William Carl Bolivar, *Library of William C. Bolivar*, Philadelphia, 1914; and Arthur A. Schomburg, *Exhibition Catalogue, First Annual Exhibition of Books, Manuscripts, Paintings, Engravings, Sculptures, etc., by the Negro Library Association*, Brooklyn, N.Y., 1918. I have a feeling that, as the black experience continues to be discovered and affirmed, we are at the beginning of a new period of interest in rare Afro-American books and other artifacts of black history. If this intuition is correct, then Gubert's collection of historic bibliographies is a particularly important and significant book as well as an interesting and useful one.

It is my hope that *Black Access* will fill several needs. By listing so many separately published bibliographies, it can serve as a convenient place to find out where to locate information on virtually every aspect of Afro-American life, culture, and history. By attempting to be comprehensive, it can provide access to obscure, specialized, and older bibliographies which might otherwise remain unknown. By cutting across the autonomy of academic disciplines, it can reveal the exciting work being done in diverse fields—folklore, for instance—with which many of us are not familiar. By bringing together nearly all bibliographic work that has been done, it can point out where the gaps are and what still needs to be done. There is no bibliography on black dance, for example, and Alice Adamczyk of the Schomburg Center is now compiling one. There is no bibliography on Afro-American photography, and Deborah Willis-Thomas, also of the Schomburg Center, is compiling a bio-bibliography on black photographers who flourished from 1840 to 1940.

In the seventy-five years since Du Bois's Tenth Atlanta Conference, the number of separately published Afro-American bibliographies has increased from four to over three thousand. This bibliography of bibliographies is now itself data, a subject for analysis, as one is able through it to trace the expansion and the development of Afro-American scholarship in this century. There are several ways in which this collection lends itself to further study. One could examine the number of bibliographies issued, their dates, and their sources as an indication of public interest in Afro-Americana. The dramatic increase in the late 1960s and early 1970s, for example, of bibliographies published by public and academic libraries shows how some American institutions responded to the militant black demands of that period. More subtle are the changing values and perspectives of the society as they are reflected in the changing content of the subject matter of these bibliographies. In other words, the patterns of what is chosen for compilation provide clues about the nature of the society at particular times. Even a cursory examination of these bibliographies suggests that such terms as prejudice, brotherhood, race relations, human relations, democracy, intergroup relations, desegregation, and so on can all be placed in time. I am sure that a number of correlations can be postulated and tested by the inherent data of these bibliographies.

Dorothy Porter is fond of saying that all bibliographies are "working" bibliographies, and that none is ever complete or completed. That is certainly true of this one. Therefore, while I am grateful for the assistance I received, it is more than the usual convention for me to say that I am aware of the limitations and incompleteness of this book and to take responsibility for them upon myself. Despite unnumbered hours of checking there are sins both of omission and commission here, but I will be pleased rather than embarrassed to have them pointed out. Charles Rosen said that *The New Grove Dictionary of Music and Musicians* was such a magnificent achievement that it should be revised without delay. While this is hardly a work of that magnitude, I do hope that it will be perceived as useful enough to deserve improvement.

Notes

1. This is reprinted in Betty K. Gubert, *Early Black Bibliographies, 1863–1918*, New York: Garland Publishing, Inc., 1982, pp. 101–102.

2. Why this is the case is an interesting question. Certainly a major reason is the existence of a strong archives and library committee of the African Studies Association, which has a newsletter, regular meetings, and a network of qualified, experienced, and committed people. There are publications specifically devoted to African bibliography, such as *Africana Journal* (formerly *African Library Journal*) published by Africana Publishing Company, a subsidiary of Holmes and Meier, and the *Current Bibliography of African Affairs* published by the African Bibliographic Center. Also, the Library of Congress indexes African periodical literature from south of the Sahara. Of course there is a multinational interest in Africa, so bibliographic resources are available from other countries, such as the Standing Committee on Library Materials from Africa (SCOLMA) in Great Britain, which publishes a quarterly periodical that includes information on works in progress. Anyone concerned with improving Afro-American bibliographic control might well examine the African model to see what could be profitably adapted.

3. I could not have compiled *Black Access* if I had not had at my disposal the unparalleled resources of the New York Public Library: the music division, the research library at 42d Street, and of course the Schomburg Center. I worked without time off from a 9–5 job, or grant money, or a secretary, but I was able to use the Library evenings, Saturdays, and on my lunch hour, and so complete the research for this project in a little over a year. I have used libraries for nearly fifty years, but I have never experienced the quality of interest, assistance, and service that I consistently received in nearly every department of NYPL.

I also visited a number of other libraries, wrote a great many letters, and made too many phone calls. The overall response, I must say, was mixed. Many researchers were glad to share their knowledge. Many librarians were friendly, responsive, and helpful; a surprising number, however, were indifferent, or uninformed, or even unaware of the public service tradition of their profession.

INTRODUCTION

Fifty Years of Collecting

DOROTHY B. PORTER

In the following pages, I will recall a few rather personal experiences encountered during five decades while developing a university research collection that concerned itself with the history and culture first of Afro-Americans, then with Africans, Afro-Brazilians, Afro-Cubans, Haitians, West Indians, as well as black people in the Spanish-speaking countries of South America.

The acquisition of various types of materials at Howard University was made possible by purchases from book publishers whenever funds were available, exchanges with other collections in libraries, visits to and correspondence with antiquarian booksellers, and gifts from known and unknown friends and private collectors of black materials. The kinds of materials collected included printed books, pamphlets, periodicals and newspapers, scrapbooks of newspaper clippings, sheet music—printed and in manuscript—record and notebooks, letters, diaries and miscellaneous documents, and audio-visual items—filmstrips, tapes, recordings, photographs, prints, artifacts, and sculpture.

In what directions would my life interests have gone (certainly not to teaching school) if I had not been offered in 1920, shortly after graduation, a position on the Howard University Library Staff to develop specifically a collection of literature by and about the Negro? Although Dr. Jesse E. Moorland had presented to Howard University the major part of his private library on the Negro in 1914, there had been no person appointed to the small library staff to be concerned exclusively with not only the Moorland Collection, but also the Lewis Tappan Collection of Anti-Slavery Materials acquired in 1873, and the few black titles and authors scattered throughout the library, cataloged and uncataloged.

While working as a student assistant in the old Carnegie library, little did I realize that I would have an opportunity to acquire a direct knowledge of the heritage of my people as I went about the serious business of organizing, collecting, cataloging, and making available for study the small collection which grew from a few thousand in 1930 to many, many thousand in 1973, when I retired.

I must confess at the onset that when I was appointed to the staff I knew very little about the history and culture of black people. But I soon learned.

My elementary and high school education was spent in a predominantly white environment. I lived in an Irish Catholic neighborhood where my white friends and I always celebrated St. Patrick's Day, not Negro History Week. In my high school graduating class there were six black students out of 250 white students at Montclair, New Jersey, High School. I was accepted and treated well, as I was the piano accompanist for the Junior High School orchestra, the only female and the only black. Sousa's "Stars and Stripes" was a favorite with the director and I can still hear him say, "Stronger left hand, Miss Burnett."

I recall that during my early youth, there were only a few books by or about Afro-Americans in our home. The poetry of Paul Laurence Dunbar was among the books on the book shelves. His poetry was very familiar, as my mother frequently recited his poetry at the Methodist church we attended. I especially remember hearing her recite "When Malindy Sings." Kelly Miller, a famous sociologist whom my father had known while he was a student at Howard University, was on occasion a guest in our home where some of his books and pamphlets were to be found. I also remember being raised up onto my father's shoulders to see Booker T. Washington on one of his speaking tours in the area. I do not remember the exact occasion, but I was told much about him and I believe most black families such as ours possessed his *Up from Slavery*. My personal copy of *Iola Leroy*, the first novel by a black woman, Frances Ellen Watkins Harper, was among my father's library, which included books on general literature and history, encyclopedias, dictionaries, medical textbooks, and histories of medicine, for my father was a physician. *Iola Leroy* is today one of the rare books in my library.

When a child, I often went to our pleasant public library where I especially enjoyed the children's room. But there I avoided *Little Black Sambo, Our Ethiopian Cousins*, and *The Pickaninny Twins*, as well as other similar titles which seemed to be the only ones in those days concerning juvenile Afro-Americans. Thank heavens the picture today has changed.

A number of black, or Negro, as we said in that day, teachers in Washington, D.C., attended Teachers College and Columbia University summer school sessions. In our home in Montclair—a delightful suburb of New York City—some of these teachers stayed for the six or more weeks, while commuting daily to and from New York City. Laura Eliza Wilkes, born in 1871, was one of these teachers. She wrote much of her book, *Missing Pages in American History*, on our porch during her summer visits. Her small booklet of ninety-one pages published in 1919 on "The Services of Negroes in the Early Wars in the United States of America, 1641–1815" is virtually unknown today.

The summer after I graduated from high school, Julia E. Brooks, Assistant Principal and Dean of Women at Dunbar High School, persuaded my mother to let me go to Washington for further education, primarily to learn what was going on among black people. So in the fall of 1923 I found myself enrolled in Miner Normal School, later Miner Teachers College, which is now merged with the University of the District of Columbia. This was the influence exerted on my mother and me by the District of Columbia teachers; however, they did not suggest I attend Howard University.

I will not bore you with my dislikes and loves of Miner Normal School, I will say only that I loved to go into the library and that my best friend was the librarian, Lula Allan, a graduate of Simmons College Library School and a former assistant librarian at Howard University from 1909 to 1920. Miss Allan, realizing my love for books, urged me, upon the receipt of my diploma from Miner Normal School in June 1925, to go to Columbia University for the summer session in library science. That fall Miss Allan went on sick leave from her library position for a year and left me in charge of the library, with the approval of the principal, Dr. Eugene Clarke. This was my first underpaid library job, but a wonderful one. Of course, I continued to study during the summer for the next two or three years, at Columbia University. In the fall of 1926, I enrolled as a full-time student at Howard University with credits from Miner Normal School and Columbia University.

While attending Columbia Summer Library School, I worked as an assistant at the 135th Street Branch Library of the New York Public Library system, from 5:00 P.M. to 9:00 P.M., part-time at the circulation desk and part-time in the Division of Negro Literature, History and Prints, as it was known then. I might add that I commuted from my home in Montclair to Columbia University by way of Hoboken, arriving at Columbia University in the morning for all-day courses and leaving the Countee Cullen Library in Harlem at 9:00 P.M., when it closed, for the trip back to New Jersey. I did not really mind this, in spite of the fact that the subway trains were often crowded. I sometimes read with a book in my left hand while standing, holding on to the overhead strap with my right hand, during the long ride from 135th Street to South Ferry where I took the Lackawanna train to New Jersey. By the time the train arrived at the Montclair depot the stars were usually out. The Milky Way, the big and little dippers, and Orion's belt were all there for my viewing.

Edward Christopher Williams, the most scholarly librarian I have ever known, was the chief librarian at Howard University when I entered it as a student. He also worked during the summer period at the 135th Street Branch Library in the Division of Negro Literature, History, and Prints. His wife, Ethel, was the daughter of Charles Waddell Chesnutt, the well-known black novelist. "E. C.," as everyone called him, was a teacher of romance languages, at Howard University in addition to his library administrative work. He was also a handsome, dapper, and a very likeable man. He introduced me to many works of Negro authorship, as well as to figures like Dante, Queen Victoria, and Benvenuto Cellini. I was not only a student in his Italian class but a student assistant in the library.

During my third summer session at Columbia University and my last week of work at the 135th Street Branch Library, I suddenly looked up one day from the circulation desk where I was working, to the stairway leading up to the

Division of Negro Literature and saw E. C. dashing down the stairway. He rushed up to me and said, "Miss Rose [who was then the librarian of the branch] has just told me she has offered you a position in the Negro Division, but I want you to come to Howard University."

As much as I would have liked to work in New York City, I felt drawn to return to the District of Columbia. Primarily, I suppose, because I had met James A. Porter, the man I later married, who had at that time been appointed an instructor in the Art Department of Howard University.

While a student assistant in the library, I learned about black writers and their works. E. C. Williams met on Wednesday evenings in the library with a few students and faculty to discuss Negro literature, particularly the novels of Charles Waddell Chesnutt. Williams always had on hand, not peanuts or jelly beans, but assorted hard candies, which we nibbled on for some of us had had no dinner. We also read and discussed works by white writers—*God's Step Children* by Gertrude Millin; *Green Thursday* by Julia Peterkin; *Dred* by Harriet Beecher Stowe; and others. While studying at the Library School at Columbia University I began to collect for my personal use the works of Langston Hughes, Countee Cullen, James Weldon Johnson, Claude McKay, and Richard Wright. Many of their works could be found then on the shelves in remainder stores near 125th Street at a much reduced price. Books by black authors were not best sellers in that day.

I would like to go back for a moment to a significant and interesting literary event in my life which occurred in 1925. As a reader of *Survey Graphic* magazine, I was excited about the March 1925 special issue, *Harlem, Mecca of the New Negro*, edited by Alain Leroy Locke, art critic and professor of philosophy at Howard University. I still have in my own library two copies which I bought fifty-one years ago for fifty cents a copy. Garland Publishing, Inc., is reprinting the issue with a new introduction at an approximate cost now of twenty dollars. Among several articles it contained "Enter the New Negro" by Alain Leroy Locke, who was later my philosophy teacher at Howard University. I was one of the three students he gave an "A" grade to in that class, probably because I typed my papers and attached a bibliography to them. Locke prepared for the *Survey Graphic* a well-rounded bibliography, "The Negro in Print: A Selected List of Magazines and Books By and About the Negro." It was helpful to me as Work's monumental bibliography of the Negro did not appear until 1928.

In November of 1925 a local club, The Literature Lovers of Washington, invited Alain Leroy Locke to be its first annual-dinner speaker. On this occasion Locke formally presented his book, *The New Negro*, to the audience, stating that "this is a Negro Renaissance." It was an exciting evening for me. Langston Hughes, the poet, was there and in his charming manner read his poetry and told us about the origin of each poem. This event strongly reinforced my desire to study and collect Negro literature for the Howard library.

My first year as a professional librarian was occupied with learning the general working procedures of the Howard University library. Most of my time was spent cataloging books under the guidance of Emma Murray, daughter-in-law of Daniel Alexander Murray, formerly one of the librarians at the Library of Congress. Cataloging, my major in library school, is a helpful foundation for bibliographical work. Unfortunately, Edward Christopher Williams died on December 24, 1929, only a year after he appointed me to his staff. His death was a great loss to me and to the library profession as a whole.

In the fall of 1930 I was appointed by the Howard University trustees "Librarian in charge of the Negro Collection." This was a challenge; it meant building a special research library for the university. From 1930 to 1931 my initial task was to search the shelves in the general library and withdraw all the books I could identify by and about the Negro for addition to the nucleus of the Moorland Collection. Fortunately, at this time I received a Rosenwald Fellowship that enabled me to return to Columbia University and complete my B.S. and M.S. in library service. My work was completed in 1932. Mollie Dunlap, former librarian of Wilberforce University, and I were the first two black women to obtain the master of science degree in library work. It is a question which one of us was first to receive the degree, but I never bothered to find out.

My required master's essay at Columbia, "Imprints by American Negro Writers, 1760–1835," was my first serious lesson in locating black Americana in various libraries and in bibliographic documentation. This essay with its accompanying checklist of writings was published in the *Papers* of the Bibliographical Society of America in October 1945. Searching for the 292 entries appended to the essay in some 32 libraries, I visited, mainly on the East Coast, provided me with invaluable experience on where, what, and how to collect early Afro-Americana. It necessitated and made possible my acquaintance with collectors, white and black, librarians, curators, and directors of large universities, public libraries, and historical societies.

Arthur Alphonso Schomburg, the well-known bibliophile and collector of works by black authors, was appointed Curator of the Negro Department, The New York Public Library, in 1931, five years after The New York Public Library, with a Carnegie grant, had purchased his private collection for $10,000. My first conversation with Mr. Schomburg, in the fall of 1931, lasted all day—just standing and walking from shelf to shelf, examining copies of the books he so dearly loved, and together, we, mostly he, talked about them.

When he showed me an almanac of Benjamin Banneker, the late eighteenth-century astronomer, he said, "I must find a copy with his portrait." When I prefaced my checklist for my Columbia University essay, a year later in 1932, I knew then of only two copies that had the wood-cut resemblance: one in the New York Historical Society and the other in the American Antiquarian Society. Others did turn up later. The February 1980 issue of the *American Historical Review* reproduced on its cover the Maryland Historical Society's copy of the title page of Benjamin Banneker's *Almanac* for 1795. It contains the wood-cut engraving of Banneker's likeness, which is nothing like the recent portrait of Banneker designed for the commemorative stamp.

On April 4, 1931, Schomburg wrote to me as follows:

My dear Mrs. Porter,

I heard you had been at Boston digging up rare material. Can you tell me, if you located Richard Allen's *Oration on the Abolition of the Slave Trade*. I know it is mentioned in Sabin, the imprint is unknown to me but the date is 1808. Will appreciate very highly your answer.

Very truly yours,

A. A. Schomburg.

Schomburg had confused Richard Allen with Absalom Jones, Allen's contemporary who did publish, in 1808 in Philadelphia, an *Oration on the African Slave Trade*, which I had included in my checklist of imprints by American Negro writers.

In the early 1930's when I first began to collect books it was necessary to write many letters, not only to antiquarian book dealers, but to authors, private collectors of Afro-Americana, and to widows who inherited some books collected as a hobby by their husbands. I suppose I may have been a bit naive when I wrote a letter to W.E.B. Du Bois seeking information from him about early rare imprints written by Afro-Americans. On April 10, 1931, he wrote to me that "If you want to locate these entries physically you will have to visit certain libraries." He then listed all the places I had already been to—such as Howard University, Cornell University, the private library of Arthur A. Schomburg, the Boston Public Library, and others—and finally he said, "You might find some in the Editorial Library of the Crisis, 69 Fifth Avenue." Of course, I had already done this. Not long thereafter, Dr. Du Bois spent several hours one afternoon in my small living room—talking to me while he sipped his favorite French wine, which I had brought back from a trip to France in the summer of 1935. He had brought a friend, Dr. Virginia Alexander, to our home for a portrait sitting. My first husband, James Amos Porter, was painting her portrait. Du Bois later dedicated his *Black Reconstruction* to her, *Ad Virginiam Salvatorem*.

Correspondence between Arthur A. Schomburg, Henry Proctor Slaughter, the Washington book collector, and Arthur Barnett Spingarn was extensive as each sought the other's help and I theirs in locating or exchanging unique items. Almost at the onset of their collecting careers, they all aimed to acquire writings by all of the black authors included in Gregoire's *An Inquiry Concerning the Intellectual and Moral Faculties and Literature of Negroes Followed With an Account of the Life and Works of Fifteen Negroes and Mulattoes, Distinguished in Science, Literature and the Arts* (1810).

This valuable work, which I found at Howard University when I was first appointed to the library staff, acquainted me with the fifteen writers included in it and I, too, sought to acquire their works for our library. While I knew the above mentioned collectors and book lovers, as well as a number of others, my collecting experience and purpose at the university was different from theirs. They acquired and possessed each book with a selfish love. My aim was to acquire rarities, preserve and exhibit them, and make them available for scholars and students.

My association with private collectors, antiquarian book dealers, and researchers was a great learning experience for me. For many years, early in my library career, I was an invited guest at the home of the collector Henry P. Slaughter. Slaughter, who had a collection of 10,000 books, was from Louisville, Kentucky. His seven-course dinners, served with the proper wines, preceded by cocktails, and followed by liqueurs or mint juleps, were held for his friends, visiting writers, and collectors, and lasted several hours. They always afforded much conversation about bookish matters. In those days I was young, but to be in the presence of Zora Neale Hurston, Langston Hughes, James Weldon Johnson, Wendell P. Dabney, Abby Mitchell, and others was a thrilling experience. Henry Slaughter was a good friend of our family. He presented my husband with a number of fine works on art and to me his collection of books about books. He was also my daughter's godfather.

On the invitation of Dr. Rufus Clement, the President of Atlanta University, I spent the month of June 1946 unpacking, organizing, and describing the Henry P. Slaughter Collection, a little fewer than 9,000 items which had been purchased shortly before by Atlanta University. The collection contained many unique items and working with it at Atlanta gave me another learning experience and broadened my knowledge of Afro-Americana. I knew well, however, the Slaughter Collection which was housed on three floors of his home at 1264 Columbia Road, N.W., in Washington. Space does not permit me to describe here his private library. However, with the assistance of a W.P.A. worker, I did record on cards all of the manuscripts, broadsides, and prints in the collection before it went to Atlanta. The card file should still be in the Moorland-Spingarn Research Center. Just a few years ago, I read an advertisement in the *Washington Post* that Bekins Moving and Storage Company was to auction boxes "unseen" of Henry P. Slaughter. This was a shock to me but not really a surprise.

Arthur Barnett Spingarn, the New York lawyer and for fifty years President of the NAACP, was my most helpful mentor from 1932 when I had just entered Columbia University Library School until his death on Dec. 1, 1971. He instructed me in the art of collecting and increased my knowledge of works not only by Afro-Americans, but also by Africans, Afro-Latin Americans, and Caribbean authors. He also discussed on many occasions with me his books by outstanding American, German, Dutch, and English writers and artists. He loved to show me his presentation copies and first editions of such literary personages as Edwin Arlington Robinson, John Galsworthy, Edwin Markham, Carl Sandburg, and others.

Parke-Bernet Galleries sold at auction in 1967, 1968, and in the 1970s rare and autographed copies of many titles from the Arthur B. Spingarn library. I attended the auction of most of the sales and have the catalogs of all of them. Spingarn's black studies material, with the bookplates of the Arthur B. Spingarn Collection of Negro Literature designed by Aaron Douglass, in original bindings and dust jackets, was sold at auction on Friday afternoon, November 6, 1970. I bid on several groups of Caribbean materials but each time was outbid. I did successfully bid on and brought home the last item listed in the catalog—*Nigger Heaven*, by Carl Van Vechten (1926), a first edition, one of 195 numbered copies on rag paper signed by Van Vechten. He had inscribed it "To my Friend Arthur Spingarn."

Arthur B. Spingarn's will, dated and signed on August 29, 1968, bequeathed to Howard University "all my books, pamphlets, manuscripts, music, musical scores written or composed by Negroes and/or relating to the Negro, and all my books written by Abraham Lincoln or written by others relating to him. It is my wish and desire that all of the above shall be added to the Arthur B. Spingarn Collection now in the Library of said Howard University and be classified as a part thereof."

Arthur Spingarn had on many occasions told me that his extensive Lincoln Collection as well as his unique collection of books on African art was to go to Howard University. These books were shelved in single rows on his book shelves; the Lincoln books in his dining room, and the African art books in his large entrance hall. The Abraham Lincoln Collection did not come directly to Howard University after Spingarn's death, but was sent to Parke-Bernet Galleries in New York City. Fortunately, I was able to go to New York and retrieve for Howard the Lincoln books before they went on the auction block.

There was no way for me to have acquired in library school courses, or otherwise, what I learned during many long evenings on visits to number 50 Gramercy Park. Arthur Spingarn seemed never to stop talking—his anecdotes and tall tales concerning his many trips to Europe and England and one to South America in search of books by black authors were priceless gems. He also shared with me many stories about his work experiences involving Langston Hughes, W.E.B. Du Bois, Zora Neale Hurston, and Gertrude Stein. A reading of the locations in Spingarn's library of many titles included in my "Early American Negro Writing" indicates the graciousness and willingness of this great bibliophile to share his vast knowledge and his literary treasures with one librarian.

It was one of the saddest moments in my life to see this friend shortly before his death sitting at one end of his long living room surrounded by empty book shelves, missing also the African sculptures and artifacts which had reposed on top of his bookcases.

Many excellent dealers of black history materials regularly issued catalogs—mimeographed and typed lists of their books, pamphlets, manuscripts, and other items. I consider a number of these catalogs, with well-annotated titles, rare today. It was always a joy for me to educate myself by reading dealers' catalogs and lists—very often these were my bedtime reading. Desirable items were always checked whether or not there were funds to purchase them. Book knowledge thus acquired enabled me to appraise collections or single items when they were offered to the library by individual collectors or booksellers. A comparison of prices for books quoted thirty years ago with those asked recently indicates prices have climbed at a startling rate.

Many acquisition librarians whose duty it is to build book collections seldom have the opportunity to discuss possible purchases with booksellers. Nearly always, they order books from catalogs and publishers' circulars. I always enjoyed visiting the major trade bookmen of Afro-Americana.

Between 1934 and 1943, Charles Egbert Tuttle, bookseller and publisher in Rutland, Vermont, introduced me to hundreds of titles among his hundreds of thousands relating to slavery, black history, and works by black authors. He was more than a salesman. His special knowledge of rare and general books in many fields marked him a scholar-collector. Through him, we at Howard acquired our largest collection of fugitive materials on slavery and black history, and at reasonable prices. Tuttle issued printed catalogs which included on the covers the running title "Tuttle's Literary Miscellany" and an engraving relating to the history of printing or to the subject of the particular catalog. Boxes and boxes of 3x5 slips containing titles of books, pamphlets, and often manuscripts relating to my interests would arrive frequently. I pulled slips with the titles I felt we had money to purchase and returned them along with the boxes to Mr. Tuttle. On many occasions I received books, pamphlets, manuscripts, prints, and documents with a note "no charge" tucked in the package.

I will always remember the warmth and hospitality of Mr. and Mrs. Tuttle's home, with its fireplace where four-foot logs burned night and day on a bed of wood ashes. On two occasions, I went to Vermont and spent a few days, each time selecting from the shelves the books and pamphlets I wanted for our library. At that time Tuttle's book stock was kept in a large section he had built adjoining his home. Tuttle's historic New-England home was next door to the house where Samuel Williams lived, a contemporary of Lemuel Haynes, the popular Rutland nineteenth-century Negro minister of a white Congregation. Williams had charge of the East Parish and Haynes served the West Parish. We are indebted to Richard Newman for recently bringing to our attention the life and sermons of Lemuel Haynes (1753–1833).

While visiting in Rutland, I enjoyed roaming around the old cemeteries with Mr. Tuttle whenever we took a rest period. Charles Egbert Tuttle died at the age of sixty-five on March 31, 1943. His son Charles E. Tuttle, Jr. still continues, with a branch office in Tokyo, the book and publishing business which his great-grandfather established in Rutland in 1832.

When Walter Goldwater, proprietor of the University Place Book Shop in New York City whose specialty is Afro-Americana, Africana, and Caribbean books, put on his letterhead "Established in 1932," one of his colleagues scoffed at him saying "You put that down the way Sotheby's says Established in 1741." I do not remember the first time I visited Goldwater's shop, but I will always be able to visualize the piles of books on tables, on the floor, and stuffed on shelves around the front room of his shop.

Goldwater printed the first catalog of his books on the Negro in 1932. His father had been a friend of Arthur Spingarn and he knew he collected books by black writers. Spingarn was a great help to Goldwater, identifying for him many authors of Negro extraction, even those with "1/16 percent Negro blood." Goldwater numbered among his friends Richard B. Moore, who had a book shop in Harlem which I visited while a student at Columbia University, C.L.R. James, George Padmore, Claude McKay, and Arthur Schomburg. Accession books in the Moorland-Spingarn Research Center record the large numbers of books by black authors purchased from the University Place Book Shop.

When Charles F. Heartman published his catalog "Americana" in 1947 in Hattiesburg, Mississippi, containing 2282 titles—annotated items— books, pamphlets, broadsides, manuscripts, and artifacts (including a Staffordshire figurine depicting Uncle Tom and Little Eva, and item no. 2174, Phillis Wheatley's 1773 London edition of *Poems on Various Subjects, Religious and Moral* bound in "Negro Skin"), I learned about many items I had no idea existed. The catalog sold for $1.00 and had an "emphasis on the subject of slavery." As I recall, Heartman wished to sell the collection as a whole and he felt it would be difficult to dispose of if he put "Negro" in the title of the catalog.

I believe Texas Southern University at Houston, Texas, purchased most of the Heartman collection of some 12,000 items—"books, pamphlets, newspapers, music scores, clippings, broadsides, and various curios."

Heartman, a bibliographer and dealer-collector issued his first news sheet, "The Charles F. Heartman Collection of Materials Relating to Negro Culture, Printed and in Manuscript," in January 1945. The seven numbers of his news sheet in my personal library contain lengthy descriptions for titles listed. News sheet no. 2, February 1945, reproduced the entire *Laws of the African Society, Instituted at Boston, Anno Domino, 1796.* Heartman published some thirty-eight bibliographies from his book farm in Hattiesburg. We are grateful to him for his publications on Phillis Wheatley and Jupiter Hammon, the first black poet.

Acquiring black materials for Howard University was a great collecting experience. I traveled to New York City and spent full days at Stechert-Hafner selecting foreign titles in Portuguese, French, German, and in African languages. Collecting books, periodicals, and photographic items from the Caribbean, South America, Europe, England, and Africa, where I visited, was always a learning experience, but also I found out which dealers were reliable and which not so reliable. Both Henry Slaughter and Arthur Spingarn requested that I look for certain "wants " each had. I remember going into Kegan Paul's while in London in the 1950s and finding a book case in a corner with a number of books by black authors which I immediately said I wanted to buy. I was told, "Those are for a special customer." I remarked, "For Arthur Spingarn?" When the answer was "Yes", I said, "Oh, that's fine."

In recent years, some of the collectors, in addition to those already mentioned, with whom I have had good relations as friends were Alain Leroy Locke, art critic and professor of philosophy at Howard University, who willed his extensive collection of books, pamphlets, periodicals, manuscripts, and photographs to Howard University; the late Glenn Carrington, formerly of Brooklyn, part of whose collection is at Howard; Charles Leroy Blockson of Norriston, Pennsylvania, whose remarkable exhibition "Of Color, Humanities and Statehood: The Black Experience in Pennsylvania over Three Centuries" opened at The Afro-American Historical and Cultural Museum in Philadelphia in October 1981; Clarence Holte, of New York City; and several young physicians who have accumulated not only books by blacks but African art.

Over the years there were many individuals with whom I became acquainted who had carefully preserved papers and photographs which documented their family histories. After some thought, they seemed grateful that our repository wished to acquire and preserve their precious documents for the use of posterity. I hope some day to tell the story of how some of these collections were acquired, such as those of John W. Cromwell, Archibald and Francis Grimké, Leigh Whipper, George William Cook, Blanch Kelso Bruce, Thomas Montgomery Gregory, Owen Dodson, Frederick Douglass, Anna Cooper, Jacob C. White, Leon Gardiner, and others.

Competition is always healthy, it has been said. On more than one occasion I competed with representatives of both the Library of Congress and the Schomburg Library for the acquisition of collections. Mary Church Terrell many years ago requested my aid in organizing her personal papers. I knew her very well and had indexed her book *A Colored Woman in a White World*, published in 1940. With the assistance of a W.P.A. worker, I arranged her speeches, letters, pamphlets, brochures, programs, and so on, and placed them in filing cabinets. She did give me from time to time a duplicate pamphlet.

Each time I visited her, she emphasized that she wanted her entire collection to go to the Library of Congress. After her death a staff member or messenger from the Library of Congress did come to her home for the Mary Church Terrell papers. The person did not scan some closets or the basement floor, however, and the six boxes of Terrell papers at Howard University, comprising some 298 items dating from 1888 to 1954, I swept off the basement floor into my shopping bags. After other salvage excursions to other basements and attics, I became known as the "bag lady."

When attending Howard University, I lived across the street from the home of the late Daniel Murray, whose "Collection of Colored Authors" is in the Library of Congress. I frequently visited his wife, Anna, before her death. She wanted Howard to purchase the Murray Collection of books, periodicals, photographs, prints, and manuscript cards which indexed the data he hoped to use in the Murray Encyclopedia. She wanted $50,000 for a collection she hardly wanted me to see. Giving away any part of the collection was unheard of. I tried unsuccessfully to persuade her to give to the University the set of *Harper's Illustrated Magazine*. After their eldest son, George Murray, who lived in the home at 928 S Street, N.W., died, the property was cleared out and put up for sale. (I still tried to acquire the collection from the only other living son, but had no success.) A real estate agent, a friend of mine, called me by telephone one very rainy day and said that there were some papers scattered around in the house and asked if I would be interested in going into the home to get whatever I wanted. He would have "to leave me there," he said and told me to "just pull the door shut when I left." There was nothing pleasant about being let alone in a large, three-story house which was empty except for trash and an old mattress where some mice had made their home. While the rain pounded on the roof I cautiously climbed to the top floor. I found there a large box containing many duplicate copies of Will W. Allen's *Life of Benjamin Banneker, The Afro-American Astronomer*, written with the assistance of Daniel Murray and published in 1921. I put as many as I could in one shopping bag and left the rest (in those days I had no help to take with me.) In the dining room on the window-sills and floor, I found photographs, programs, and post cards. In the fireplace in the living room, there were papers partially burned. Others were in good condition. More than one hundred items—legal documents, correspondence, reports, periodicals, newspaper clippings—all dating from 1872 to 1937 were salvaged. My unsuccessful efforts of many years to acquire the Murray Collection is a story for another time. Recently, the Collection has been put on microfilm by the Wisconsin State Historical Society which acquired it.

A collection I was able to save just before it was on its way to the trash dump was the papers of the local, or D.C., branch of the NAACP. I received a telephone call one day informing me that the papers were to be discarded and that there were several wooden vertical files. My bags were of no use here. I was able to get the university truck to pick them up for me. When my preliminary container list was made, it consisted of 984 folders in 53 manuscript boxes. I have often wondered what has happened to local NAACP files in other cities.

My joys of collecting were and still are many. Collecting was always a personal affair with me. Whenever I traveled to Europe, England, Ireland, Scotland, Africa, the Caribbean, and Latin America, I always selected books and made arrangements for them to be sent to the Moorland-Spingarn Collection. For myself, I picked up a few posters, stamps, prints, money (bills beautifully engraved with African portraits), and small artifacts.

Too much of our heritage, until recently, has been lost because there were not enough collectors among us. It is not too late to start today. Richard Newman's bibliography, *Black Access*, indicates many rich resources in the field of black bibliography. As we all know, no bibliography is ever completed, but this one should be the standard for a good many years to come.

BLACK ACCESS

THE BIBLIOGRAPHY

A

A1. Aasland, Benny H. "Glimtar av en unik hertig [Edward (Duke) Ellington]." *Orkester journalen* 42 (July/Aug. 1974), 8+.

A2. Aasland, Benny H. *The "Wax Works" of [Edward] Duke Ellington: an up-to-date discography.* Stockholm, Sweden: Foliotryck, 1954, 173 pp.

A3. Aasland, Benny H. *The "Wax Works" of [Edward] Duke Ellington: the 6th March 1940–30 July 1942 RCA Victor Period.* Jarfalla, Sweden: Dems, c. 1978, 81 pp.

A4. Abajian, James de T. *Blacks and Their Contribution to the American West: a bibliography and union list of library holdings through 1970.* For the Friends of the San Francisco Public Library in cooperation with the American Library Association. Boston, Mass.: G.K. Hall, 1974, 488 pp.

A5. Abajian, James de T. *Blacks in Selected Newspapers, Censuses and Other Sources: an index to names and subjects.* Boston, Mass.: G.K. Hall, 1977, 3 vols.

A6. *Abolition and Emancipation Literature.* Annual Report of the American Historical Association for the year 1930. Vol. 3. Washington, D.C.: American Historical Association, 1932, pp. 405–572.

A7. *About Black Americans.* Philadelphia, Pa.: Free Library of Philadelphia, Office of Work with Children, 1970.

A8. *About 100 Books: gateway to better group understandings.* New York: American Jewish Committee, Institute of Human Relations.

* Abrahams, Roger D. See S299.

A9. "Access to Black Literature." *American Libraries* 4 (Feb. 1973), 90.

A10. Ackerman, P. "Mother Lode in the Archives [Blues]." *Billboard* 79 (June 24, 1967), 71.

A11. *Acquisitions in Black Material.* Norfolk, Va.: Norfolk Public Library, Minority Materials Committee, 1974, 27 pp.

A12. Adair, Thelma. "Choices, Choices, Choices! Peak Experiences from the Afro-American Heritage." *Childhood Education* 46 (Apr. 1970), 355–64.

A13. Adams, John R. "Harriet Beecher Stowe." *American Literary Realism* 2 (Summer 1969), 160–4.

A14. Addo, Linda D. *The Negro in American History: a selected bibliography*. Greensboro, N.C.: Greensboro Tri-College Consortium, 1970, 49 pp.

A15. Adger, Robert M. *Catalogue of Rare Books on Slavery and Negro Authors on Science, History, Poetry, Religion, Biography, etc*. Philadelphia, Pa.: Privately printed, 1904, 14 pp. Reprinted in Wendy Ball and Tony Martin. *Rare Afro-Americana: a reconstruction of the Adger Library*. Boston, Mass.: G.K. Hall, 1981, pp.57–71. Reprinted in Betty Kaplan Gubert. *Early Black Bibliographies, 1863–1918*. New York: Garland, 1982, pp.75–89.

A16. Adger, Robert M. *A Portion of a Catalogue of Rare Books and Pamphlets, Collected by R.M. Adger, Philadelphia, Upon Subjects Relating to the Past Condition of the Colored Race and the Slavery Agitation in this Country*. Philadelphia, Pa.: Privately printed, 1894, 4 pp. Reprinted in Betty Kaplan Gubert. *Early Black Bibliographies, 1863–1918*. New York: Garland, 1982, pp. 67–74.

A17. Adinarayaniah, S.P. "Research in Colour Prejudice." *British Journal of Psychology* 31 (Jan. 1941), 228–9.

A18. Adler, Patricia. *Ethnic and Political Minorities in the Los Angeles Area: a bibliography of doctoral dissertations and master's theses at the University of Southern California, 1912–1969*. Los Angeles, Cal.: University of Southern California, Department of History, 1970, 25 pp.

A19. Aery, William A. "Negro Problems and Progress." *Survey* 41:11 (Dec. 14, 1918), 357.

A20. *African and Afro-American Arts*. Houston, Tex.: Houston Public Library, Fine Arts Department, 120 pp. A 10 pp. supplement was issued in 1972, and a 12 pp. supplement in 1974.

A21. "African and Other Source Material of the Schomburg Collection—a Selection of Typical Items." *Branch Library Book News—Supplement to the Bulletin of The New York Public Library* 12:5 (May 1935), 92–3.

A22. *Africans in the U.S., 1961–1962: a selected current reading list based on articles listed in our catalogs*. Cumulated Reading List Series vol. 2, no. 4 Washington, D.C.: African Bibliographic Center, 1964, 4 pp.

A23. *Afro-American and Mexican-American Bibliography: a selected guide to materials in the California State Polytechnic College Library*. San Luis Obispo, Cal.: California State Polytechnic College, Dexter Memorial Library, 1969, 155 pp.

A24. "Afro-American Bibliography." *The Instructor* 78 (Mar. 1969), 101 + .

A25. *Afro-American Culture and History*. Cleveland, Ohio: Cleveland Public Library, 1967.

A26. "Afro-American History Week." *Read, See and Hear* 24:5 (Feb. 7, 1975), 2 pp. A supplement appeared in vol. 25:2 (Feb. 2, 1976).

A27. *The Afro-American in Books for Children*. Washington, D.C.: District of Columbia Public Library, Children's Service, 1974, 71 pp. This is a revised edition of *The Negro in Books for Children*, 32 pp., published by the library in 1968. Published by Readers Advisory Service in 1976.

A28. *Afro-American Resources of the El Camino College Library*. El Camino, Cal.: El Camino College Library, 1969, 55 pp.

A29. "Afro-American Studies: a bibliographic key for 1976."*In* Herman L. Totten. *Bibliographic Control of Afro-American Literature*, Vol. 1. Eugene, Ore.: University of Oregon, School of Librarianship, 1976, pp. 122–59.

A30. *Afro-American Studies: a guide to resources in the Harvard University Library*. Preliminary edition. Cambridge, Mass.: Harvard University, Houghton Library, 1969, 21 pp. An edition of 32 pp. was issued in 1976.

A31. *Afro-Americana, 1553–1906: author catalog of the Library Company of Philadelphia and the Historical Society of Pennsylvania*. Boston, Mass.: G.K. Hall, 1973, 714 pp.

A32. *Afro-Americans*. Sacramento, Cal.: American River College Library, 1969, 18 pp.

A33. *Afroamericans and Homosexuality*. Bloomington, Ind.: Institute for Sex Research, 1976, 1 p.

A34. *Afro-Americans in Literature*. Tacoma, Wash.: Tacoma Public Library.

A35. *Afro-Americans in the U.S.: a selected bibliography*. Pasadena, Cal.: Pasadena Public Library, 1939, 6 pp.

A36. Agostinelli, Anthony J. *The Newport Jazz Festival, Rhode Island, 1954–1971: a bibliography, discography and filmography*. Providence, R.I.: Author, 1977, 64 pp.

* Ahler-Buuk, Margot. See B227.

A37. Ahlström, T. "Jazz-diskoteket: [Ferdinand] Jelly Roll Morton." *Musikrevy* 27:5 (1972), 314–8.

* Aiken, Richard S. See H66.

A38. Airall, Jacqueline, Ernestine Snead, and Patricia White. "Finding Afro-American Materials in the Michigan State University Libraries." RAS 11. *Readers Advisory Service* 1 (1974), 12 pp.

A39. Akeroyd, Richard. *Bibliographies for Black Studies*. Storrs, Conn.: University of Connecticut, Wilbur Cross Library, 1970.

A40. Akeroyd, Richard. *Black Voices of the Sixties*. Wilbur Cross Library Booklist no. 1. Storrs, Conn.: University of Connecticut, Library Committee on Black Studies, 1970, 8 pp.

A41. Akeroyd, Richard. *Wilbur Cross Library Black Studies Guide*. Storrs, Conn.: University of Connecticut, Wilbur Cross Library.

* Albrecht, Otto E. See W56A.
* Alden, Barbara. See F36.
* Alexander, Albert A. See B305.
A42. Alexander, Jean A. "Black Literature for the 'Culturally Deprived' Curriculum: who are the losers?" *Negro American Literature Forum* 4 (Fall 1970), 96–103.
* Alexander, Mary Linse. See A98.
* Alexander, S. Kern. See S167.
A43. *All Winds Blow Free: the American Negro in books for boys and girls, a selected list.* Pittsburgh, Pa.: Carnegie Library, 1968, 12 pp. A publication of 22 pp. with the same title was issued in 1970.
A44. Allard, Ursula. *The Black Man: a bibliography.* St. Paul, Minn.: College of St. Thomas, O'Shaughnessy Library.
A45. Allee, Mrs. M.H. "Books Negro Children Like." *Horn Book* 14 (Mar.-Apr. 1938), 81–7.
A46. Allen, Daniel. *Bibliography of Discographies.* Vol. 2, Jazz. New York: R.R. Bowker Co., 1981, 200 pp.
A47. Allen, E.H. "Selected Annotated Bibliography on the Health Education of the Negro." *Journal of Negro Education* 6 (July 1937), 578–87.
* Allen, Kathleen S. See C118.
A48. Allen, Richard B. "The Archive of New Orleans Jazz." *Yearbook of American Music Research* 3 (1968), 141–7.
A49. Allen, Walter C. "A Discography of [Joseph] King Oliver's 1923 Okeh Recordings." *Journal of Jazz Studies* 3 (Spring 1976), 46.
A50. Allen, Walter C. "Hendersonia [Fletcher Henderson]." *Record Research* 55 (Sept. 1963), 14; 56 (Nov. 1963), 12.
A51. Allen, Walter C. *Hendersonia: the music of Fletcher Henderson and his musicians, a bio-discography.* Stanhope, N.J.: Jazz Monographs, 1973, 651 pp.
A52. Allen, Walter C. *King Joe Oliver.* Stanhope, N.J.: Privately printed, 1955, 1956, 224 pp. London: Sedgwick and Jackson, 1959.
A53. Allen, Walter C. *Studies in Jazz Discography I.* Procedings of the First and Second Annual Conference on Discographical Research, 1968–1969, and of the Conference on the Preservation and Extension of the Jazz Heritage, 1969. New Brunswick, N.J.: Rutgers, the State University, Institute of Jazz Studies, 1971, 112 pp. Reprinted by Greenwood.
A54. Allport, Gordon W. "Books [Race]." *Scientific American* 182 (June 1950), 56–8.
A55. "American and Foreign Books and Articles Bearing on the Negro." *Journal of Negro History* 20 (Jan. 1935), 100–10.
A56. *The American Civil Liberties Union Records and Publications, 1917–1975: a guide to the microfilm collection.* Glen Rock, N.J.: Microfilming Corporation of America, 1977.
A57. *The American Colonization Society: a register of its records in the Li-*

brary of Congress. Washington, D.C.: Library of Congress, Manuscript Division, 1979, 34 pp.

A58. Not used.

A59. *American Missionary Association Archives in Fisk University Library.* Nashville, Tenn.: Fisk University, 1947, 11 pp.

A60. *The American Negro: a selected bibliography.* Berkeley, Cal.: Berkeley Public Library, 1966.

A61. *The American Negro and African Studies: a bibliography on the special collections in Carnegie Library, Livingstone College.* Salisbury, N.C.: Livingstone College, Carnegie Library, 1968.

A62. *The American Negro: history and achievement.* Akron, Ohio: Akron Public Library, 1968, 12 pp.

A63. *The American Negro in Contemporary Society: an annotated booklist.* Berkeley, Cal.: California Library Association, Young Adult Librarians' Round Table, 1966, 26 pp.

A64. "American Negro Music." *International Review of Missions* 15 (1926), 748–53.

A65. *The American Negro: some recent titles for elementary schools.* Oklahoma City, Ok.: Oklahoma Department of Education, Library Resources Division, 1971, 10 pp.

A66. *The American Negro: some recommended titles for secondary schools.* Oklahoma City, Ok.: Oklahoma Department of Education, Library Resources Division, 1971, 23 pp.

A67. *The American Negro Speaks to Young Americans.* Providence, R.I.: Providence Public Library.

A68. *American Negro Writing.* Akron, Ohio: Akron Public Library, 8 pp.

A69. *Americans All: an intercultural bibliography.* New York: Bank Street College of Education, Curriculum, Consultation Service.

* Amin, Karima. See S238.

A70. Amoroso, Doreen. *List of Materials for Ethnic Studies Laboratory.* Tacoma, Wash.: Tacoma Community College, Pearl A. Wanamaker Library.

A71. Amos, Preston E. *One Hundred Years of Freedom: a selected bibliography of books about the American Negro.* Washington, D.C.: Association for the Study of Negro Life and History, 1963, 53 pp.

A72. *Analytical Guide and Indexes to "Alexander's Magazine," 1905–1909.* Rose Bibliography Project, George Washington University. Westport, Conn.: Greenwood Publishing, 1974, 204 pp.

A73. *Analytical Guide and Indexes to "The Colored American Magazine," 1900–1909.* Rose Bibliography Project, George Washington University. Westport, Conn.: Greenwood Publishing, 1974, 2 vols.

A74. *Analytical Guide and Indexes to "The Crisis: a record of the darker races," 1910–1960.* Rose Bibliography Project, George Washington University. Westport, Conn.: Greenwood Publishing, 1975, 3 vols.

A75. *Analytical Guide and Indexes to "The Voice of the Negro," 1904–1907.* Rose Bibliography Project, George Washington University. Westport, Conn.: Greenwood Publishing, 1974, 451 pp.

A76. Anders, P.A. "Good Reading for Disadvantaged Youth." *Southeast Librarian* 18 (Winter 1968), 257–68.

A77. Anderson, Barbara. *Afro-American Master's Theses* [Written at San Francisco State College through 1969]. San Francisco, Cal.: San Francisco State College.

A78. Anderson, Dorothy W., et al. *Recent Notable Books: a selective bibliography in honor of Dorothy Burnett Porter.* Washington, D.C.: Howard University, Moorland-Spingarn Research Center, 1974, 15 pp.

A79. Anderson, Edith F. *Book List.* Dayton, Ohio: Sinclair Community College, Learning Resource Center.

A80. Anderson, John Parker. Description of Harriet Beecher Stowe exhibit. *In* Karte Brannon Knight. *History of the Work of Connecticut Women at the World's Columbian Exposition, Chicago 1893.* Hartford, Conn.: Case, Longwood and Brainard, 1898, pp. 107–23.

A81. Anderson, Marian Posey. *Books to Grow On: helping the very young explore their world and its people.* New York: American Jewish Committee, 1961, 40 pp.

A82. Andrew, Ann. *Children's Books for and about Blacks.* Ypsilanti, Mich.: Eastern Michigan University Library, 15 pp.

A83. Andrews, Regina M. *Intergroup Relations in the U.S.: a compilation of some materials and service organizations.* New York: Human Relations Committee, National Council of Women of the U.S., 1956, 47 pp. An expanded edition of 1959 contains 74 pp.

A84. Andrews, William L. "Charles W. Chesnutt: an essay in bibliography." *Resources for American Literary Study* 6 (Spring 1976), 3–22.

A85. Andrews, William L. "The Works of Charles W. Chesnutt: a checklist." *Bulletin of Bibliography* 33:1 (Jan. 1976). 45 + .

A86. *Annotated Bibliography: Afro-American, Hispano and Amerind (Aboriginal Indian and Eskimo).* Denver, Col.: Colorado Department of Education, Human Relations Task Force Committee, 1969, 45 pp.

A87. *Annotated Bibliography, 1920–1950 [by and about] Cedric Dover,* 14 pp.

A88. *Annotated Bibliography of Materials Relevant to Racial Occupancy Patterns in Public Housing Projects,* 6 pp.

A89. "Annotations of Outstanding Books and Articles Dealing with the Problems of Negroes and Other Minority Groups in a World at War." *Fisk Comment* 3 (Feb. 1943), 1–3.

A90. Anthony, Elizabeth, V., and Gladys B. Sheppard. *Bookshelf of Negro History.* Baltimore, Md.: Roebuck, 1944, 11 pp.

A91. Anthony, Ernestine. *The Negro in the North during Wartime: select bibliography,* 6 pp.

A92. Anthony, M.E. "Selected Bibliography." *Journal of Educational Sociology* 17 (Jan. 1944), 312–20.

A93. [Antoine "Fats" Domino Discography]. *Record Exchanger* 1:3 (June 1970), 10–1. A list of additions appeared in 1:4 (Aug.-Sept. 1970), 22.

A94. Aptheker, Herbert. *Annotated Bibliography of the Published Writings of W.E.B. Du Bois*. Millwood, N.Y.: Kraus-Thompson Org., 1973, 626 pp.

A95. Aptheker, Herbert. "Some Unpublished Writings of W.E.B. Du Bois." *Freedomways* 5 (Winter 1965), 103–28.

A96. Aptheker, Herbert. "The W.E.B. DuBois Papers." *Political Affairs* 45:3 (Mar. 1966), 36–45.

A97. Arata, Esther Spring, and Nicholas John Rotoli. *Black American Playwrights, 1800 to the Present: a bibliography*. Metuchen, N.J.: Scarecrow Press, 1976, 302 pp.

A98. Arata, Esther Spring, Marlene J. Erickson, Sandra Dewitz, and Mary Linse Alexander. *More Black American Playwrights: a bibliography*. Metuchen, N.J.: Scarecrow Press, 1978, 335 pp.

* Arata, Esther Spring. See also R148.

A99. Archer, Jill A. *Black American Folklore: a bibliography*. Bloomington, Ind.: Indiana University Library, Circulation Department, 1968.

* Archer, Jill A. See also S290.

A100. Archibald, Helen A. *Negro History and Culture: selected material for use with children*. Chicago City Missionary Society, 1965.

* Arenstein, Misha. See H97.

A101. Armagnac, Perry, and Carl A. Kendoziora, Jr. "Perfect Dance and Race Catalog (1922–1930)." *Record Research* 51–2 (May-June 1963), 48 pp. (whole issue).

A102. Armstrong, Douglas, and Marian Dworaczek. *A Selected Bibliography on Human and Civil Rights*. Toronto, Ont.: Ontario Ministry of Labour, Research Library, 1973, 20 pp.

A103. "Arna Bontemps: Dedication and Bibliography." *Black World* 20:11 (Sept. 1971), 78–9.

* Arnaud, Gerald. See R147.

A104. Arnold, A.L. "Books Written for Children by Black Authors Available in the Lewis Carroll Room of the Cleveland Public Library: an annotated bibliography." Research paper, Kent State University, 1975, 48 pp.

A105. *Art Slide Catalogue 1974–1975*. Mobile, Ala.: University of Southern Alabama, College of Arts and Sciences. Ethnic American Art Slide Library, 1975, 134 pp. Supplements an earlier publication in 1971–1972. A list of additions was published in 1976.

A106. *The Arthur B. Spingarn Collection of Negro Authors* Washington, D.C.: Howard University, Carnegie Library, Moorland Foundation, 1948, 12 pp.

A107. [(Arthur James) Zutty Singleton Discography]. *Record Research* 2:3 (July–Aug. 1956), 13.

A107A. Asher, Robert. "Documents of the Race Riot of East St. Louis."

Journal of the Illinois State Historical Society 65:8 (Autumn 1972), 327–36.

A108. Ashford, F.G., Catherine Long, and Robert Thompson. *Listing of All Books by and about the Negro in the Inman E. Page Library*. Jefferson City, Mo.: Lincoln University, Inman E. Page Library.

A109. Ashton, Jean W. *Harriet Beecher Stowe: a reference guide*. Boston, Mass.: G.K. Hall, 1977, 168 pp.

A110. "Aspects of Integration." *Library Journal* 80 (Apr. 15, 1955), 837–9.

A111. Atkins, H.D., and M.R. Bowles. *A Selected Bibliography of Subject Bibliographies in the Fisk University Library*. Nashville, Tenn.: Fisk University Library, 1950.

* Atkins, Ronald. See H31.

A112. Auer, Margaret, and Lois Bailey. *Bibliography* [of book and audio–visual materials on the elementary and secondary levels available from the University of Detroit Instructional Center]. Detroit, Mich.: University of Detroit, Instructional Center.

A113. Aurback, Herbert A. *A Selected Bibliography on Socio-Culturally Disadvantaged Children and Youth and Related Topics*. ERIC Document no. ED 010–523. Pittsburgh, Pa.: University of Pittsburgh, Learning Research and Development Center, 1966.

A114. Austin, Mary. "The Negro Problem." *The Young Woman Citizen*. New York: Women's Press, 1918, pp. 173–4.

A115. "The Availability of Negro Source Material in Philadelphia." *Negro History Bulletin* 32 (Mar. 1968), 17.

A116. Avakian, George. "Bessie Smith on Records." *Jazz Record* 58 (Sept. 1947), 5 + .

A117. Avakian, George. *Jazz from Columbia: a complete jazz catalog*. New York: Columbia Records, 1956.

A118. Avery, Carol. "Black Americans—Biography." RAS 406. *Readers Advisory Service: selected topical booklists* 6:2 (1979), 406–1—406–2.

A119. Awamura, Masaaki, *Jazu Rekōdo Bukku* [*Jazz Record Book*]. Tokyo, Japan: Ongaka no Tomo, 1968, 208 pp.

A120. Axelrod, Steven. "Colonel [Robert Gould] Shaw in American Poetry: 'For the Union Dead' and its predecessors." *American Quarterly* 24:4 (Oct. 1972), 523–37.

B

* Baatz, Wilmer H. See K78, Mc6.

B1. Babb, Inez Johnson. "Bibliography of Langston Hughes, Negro Poet." Unpublished paper, Pratt Institute Library School, 1947, 13 pp.

* Babcock, Janice. See T86.

B2. Bachus, Edward J. *Recent Acquisitions: a list of books dealing with the black man in America*. Saratoga Springs, N.Y.: Skidmore College, Lucy Scribner Library.

B3. Baden, Anne L. *Immigration in the U.S.: a selected list of recent references*. Washington, D.C.: Library of Congress, 1943, 94 pp.

B4. Bagganaes, Roland, and John Norris, "Discography [Dollar Brand]." *Coda* 11 (Feb. 1973), 5–6.

B5. Bailey, G.E. *America's Black Writers*. Reading list no. 52. Pocatello, Idaho: Idaho State University Library, 1969, 5 pp.

B6. Bailey, Joe H. *Black Studies*. Denton, Tex.: North Texas State University Library.

B7. Bailey, Leonard P. *Broadside Authors and Artists: an illustrated biographical directory*. Detroit, Mich.: Broadside Press, 1974, 125 pp.

* Bailey, Lois. See A112.

B8. Bailey, M.E. "Some New Books on the Negro." *Bookman* 52 (Jan. (1921), 301–6.

B9. Baily, Lugene, and Frank E. Moorer. "A Selected Checklist of Material by and about Ralph Ellison." *Black World* 20 (Dec. 1970), 126–30.

* Baily, Lugene. See also M130.

B10. Bakalas, A. "Cat Anderson." *Le Point du Jazz* 6 (Mar. 1972), 65–70.

B10A. Baker, Augusta B. "The American Negro." *American Unity* 12:2 (Nov.-Dec. 1953), 17–19.

B10B. Baker, Augusta B. "The American Negro." *One World in Children's Books*. New York (?): Educational Press Association of America, 1953, pp.20–3.

B11. Baker, Augusta B. *The Black Experience in Children's Books*. Sponsored by Countee Cullen Regional Branch, North Manhattan Project. New York: The New York Public Library, Office of Children's Services, 1971, 109 pp.

B12. Baker, Augusta B. "The Black Experience in Children's Books: an introductory essay to the annotated booklist." *Bulletin of The New York Public Library* 75:3 (Mar. 1971), 143–6. A slightly revised version appeared in *Bookmark* 30 (July 1971), 309–11. This essay originally appeared as the introduction to B11.

B13. Baker, Augusta B. *Books about Negro Life for Children*. New York: Bureau for Intercultural Education, 1946, 16 pp. An earlier version was issued in 1939.

B14. Baker, Augusta B. *Books about Negro Life for Children*. New York: The New York Public Library, 1949, 16 pp.; 1957, 24 pp.; 1961, 31 pp.; 1963, 33 pp.

B15. Baker, Augusta B. "The Changing Image of the Black in Children's Literature." *Horn Book* 51:1 (Feb. 1975), 79–88.

B16. Baker, Augusta B. "Reading for Democracy." *Wilson Library Bulletin* 18 (Oct. 1943), 141–4. Reprinted as a pamphlet entitled *Books about the Negro for Children*.

* Baker, Barbara. See C213.

B17. Baker, John H. "Further Clarence Williams Documentation." *Playback* 2:1 (Jan. 1949), 21–2.

B18. Baker, O.J. *Masters' Theses of Prairie View State College, 1938–1944*. Prairie View, Tex.: Prairie View University, 1945, 16 pp.

B19. Bakewell, Dennis C. *Black-Brown Bibliography*. Northridge, Cal.: San Fernando Valley State College Library, 1969, 86 pp.

B20. Bakewell, Dennis C. *The Black Experience in the U.S.: a bibliography based on the collection of the San Fernando Valley State College Library*. Northridge, Cal.: San Fernando Valley State College Foundation, 1970, 162 pp.

* Bakish, David. See M14, M14A.

B21. Bakker, Dick M. *Billie [Holiday] and Teddy [Wilson] on Microgroove, 1932–1944*. Alphen aan de Rijn, Netherlands: Micrography, 1975.

B22. Bakker, Dick M. *[Edward] Duke Ellington on Microgroove, 1923–1942*. Alphen aan de Rijn, Netherlands: Micrography, 1974, 52 pp.

* Bakker, Dick M. See also K92.

B23. Baldwin, Lewis V. *Resources for the Study of Afro-American Religion: a guide to selected North Shore libraries*. Evanston, Ill.: Garrett-Evangelical Theological Seminary, Institute for Black Religious Research, 1980.

B24. Baldwin, Lewis V. *Resources for the Study of Blacks in Methodism: a guide to Garrett-Evangelical Theological Seminary and Northwestern University libraries*. Evanston, Ill.: Garrett-Evangelical Theological Seminary, Institute for Black Religious Research, 1980.

B25. Ball, Wendy, and Tony Martin. *Rare Afro-Americana: a reconstruction of the Adger library*. Boston, Mass.: G.K. Hall, 1981, 235 pp.

* Ball, Wendy. See also A15.

B25A. Balliet, Conrad A. "White on Black: a check list of poetry by White Americans about the black experience." *Bulletin of The New York Public Library* 75:9 (Nov. 1971), 424–64.

B26. Banfield, Beryle. "Bibliography of Afro-American History." *Grade Teacher* (Oct. 1968).

B27. Bangs, Lester. "[Bob] Marley and [Peter] Tosh: progress report on reggae." *Stereo Review* 39:3 (Sept. 1977), 96.

B28. Banks, James A. "Developing Racial Tolerance with Literature on the Black Inner City." *Social Education* 34 (May 1970), 549–52.

B29. Banks, Vera J., Elsie S. Manny, and Nelson L. LeRoy. *Research Data on Minority Groups: an annotated bibliography of Economic Research Service reports, 1955–1965*. Washington, D.C.: U.S. Department of Agriculture Economic Research Service, 1966, 25 pp.

* Banner, James M., Jr. See Mc39.

B30. Barabas, Jean. *The Assessment of Minority Groups: an annotated bibliography (with subject index)*. ERIC Document no. ED 083–325. Selected topical booklists, 84. Readers Advisory Service. ERIC Information Retrieval Center on the Disadvantaged. Urban Disadvantaged Series no. 34. New York: Science Associates, 1975, 29 pp.

* Baraka, Imamu Amiri. See C113.

* Barbour, Floyd B. See N104.

B31. Barbour, James, and Robert E. Fleming. "A Checklist of Criticism on Early Afro-American Novelists." *College Language Association Journal* 8 (1977), 21–6.

B32. Barbour, James, and Robert E. Fleming. "Nineteenth Century Black Novelists: a checklist." *Minority Voices* 3:2, pp. 27–43.

B33. Barbrook, A.T. "Archive [of jazz reissues]." *Pieces of Jazz* 7 (1969), 7–19.

* Barker, Carroll G. See J96.

B34. Barksdale, Gaynelle W. *Graduate Theses of Atlanta University, 1954–1959*. Atlanta, Ga.: Atlanta University Library, 1962.

B35. Barksdale, Gaynelle W. *Graduate Theses of Atlanta University, 1943–1947*. Atlanta, Ga.: Atlanta University Library, 1948, 58 pp.

B36. Barksdale, Gaynelle W. *Graduate Theses of Atlanta University, 1931–1942*. Atlanta, Ga.: Atlanta University Library, 1944, 71 pp.

B37. Barksdale, Gaynelle W., and Edward B. Miller. *Graduate Theses of Atlanta University, 1948–1953*. Atlanta, Ga.: Atlanta University Library, 1955, 102 pp.

B38. Barnard, Henry. *Slavery, Part 1: a bibliography of the microfilm collection*. Sanford, N.C.: Microfilming Corporation of America, 1980.

B39. Barnes, Nell D. *Black Aging: an annotated bibliography*. Public Administration Series Bibliography P–167. Monticello, Ill.: Vance Bibliographies, 1979, 18 pp.

B40. Barnes Willard. *The Negro in America*. Moscow, Idaho: University of Idaho Library, 1968, 28 pp.

B41. Barrett, Virginia, Dorothy Evans, Lorraine Henry, Jennifer Jordan, and Vattel Rose. "An Annotated Bibliography of Afro-American Literature, 1975; with selected bibliographies of African and Caribbean literature." *College Language Association Journal* 20: (Sept. 1976), 94–121.

* Barrett, Virginia. See also R112.

* Barringer, Patricia. See P73.

B42. Barry, F. "What Black Students are Reading"[Letter]. *Wilson Library Bulletin* 44 (Jan. 1970), 504.

B43. Barry, Thomas E., Michael G. Harvey, and Michael E. McGill. *Marketing and the Black Consumer: an annotated bibliography*. Chicago, Ill.: American Marketing Association, 1976, 40 pp.

B44. Bartal, K.M., et al. "Black vs. White Leaders: a comparative review of the literature." *Academy of Management Review* 3 (Apr. 1978), 293–304.

B45. Bartlett, John Russell. *The Literature of the Rebellion: a catalogue of books and pamphlets relating to the Civil War in the U.S., and with subjects growing out of that event, together with works on American slavery and essays from reviews and magazines on the same subjects.* Boston, Mass.: Draper and Halliday; Providence, R.I.: Sidney S. Rider, 1866, 477 pp. Reprinted, Westport, Conn.: Negro Universities Press, A Division of Greenwood Press, 1970.

B46. Barton, Josef J. *Brief Ethnic Bibliography: an annotated guide to the ethnic experience in the U.S.* Cambridge, Mass.: Langdon Associates, 1976, 51 pp.

B47. "Basie Discography." *Down Beat* 17:23 (Nov. 17, 1950), 14.

B48. Baskin, Alex. *The American Civil Liberties Union Papers: a guide to the records, ACLU cases, 1912–1946.* Stony Brook, N.Y.: Archives of Social History, 1971, 87 pp.

B49. Bassett, Robert J. *Afro-American Collection in the Undergraduate Library.* Knoxville, Tenn.: University of Tennessee, Undergraduate Library.

B50. Batcheldor, M.L. *Digest of the Laws of the Various States relating to the Ku Klux Klan.* Albany, N.Y.: New York State Library, Legislative Reference Section, 1923, 7 pp.

B51. Bates, M. B. "Analysis of Periodical Articles on Negro Librarianship." M.S.L.S. thesis, Atlanta University, 1958, 67 pp.

B.52. Baxandall, Lee. "Africans and Afro-Americans." *Marxism and Aesthetics: a selected annotated bibliography.* New York: Humanities Press, 1968, pp. 8–16.

B53. Baxter, Camille, and Sylvia Lamont. *Afro-American Materials in the Los Angeles Harbor College Library.* Wilmington, Cal.: Los Angeles Harbor College Library, 29 pp.

B54. Baxter, Katherine. *The Black Experience and the School Curriculum: teaching materials for grades K–12, an annotated bibliography.* Philadelphia, Pa.: Wellsprings Ecumenical Center, 1968, 52 pp.

B55. Bayles, M. "On Busing in Boston." *Harpers* 261 (July 1980), 77–9.

* Bayne, P.S. See E24A.

B56. Beach, Mark. *Desegregated Housing and Interracial Neighborhoods: a bibliographic guide.* Philadelphia, Pa.: National Neighbors, 1975, 91 pp.

B57. Beach, Mark. *Interracial Neighborhoods in American Cities.* Public Administration Series Bibliography P–352, Monticello, Ill.: Vance Bibliographies, 1979, 16 pp.

* Beatty, Jane N. See H18.

* Bebenburg, Walter von. See E15.

B58. Becker, M.L. "A Book Study of American Negro Spirituals." *Saturday Review of Literature* 8 (Jan. 30, 1932), 497.

B59. Becker, M.L. "Negro Writers of Prose and Poetry Publishing within the Last Ten Years." *Saturday Review of Literature* 5 (Mar. 16, 1929), 787.

B60. Becker, M.L. "Recent Novels by Colored Authors." *Saturday Review of Literature* 8 (Mar. 5, 1932), 577.

* Beckwith, Charles. See Q6.
* Beech, Mollie L. See P46.
* Beggs, David W. See S167.
B61. Begum, Marcia J. *Contributions of the Negro to American Life: a list of books*. Providence, R.I.: Providence Public Library, 1970 (?), 12 pp. An earlier edition of 8 pp. was published in the 1960s.
B62. Bell, Barbara L. *Black Biographical Sources: an annotated bibliography*. New Haven, Conn.: Yale University Library, Reference Department, 1970, 20 pp.
B63. Bell, Dorothy. *Canadian Black Studies Bibliography*. London, Ont.: Author, 1971, 105 pp.
B64. Bell, Dorothy, et al. *Canadian Black Studies Bibliography*. Toronto, Ont.: Cross Cultural Learners Workshop, 1971.
* Bell, Michael D. See Mc39.
B65. Bellamy, V. Nelle. "The Liberia Papers: library and archives of the Church Historical Society." *Historical Magazine of the Protestant Episcopal Church* 37 (Mar. 1968), 77–82.
* Belle, Cecil S. See W101A.
* Bellemain, Daniel. See M117.
B66. Bellerby, V. "[Edward (Duke)] Ellington's Legacy on Record." *Melody Maker* 49 (June 1, 1974), 37.
* Belli, Donna. See S35, S36, S37.
B67. Bengelsdorf, Winnie, Susan Norwitch, and Louise Vrande. *Ethnic Studies in Higher Education: state of the art and bibliography*. Washington, D.C.: American Association of State Colleges and Universities, 1972, 261 pp.
B68. Benjamin, Hazel C. *Employment Testing and Title VII: selected references*. Princeton, N.J.: Princeton University, Industrial Relations Section, 1968, 4 pp.
B69. Bennett, Bruce L. "Bibliography on the Negro in Sports." *Journal of Health, Physical Education, Recreation* 41 (Jan.1970), 77 + .
B70. Bennett, Elaine C. *Calendar of Negro-related Documents in the Records of the Committee for Congested Production Areas in the National Archives*. Prepared for the Committee on Negro Studies of the American Council of Learned Societies. Washington, D.C.: American Council of Learned Societies, 1949, 100 pp. Reprinted by Scholars, 1976.
B71. Benoit, Bernard, and Michael Fabre. "A Bibliography of Ralph Ellison's Published Writings." *Studies in Black Literature* 2:3 (Autumn 1971), 25–8
B72. Berg, Arne. *Jazz Rhythm and Blues: panorama special [Sam] Lightnin' Hopkins discography*. Stockholm, Sweden: Author, 196?.
* Berg, James M. See T118.
B73. Berger, Edward. "Benny Carter. Part I: a discographical appraisal." *Journal of Jazz Studies* 4:1 (Fall/Winter 1977), 47–74. "Part II: Benny

Carter's Arrangements: recordings by other artists.'' 5:1 (Fall/Winter 1978), 36–80.

B74. Bergman, Peter M. ''Bibliography of Bibliographies.'' *The Chronological History of the Negro in America*. New York: Harper and Row, 1969, pp. 617–24.

B75. Bergman, Peter M., and Jean McCarroll. *The Negro in the Congressional Record*. New York: Bergman Publishers, 1969.

* Bernstein, Diana. See C127.

B76. Berry, Almedius B. *Reference Materials on and about the Negro*. Syracuse, N.Y.: Syracuse University, School of Library Science, 1945, 15 pp.

B77. Berry, Jason. ''Jazz Literature.'' *Southern Exposure* 6:3 (Fall 1978), 40–9.

B78. Best, Jack L. *Records of the Assistant Commissioner for the State of North Carolina Bureau of Refugees, Freedmen, and Abandoned Lands 1865–1870*. National Archives Microfilm Publications Pamphlet M843. Washington, D.C.: National Archives and Records Series, General Services Administration, 1973, 18 pp.

B79. ''Best R & B Records and Artists of 1964.'' *Cash Box* (Dec. 26, 1964), 36.

B80. Bethel, Elizabeth, Sarah Dunlap, and Lucille Pendell. *Preliminary Checklist of the Records of the Bureau of Refugees, Freedmen, and Abandoned Lands, 1865–1872*. Washington, D.C.: National Archives, War Records Office, 1946, 64 pp.

* Bhana, S. See T112.

B81. *Bibliographic Guide to Black Studies: 1975*. Boston, Mass.: G.K. Hall, 1976, 318 pp. This series is an annual supplement to the *Dictionary Catalogue of the Schomburg Collection*, The New York Public Library. The succeeding *Guides* carry the same imprint date as in the title: *1976*, 340 pp.; *1977*, 257 pp.; *1978*, 183 pp.; *1979*, 220 pp. The *1980* volume, however, was issued in 1981; it contains 424 pp. The *1981* volume, of 190 pp. was published in 1982.

B82. *Bibliographical Suggestions for the Study of Negro History*. Washington, D.C.: Association for the Study of Negro Life and History, 1958(?), 11 pp.

B83. ''Bibliographie: jazz, blues, worksong, spirituals, gospel songs.'' *Musik und Bildung* 5:4 (Apr. 1973), 198–202.

B84. *Bibliographies of Materials on American Negro History and Culture for All Grade Levels*. Raleigh, N.C.: North Carolina Department of Public Instruction, Division of Educational Media, 1970, 8 pp.

B85. *Bibliographies: selected references on housing of minorities*. Washington, D.C.: U.S. National Housing Agency, Office of the Administrator, 1946.

B86. *Bibliography and Index of the Life and Works of Paul Laurence Dunbar on Microfilm*. St. Paul, Minn.: 3M Co., International Microfilm Press, 1969, 7 pp.

B87. *Bibliography and Resource Guide: an aid to understanding in intergroup relations, Negro history and aspiration, the civil rights struggle and the crisis in our cities*. Madison, Wis.: Wisconsin Department of Industry, Labor and Human Relations/Human Rights Division, 1968, 7 pp.

B88. *Bibliography for Educational Integration*. Baltimore, Md.: Urban League, 1954, 8 pp.

B89. *Bibliography for Educators: the American Negro*. Lansing, Mich.: Michigan Education Department, Educational Services Bureau, Library Division, 1968, 8 pp.

B90. "Bibliography: literature on the South." *Freedomways* 4 (Winter 1967), 149–67.

B91. "A Bibliography of African and Afro-American Religions." *Black Books Bulletin* 4 (Spring 1976), 68–71.

B92. *A Bibliography of African and Afro-American Religions*. Princeton, N.J.: The Fund for Theological Education, 1971, 38 pp.

B93. *Bibliography of Afro-American Culture*. Detroit, Mich.: Board of Education of the City of Detroit, 1971, 17 pp.

B94. *Bibliography of Afro-American Fiction, 1853–1970*. Fredericksburg, Va.: Mary Washington College, Department of English, 1970, 88 pp.

B94A. *A Bibliography of Bibliographies on the Negro contained in the Libraries of the University of Michigan: a tentative list*. Ann Arbor, Mich.: University of Michigan, General Library, 1970 (?), 21 pp.

B95. *Bibliography of Black Literature*. Battle Creek, Mich.: Kellogg Community College, Emory W. Morris Library.

B96. *A Bibliography of Black Studies Resources in the Library*. Buffalo, N.Y.: SUNY-Buffalo, Urban Center, 1969.

B97. *Bibliography of Books and Periodicals by and about Blacks in the University of Arkansas Library*. Fayetteville, Ark.: University of Arkansas Library, Reference Department, 1970, 27 pp.

B97A. *Bibliography of Books by and about Negroes*. Jefferson City, Mo.: Lincoln University, Inman E. Page Library, 1970. Supplements were issued in March 1971; Spring 1973, Fall 1974, and Spring 1976.

B98. "Bibliography of Charles Henry Turner." *Journal of Negro Education* 9 (Oct. 1940), 657–60.

B99. *Bibliography of Contributions of Negro Women to American Civilization*. New York: Schomburg Library, 1952, 4 pp. Based on a list of 1 p. compiled in 1940 by Catherine A. Latimer.

B100. *A Bibliography of Doctoral Research on the Negro*. Supplement 1967–1977. Ann Arbor, Mich.: University Microfilms, 1970 (?), 26 pp. A supplement to Earle H. West's list of 1969. Supersedes a 1967–1977 supplement of 65 pp. issued in 1978.

B101. *Bibliography of Horace Mann Bond*. Atlanta Ga., 197?, 7 pp.

B102. *Bibliography of Master's Theses, 1937–1962*. Petersburg, Va.: Virginia State College Library, Reference Department, 1963, 48 pp. Reprinted from *Virginia State College Gazette* 69:3 (Sept. 1963).

B103. *Bibliography of Melville J. Herskovits*. Evanston, Ill. (?): 1963 (?), 33 pp.

B104. *Bibliography of Minorities, Blacks and Mexican-Americans*. San Jose, Cal.: San Jose State College, 1968, 29 pp.

B105. *Bibliography of Negro Life*. Newark, N.J.: Essex County Community College Library, Readers' Services Department, 1969.

B106. *Bibliography of Published Works by Robert C. Weaver, Secretary, U.S. Department of Housing and Urban Development*. Washington, D.C.: U.S. Department of Housing and Urban Development, 1966, 9 pp. An edition of 1967 contained 12 pp.

B107. *Bibliography of References and Resource Materials Related to Black Childrearing and Family Life*. St. Louis, Mo.: Institute of Black Studies, 75 pp.

B108. *Bibliography of Required Materials for Teacher Training Centers, Dedicated to the Second International Conference of African People, San Diego, Cal., Aug. 31–Sept. 4, 1972*. New York: Conference of African People, Eastern Regional Conference, Action Library, 1972, 10 pp.

B109. *A Bibliography of Resource Materials about the American Negro and Other American Minority Groups*. Olympia, Wash.: Office of the Superintendent of Public Instruction, 1968.

B110. "Bibliography [of Songs and Music]." *Music Educators Journal* 58 (Jan. 1970), 113+.

B111. *Bibliography of Sources by and about Blacks Compiled by the Interns in the Internship Librarian Program*. Internship in Ethnic Studies Librarianship. Oct. 21–Dec. 13, 1974. Sponsored by Fisk University Library in cooperation with the University of Southern California and Oklahoma City University. Nashville, Tenn.: Fisk University Library, 1974, 101 pp.

B112. *Bibliography of Student Movements Protesting Segregation and Discrimination, 1960*. Tuskegee, Ala.: Tuskegee Institute, Department of Records and Research, 1961, 10 pp.

B113. *A Bibliography of Studies on Negroes, West Virginia Tech Collection*. Montgomery, W. Va.: West Virginia Institute of Technology, 1970, 24 pp.

B114. *Bibliography of the Negro Press*. Jefferson City, Mo.: Lincoln University, 1946, 11 pp.

B115. *A Bibliography of Thomas Wentworth Higginson*. Cambridge, Mass.: Cambridge Public Library, 1906, 47 pp.

B116. "Bibliography on Afro-American History and Culture." Prepared by the Staff, Department of Social Studies, Detroit, Mich., Public Schools. *Social Education* 33:4 (Apr. 1969), 447–61. Reprinted by the National Council for the Social Studies.

B117. *Bibliography on Black Studies*. Newark, N.J.: Essex County Community College Library, Readers' Services Department, 1971, 39 pp. A 23 pp. supplement was issued in 1972.

B118. *Bibliography on Education of the Negro*. Bulletin, 1931, no. 17. Washington, D.C.: U.S. Department of the Interior, Office of Education, 1931, 34 pp.

B119. *Bibliography on Fair Employment Practice Law*. Los Angeles, Cal.: Los Angeles County Law Library, 1960, 5 pp.

B120. *Bibliography on Negro Labor*. Washington, D.C.: U.S. Bureau of Statistics, 1937, 34 pp.

B121. *Bibliography on Negro Life and History*. Lansing, Mich.: Michigan Department of Education, Cooperative Curriculum Program, Committee on Elementary Education, 24 pp.

B122. "Bibliography on Negro Nursing." *National Negro Health News* 6 (Apr.– June 1939), 26–7.

B123. *Bibliography on Negroes*. Rutherford, N.J.: Fairleigh Dickinson University, Messler Library.

B124. *Bibliography on Racism*. DHEW Publication no. (HSM)73–9012. Rockville, Md.: U.S. National Institute of Mental Health, Center for Minority Group Mental Health Programs, 1972.

B125. *Bibliography on the Negro in Industry*. Washington, D.C.: President's Commission on Fair Employment Practice, Division of Review and Analysis, 4 pp.

B126. *Bibliography Part I: the black American*. Walnut, Cal.: Mt. San Antonio College Library, 1969, 2 pp.

B127. Bicknell, Marguerite Elizabeth, and Margaret C. McCulloch. *Guide to Information about the Negro and Negro-White Adjustment*. Memphis, Tenn.: Brunner Printing Co., 1943, 39 pp.

B128. Biddle, Stanton F. *Library Resources for Research on Black Families in New York State*. Buffalo, N.Y.: Author, 1982, 1 p.

B129. Biddle, Stanton F. "The Schomburg Center for Research in Black Culture: documenting the black experience." *Bulletin of The New York Public Library* 76 (1972), 21–35.

B130. Bierman, June, and Marjorie Knapp. *A Selected Bibliography of Afro-American Literature*. Van Nuys, Cal.: Los Angeles Valley College Library.

B131. Bigala, John C.B. *An Annotated Bibliography for Teaching Afro-American Studies at Secondary and College Levels*. Tipsheet no. 5. New York: Columbia University, National Center for Research and Information on Equal Educational Opportunity, 1971, 47 pp.

B132. Bigley, Eleanor, Forrest Sloan, Ruth Heggerness, and Helen E. Holcomb. *A Bibliography to Promote Better Human Understandings*. Washington [State] Education Association, Department of Classroom Teachers, 1953, 16 pp.

B133. Bikshapathi, Adepu. *Health and the Urban Poor: a bibliography.* ERIC Document no. ED 114–445. New York: ERIC Clearinghouse on the Urban Disadvantaged, 1978.

B134. *Bird [Parker] and Diz [Gillespie]: a bibliography.* New York: New York Jazz Museum, 197?.

B135. Birkos, Alexander S., and Lewis A. Tambs, *African and Black American Studies.* Academic Writer's Guide to Periodicals, Vol. 3. Littleton, Col.: Libraries Unlimited, 1975, 205 pp.

B136. Birtha, Becky. *Literature by Black Women.* Philadelphia, Pa.: Author, 1981.

B137. Birtha, Jessie M. "Portrayal of the Black in Children's Literature." *Pennsylvania Library Association Bulletin* 24 (July 1969), 187–97. Reprinted in *Top News* 26 (June 1970), 395–408. Reprinted in *Kansas Library Bulletin* 40:2 (1971), 10–15.

B138. Birtha, Jessie M., Carol Grustas, Helen Jenkins, and Sylvia Sprinkle. *About Black Americans.* Philadelphia, Pa.: Free Library of Philadelphia, 1970 (?), 6 pp.

B139. Bischoff, Phyllis. *Ethnic Studies: a selected guide to reference materials at Berkeley.* Berkeley, Cal.: University of California at Berkeley, 1974.

B140. *Black.* Akron, Ohio: Akron Public Library, 1970, 16 pp.

B141. Black, Frederick R. "Bibliographical Essay: Benjamin Drew's 'Refugee' and the Black Family." *Journal of Negro History* 57:3 (July 1972), 284–9.

B142. Black, P.C. *Survey of Books by and about the Negro in the U.S. Available in Selected Mississippi Public Libraries.* M.A. thesis, Emory University, 1968, 58 pp.

B143. *Black America.* Baltimore, Md.: Baltimore County Public Library, 1969.

B144. *Black America: a selected bibliography of books.* New York: Columbia University, Teachers College Library.

B145. *The Black American.* Cleveland, Ohio: Cleveland Public Library, Government, Education and Social Science Department, 8 pp.

B146. *The Black American: a selected list of books at the U.S.A.F.E. Library and W.A.B. Library.* Wiesbaden, Germany: Lindsey Air Station Library, Wiesbaden Air Base Library, 1973, 44 pp.

B146A. *The Black American: a selective bibliography.* Santa Barbara, Cal.: Santa Barbara Public Library, Reference Division, 1971, 19 pp.

B147. *The Black American, and Africa—Evolutionary Continent; a compendium in two parts.* Corning, N.Y.: Arthur A. Houghton, Jr., Library, 1964.

B148. *Black American Bibliography: books about the black man in America.* Berkeley, Cal.: Berkeley Public Library, 1969, 5 pp.

B149. Black American Culture Bibliography: a list of books and periodicals on black American culture located in the Belk Library. Boone, N.C.: Appalachian State University, Belk Library, Acquisitions Department, 1972, 316 pp.

B150. *Black Americana: a selected list.* East Cleveland, Ohio: East Cleveland Public Library, 1971, 6 pp.

B151. *Black Americana: a selected list of recent and older books on Negro life and culture from the collections of the Detroit Public Library.* Detroit, Mich.: Detroit Public Library, 1970, 27 pp. The library issues annual publications with this title, most notably *Black Americana: selected books of the seventies,* 1980. No list was issued in 1981, but the series was resumed with *Black Americana: a selected list of recent books,* 1982, 8 pp.

B152. "Black Americans." *Booklist* 69 (May 1, 1973), 835–45. American Library Association, American Association of School Librarians, Committee on Treatment of Minority Groups in Library Books and Other Instructional Materials.

B153. *The Black Americans: books for children.* Oakland, Cal.: Oakland Public Schools, Division of Instructional Media, Library Department, 1970, 27 pp.

B154. *Black and Brown Bibliography: history; a selected list of books relating to the history of Afro-Americans and Mexican–Americans.* San Bernardino, Cal.: San Bernardino State College, 1970, 39 pp.

B155. *Black and Brown Bibliography: literature, art, music, theatre; a selected list of books relating to the culture of Afro-and Mexican-Americans.* San Bernardino, Cal.: San Bernardino State College Library, 1970, 16 pp.

B156. *Black and Brown Bibliography: philosophy, social sciences, political science, education; a selected list of books relating to the culture of Afro-Americans and Mexican-Americans.* San Bernardino, Cal.: San Bernardino State College Library, 1970, 13 pp.

B157. *Black and White: What Delight: a list of books for the young child about understanding himself and others.* Raleigh, N.C.: North Carolina State Library, Library Development Division, 1971, 4 pp.

B158. *A Black Bibliography.* Beloit, Wis.: Beloit College Libraries, 1968, 19 pp.

B159. *Black Bibliography.* New Brunswick, N.J.: Rutgers University, Livingston College, Kilmer Area Library, 1973, 53 pp. The second supplement to an original publication of the same title.

B160. *Black Bibliography.* Salt Lake City, Utah: University of Utah, Marriott Library, 1974, 825 pp. A supplement of 458 pp. was published as *Supplement to Black Bibliography* in 1977. *Black Bibliography: a selective listing* was published in 1970.

B161. *Black Bibliography: a selected list of books on Africa, Africans, and Afro-Americans.* Long Beach, Cal.: California State College at Long Beach, 1969, 88 pp.

B162. *Black Bibliography: a selected list of sources.* Little Rock, Ark.: Arkansas Library Commission, 1970.

B163. *Black Bibliography: a selected listing from the Law Library.* Salt Lake City, Utah: University of Utah Libraries.

B164. *A Black Bibliography for White Students.* Nashville, Tenn.: Fisk University, Amistad Center and Race Relations Department, 23 pp.

B165. *Black Bibliophiles—Preservers of Black History.* Washington, D.C.: Howard University, Moorland-Spingarn Research Center, 1982, 18 pp.

B166. "The Black Church in the U.S.: a resource guide." *Renewals: a bibliographic newsletter of the Boston Theological Institute Libraries* 2:4 (Feb. 1979), 1–6.

B167. *Black Contributions in the Development of America.* Columbus, Ohio: Ohio State Library, 1970 (?), 8 pp. An edition of 4 pp. was published in 1968.

B168. *Black Culture: a selected bibliography for children.* Chicago, Ill.: Chicago Public Library, 1969, 20 pp.

B169. *Black Culture and the Arts.* Akron, Ohio: Akron Public Library, 7 pp.

B170. *Black Culture: resources on Negro history.* Columbus, Ohio: Capitol University Library, 1969, 28 pp.

B171. "Black Culture Series for Young Readers." *The Ebony Handbook.* Chicago, Ill.: Johnson Publishing Co., 1974, pp. 190–3.

B172. *The Black Experience: films, filmstrips and recordings on the Afro-American.* Cleveland, Ohio: Cuyahoga County Public Library, 35 pp.

B173. *The Black Experience in America from Colonial Times to the Present: an exhibition of books, pamphlets, and manuscripts from the historical collection of Charles L. Blockson.* Sponsored by the Black Studies Program, Pennsylvania State University, University Park, Pa., Feb. 2–15, 1976.

B174. "The Black Experience in Sight and Sound." *Read, See and Hear* 21:4 (Jan. 15, 1973), 4 pp. Issued by the Newark, N.J., Board of Education, Department of Libraries and Audiovisual Education. Supplemented by 21:5 and 24:5.

B175. *Black Films: a selected list.* Rev. ed. New York: The New York Public Library, Office of Adult Services, 1971, 13 pp.

B176. *Black Heritage.* Jamaica, N.Y.: Queensborough Public Library, 1970.

B177. *Black Heritage Resource Guide: a bibliography of the Negro in contemporary America.* New York: National Council of the Churches of Christ in the U.S.A., Department of Educational Development, 1970.

B178. *Black Heritage: the American experience; a selected annotated bibliography.* ERIC Document no. 072–824. Washington, D.C.: Bureau of Naval Personnel, 1970. A publication of the same title was issued by the Human Resource Development Project Office of the Department of the Navy in 1972; it contained 57 pp.

B179. *Black History*. San Francisco, Cal.: San Francisco Unified School District.

B180. *Black History*. Westerville, Ohio: Otterbein College, Centennial Library.

B181. *Black History and Other Materials in the Glen Rock Library*. Glen Rock, N.J.: Glen Rock Public Library, 11 pp.

B182. *Black History Bibliography*. Toledo, Ohio: Toledo Board of Education, Afro-American Resource Center, 1970, 8 pp.

B183. *Black History Viewpoints: a selected bibliographical guide to resources for Afro-American and African history*. Westport, Conn.: Negro Universities Press, 1969, 71 pp.

B184. *The Black Index: a bibliographical index of major studies, articles, and information dealing with black media marketing*. Arlington, Va.: Sheridan Broadcasting Network, 1980.

B185. *Black is . . . . : a list of children's books from the library*. Baltimore, Md.: Enoch Pratt Free Library, Office of Work with Children, 1972, 57 pp.

B186. *Black-Jewish Relations Series*. New York: 92nd St. YM-YWHA, 1980, 1 p.

B187. *Black Life and Literature for Children*. Gary, Ind.: Gary Public Library, 24 pp.

B188. *Black Literature*. Schenectady, N.Y.: Schenectady County Public Library, 1970, 6pp.

B189. *The Black Man in Africa and America*. Upper Montclair, N.J.: Montclair State College Library, Reference Department, 1970.

B190. *The Black Man in America: a selected list of books*. Los Angeles, Cal.: Los Angeles Public Library, Young Adult Services, 1969, 6 pp.

B191. *The Black Man's Past in America: a selected reading list*. Baltimore, Md.: Enoch Pratt Free Library, 1968.

B192. *Black Music: a selected discography*. Sacramento, Cal.: Sacramento State College Library, 1971, 35 pp.

B193. "Black Newspaper Archives." *American Libraries* 8 (Apr. 1972), 172.

B194. *Black on Black and Other Suggested Reading for Negro History Week 1970*. Jamaica, N.Y.: Queensborough Public Library, 4 pp.

B195. *Black Perspectives: a bibliography*. New York: Community College Press, 1971, 68 pp.

B196. *Black Reading Power*. Jamaica, N.Y.: Queensborough Public Library, 1971, 4 pp.

B197. "Black Related Items." *American Libraries* 13 (Feb. 1982), 145–7.

B198. *Black Sociologists*. Bibliographies in Black Studies no. 2. Chicago, Ill.: Chicago Center for Afro-American Studies and Research, Inc., 88 pp.

B199. *The Black Story: an annotated multi-media list for secondary schools*. Rockville, Md.: Rockville Department of Educational Media and Technology, 1969, 97 pp.

B200. *Black Studies*. Selected Catalog of National Archives and Records Service Microfilm Publications. Washington, D.C.: National Archives and Records Service, 1973, 70 pp.

B201. *Black Studies: a selective list of resources for teachers.* St. Louis, Mo.: St. Louis Public Library, 1969, 3 pp.

B202. *Black Studies Bibliography.* Eugene, Ore.: Lane Community College, Learning Resource Center, 53 pp.

B203. "Black Studies Collections." *Australian Library Journal* 26 (Apr. 15, 1977), 92.

B204. *Black Studies in the U.S.: a selected guide to research materials in the University of California at Santa Barbara Library.* Rev. ed. Santa Barbara, Cal.: University of California at Santa Barbara Library, Reference Department, 1970, 40 pp.

B205. *Black Studies: selected catalog of National Archives and Records Services microfilm publications.* Washington, D.C.: National Archives and Records Services, 1973, 71 pp.

B206. *Black Voices: a selected list of achievements of black writers.* San Diego, Cal.: San Diego Public Library, Literature and Languages Section, 1972.

B207. *Black Writing from Africa, the Caribbean and the U.S.: [catalogue of an exhibition] prepared for the second World Black and African Festival of Arts and Culture, Lagos, 22nd Nov.–20th Dec. 1975.* London, England: National Book League, 1975, 36 pp.

B207A. Blackledge, Jacqueline. "The Afro-American in Florida History: a compilation of materials in libraries in the Nashville area." *Bibliography of Sources by and about blacks compiled by Interns in the Internship in Black Studies Librarianship Program.* Nashville, Tenn.: Fisk University Library, 1974 (?), pp. 2–25.

* Blackstone, Judith, See C15.

B208. Blackstone, Orin. *Index to Jazz.* New Orleans, La.: Gordon Gullickson, 1947, 4 vols.

B209. Blackwell, Jean. *The Negro in the American Scene: a selective bibliography.* New York: City-Wide Citizens Committee on Harlem, 9 pp.

* Blackwell, Jean. See also Hutson, Jean Blackwell.

* Blake, Elias, Jr. See G92.

B210. Blanck, Jacob. "Charles Waddell Chesnutt." *Merle Johnson's American First Editions.* 4th ed. Waltham, Mass.: Mark Press, 1965, p. 106.

B211. Blanck, Jacob. "Harriet Beecher Stowe." *Merle Johnson's American First Editions.* 4th ed. Waltham, Mass.: Mark Press, 1965, pp. 481–4.

B212. Blanck, Jacob. "Paul Laurence Dunbar." *Bibliography of American Literature*, Vol. II. New Haven, Conn.: Yale University Press, 1955–69, pp. 498–505.

B213. Blanck, Jacob. "Paul Laurence Dunbar." *Merle Johnson's American First Editions.* 4th ed. Waltham, Mass.: Mark Press, 1965, pp. 156–7.

B214. Blassingame, John W., and Mae G. Henderson. *Antislavery Newspapers and Periodicals: an annotated index of letters 1817–1871*. Vol. 1: 1817–1845; annotated index of letters in the "Philanthropist," "Emancipator," "Genius of Universal Emancipation," "Abolition Intelligencer," "African Observer," and the "Liberator." Vol. 2: 1835–1865; annotated index of letters in the "Liberator," "Anti-Slavery Record," "Human Rights," and the "Observer." Vol. 3: 1835–1854; annotated index of letters in the "Friend of Man," "Pennsylvania Freeman," "Advocate of Freedom," and "American and Foreign Anti-Slavery Reporter." Boston, Mass.: G.K. Hall, 1980, 586 pp; 1980, 636 pp.; 1981, 557 pp.

B215. Blau, George. "W.C. Handy." *Music Memories* 3:2 (Apr. 1963), 18.

B216. Blazek, Ron, Janice Fennell, and Frances M. McKinney. *The Black Experience: a bibliography of bibliographies, 1970–1975*. Chicago, Ill.: American Library Association, Reference and Adult Services Division, 1978, 67 pp.

* Blazek, Ron. See also J137.

B217. Blinn, Eleanor. *Bibliographies of Current Acquisitions for Black Studies Programs, 1968–1969*. San Francisco, Cal.: City College of San Francisco Library.

B218. Blockson, Charles. "Roots and Branches." *Philadelphia* 69 (Sept. 1979), 95+.

B219. *Blowing in the Wind: the changing image of Black America*. San Francisco, Cal.: San Francisco Public Library.

B220. Blue, Thomas, and Mrs. R.D. Harris. "Negro Authors [and Composers]." Louisville, Ky.: Louisville Public Library, 1921, 11 pp.

B221. *Blues*. Washington, D.C.: Library of Congress, Music Division, 1969, 9 pp.

B222. *The Blues: a list of recordings*. New York: The New York Public Library, 8 pp.

B223. "Blues Labels: Yazoo." *Jazz Podium* 21 (Jan. 1972), 16–8.

B224. Blum, Zahava D., and Peter H. Rossi. *Social Class and Poverty: a selected and annotated bibliography*. Boston, Mass.: American Academy of Arts and Sciences, 1976, 71 pp. An Addendum of 2 pp. was issued in Jan. 1977.

B225. Blum, Zahava D., and Peter H. Rossi. *Social Class Research and Images of the Poor: a bibliographic review*. ERIC Document no. ED 020–294. Baltimore, Md.: Johns Hopkins, 1968.

* Blum, Zahava D. See also B283.

B226. Blumer, Herbert. "Research on Racial Relations: United States of America." *International Social Science Bulletin* 10 (1967), 403–47.

B227. Blunck, Malwine, Anette Ziegler, and Margot Ahler-Buuk. "Articles in 'Der Spiegel' about Black Musicians, 1948–1976," "Reviews of 'Porgy and Bess' in German Newspapers and Periodicals." *In* "Black Music in Germany: two bibliographies." *Black Perspectives in Music* 5:2 (Fall 1977), 161–72.

B227A. Boardman, Neil S. *From Head Start to Upward Bound: a bibliography.* 1971, 20 pp.

B228. Boddy, I.M. "Catalog of Selected Audiovisual Materials for Human Relations." *Journal of Human Relations* 1 (Summer 1953), 19–42.

* Boelke, Joanne. See C167.

B229. Bogaert, Karel. *Blues Lexicon: blues, cajun, boogie woogie, gospel.* Antwerp, Belgium: Standaard, 1972, 480 pp.

* Bogle, Enid. See R112.

* Bohanan, R.D. See P6.

B230. Bohrn, Harald. *Gunnar Myrdal: a bibliography, 1919–1976.* Stockholm, Sweden: Acta Bibliothecae Regiae Stockholmiensis, 1976, 188 pp.

B231. Bolan, Lewis. *The Role of Urban Planning in the Residential Integration of Middle Class Negroes and Whites.* Exchange Bibliography no. 41. Monticello, Ill.: Council of Planning Librarians, 1968.

B232. Boles, Nancy G. "Notes on Maryland Historical Society Manuscript Collections: black history collections." *Maryland Historical Magazine* 66:1 (Spring 1971), 72–8.

B233. Bolivar, William Carl. *Library of William C. Bolivar, Philadelphia, Pennsylvania. Together with Printed Tracts, Magazines, Articles, Reports, Addresses and Miscellaneous not enumerated; Americana, Negroana, Manuscripts, Autograph Letters, Lincolniana, Rare Phamphlets (sic), Travels, Africana, etc.* Philadelphia, Pa., 1914, 32 pp. Reprinted in Betty Kaplan Gubert. *Early Black Bibliographies, 1863–1918.* New York: Garland, 1982, pp. 293–328.

B234. Bolner, James. *Racial Imbalance in Public Schools: a basic annotated bibliography.* Baton Rouge, La.: Louisiana State University and Agricultural and Mechanical College, 1968, 73 pp.

B235. Bond, Horace Mann. "Negro Education: bibliographies and general sources." *Encyclopedia of Educational Research.* New York: Macmillan, 1941, pp. 746–72.

B236. Bone, Robert A. "Short Story Collections by Afro-American Authors, 1895–1935." *Down Home: a history of Afro-American short fiction from its beginnings to the end of the Harlem Renaissance.* New York: G.P. Putnam's Sons, 1975, pp. 307–14.

B237. Boner, Marian D. *Poverty and Housing: a selected bibliography.* Exchange Bibliography no. 128. Monticello, Ill.: Council of Planning Librarians, 1970.

B238. Bonner, Gretchen. "Books for Children and Young People: Negro history." *Wilson Library Bulletin* 63 (Jan. 1967), 59.

B239. Bontemps, Arna. *American Missionary Association Archives in Fisk*

University Library. Nashville, Tenn.: Fisk University Library, 1947, 12 pp.

B240. Bontemps, Arna. *Charles W. Chesnutt Collection, founded by Helen M. Chesnutt, 1952*. Nashville, Tenn.: Fisk University, 3 pp.

B241. Bontemps, Arna. "Chesnutt Papers Go to Fisk." *Library Journal* 77 (Aug. 1952), 1288–9.

B242. Bontemps, Arna. *Color in a Shrinking World*, 1943, 4 pp.

B243. Bontemps, Arna. "The James Weldon Johnson Memorial Collection of Negro Arts and Letters." *Yale University Library Gazette* 18 (Oct. 1943), 1926.

B244. Bontemps, Arna. "Special Collections of Negroana."*Library Quarterly* 14 (July 1944), 187–206.

B245. Booher, David E. *Poverty in an Urban Society: a bibliography*. Exchange Bibliography no 246. Monticello, Ill.: Council of Planning Librarians, 1971.

B246. *Booker T. Washington: a register of his papers in the Library of Congress*. Washington, D.C.: Library of Congress, Manuscript Division, Reference Department, 1958, 105 pp.

B247. "Books about the Negro." *Bulletin of The New York Public Library; Branch Library Book News* 2:9 (Dec. 1925), 131–6.

B248. *Books about the Negro People*. Spokane, Wash.: Spokane Public Library, 13 pp.

B249. "Books and Pamphlets on Negroes and Race Relations." *Youth Leaders Digest* 7 (Jan. 1945), 139–43.

B250. *Books and the New Era: the Negro*. Columbus, Ohio: Methodist Book Concern, 1913.

B251. *Books by and about Negroes*. Columbia, S.C.: South Carolina Department of Education, 1969, 15 pp. A 4 pp. supplement was issued in 1970.

B252. *Books by and about Negroes: a special paperback collection*. Washington, D.C.: District of Columbia Public Library, 1969.

B253. "Books by and about Negroes, 1943–1944." *A Monthly Summary of Events and Trends in Race Relations* 3 (Aug.-Sept. 1945), 64–5.

B254. "Books by and about the American Negro." *Library Journal* 95 (Jan. 15, 1970), 218+ ; *School Library Journal* 17 (Jan. 1970), 34+ .

B255. *Books by and about the American Negro: a selected list for young adults*. New York: The New York Public Library, Countee Cullen Branch, North Manhattan Project, 1966, 14 pp.

B256. *Books by and about the American Negro for Elementary, Intermediate, Junior, and Senior High School Libraries*. New York: New York City Board of Education, Bureau of Libraries, 1969. Supersedes *Focus on One America*.

B257. *Books by and about the Negro: a selected bibliography*. Raleigh, N.C.: North Carolina Department of Public Instruction, 1944, 3 pp.

B258. *Books, Films, Recordings by and about the American Negro: a selected* list for young adults. New York: The New York Public Library, Countee Cullen Branch, North Manhattan Project, 1968, 24 pp.

B259. *Books for Brotherhood*. New York: National Conference of Christians and Jews.

B260. *Books for Children: black and white, a selected bibliography*. New York: NAACP, 1972 (?).

B261. Not used.

B262. *Books for Multi-Ethnic Studies*. Jericho, N.Y.: Nassau County, N.Y., Board of Cooperative Educational Services, Research and Development Division, 1970, 51 pp.

B263. *Books for Negro History Week*. Chicago, Ill.: Chicago Public Schools, Division of Libraries, 1963.

B264. *Books for School and the Treatment of Minorities*. Washington, D.C.: U.S. Congress, House of Representatives, 89th Congress, 2nd Session, Committee on Education and Labor, 1966, 828 pp.

B265. *Books in Russian on the U.S. Race Problem in the Lenin State Library*. Moscow, U.S.S.R., 1955, 2 pp.

B266. *Books in the Julius Rosenwald Fund Library*. Chicago, Ill.: Julius Rosenwald Fund Library, 1941, 48 pp.

B267. "Books, Magazine Articles, Pamphlets, Reports: covers housing, education, civil rights, etc." *Race Relations Law Reporter* 5 (Winter 1960), 1287–93.

B268. "Books Most Requested in the Fillmore Street Reference Project [San Francisco Public Library]." *Wilson Library Bulletin* 43 (May 1969), 875.

B269. *Books on Africa and the Negro at the 135th Street Branch*. New York: New York Public Library, 1921, 8 pp.

B270. "Books on Minority Groups: Afro-Americans." *Catholic Library World* 41:5 (Jan. 1970), 319–21.

B271. *Books Promote Understanding: children's books on Negro life and history*. Cincinnati, Ohio: Public Library of Cincinnati and Hamilton County, Children's Department, 1971.

B272. *Books Transcend Barriers: a bibliography of books about Negroes for elementary school children*. Seattle, Wash.: Seattle Public Schools, 1967, 53 pp.

B273. Boone, Dorothy Deloris. "A Historical Review and a Bibliography of Selected Negro Magazines, 1910–1919." Ed.D. thesis, University of Michigan, 1970, 146 pp.

B274. Booth, Robert S., et al. *Culturally Disadvantaged: a bibliography and key word out-of-context (KWOC) index*. Detroit, Mich.: Wayne State University Press, 1967.

B275. Borders, Florence E. *Guide to the Microfilm Edition of the Countee Cullen Papers, 1921–1969*. New Orleans, La.: Amistad Research Center, 1975, 49 pp.

B276. Borneman, Ernest. *A Bibliography of African and Afro-American Music*. London, England: Royal Empire Society, 1940.

B276A. Borneman, Ernest. "A Selective Chronology of Ragtime, Blues and Pop Tunes That Influenced Jazz History." *Record Changer* (Oct. 1945), 31.

B277. Boubel, Margaret, et al. *From Africa to America: a list of materials in the Chabot College Library Relating to the History of Black People in America*. Hayward, Cal.: Chabot College Library, 1969, 18 pp.

B278. Bouknight, L. Marie. *Records of the Assistant Commissioner for the State of Mississippi Bureau of Refugees, Freedmen, and Abandoned Lands, 1865–1869*. National Archives Microfilm Publications Pamphlet Describing M826. Washington, D.C.: National Archives and Records Service, General Services Administration, 1973, 14 pp.

* Bowles, M.R. See A111.

B279. Bowling, Charles H. "Bibliography of Negro Ante-Bellum Songs as Found in the Sheet Music Collection of the Duke University Library, Durham, North Carolina." M.A. thesis, North Carolina College, 1960, 77 pp.

B280. Boyce, Byrl N., and Sidney Turoff. *Minority Groups and Housing: a bibliography, 1950–1970*. Morristown, N.J.: General Learning Press, 1972, 202 pp. An enlarged edition of a 1968 work by Stephen D. Messner.

B281. Boyd, Sandra H. *Blacks and Religion in America: an annotated bibliography of bibliographies*. Cambridge, Mass.: Episcopal Divinity School/Weston School of Theology. Prepared for Black History Month, Feb. 1979, 2 pp. Revised 1980.

B282. Brachet, Viviane, Zahava D. Blum, and Peter H. Rossi. *Social Stratification and Poverty: a selected and annotated bibliography*. Madison, Wis.: University of Wisconsin, Institute for Research on Poverty, 1973.

B283. Bradley, Gladyce Helene. *Selected Bibliography on Desegregation and Integration in the Public Schools of the United States*. Baltimore, Md.: Morgan State College, 1955, 11 pp.

* Bradley, Jack. See M141.

B284. Brasch, Ila Wales, and Walter Milton Brasch. *A Comprehensive Annotated Bibliography of American Black English*. Baton Rouge, La.: Louisiana State University Press, 1974, 289 pp.

B285. Brasch, Ila Wales, and Walter Milton Brasch. "A Review of Black English Research and Discussion of the Development of the Black English Bibliography." Paper, Linguistics Colloquium on Black English, Ohio University, Athens, Ohio, Jan. 23, 1973.

* Brasch, Walter Milton. See B284, B285.

B286. Braun, Mary, and R. Lawrence Martin. *The Negro in American Life: a selected bibliography of materials available in the Ferris State College Library* Big Rapids, Mich.: Ferris State College Library, 1968.

* Bravard, Robert S. See P47.

B287. Brawley, Benjamin G. *Early Negro American Writers: selections with biographical and critical introductions.* Chapel Hill, N.C.: University of North Carolina Press, 1935, 305 pp.

B288. Brawley, Benjamin G. "The Negro in Contemporary Literature." *English Journal* (high school and college edition) 18 (Mar. 1929), 194–202

B289. Brazell, Troy. *The Black American Musical Heritage.* Ypsilanti, Mich.: Eastern Michigan University Library, 12 pp.

* Breckenridge, W.C. See S12.

* Breit, Marquita. See F71.

* Brenford, Robert J. See M53, M54.

B290. Brewer, J. Mason. "Negro Folklore in North America: a field of research." *The New Mexico Quarterly Review* 16 (Spring 1946). A slightly modified version appeared as "Afro-American Folklore." *Journal of American Folklore* 60 (Oct.–Dec. 1947), 377–82.

B291. Breyfoyle, Donna, and M. Dworaczek. *Blacks in Ontario: a selected bibliography, 1965–1976.* Bibliographic Series no. 8. Ottawa, Ont.: Ontario Ministry of Labour, 1977, 27 pp.

B292. Brickman, W.W. "Light on the Segregation Issue." *School and Society* 83 (Apr. 14, 1956), 135–6.

B293. Bridges, [Leonard] Hal. *Civil War and Reconstruction.* Publication no. 5. Washington, D.C.: American Historical Association, Service Center for Teachers of History, 1957, 25 pp. A second edition of 25 pp. was issued in 1962.

B294. *A Brief List of Materials Relating to the Blues.* Washington, D.C.: Library of Congress, Music Division, Archives of Folk Song, Nov. 19, 1969.

B295. Brignano, Russell Carl. *Black Americans in Autobiography: an annotated bibliography of autobiographies and autobiographical books written since the Civil War.* Durham, N.C.: Duke University Press, 1974, 118 pp.

B296. Brignano, Russell Carl. "Richard Wright: a bibliography of secondary sources." *Studies in Black Literature* 2 (Summer 1971), 19–25.

B297. Brimmer, Andrew F., and Harriett Harper. "Economist's Perception of Minority Problems: a view of emerging literature." *Journal of Economic Literature* 8:3 (Sept. 1970), 783–806.

B298. Briscoe, Dorothy L., et al. *A Bibliography of Research on the Negro in Higher Education, 1932–1969.* Normal, Ala.: Alabama A & M University, Joseph F. Drake Library, 36 pp.

B299. Britton, Jean E. *Selected Books about the Afro-American for Very Young Children, K–2.* Boston, Mass.: Massachusetts Department of Education, Bureau of Curriculum Innovation, 1969, 15 pp.

B300. Broadhead, Clare A. *The Negro Freedom Movement, Past and Present: an annotated bibliography*. Detroit, Mich.: Wayne Co. Intermediate School District, Desegregation Advisory Project, 1967, 101 pp.

B301. Brock, W.R. "Race and the American Past: a revolution in historiography." *History* [Great Britain] 52:174 (1967), 49–59.

B302. Broderick, Dorothy May. "The Image of the Black in Popular and Recommended American Juvenile Fiction, 1827–1967." Ph.D. dissertation, Columbia University, 1971, 556 pp. Published as *Image of the Black in Children's Fiction*, New York: R.R. Bowker, 1973, 219 pp.

B303. Brokaw, John W. "The Minstrel Show in the Hoblitzelle Theatre Arts Library." *Library Chronicle of the University of Texas* 4 (1972), 23–30.

B304. Bronte, Diana Lydia. *A More Perfect Union: time out for man*. Princeton, N.J.: National Humanities Series, 1972, 12 pp.

B305. Brooks, Alexander D., Albert A.Alexander, and Virginia H. Ellison. *Civil Rights and Liberties in the U.S.: an annotated bibliography. With a selected list of fiction and the audio-visual materials*. New York: Civil Liberties Educational Foundation, 1962, 151 pp.

* Brooks, Elaine C. See P46.

B306. Brooks, Georgia M. *Bibliography on Ann Allen Shockley*, 1980, 1 p.

B307. Broomer, Stu. "Albert Ayler on Record: free spiritual music." *Coda* 8:1 (Apr.-May 1967), 2–5.

B308. "Brotherhood Week . . . : annual multicultural list of books for children and young people: 1980." *Read, See and Hear* 29:4, 4 pp. Issued by the Newark, N.J., Board of Education, Bureau of Libraries and Audiovisual Education.

B309. "Brotherhood Week . . . : multicultural books for children and young people." *Read, See and Hear* 28:5, 5 pp. Issued by the Newark, N.J., Board of Education, Bureau of Libraries and Audiovisual Education.

B310. Brotherhood Week . . . : multicultural books for children and young people, 1977 [sic]." *Read, See and Hear* 27:5 (Feb. 13, 1978), 4 pp. Issued by the Newark N.J., Board of Education, Bureau of Libraries and Audiovisual Education.

B311. Brouner, Terre, and Mimi Grindon. *Discrimination Today in the U.S.A. Tools for Research: directory of human relations agencies and bibliography on human rights*. Social Action Series 1, no. 8. Purchase, N.Y.: Manhattanville College of the Sacred Heart, Social Action Secretariat, 1961, 28 pp.

B311A. Brousseau, Bill, and Carol Klein. *Affirmative Action, Equal Employment Opportunity in the Criminal Justice System: a selected bibliography*. Washington, D.C. (?): National Institute of Justice, 1980, 49 pp.

* Brown, Ann Duncan. See L102.

B312. Brown, Barbara, Deborah A. MacDonald, and Arnell J. Marshall. *The

Contemporary black Woman in Africa and America: a selected bibliography of books and periodical articles published from 1960–1975. Washington, D.C.: Howard University Library, 1975, 55 pp.

B313. Brown, Carol. *Afro-American History.* Focus: Black American Bibliography Series. Bloomington, Ind.: Indiana University Libraries, 1969, 43 pp.

* Brown, Cheryl Luvenia. See S263.

* Brown, Clifton L. See W106, W107.

B314. Brown, Ernest James. "An Annotated Bibliography of Selected Solo Music Written for the Piano by Black Composers." D.M.A. dissertation, University of Maryland, 1976, 110 pp.

B315. Brown, H.D. "Brief Survey of the Holdings of Michigan Institutions and Activities in the Field of Negro Life and History." *Negro History Bulletin* 26 (Oct. 1962), 5 + .

B316. Brown, Martha H. "A Listing of Non-Print Materials on Black Women." *In* Gloria T. Hull, Patricia Bell Scott, and Barbara Smith, eds. *But Some of Us Are Brave: Black women's studies.* Old Westbury, N.Y.: Feminist Press, 1982, pp. 307–26.

B317. Brown, Myland R. *Bibliography; history of the Negro.* Orangeburg, S.C.: South Carolina State College, Miller F. Whittaker Library.

B318. Brown, Rae Linda. *Music, Printed and Manuscript, in the James Weldon Johnson Memorial Collection of Negro Arts and Letters, Yale University: an annotated catalog.* New York: Garland, 1982, 322 pp.

* Brown, Robert T. See S43.

B319. Brown, Warren. *Checklist of Negro Newspapers in the U.S., 1827–1946.* School of Journalism Series no. 2. Jefferson City, Mo.: Lincoln University, School of Journalism, 1946, 37 pp.

B320. Browne, Robert S. *Black Economic Development: a bibliography.* New York: Afram Associates, 1970.

B321. Brownell, Jean B. *Negroes in Oregon before the Civil War.* Typescript in the Oregon Historical Society Library, 25 pp.

* Bruccoli, Matthew J. See C105, C106, C180, D176, K37.

B322. Brucker, Joan W. *An Annotated Bibliography of White Racism in Public School Education Today: sources for awareness and action.* New York: Foundation for Change, 1972, 4 pp.

* Brunner, G. Allen. See W143.

B323. Bruno, Louis. *Preliminary List of Resource Materials on Minority Groups.* Olympia, Wash.: State Superintendent of Public Instruction, 1968.

B324. Bruyninckx, Walter. *Fifty Years of Recorded Jazz, 1917–1967.* Mechelen, Belgium: Author, 1968, 1000 pp.

*Bryen, D.N. See H19.

B325. Bryer, Jackson R. "Richard Wright." *In* Louis D. Rubin. *A Bibliographical Guide to the Study of Southern Literature.* Baton Rouge, La.: Louisiana State University Press, 1969, pp. 333–34.

B326. Bryer, Jackson R. "Richard Wright (1908–1960): a selected checklist of criticism." *Wisconsin Studies in Contemporary Literature* 1 (Fall 1960), 22–3.

* Bryer, Jackson R. See also D1, D10, G36, I16, K80, M83, M84, M85, R66, T110A.

B327. Bryl, Susan, and Erwin K. Welsch. *Black Periodicals and Newspapers: a union list of holdings in the libraries of the University of Wisconsin and library of the State Historical Society of Wisconsin.* Madison, Wis.: University of Wisconsin, Memorial Library, 1975, 80 pp.

* Bryl, Susan. See also S265.

* Buchanan, Catherine. See K73.

* Buchmier, J.O. See P70.

B328. Buck, James E. *A Bibliography of Negro Literature Held by Washburn University.* Topeka, Kan.: Washburn University Library.

B329. Buckley, Richard Dale. "Negro Periodicals: historical notes and suggestions for use." *Social Education* 33 (Apr. 1969), 426–8.

B330. Bullen, George. "Bibliography." *Uncle Tom's Cabin.* Boston, Mass.: Houghton, Osgood and Co., 1878, pp. xxxix-lviii. Holdings of the British Museum.

B331. Bullock, Julia Amanda. *The Role of the Negro in Eighteenth Century America: a bibliography.* Boston, Mass.: Simmons College School of Library Science, 1942, 9 pp.

B332. Bullock, Penelope L. "The Negro Periodical Press in the United States, 1838–1909." Ph.D. dissertation, University of Michigan, 1971, 455 pp. Published by Louisiana State University Press, 1981, 330 pp.

B333. "Bunk [Johnson] Discography." *Down Beat* 16 (Aug. 26, 1949), 6.

B334. Burdex, Monica J. *Black Women and the Women's Liberation Movement, 1960-present.* Readers Advisory Service. Selected Topical Booklists 152. Chicago, Ill.: Science Research Associates, 1976, 2 pp.

* Burgess, R. See S134.

B334A. Burkett, Randall K. "Afro-American Religious History: articles published during 1976." *Newsletter of the Afro-American Religious History Group of the American Academy of Religion* 1:2 (Winter 1977), 5–11.

B335. Burkett, Randall K. "A Checklist of Books and Pamphlets by Afro-American Episcopal Clergymen Ordained to 1865." *Newsletter of the Afro-American Religious History Group of the American Academy of Religion* 5:1 (Fall 1980), 7–10.

B336. Burkett, Randall K. "Checklist of *Minutes of the A.M.E.Z. Church,* 1830–1840." *Newsletter of the Afro-American Religious History Group of the American Academy of Religion* 1:1 (Fall 1976), 4–5.

B336A. Burkett, Randall K. "Recent Works on Afro-American Religious History: a listing from 'America: history and life.' " *Newsletter of the Afro-American Religious History Group of the American Academy of Religion* 2:1 (Fall 1977), 5–7.

B337. Burkett, Randall K. "Sources for Biographical Sketches of Afro-American Religious Leaders." *Newsletter of the Afro-American Religious History Group of the American Academy of Religion* 3:1 (Fall 1978), 5–9.

B338. Burks, Mary Fair. "A Survey of Black Literary Magazines in the U.S." Ed.D. dissertation, Columbia University Teachers College, 1975, 452.pp.

B339. Burns, Jim. "Dexter Gordon, 1942–1952." *Jazz Journal* 25 (Apr. 1972), 39.

B340. Burns, Jim. "Early [John] Birks [Dizzy Gillespie]." *Jazz Journal* 24:3 (Apr. 1971), 18+

B341. Burns, Jim. "[John Birks] Dizzy Gillespie, 1945–1950." *Jazz Journal* 25 (Jan. 1972), 14.

B342. Burr, Nelson, James Ward Smith, and A. Leland Jamieson. "The Negro Church," Vol. 4, parts 1 and 2, pp. 348–81; "The Anti-Slavery Crusade," Vol. 4, parts 3, 4, and 5, pp. 683–93; "Negro Religious Literature," Vol. 4, parts 3, 4, and 5, pp. 938–43. *A Critical Bibliography of Religion in America*. Princeton, N.J.: Princeton University Press, 1961.

B343. Burrell, Anna P. *Partial Bibliography for Human Relations*. Buffalo, N.Y.: SUNY, College for Teachers, Edward H. Butler Library, 1953, 45 pp.

B344. Burris, Andrew M. "American First Editions: Charles W. Chesnutt, 1858–1932." *Publishers Weekly* 131 (May 15, 1937), 2033.

B345. Burris, Andrew M. "A Bibliography of Works by Paul Laurence Dunbar, Negro Poet and Author, 1872–1906." *The American Collector* 5 (Nov. 1927), 68–73.

B346. Burstein, Rose Ann. *Selected List of Black Studies Books Currently in the Sarah Lawrence College Library*. Bronxville, N.Y.: Sarah Lawrence College Library, 1970, 17 pp.

* Burton, Warren. See S157.

B347. Busacca, Basil. "Checklist of Black Playwrights, 1823–1970." *Black Scholar* 5:1 (Sept. 1973), 48–54.

B348. Bush, Robert D., and Blake Touchstone. "A Survey of Manuscript Holdings in the Historic New Orleans Collection." *Louisiana History* 16:1 (1975), 89–96.

B349. Butterfield, Mary. *Civil Rights in the '60's: from sit-in to black power*. Ypsilanti, Mich.: Eastern Michigan University Library, 20 pp.

B350. Buttlar, Lois, and Lubomyr R. Wynar. *Building Ethnic Collections: an annotated guide for school media centers and public libraries*. Littleton, Col.: Libraries Unlimited, 1977, 434 pp.

B351. Buzelin, Jean, and Alex Dutilh. "Discographie—Archie Shepp." *Jazz Hot* 42 (Mar. 1976), 24–7.

C

C1. Cabiness, Togo. *Books by Negro Writers*. Morristown, Tenn.: Morristown College, Carnegie Library, 2 pp.

C2. Cabiness, Togo. *Books on Negro Life and History*. Morristown, Tenn.: Morristown College, Carnegie Library, 8 pp.

C3. *Calendar of the Gerrit Smith Papers in the Syracuse University Library, General Correspondence, Vol. I, 1819–1846*. Albany, N.Y.: U.S. Works Progress Administration, Historical Records Survey, Division of Community Service Programs, 1941, 290 pp.

C4. *Calendar of the Manuscripts in the Schomburg Collection of Negro Literature, Located at 135th Street Branch, New York Public Library*. Compiled by the Historical Records Survey, Work [sic] Projects [sic] Administration, New York City, 1942, 3 vols. Reprinted, New York: Andronicus [1970], 548 pp.

C5. *Calendar of the Writing of Frederick Douglass, in the Frederick Douglass Memorial Home, Anacosta, D.C.* Washington, D.C.: Historical Records Survey, Division of Professional and Service Projects, Work Projects Administration [sic]; 1940, 93 pp.

C6. Not used.

C7. Caliver, Ambrose. *Sources of Instructional Materials on Negroes*. Washington, D.C.: Federal Security Agency, Office of Education, 1944, 19 pp.

C8. Caliver, Ambrose, and Ethyl Graham Greene. *Education of Negroes: a five-year bibliography, 1931–5*. 1937. No. 8. Washington, D.C.: Office of Education, 1937, 63 pp.

C9. Caliver, Ambrose, and Ethyl Graham Greene. *Good References on the Life and Education of Negroes*. Bibliography no. 68. Washington, D.C.: Office of Education, 1940, 13 pp.

C10. Caliver, Ambrose, and Theresa B. Wilkins. *Sources of Instructional Materials on Negroes*. Rev. ed. Committee for the Defense of Democracy through Education, and the Joint Committee of the National Education Association and the American Teachers Association. Washington, D.C.: National Education Association, 1946, 23 pp.

C11. Calkins, David L. "Nineteenth Century Black History [of Cincinnati]: a bibliography." *Cincinnati Historical Society Bulletin* 28:4 (1970), 336–43.

C12. Calloway, Ina Elizabeth. "Annotated Bibliography of Books in the Trevor Arnett Library Negro Collection Relating to the Civil War." M.S. in L.S. thesis, Atlanta University, 1963, 41 pp.

C13. Cameron, Colin. *Attitudes of the Poor and Attitudes toward the Poor: an annotated bibliography*. Madison, Wis.: University of Wisconsin, Institute for Research on Poverty, 1975, 182 pp. A supplement of 157 pp. by Cameron and Mara O'Neill was issued in 1977.

C14. Cameron, Colin. *Discrimination in Testing Bibliography*. Rev. ed. ERIC Doc. no. ED 086–736. Madison, Wis.: University of Wisconsin, Institute for Research on Poverty, 1973, 141 pp.

C15. Cameron, Colin, and Judith Blackstone. *Minorities in the Armed Forces: a selected, occasionally annotated bibliography*. Madison, Wis.: University of Wisconsin, Institute for Research on Poverty, 1970, 32 pp.

C16. Cameron, Colin, and Anila Bhatt Menon. *Hard Core Unemployment: a selected, annotated bibliography*. ERIC Doc. no. ED 039–323. Madison, Wis.: University of Wisconsin, Institute for Research on Poverty, 1969, 28 pp.

C17. Cameron, Colin, Mara O'Neill, and Jane Pearlmutter. *Poverty-Related Topics found in Dissertations*. Madison, Wis.: University of Wisconsin, Institute for Research on Poverty, 1976, 74 pp.

C18. Cameron, Dee Birch. "A Maya Angelou Bibliography." *Bulletin of Bibliography* 36:1 (Jan.–Mar. 1979), 50–2.

C19. Campbell, Agnes. *Negro Housing in Towns and Cities, 1927–37*. Bull. No. 46. New York: Russell Sage Foundation Library, 1937, 5 pp.

C19A. Campbell, D.W. "Black Genealogy and the Public Library: a bibliography." *Public Libraries* 19 (Spring 1980), 22–4.

C19B. Campbell, Dorothy. *Index to Black American Writers in Collective Biographies*. Littleton, Col.: Libraries Unlimited, 1983, 162 pp.

C20. Campbell, Georgetta Merritt. "Extant Collections of Black Newspapers 1880–1915 in the Libraries of the U.S.: the need for a scholarly index." Ed.D. thesis, Fairleigh Dickinson University, 1978, 399 pp.

C21. Campbell, Georgetta Merritt. *Extant Collections of Early Black Newspapers: a research guide to the black press, 1880–1915, with an index to the Boston "Guardian," 1902–1904*. Troy, N.Y.: Whitston Publishing Co., 1981, 401 pp.

C22. Campbell, Mrs. M.V., and J.A. Hulbert. *A Bibliography of Graduate Masters Theses Written at Virginia State College, 1937–49*. Petersburg, Va.: Virginia State College, Johnson Memorial Library, 1949, 29 pp.

C23. *Canadian Black Studies Bibliography*. London, Ont.(?), 1971, 96 pp.

C24. Cannon, Helen. "Cornrows and Braids: a bibliography." *Unabashed Librarian* 36 (1980), 10. Reprinted from *BARC Notes*, June 1980.

C25. Capouya, E. "Documents of the Struggle for Public Decency." *Saturday Review* 47 (July 25, 1964), 13 + .

C26. Carey, D., F. Dutton, and G. Hulme. "Jelly Roll's [Morton] Victor Jazz." *Jazz Journal* 15 (June 1962), 8–10; (July 1962), 9–10.

C27. Carey, Dave, Albert J. McCarthy, and Ralph G.V. Venables. *The Directory of Recorded Jazz and Swing Music*. Alphabetically through "Longshaw." Continued by Jepsen and McCarthy. Fordingbridge, Hamps., England: The Delphic Press, 1948, 1112 pp. in six volumes.

C28. Carey, Elizabeth L., and Corienne K. Robinson. *A Selected List of References on Housing for Negroes*. Washington, D.C.: National Housing Agency, Federal Public Housing Authority Library, 1945, 17 pp.

C29. Carey, Emily A., Olivia M. Espin, and Doris Munos. *Women, Ethnicity and Counseling: a resource list*. Boston, Mass.: Womanspace Feminist Therapy Collective, 1977.

C30. Carithers, Martha W. "School Desegregation and Racial Cleavage, 1954–70: a review of the literature." *Journal of Social Issues* 26 (Autumn 1970), 25–47.

C31. Carl Gregor, Herzog zu Mecklenburg [Duke of Mecklenburg]. *International Jazz Bibliography: jazz books from 1919 to 1968*. Sammlung musikwissenschaftlichter Abhandlungen 49. Strasbourg: P.H. Heitz, 1969, 198 pp.

C32. Carl Gregor, Herzog zu Mecklenburg [Duke of Mecklenburg]. *1970 Supplement to International Jazz Bibliography and International Drum and Percussion Bibliography*. Beiträge zur Jazzforschung, 3. Graz: Universal Edition, 1971.

C33. Carl Gregor, Herzog zu Mecklenburg [Duke of Mecklenburg]. *1971/72/73 Supplement to International Jazz Bibliography and Selective Bibliography of Some Jazz Background Literature and Bibliography of Two Subjects Previously Excluded* [Poetry and fiction, and cartoons and drawing]. Beirtäge zur Jazzforschung, 6. Graz: Universal Edition, 1975.

C34. *Carl Van Vechten, 1880–1964; a memorial exhibition of his life and work from the collection of Paul Padgette*. San Francisco, Cal.: San Francisco Public Library, 1965, 22 pp.

C35. "Carl Van Vechten 17 June 1880: 17 June 1980 A Centenary Exhibition of Some of His Gifts to Yale. Arranged by Donald Gallup." *Yale University Library Gazette* 55:2 (Oct. 1980). Reprinted as a pamphlet.

C36. Carlos, Luis. *Black Bibliography 1970*. Monterey, Cal.: Monterey Peninsula College Library, 1970, 29 pp.

C37. Carlson, Alvar W. "A Bibliography of the Geographical Literature on the American Negro, 1920–71." *The Virginia Geographer* 7 (Spring-Summer 1972), 12–8.

C38. Carlson, K. "Equalizing Educational Opportunities." *Review of Educational Research* 42 (Fall 1972), 453–75.

C39. Carmela, Margaret. *The American Negro in Periodicals, 1964–70*. Convent Station, N.J.: College of St. Elizabeth, Mahoney Library.

C40. Carmela, Margaret. *The Life and History of Black America*. Convent Station, N.J.: College of St. Elizabeth, Mahoney Library, 1970, 16 pp.

C41. Carmela, Margaret. *Negro Authors*. Convent Station, N.J.: College of St. Elizabeth, Mahoney Library, 1970, 5 pp.

C42. Carney, M. "Doctoral Dissertations and Projects Related to the Education of Negroes." *Advanced School Digest* 7 (Feb. 1942), 43–4.

C43. Carr, Crystal. *Ebony Jewels: a selected bibliography of books by and about black women*. Rev. ed. Inglewood, Cal.: Crenshaw-Imperial Branch Library, 1975.

* Carr, John C. See G37, G66.

C44. Carr, M.L., and M. Jenkins. "Multi-ethnic Materials." *Wisconsin Library Bulletin* 68 (July 1972), 251–4.

C45. Carriere, Claude. "Stomp [sic], Look, and Listen: discographie sélective des microsillons du Duke [Ellington]." *Jazz Hot* 298 (Oct. 1973), 22 + .

C46. Carroll, Clifford. *Crosby Library—Books on Negroes*. Spokane, Wash.: Gonzaga University, Crosby Library, 1968, 25 pp.

* Carson, Chris. See Q6.

C47. Carter, George E., and C. Peter Ripley. *Black Abolitionist Papers, 1830–1865: a guide to the microfilm edition*. Sanford, N.C.: Microfilming Corporation of America, 1980.

C48. Carter, Purvis M. "The Negro in Periodical Literature, 1970–1972." *Journal of Negro History* 63:1 (Jan. 1978), 87–92; 63:2 (Apr. 1978), 161–89; 63:3 (July 1978), 262–306.

* Cartwright, William S. See V54, V55.

C49. Cary, Reby. *Black Leadership in U.S. History: princes shall come out of Egypt*. Arlington, Tex.: University of Texas at Arlington Library.

C50. Caselli, Ron, et al. *The Minority Experience; a basic bibliography of American ethnic studies*. Santa Rosa, Cal.: Sonoma County Superintendent of Schools, 1970, 61 pp. Revised and enlarged in 1975 to 106 pp.

C51. Cashman, Marc, and Barry Klein. *Bibliography of American Ethnology*. Rye, N.Y.: Todd Publications, 1976, 304 pp.

C52. Cassata, Mary B. "Who Are the Users of Afro-American Literature and How Is That Literature Used?"*In* Herman L. Totten, ed. *Bibliographical Control of Afro-American Literature*, Vol. 1. Eugene, Ore.: University of Oregon, School of Librarianship, 1976, pp. 1–30.

C53. Cassidy, Rita M. "Black History: some basic readings." *History Teacher* 2:4 (1969), 36–9.

C54. Caster, Lillie D. *Negro History and Literature: selected lists*. Glassboro, N.J.: Glassboro State College. Reprinted by the New Jersey State Library, Trenton.

C55. *Catalog of Books on the War of the Rebellion and Slavery, in the Library of the State Historical Society of Wisconsin*. Madison, Wis.: State Historical Society of Wisconsin, 1887, 61 pp.

C56. *Catalog of Publications, 1964*. Washington, D.C.: U.S. Commission on Civil Rights, 1964.

C57. *Catalog of the Negro Collections in the Florida Agricultural and Mechanical University Library and the Florida State University Library*. Tallahassee, Fla.: Friends of the F.S.U. Library, 1969, 80 pp.

C58. *Catalog of the Old Slave Mart Museum and Library*. Charleston, S.C. Boston, Mass.: G.K. Hall, 1978, 2 vols.

C59. *Catalogue, Heartman Negro Collection, Texas Southern University*. Houston, Tex.: Texas Southern University, 1957, 325 pp.

C60. Not used.

C61. *Catalogue of the E. Azalia Hackley Memorial Collection of Negro Music, Dance and Drama in the Detroit Public Library.* Boston, Mass.: G.K. Hall, 1979, 1 vol.

C62. *Catalogue of the Special Negro and African Collection, Vail Memorial Library, Lincoln University.* Lincoln, Pa.: Lincoln University, Vail Memorial Library, 2 vols. A microfilm supplement covers acquisitions from 1970 to June 1977.

C63. "The Cause Is Mankind: a booklist." *Minnesota Libraries* 21 (Dec. 1965), 234–8.

C64. Cawthorne, Edythe O. *We Walk in Proud Shoes.* Iowa State Travelling Library, 1968.

C65. [Cecil Taylor Discography]. *Coda* (Mar. 1975), 8.

C66. Cederholm, Theresa Dickason. *Afro-American Artists: a bio-bibliographical directory.* Boston, Mass.: Boston Public Library, 1973, 348 pp.

C67. Cerri, Livio. *Jazz in microsolco.* Pisa: Nistri-Lischi, 1963, 505 pp.

C68. Chamberlain, Alexander F. "Record of Negro Folk-lore." *Journal of American Folk-lore* 16 (July-Sept. 1903), 273–4; 17 (Jan.-Mar. 1904), 77–9; 18 (Apr.-June 1905), 156; 18 (July-Sept. 1905), 244; 19 (Jan.-Mar. 1906), 75–7; 21 (Apr.-Sept. 1908), 263–7; 22 (Jan.-Mar. 1909), 102–4.

C69. Chamberlain, G.L. "On Being Black and Being American." *America* 128 (Jan. 20, 1973), 42–3.

C70. Chambers, Frederick. *Black Higher Education in the United States: a selected bibliography on Negro higher education and historically black colleges and universities.* Westport, Conn.: Greenwood Publishing, 1978, 268 pp.

C71. Chandler, Sue. "A Bibliography of Sources in the Fisk University Library about Aaron Douglas." *BANC!* 4:2/5:1 (Sept. 1974/June 1975), 22–4.

C71A. Chandler, Sue. "Books about the Fisk Jubilee Singers in the Fisk University Library Special Collections: materials on or writings by the Fisk Jubilee Singers to be found in selected titles." *BANC!* 2:1 (Dec. 1971), 3–5.

C71B. Chandler, Sue. "Books and Articles by John Wesley Work III in the Fisk University Library Special Collections: selected items about John Wesley Work appearing in the Fisk University Library Special Collections." *BANC!* 3:1 (Dec. 1972), 18–9.

C72. Chandler, Sue. "A Selected Annotated List of Reference Books Reflecting the Black Experience." *In* E.J. Josey and Ann Allen Shockley, eds. *Handbook of Black Librarianship.* Littleton, Col.: Libraries Unlimited, 1977, pp. 134–42.

* Chang, Sally. See E2A.

C73. *Changing Patterns: the Negro in America.* Boston, Mass.: Boston Public Library, 1967.

C74. *Chaos or Community?* Toledo, Ohio.: Toledo Public Library, 1968.

C75. *Chaos to Community; dream to reality.* Syracuse, N.Y.: Onondaga County Library System.

C76. Chapman, Abraham. *The Negro in American Literature, and a Bibliography of Literature by and about Negro Americans.* Special publication no. 15. Oshkosh, Wis.: Wisconsin Council of Teachers of English, 1966, 135 pp.

C77. Chapman, Dorothy. *Index to Black Poetry.* Boston, Mass.: G.K. Hall, 1974, 541 pp.

C78. *Charles Spurgeon Johnson: a bibliography.* Nashville, Tenn.: Fisk University Library, 1947, 16 pp.

C79. [Charlie Mingus Discography]. *Hi Fi Stereophonic* (July 1975), 701.

C80. [Charlie Parker Discography]. *Hi Fi Stereophonic* (Feb. 1975), 136–9.

C81. [Charlie Parker. Radio Transcriptions]. *Record Research* 2:3 (May-June 1956), 24.

* Chase, L. See S194.

C82. Chauvard, M., and J. Démètre. "Down Excello Way." *Jazz Monthly* 8 (Nov. 1962), 3–6. Reprinted from "Du côté de chez Excello." *Jazz Hot* (Apr. 1962), 14–7.

C83. Chauvard, M., and J. Démètre. "Pour une discothèque de blues [Arhoalie label.]" *Jazz Hot* 180 (Oct. 1962), 13 + .

* Chauvard, M. See also D77, M115.

* Chaves, Antonio F. See G92.

C84. Cheatham, Mary L. *Afro-Americana.* Clarksville, Ark.: College of the Ozarks, Dobson Memorial Library, 1969.

C85. *A Check List of an Exhibition of John Brown, 1800–1859, and a Note on John Brown by Richard B. Harwell.* Lawrence, Kan.: University of Kansas Libraries, 1959, 15 pp.

C86. *A Checklist of Colby's Elijah Parish Lovejoy Collection.* Waterville, Me.: Colby College Library, 1944, 11 pp.

C87. *A Checklist of Selected Writings by Richard A. Long.* CAAS Bibliographies No. 12. Atlanta, Ga.: Center for African and African-American Studies, 12 pp.

* Cheney, Francis. See T10.

C88. Cherrington, George, and Brian Knight. *Jazz Catalogue: a discography of all British jazz releases complete with full personals and recording dates.* London: Jazz Journal, 1960–71, 10 vols.

C89. *The Chicago Afro-American Union Analytic Catalog: an index to materials on the Afro-American in the principal libraries of Chicago.* Boston, Mass.: G.K. Hall, 1972, 5 vols.

C90. *Children's Bibliography on Human and Race Relations.* Washington, D.C.: Analysis Press, 1973, 32 pp.

C91. Chilton, John. *Bill Coleman on Record.* London, England: Steve Lane, 1966, 18 pp.

C92. Chilton, John. *McKinney's Music: a bio-discography of McKinney's Cotton Pickers*. London, England: Bloomsbury Book Shop, 1978, 68 pp.

* Chisholm, Jonell. See K73.

C93. Chmura, Helene F. "Lead Belly's [Huddie Ledbetter] American Record Company Recordings." *The Discophile* 47 (Apr. 1956), 4–5.

C94. Chobanian, Peter, and Eleanor Colbert. *A Bibliography in the Lane Library on Black Studies*. Ripon, Wis.: Ripon College, Lane Library, 1970.

C95. Cholinski, Henryk. "Charlie Parker Discography." *Jazz Forum* (Mar.-May 1975).

C96. Cholinski, Henryk. "[Edward] Duke Ellington on LP's." *Jazz Forum* 23–6 (June-Dec. 1973).

C97. Cholinski, Henryk. "Louis Armstrong on LP's." *Jazz Forum* 17 (June 1972); 18 (Aug. 1972).

C98. Christensen, Carol, and Carol Hansen. *Minority Groups in the U.S.: a bibliography of books in the Bethel College Library*. St. Paul, Minn.: Bethel College, 1970, 50 pp.

C99. Christiansen, Dorothy. *Busing; a Center for Urban Education bibliography*. ERIC Doc. no. ED 061–378. New York: Center for Urban Education, 1971.

C100. Christiansen, Dorothy. "Desegregation, Integration: references in the collection of the library of the Center for Urban Education." *The Center Forum* (Dec. 23, 1968), 19–20.

C101. Christie, Richard E., and Peggy Cook. "A Guide to Published Literature Relating to the Authoritarian Personality through 1956." *Journal of Psychology* 45 (1958), 171–99.

C102. "A Chuck Berry Discography." *Rock It with Aware Magazine* 2:4 (1976), 22–4.

C103. Chung, Inso, and Bruce Smithson. *Black Bibliography*. Hayward, Cal.: California State College at Hayward Library, 1969 (?), 143 pp.

* Churchill, Frances O. See J103.

C103A. Clack, Doris H. *Black Literature Resources: analysis and organization*. New York: M. Dekker, 1975, 207 pp.

C103B. Clack, Doris H. "The Cataloging of Afro-American Literature: subject headings and classification." *In* Herman L. Totten, ed. *Bibliographical Control of Afro-American Literature*, Vol. 1. Eugene, Ore.: University of Oregon, School of Librarianship, 1976, pp. 160–98.

C103C. *The Clarence L. Holte Collection of Africana*. Festac '77. N.p: 2nd World Black and African Festival of Arts and Culture, 1977, 20 pp.

C104. Clark, A. Zane. *Afro- and Mexican-Americana: books and other materials in the library of the Fresno State College relating to the history, culture and problems of Afro-Americans and Mexican-Americans*. Fresno, Cal.: California State College at Fresno Library, 1969, 109 pp.

C105. Clark, C.E. Frazer, Jr. "[Everett] LeRoi Jones 1934-[Imamu Amiri Baraka]." *In* Matthew J. Bruccoli, ed. *First Printings of American Au-*

thors: contributions toward descriptive bibliography. Vol. 1. Detroit, Mich.: Gale Research, 1977, pp. 197–207.

C106. Clark, C.E. Frazer, Jr. "Richard [Nathaniel] Wright 1908–1960." *In* Matthew J. Bruccoli, ed. *First Printings of American Authors: contributions toward descriptive bibliography.* Vol. 1. Detroit, Mich.: Gale Research, 1977, pp. 427–30.

C107. Clark, D. "Toward Equality." *Commonweal* 80 (July 24, 1964), 518–9.

C108. Not used.

* Clark, Georgia, See V47.

C109. Clark, Geraldine. "Afro-American Authors Represented on the ALA Notable Books List." *In* E.J. Josey and Ann Allen Shockley, eds. *Handbook of Black Librarianship.* Littleton, Col.: Libraries Unlimited, 1977, pp. 156–60.

C110. Clark, H.B. "Basic Sources of Race Relations Literature." *Union Seminary Quarterly Review* 20 (Mar. 1965), 281–8.

C111. Clark, Vernon L. *A Bibliographic Guide to the Study of Black History.* ERIC Document no. 094–880. Chapel Hill, N.C.: University of North Carolina, Frank Porter Graham Center, 1974, 23 pp.

C112. Clark, Veve A. "Enough of the Blues: the year's work in black theatre, 1978, a biblioreview." *The Black Scholar* 11 (Sept.-Oct. 1979), 69–80.

* Clark, Viola Jones. See D93.

C113. Clarke, J.H. "Dimensions of the Black Experience: bibliography." *In* LeRoi Jones, ed. *African Congress: a documentary of the first modern Pan-African Congress.* New York: Morrow, 1972, pp. 436–45.

C114. Clarke, John Henrik. *Black Heritage: a history of Afro-Americans, a selected bibliography.* New York: WCBS-TV, 10 pp.

* Clark, John Henrik. See also K15, K23, K25.

C115. Clarke, Tobin. *Afro-American Heritage.* Ethnic Culture Series no. 6. Stockton, Cal.: Stockton-San Joaquin County Library, 1969, 21 pp.

C116. Not used.

C117. Not used.

C118. Clayton, Mayme A., and Kathleen S. Allen. *Index to the Afro-American Rare Book Collection* [of the Western States Black Research Center, Los Angeles, Cal.]. Denver, Col.: Information Resources, 1977, 61 pp.

C119. Cleaves, Mary W., and Alma L. Gray. *A Bibliography of Negro History and Culture for Young Readers.* Miles M. Jackson, ed. Pittsburgh, Pa.: University of Pittsburgh Press, 1968.

* Cleaves, Mary W. See also J25.

C120. Clifford Brown Discography." *Les Cahiers du Jazz* 2, pp. 91–6.

C121. Clouzet, J. "Les éditions phonographiques aux États-Unis." *Jazz Magazine* 176 (Mar. 1970), 34–6.

C122. Cobb, W. Montague. "Problems in Physical Anthropology." *ACLS Bulletin* 32 (Sept. 1941), 90–100.

C123. Cobb, W. Montague. "Publications of Charles R. Drew." *Negro History Bulletin* 13 (June 1950), 213.

* Cogni, Giulio. See L15.

C124. Cogswell, Robert. "A Discography of Blackface Comedy Dialogs." *JEMF Quarterly* 15, pp. 166–79.

* Cohen, D. See M155.

C125. Cohen, Iva. *Civil Liberties and Civil Rights in the U.S. Today: a selected bibliography.* New York: American Jewish Committee, 1956, 36 pp.

C126. Cohen, Iva. *Intergroup Relations: a selected bibliography.* New York: American Jewish Committee, 1954, 14 pp.

C127. Cohen, Iva, and Diana Bernstein. *Civil Rights Today: a selected bibliography.* New York: American Jewish Committee, 1948, 15 pp. Rev. 1948, 17 pp.; 1949, 23 pp.; 1951, 31 pp.

C128. Cohn, Alan M. "Additions to [Letitia] Dace's LeRoi Jones [Imamu Amiri Baraka]." *Papers of the Bibliographic Society of America* 70, pp. 537–8.

C129. Cohn, F. "Exhibit Report; An Estimate of Importance; Books on Negro Life and History." *Negro History Bulletin* 31 (Dec. 1968), 6–7.

* Colbert, Eleanor. See C94.

C130. Cole, Donald B. *A Bibliography for the History of Black Americans.* Exeter, N.H.: Author (?), 1968, 5 pp.

C131. Cole, Johnetta B. "Black Women in America: an annotated bibliography." *Black Scholar* 3:4 (Dec. 1971), 41–53.

C132. Coleman, Maude B. *Bibliography and Information on Interracial Programs in the U.S.* Harrisburg, Pa.: Pennsylvania Department of Welfare, Bureau of Community Work, 1947, 34 pp.

C133. *Collection of Afro-American Literature: acquisitions list.* Boston, Mass.: Suffolk University, Museum of Afro-American History, 1979, 14 pp. A list of 9 pp. appeared in 1980.

C134. *Collection of Afro-American Literature: checklist of books by and about black writers associated with New England in the college library.* Boston, Mass.: Suffolk University, Museum of Afro-American History, 1977, 17 pp.

C135. Coller, Derek. "Big Bill Broonzy." *Matrix* 33, pp. 3–6.

C136. Collins, L.M. *Books by Black Americans.* Notes for Lib. Sci. 301 and Lib. Sci. 303. Institute on the Selection, Organization, and Use of Materials by and about the Negro, June 15-July 24, 1970. Nashville, Tenn.: Fisk University, 1970, 54 pp.

C137. Collins, Robert O., and Peter Duignan. *Americans in Africa: a preliminary guide to American missionary archives and library manuscript collections on Africa.* Hoover Institution Bibliographical Series: XII. Stanford, Cal.: Stanford University, The Hoover Institution on War, Revolution, and Peace, 1963, 96 pp.

C138. Collura, Maureen. *Afro-American Bibliography.* Buffalo, N.Y.: SUNY College at Buffalo, Edward H. Butler, 1971(?).

C139. "Colonization." *New York Public Library Bulletin* 6 (1902), 256–9.

C140. Colpitts, Corinne. *Black Authors Whose Works Are Represented in the Oklahoma State University Library.* Stillwater, Ok.: Oklahoma State University Library.

* Colton, Bob. See S126.

C141. Columbato, Donatello. "Muddy Waters Discography."*Blues Power* 1:4 (1974), 13–4.

C142. Colvig, Richard. "Black Music." *Choice* 6 (Nov. 1969), 1169–79.

C143. Colvig, Richard. *Black Music: a checklist of books.* Oakland, Cal.: Oakland Public Library, Music Division, 1969, 20 pp.

C144. *Combatting Racism.* College Park, Md.: Urban Information Interpreters, 1972, 55 pp.

C145. Combined Paperback Exhibit. *Red, White and Black (and Brown and Yellow) Minorities In America.* Briarcliff Manor, N.Y.: The Combined Book Exhibit, Inc., 1970, 31 pp.

C146. Combined Paperback Exhibit. *Red, White and Black Minorities in America: a collection of paperbacks with a selected list of bibliographies.* Briarcliff Manor, N.Y.: The Combined Book Exhibit, Inc., 1969, 33 pp.

C147. Committee to Investigate Assassinations. *American Political Assassinations: a bibliography of works published 1963–1970, related to the assassination of John F. Kennedy, Martin Luther King, Robert F. Kennedy.* Washington, D.C.: Georgetown University Library, Special Collections Division, 1973, 28 pp.

C148. *Common Ground: a guide to intergroup education, 1965.* Fairfax, Va.: Fairfax County Schools.

C149. Commons, John R. "Bibliography." *Chautauquan* 38 (Nov. 1903), 234.

C150. *Community Organization and Intergroup Relations: a selected bibliography.* Bibliographic series no. 6. Chicago, Ill.: American Council on Race Relations, 1949, 5 pp.

C151. *Company Experience with the Employment of Negroes.* Selected References no. 60. Princeton, N.J.: Princeton University, Department of Economics and Social Institutions, Industrial Relations Section, 1954, 4 pp.

C152. Condon, Rita. "Fifty Books for School Libraries on the Blacks." *Wilson Library Bulletin* (Mar. 1969), 657–64. Discussion, June 1969, p. 946.

* Cone, James H. See E2.

C153. Connor, Donald Russell, et al. *Twenty Years of the Duke [Ellington]*. Pt. 1: 1933–1955. Carnegie, Pa.: Pope's Records Unlimited, 1966, 12 pp.

C154. Conover, Helen F. *Interracial Relations in the U.S.: a selected list of references*. Washington, D.C.: Library of Congress, General Reference and Bibliography Division, 1945, 21 pp.

C155. Conover, Helen F. *Race Relations: selected references for the study of the integration of minorities in American labor*. Washington, D.C.: Library of Congress, General Reference and Bibliography Division, 1944, 38 pp.

C156. Conrad, Gerhard. [Coleman Hawkins Discography]. *Jazzfreund* 16 (Sept. 1974), 30–1.

C157. Contant, Florence. *Community Development Corporations: an annotated bibliography*. Exchange Bibliography no. 530. Monticello, Ill.: Council of Planning Librarians, 1974, 40 pp.

C158. *The Contemporary Negro*. Harrisburg, Pa.: Pennsylvania State Library, General Library Bureau, 1970, 24 pp.

C159. Cook, Katherine M., and Florence E. Reynolds. *The Education of Native and Minority Groups: a bibliography, 1923–1932*. Washington, D.C.: U.S. Department of the Interior, Office of Education, 1933, 57 pp. A supplementary volume of 25 pp. covering 1932–1934 was issued in 1935 as U.S. Office of Education pamphlet no. 63.

C160. Cook, P.A.W. "Guide to the Literature on Negro Education." *Teachers College Record* 34 (May 1933), 671–7.

* Cook, Peggy. See C101.

C161. Cooke, A.L. *Black Studies*. Jackson, Tenn.: Lane College, J.K. Daniels Library, 17 pp.

C162. Cooke, A.L. *Negro Collection*. Jackson, Tenn.: Lane College, J.K. Daniels Library, 1965, 23 pp.

C163. Cooke, Ann. "Max Roach: a name discography." *Jazz Monthly* 9 (June 1963), 15–8.

C164. Cooke, Jack. " 'We insist!' The Max Roach Group Today and the 'Freedom Now Suite.' " *Jazz Monthly* 8 (July 1962), 3–4.

* Cooke, Jack. See also H31.

* Cooke, Roy. See D19.

C165. Cooper, David Edwin. *International Bibliography of Discographies: classical music and jazz and blues, 1962–1972; a reference book for record collectors, dealers and libraries; with a preface by Guy A. Marco*. Keys to Music bibliography no. 2. Littleton, Col.: Libraries Unlimited, 1975, 272 pp.

C166. Copeland, George Edward. "James Weldon Johnson: a bibliography." M.A. thesis, Pratt Institute Library School, 1951, 79 pp.

C167. Copenhaver, Christina, and Joanne Boelke. *Library Service to the Dis-*

advantaged: a bibliography. Bibliographic series no. 1. Minneapolis, Minn.: ERIC Clearinghouse for Library and Information Sciences, 1968, 19 pp.

C168. Cordasco, Francesco, et al. *The Equality of Educational Opportunity: a bibliography of selected references.* Totowa, N.J.: Littlefield, Adams, 1973.

C169. Cordell, John A. "Jackie Wilson Discography." *Time Barrier Express* 3:4 (consecutive issue no. 24) (Apr./May 1979), 31–2.

C170. Cornwell, Sophy. *Malcolm X: a selected bibliography.* Lincoln, Pa.: Lincoln University, Vail Memorial Library, 1969, 5 pp. Rev. ed., 1970, 6 pp.

C171. Cornwell, Sophy, and Richard Hawes. *Harlem Renaissance Bibliography.* Lincoln, Pa.: Lincoln University, Vail Memorial Library, 1976, 6 pp.

C172. Cornwell, Sophy, and Deborah Williams. *Vail Memorial Library: Guide to Reference Books in the Special Negro and African Collections.* Lincoln, Pa.: Lincoln University, 1972, 15 pp.

C173. Corrigan, Robert A. "Afro-American Fiction: a checklist 1853–1970." *American Studies Journal* 11:2 (Fall 1970), 114–35. Errata and additions, 12 (Spring 1971), 69–73.

C174. Corrigan, Robert A. "Afro-American Fiction Since 1970." *American Studies Journal* 14 (Fall 1973), 85–90.

C175. Corrigan, Robert A. "Bibliography of Afro-American Fiction 1853–1970." *Studies in Black Literature* 1:2 (Summer 1970), 51–86.

C176. Corrigan, Robert A., and Charles T. Davis. *Census of Afro-American Poetry.* Iowa City, Iowa: University of Iowa, American Civilization Program.

C177. Corrigan, Robert A., and Donald B. Gibson. *Richard Wright's Fiction: the critical response, 1940–1971.* Iowa City, Iowa: University of Iowa, 1971.

C178. Coughlan, Margaret N. *Folklore from Africa to the U.S: an annotated bibliography.* Washington, D.C.: Library of Congress, 1976, 161 pp.

* Countee, Thomas H., Jr. See G30A.

C179 "The Countee Cullen Memorial Collection." *Atlanta University Bulletin* (Dec. 1950), 20 + .

* Courtney, Terence. See M117.

C180. Covici, Allan. "Zora Neale Hurston 1903–1960." *In* Matthew J. Bruccoli, ed. *First Printings of American Authors: contributions toward descriptive checklists,* Vol. 1. Detroit, Mich.: Gale Research, 1977, pp 191–2.

* Covici, Allan. See also W104.

C181. Covo, Jacqueline. *The Blinking Eye: Ralph Waldo Ellison and his American, French, German and Italian Critics, 1952–1971: biblio-*

graphic essays and a checklist. Metuchen, N.J.: Scarecrow Press, 1974, 214 pp.

C182. Covo, Jacqueline. "Ralph Ellison in France: a bibliographic essays and a checklist of French criticism, 1954–1971." *College Language Association Journal* 16 (June 1973), 519–26.

C183. Covo, Jacqueline. "Ralph Waldo Ellison: bibliographic essays and a finding list of American criticism, 1952–1964." *College Language Association Journal* 15:2 (Dec. 1971), 171–96.

C184. Cowan, Robert Granniss. *Admission of the 31st State by the 31st Congress: an annotated bibliography of Congressional speeches upon the admission of California*. Author, 1962, 139 pp.

C185. Cowlyn, Martin. "The Blues Shouters: Part 1—Jimmy Witherspoon." *Blues-Link* 4 (1974), 5–7.

C186. Cowlyn, Martin. "The Blues Shouters: Part 2—Jimmy Rushing." *Blues-link* 5 (1974), 20–2.

C187. Crayton, James E. "A Case for Afro-American Collections." *California Librarian* 37:1 (1976), 18–21.

C188. "Cream of the Blues Catalog." *Billboard* 79 (June 24, 1967), 74–82 + .

C189. *Crisis, Black and White: Negro history, culture and protest*. Los Angeles, Cal.: Los Angeles Public Library, Community Discussion Program.

C190. *Crisis for Black and White*. Pittsburgh, Pa.: Carnegie Library, 1968, 12 pp.

* Crisman, Marjorie S. See S50.

* Cromer, Susan. See M45A.

C191. Cromwell, John W. "The American Negro Bibliography of the Year." *Papers of the American Negro Academy . . . read at the 19th annual meeting of the American Negro Academy . . . Washington, D.C., Dec. 28 and 29, 1915*, pp 73–8.

C192. Cromwell, Otelia, L.D. Turner, and E.B. Dykes. *Readings from Negro Authors for Schools and Colleges with a Bibliography of Negro Literature*. New York: Harcourt, Brace and Co., 1931.

C193. Crosbie, Ian. "Twentieth Century Gabriel [Erskine Hawkins]." *Jazz Journal* 25 (Aug. 1972), 16.

C194. Crosby, Muriel. *Reading Ladders for Human Relations*. 4th ed. Washington, D.C.: American Council on Education, 1963, 242 pp.

C195. Cross, Addie F. *Faculty Publications: first listing, 1940–1959, Hampton Institute, Hampton, Va*. Hampton, Va.: Hampton Institute, Huntington Library, 1959, 36 pp.

C196. Crouch, Barry A. "Hidden Sources of Black History: the Texas Freedmen's Bureau as a case study." *Southwest History Quarterly* 83 (Jan. 1980), 211–26.

C197. Crouchett, Lawrence. *Bibliography (Topical) on Afro-American His-*

tory, Culture, and Education. Pleasant Hill, Cal.: Diablo Valley College.

C198. Crouchett, Lawrence. *The Negro in U.S. History: a bibliography of books, pamphlets, periodicals, and articles*. Pleasant Hill, Cal.: Diablo Valley College, 1965, 35 pp.

C199. Crumb, Laurence N. *Mind and Soul: a checklist of sources for black studies available in the Library-Learning Center, University of Wisconsin-Parkside*. Kenosha, Wis.: University of Wisconsin-Parkside, 1976, 381 pp.

* Crump, Charlie. See S233, S234.

C200. Cullaz, Maurice. "Blues." *Jazz Hot* 264 (Sept. 1970), 37–8.

C201. Cullaz, Maurice. *Guide des Disques de Jazz*. Paris: Buchet/Chastel, 1971, 347 pp.

C202. *The Culture and Historical Contributions of American Minorities: a bibliography*. Buffalo, N.Y.: Buffalo Public Schools, 1967.

C203. *Cultures, Races, and Ethnic Groups*. Special Bibliography no. 31. Ft. Leavenworth, Kan.: U.S. Army Command and General Staff College, Library Division, 1973, 23 pp.

C204. Cunningham, Joan. "Secondary Studies on the Fiction of Charles W. Chesnutt." *Bulletin of Bibliography* 33:1 (Jan. 1976), 48–52.

C205. Cunningham, Scott. *A Bibliography of the Writings of Carl Van Vechten*. Centaur bibliographies no. 5. Philadelphia, Pa.: The Centaur Book Shop, 1924, 52 pp.

C206. Cunningham, Scott. *A Bibliography of the Writings of Carl Van Vechten*. With an overture in the form of a funeral march by Carl Van Vechten. Folcroft, Pa.: Folcroft Library Editions, 1972, 52 pp.

C207. Curl, Charles H. "Black Studies: form and content." *College Language Association Journal* 13 (Sept. 1969), 1–9.

C208. *Current Books about Negro Life in America*. Trenton, N.J.: Free Public Library, Children's Department, 1968.

C209. *Current Books about Negroes in America*. Trenton, N.J.: Free Public Library, Area Reference Library, Children's Department, 1969, 12 pp.

C210. Curry, Prudence L. *Books by and about the Negro available in the George Washington Carver Branch: supplemented by a list of books on the subject at the main library*. San Antonio, Tex.: San Antonio Public Library, 1941(?), 19 pp.

C211. Cusack, Thomas. [*Ferdinand*] *Jelly Roll Morton: an essay in discography*. London, England: Cassell, 1952, 40 pp

C212. Cushman, William Mitchell. *Equal Opportunity and the Urban Blight: an analysis of public policy and its implications for urban planning*. Exchange Bibliography no. 634. Monticello, Ill.: Council of Planning Librarians, 1974, 18 pp.

* Cypher, Irene F. See S40.

C213. Cyr, Helen, Barbara Baker, and George Noone. *Cultural Diversity: li-*

brary and audio visual materials for in-service education. Oakland, Cal.: Oakland Public Schools, 1964, 39 pp.

D

D1. Dace, Letitia. "Amiri Baraka (LeRoi Jones)." *In* M. Thomas Inge, Jackson R. Bryer, and Maurice Duke, eds. *Black American Writers, Bibliographic Essays*, Vol. 2. New York: St. Martin's Press, 1978, pp. 121–8.

D2. Dace, Letitia. *LeRoi Jones (Imamu Amiri Baraka): a checklist of works by and about him.* London, England: The Nether Press, 1971, 196 pp.; La Jolla, Cal.: Laurence McGilvery, 1971, 196 pp.

* Dace, Letitia. See also C128.

D3. Daguerre, Pierre. "Discographie de Otis Redding." *Soul Bag* 68 (1978), 14–23.

D4. Daguerre, Pierre, Kurt Mohr, and Jacques Perin. "Ike and Tina Turner Discographie." *Soul Bag* 55 (Oct. 1976), 19–29.

D5. Dain, Bernice, and David Nevin. *The Black Record: a selected discography of Afro-Americans on audio discs held by the Audio Visual Department, John M. Olin Library.* ERIC Document no. 094-081. Seattle, Wash.: Washington University, John M. Olin Library, 1973, 26 pp.

D6. Dakan, Norman E. *Black Literature.* CINCPACAF (DPSR) Director PACAF Libraries. APO San Francisco, Cal.: U.S. Pacific Air Forces, 1970, 69 pp.

D7. Dalquist, Janet A. *Suomi College Library Black Studies Bibliography.* Hancock, Mich.: Suomi College Library.

D8. Dalva, Harry, M. Kay Ogman, et al. *Words Like Freedom: a multi-cultural bibliography.* Burlingame, Cal.: California Association of School Librarians, Human Relations Committee, 1975, 77 pp.

D9. Damon, S. Foster. "The Negro in Early American Songsters." *Papers of the Bibliographic Society of America* 28 (1934), 132–63. Reprinted for private circulation.

D10. Dance, Daryl. "James Baldwin." *In* M. Thomas Inge, Jackson R. Bryer, and Maurice Duke, eds. *Black American Writers, Bibliographic Essays*, Vol. 2. New York: St. Martin's Press, 1978, pp. 73–120.

D11. Dance, Stanley, "Jazz in the Twenties." *The Saturday Review* 48 (Mar. 13, 1965), 136.

D12. Dandridge, Rita B. "On The Novels Written by Selected Black American Women: a bibliographical essay." *In* Gloria T. Hull, Patricia Bell Scott, and Barbara Smith, eds. *But Some of Us Are Brave: black women's studies.* Old Westbury, N.Y.: Feminist Press, 1982, pp. 261–79.

D12A. Daniel, Elenor Murphy, and Adine McClarty Rollins. *Index to Black Newspapers.* Wooster, Ohio: Micro Photography Division, Bell and Howell.

D13. Daniel, Jack L., and Linda F. Wharton. *Black American Rhetoric: a selected bibliography*. Arlington, Va.: ERIC (EDRS), 1976, 9 pp.

* Daniels, Belinda S. See D61.

* Danky, James P. See S265.

D14. Danner, Vinnie M. *A Bibliography of Published and Unpublished Materials on the Health Status of Blacks, Minorities and the Poor*. Nashville, Tenn.: Center for Health Care Research of Meharry Medical College, 1972, 40 pp.

D15. Darden, Joe T. *Ghetto: a bibliography*. Exchange Bibliography no. 1310. Monticello, Ill.: Council of Planning Librarians, 1977, 25 pp.

D16. Daughtery, Willia E. "Sissieretta Jones [Black Patti]: profile of a black artist." *Musical Analysis* 1:1 (Winter 1972), 12–18.

D17. Davies, John R. T. "The Alternate Earl Hines." *Storyville* 40 (Apr.-May 1972), 127–30.

D18. Davies, John R.T., and Roy Cooke. *The Music of [Thomas] Fats Waller*. London, England: Century Press, 1950, 40 pp. A second edition appeared in 1953.

D19. Davies, John R.T., and Laurie Wright. *Morton's Music: [Ferdinand] Jelly Roll Morton discography*. Chigwell, Essex, England: Storyville Publications, 1968, 40 pp. Addenda in *Storyville* 17 (June-July 1968), 29–30.

* Davies, Marshall W. See H118.

D20. Davies, Ron, Dan Mahony, and H. Meunier Harris. "The Records of Ethel Waters." *Playback* 2:6 (June 1949), 26–9.

* Davis, Charles T. See C176, F4.

D21. Davis, Ira. *A Pioneer in Black Literature—Charles Waddell Chesnutt*. Orangeburg, S.C.: South Carolina State College, Miller F. Whittaker Library.

D22. Davis, J.E. "'Southern Workman' Articles Special Index." *The Hampton Leaflets* 6:7 (1912), 30 pp.

D23. Davis, Lenwood G. "Bibliographic Material [housing]." *Negro History Bulletin* 39 (Apr. 1976), back cover.

D24. Davis, Lenwood G. *The Black Aged in the U.S.: an annotated bibliography*. Westport, Conn: Greenwood Publishing, 1980, 200 pp.

D25. Davis, Lenwood G. *Black Businesses, Employment, Economics and Finance in Urban America: a selective bibliography*. Exchange Bibliography no. 629. Monticello, Ill.: Council of Planning Librarians, 1974, 39 pp.

D26. Davis, Lenwood G. *Black Capitalism in Urban America*. Exchange Bibliography no. 630. Monticello, Ill.: Council of Planning Librarians, 1974, 53 pp.

D27. Davis, Lenwood G. *The Black Family in the U.S*. Exchange Bibliography no. 808–9. Monticello, Ill.: Council of Planning Librarians, 1975, 84 pp.

D28. Davis, Lenwood G. *The Black Family in the U.S.: a selected bibliography of annotated books, articles and dissertations on black families in America*. Westport, Conn.: Greenwood Publishing, 1978, 132 pp.

D29. Davis, Lenwood G. *The Black Family in Urban Areas of the U.S.: a bibliography of published works*. Exchange Bibliography no. 471. Monticello, Ill.: Council of Planning Librarians, 1973, 60 pp. A second edition, Exchange Bibliography no. 808–9, of 84 pp. was issued by the Council in 1975.

D30. Davis, Lenwood G. "The Black Woman in America: autobiographical and biographical material." *Northwest Journal of African and Black American Studies* 2 (Winter 1974), 27–9.

D31. Davis, Lenwood G. *The Black Woman in American Society: a selected annotated bibliography*. Boston, Mass.: G.K. Hall, 1975, 160 pp.

D32. Davis, Lenwood G. *Black Women in the Cities, 1872–1972: a bibliography of published works on the life and achievements of black women in the cities in the U.S.* Exchange Bibliography no. 336. Monticello, Ill.: Council of Planning Librarians, 1972, 53 pp. A second edition, Exchange Bibliography no. 751/752, of 75 pp., was issued by the Council in 1975.

D33. Davis, Lenwood G. *Blacks in Politics: an exploratory bibliography*. Exchange Bibliography no. 926. Monticello, Ill.: Council of Planning Librarians, 1975, 19 pp.

D34. Davis, Lenwood G. *Blacks in Public Administration: a preliminary survey*. Exchange Bibliography no. 973. Monticello, Ill.: Council of Planning Librarians, 1976, 11 pp.

D35. Davis, Lenwood G. *Blacks in the American West: a working bibliography*. Exchange Bibliography no. 582. Monticello, Ill.: Council of Planning Librarians, 1974, 42 pp. A second edition of 50 pp., Exchange Bibliography no. 984, was issued by the Council in 1976.

D36. Davis, Lenwood G. *Blacks in the Cities, 1900–1972: a bibliography*. Exchange Bibliography no. 329. Monticello, Ill.: Council of Planning Librarians, 1972, 42 pp. A second edition of 42 pp., Exchange Bibliography no. 787/788, updates the material to 1974 and was issued by the Council in 1975.

D37. Davis, Lenwood G. *Blacks in the Pacific Northwest, 1788–1972: a bibliography of published works and of unpublished source materials on the life and contributions of black people in the Pacific Northwest*. Exchange Bibliography no. 335. Monticello, Ill.: Council of Planning Librarians, 1972, 53 pp. A second edition of 93 pp., Exchange Bibliography no. 767/768, was issued by the Council in 1975. It updates the material to 1974.

D38. Davis, Lenwood G. *Blacks in the State of Ohio, 1800–1976: a preliminary survey*. Exchange Bibliography no. 1208/1209. Monticello, Ill.: Council of Planning Librarians, 1977, 68 pp.

D39. Davis, Lenwood G. *Blacks in the State of Oregon, 1788–1971: a bibliography of published works and of unpublished source materials on the life and achievements of black people in the Beaver State*. Exchange Bibliography no. 229. Monticello, Ill.: Council of Planning Librarians, 1971, 54 pp. A second edition of 85 pp., Exchange Bibliography no. 616, which updates the material to 1974 was published by the Council in 1974.

D40. Davis, Lenwood G. *Blacks in the State of Utah: a working bibliography*. Exchange Bibliography no. 661. Monticello, Ill.: Council of Planning Librarians, 1974, 11 pp.

D41. Davis, Lenwood G. *Crime in the Black Community: an exploratory bibliography*. Exchange Bibliography no. 852. Monticello, Ill.: Council of Planning Librarians, 1975, 26 pp.

D42. Davis, Lenwood G. *Deviant Behavior in the Black Community: an exploratory survey*. Exchange Bibliography no. 1057. Monticello, Ill.: Council of Planning Librarians, 1976, 15 pp.

D43. Davis, Lenwood G. *Ecology of Blacks in the Inner City: an exploratory bibliography*. Exchange Bibliography no. 785/786. Monticello, Ill.: Council of Planning Librarians, 1974, 16 pp.

D44. Davis, Lenwood G. *A History of Black Religion in Northern Areas: a preliminary survey*. Exchange Bibliography no. 734. Monticello, Ill.: Council of Planning Librarians, 1975, 5 pp.

D45. Davis, Lenwood G. *A History of Black Religion in Southern Areas: a preliminary survey*. Exchange Bibliography no. 733. Monticello, Ill.: Council of Planning Librarians, 1975, 6 pp.

D46. Davis, Lenwood G. *A History of Black Self-Help Organizations and Institutions in the U.S., 1776–1976: a working bibliography*. Exchange Bibliography no. 1207. Monticello, Ill.: Council of Planning Librarians, 1977, 11 pp.

D47. Davis, Lenwood G. *A History of Blacks in Higher Education, 1875–1975: a working bibliography*. Exchange Bibliography no. 720. Monticello, Ill.: Council of Planning Librarians, 1975, 10 pp.

D48. Davis, Lenwood G. *A History of Journalism in the Black Community: a preliminary survey*. Exchange Bibliography no. 862. Monticello, Ill.: Council of Planning Librarians, 1975, 35 pp.

D49. Davis, Lenwood G. *A History of Public Health, Health Problems, Facilities and Services in the Black Community: a working bibliography*. Exchange Bibliography no. 844. Monticello, Ill.: Council of Planning Librarians, 1975, 20 pp.

D50. Davis, Lenwood G. *A History of Selected Diseases in the Black Community: a working bibliography*. Exchange Bibliography no. 1059. Monticello, Ill.: Council of Planning Librarians, 1976, 28 pp.

D51. Davis, Lenwood G. *A History of Tuberculosis in the Black Community: a working bibliography*. Exchange Bibliography no. 859. Monticello, Ill.: Council of Planning Librarians, 1975, 13 pp.

D52. Davis, Lenwood G. *Housing in the Black Community: a selected bibliography of published works on housing laws, problems, planning and covenants in the black community.* Exchange Bibliography no. 925. Monticello, Ill.: Council of Planning Librarians, 1975, 19 pp.

D53. Davis, Lenwood G. *Index to Council of Planning Librarians Bibliographies on Blacks, Related to Blacks, on Africa, and Related to Africa: numbers 869–1310.* Exchange Bibliography no. 1374. Monticello, Ill.: Council of Planning Librarians, 1977, 5 pp.

D54. Davis, Lenwood G. *The Mental Health of the Black Community: an exploratory bibliography.* Exchange Bibliography no. 958. Monticello, Ill.: Council of Planning Librarians, 1975, 25 pp.

D55. Davis, Lenwood G. *Pan-Africanism: a selected bibliography.* Portland, Ore., (1972), 49 pp.

D56. Davis, Lenwood G. "Pan-Africanism: an extensive bibliography." *Geneva-Africa* [Geneva, Switzerland] 12:1 (Part 2) (Fall 1973), 103–20.

D56A. Davis, Lenwood G. *A Paul Robeson Research Guide: a selected annotated bibliography.* Westport, Conn.: Greenwood Publishing, 1982, 879 pp.

D57. Davis, Lenwood G. *Poverty and the Black Community: a preliminary survey.* Exchange Bibliography no. 965. Monticello, Ill.: Council of Planning Librarians, 1975, 22 pp.

D58. Davis, Lenwood G. *Psychology and the Black Community.* Exchange Bibliography no. 1060. Monticello, Ill.: Council of Planning Librarians, 1976, 17 pp.

D59. Davis, Lenwood G. *Sickle Cell Anemia: a preliminary survey.* Exchange Bibliography no. 763. Monticello, Ill.: Council of Planning Librarians, 1975. A second edition of 97 pp., Exchange Bibliography no. 1042/1043, was issued by the Council in 1976. A publication by Davis entitled *Sickle Cell Anemia: a selected, annotated bibliography* was published in 1978 by the National Black Bibliographic and Research Center, Newark, Del.

D60. Davis, Lenwood G. *A Working Bibliography on Published Materials on Black Studies Programs in the U.S.* Exchange Bibliography no. 1213. Monticello, Ill.: Council of Planning Librarians, 1977, 31 pp.

D61. Davis, Lenwood G., and Belinda S. Daniels. *Black Athletes in the U.S.: a bibliography of books, articles, autobiographies, and biographies on professional black athletes in the U.S., 1800–1981.* Westport, Conn.: Greenwood Publishing, 1981, 265 pp.

D62. Davis, Lenwood, G., and Janet Sims. *Black Artists in the U.S.: an annotated bibliography of books, articles, and dissertations on black artists, 1779–1979.* Westport, Conn.: Greenwood Publishing, 1980, 138 pp.

D63. Davis, Lenwood G., and Janet Sims. *Marcus Garvey: an annotated bibliography.* Westport, Conn.: Greenwood Publishing, 1980, 192 pp.

* Davis, Lenwood G. See also D133, H110.

D64. Davis, Morris E., and Andrew Roland. *The Occupational Health of Black Workers: a bibliography.* Public Administration Series No. 492. Monticello, Ill.: Vance Bibliographies, 1980, 21 pp.

D65. Davis, Nathaniel. *Afro-American Studies: a bibliography of doctoral dissertations and master's theses completed at the University of California, Los Angeles, from 1942 to 1980.* Los Angeles, Cal.: UCLA Center for Afro-American Studies, 1981, 50 pp.

D65A. Davis, Susan E. "Collection Development and the Special Subject Repository [The Schomburg Center for Research in Black Culture]." *Bookmark* 39:2 (Winter 1981), 100–4.

D66. Davison, Ruth A., and April Legler. *Government Publications on the Negro in America, 1948–1968.* Focus: Black American Bibliography Series. Bloomington, Ind.: Indiana University Libraries, 1969, 29 pp.

D67. Deahn, Jean. *The American Negro: his history, his education, his music, his family life and social condition, in politics.* Littleton, Col.: Arapahoe Community College Library, 1 p.

D68. Debroe, Georges. "Edward [Duke] Ellington in Question." *Point de Jazz* 10 (Oct. 1974), 95–6.

* Dees, Robert. See R86.

D69. Deiss, William A. *The Black Record: a selected discography of Afro-Americans on audio.* St. Louis, Mo.: Washington University Library.

D70. Delaunay, Charles. *Hot Discography.* New York: Commodore Record Co., 1943, 416 pp. Reprint of 1938 edition. There was also an edition in 1940. A publication of the same title also by Delaunay was issued in Paris by Le Hot Club de France with editions in 1936, 217 pp.; 1938, 408 pp.; and 1943, 540 pp.

D71. Delaunay, Charles. *New Hot Discography: the standard dictionary of recorded jazz.* New York: Criterion, 1948, 1963, 608 pp.

D72. DeLerma, Dominique-René. *Bibliography of Black Music:* Vol. 1, *Reference Materials;* Vol. 2, *Afro-American Idioms.* Westport, Conn.: Greenwood Publishing, 1981, 124 pp., 218 pp. Vol. 3, *Geographical Studies*, 1982, 284 pp.

D73. DeLerma, Dominique-René. *Black Concert and Recital Music: a provisional repertoire list.* Bloomington, Ind.: Indiana University, 1975.

D74. DeLerma, Dominique-René. "Black Music: a bibliographic essay." *Library Trends* 23 (Jan. 1975), 517–32.

D75. DeLerma, Dominique-René. *A Discography of Concert Music by Black Composers.* Minneapolis, Minn.: Afro-American Music Opportunities Association Press, 1973, 29 pp.

D76. Delormé, M. "Discographie commentée des enregistrements publics de Charlie Parker." *Jazz Hot* 207 (Mar. 1965), 30 + .

D77. Démètre, J., and M. Chauvard. "Pour une discothèque de blues." *Jazz Hot* 183 (Jan. 1963), 24–5; 184 (Feb. 1963), 22–3.

* Démètre, J. See also C82, C83.

D78. Demeusy, Bertrand. "Elmer Snowden Discography." *Jazz Journal* 16:4 (Apr. 1963), 15–6.

D79. Demeusy, Bertrand, and Otto Flückiger. *Arnett Cobb, with Discography: the wild man of the tenor sax.* Basel, Switzerland: Jazz Publications, 1962, 22 pp.

D80. Demeusy, Bertrand, and Otto Flückiger. *Discography of Lionel Hampton Orchestra, 1954–1958.* Basel, Switzerland: Jazz Publications, 1963, 30 pp.

D81. Demeusy, Bertrand, Otto Flückiger, Jorgen Grunner Jepsen, and Kurt Mohr. *[Oran] Hot Lips Page.* Basel, Switzerland: Jazz Publications, 1961, 30 pp. A 1 p. supplement was issued in 1962.

D82. DeMichael, D. "Jazz on Tape: a survey of the year's prerecorded stereo jazz tapes." *Down Beat* 32 (Dec. 2, 1965), 15 + .

D83. *Democracy Unlimited for America's Minorities.* California Federation for Civic Unity Collection. Los Angeles, Cal.: Los Angeles Public Library, 1944, 8 pp.

D84. Dempsey, D. "Uncle Tom's Ghost and the Literary Abolitionists." *Antioch Review* 6 (Sept. 1946), 442–8.

D85. Denby, Robert V. "Literature by and about Negroes for the Elementary Level." *Elementary English* 46 (Nov. 1969), 909–13.

D86. Dengel, Ray E., Dennis P. Leeper, and Mary Hindle. *Hamilton Library Afro-American Bibliography.* Edinboro, Pa.: Edinboro State College, Hamilton Library.

D87. Denham, Bernard J., Elizabeth Rebman, and Richard Pollard. *Afro-American Collection Shelf List.* Stanford, Cal.: Stanford University, Meyer Memorial Library.

D88. Deodene, Frank, and William P. French. *Black American Fiction Since 1952: a preliminary checklist.* Chatham, N.J.: The Chatham Bookseller, 1970, 25 pp.

D89. Deodene, Frank, and William P. French. *Black American Poetry Since 1944: a preliminary checklist.* Chatham, N.J.: The Chatham Bookseller, 1971, 41 pp.

D90. *The Desegregation Literature: a critical appraisal.* Washington, D.C.: U.S. Department of Health, Education, and Welfare, National Institute of Education, Desegregation Studies Staff, 1976, 160 pp.

D91. Deskins, Donald R., Jr. "Geographical Literature on the American Negro, 1949–1968: a bibliography." *Professional Geographer* 21:3 (1969), 145–9.

D91A. Deutsch, Leonard J. "A Corrected Bibliography for Rudolph Fisher." *Bulletin of Bibliography* 35:1 (Jan.-Mar. 1978), 30–3.

D92. DeVeaux, Diane. *A Guide to Books and Periodicals about the Nation of Islam in the Mid-Manhattan Library [NYPL].* New York: New York Public Library, 1974. 6 pp.

D93. DeVeaux, Diane, Marilyn Berg Iarusso, and Viola Jones Clark. *The Black*

Experience in Children's Audiovisual Materials. New York: The New York Public Library, Countee Cullen Branch, North Manhattan Project, Office of Children's Services, 1973, 32 pp.

D94. DeWitt, Josephine. *The Black Man's Point of View: a list of references to material in the Oakland Free Library*. Oakland, Cal.: Acorn Club of Oakland and the Oakland Free Library, 1930, 30 pp.

* Dewitz, Sandra. See A98.

D95. Dibbern, U., and H. Ihde. "Das Echo der Kultur und des Freiheitskampfer der nordamerikanischen Neger in der DDR, 1945–1949: eine Bibliographie." *Zeitschrift fuer Anglistik und Amerikanistik* 20:4 (1972), 429–42.

* Dick, Daniel. See P66.

D96. Dickinson, Donald C. *A Bio-Bibliography of Langston Hughes, 1902–1967*. Hamden, Conn.: Archon Books, 1967, 267 pp. A revised edition of 273 pp. was issued in 1972. Based on Dickinson's 1964 Ph.D. dissertation of 303 pp. at the University of Michigan.

D97. Dickinson, Donald C. "Books in the Field: black bibliography." *Wilson Library Bulletin* 44 (Oct. 1969), 184–7.

D98. Dickinson, Elizabeth M. *Selected Bibliography: the Negro in American theatre*, 1965 (?), 14 pp.

D99. *Dictionary Catalog of the Arthur B. Spingarn Collection of Negro Authors, Howard University Libraries, Washington, D.C.* Boston, Mass.: G.K. Hall, 1970, 2 vols.

D100. *Dictionary Catalog of the George Foster Peabody Collection of Negro Literature and History, Collis P. Huntington Memorial Library, Hampton Institute*. Westport, Conn.: Greenwood Publishing, 1972, 2 vols.

D101. *Dictionary Catalog of the Jesse E. Moorland Collection of Negro Life and History, Howard University Libraries, Washington, D.C.* Boston, Mass.: G.K. Hall, 1970, 9 vols. A supplement of 3 vols. was published in 1976.

D102. *Dictionary Catalog of the Negro Collection of the Fisk University Library*. Boston, Mass.: G.K. Hall, 1974, 6 vols.

D103. *Dictionary Catalog of the Schomburg Collection of Negro Literature and History. The New York Public Library*. Boston, Mass.: G.K. Hall, 1962, 9 vols. A *First Supplement* of 2 vols. was published in 1967; *Second Supplement*, 4 vols., 1972; *Supplement 1974*, 1 vol., 1976. The catalog is currently supplemented by the annual *Bibliographic Guide to Black Studies*.

D104. *Dictionary Catalog of the Vivian G. Harsh Collection of Afro-American History and Literature, Chicago Public Library*. Boston, Mass.: G.K. Hall, 1978, 4 vols.

* Dill, Augustus Granville. See D151, D152, D153, D154, D154A.

D105. Dillard, J.L. "Toward a Bibliography of Works Dealing with the Creole Languages of the Caribbean Area, Louisiana, and the Guianas.'' *Caribbean Studies* 3:1 (1963), 84–95.

* Dillon, Barbara. See H74.

D106. Dillon, Merton L. ''The Abolitionists: a decade of historiography, 1959–1969.'' *Journal of Southern History* 35 (Nov. 1969), 500–22.

D107. Dimitroff, Lillian. *Annotated Bibliography of Audio-Visual Materials Related to Inner-City Educational Problems.* Chicago, Ill.: Chicago State College Library, 1968, 7 pp.

D108. Dinniman, Andrew E., and Farah E. Rivoir. *Guide to Materials on Afro-American Studies in the Francis Harvey Green Library.* Westchester, Pa.: Westchester State College Library, 1977, 46 pp.

D109. *Directory of Data Sources on Racial and Ethnic Minorities.* BLS Bulletin 1879. Washington, D.C.: U.S. Department of Labor, Bureau of Labor Statistics, 1975, 86 pp.

D110. ''Discographies of Ragtime Recordings.'' *Jazz Forum* 4 (Apr. 1947), 7–8.

D111. *Discography of Charlie Parker.* Basel, Switzerland: Jazz Publications, 1962, 9 pp.

D112. [Discography of Diana Ross and the Supremes]. *Billboard* (Mar. 20, 1976), p. D–63.

D113. *Discography of Jimmy Smith and Leo Parker.* Basel, Switzerland: Jazz Publications, 1962, 8 pp.

D114. *Discrimination in Civil Rights: a selected bibliography.* Lansing, Mich.: Michigan State Library, 1964, 6 pp.

D115. *Discrimination in Education: a selected bibliography.* Chicago, Ill.: American Council on Race Relations, 1948, 3 pp.

D116. *Discrimination in Employment: a selected bibliography.* Chicago, Ill.: American Council on Race Relations, 1949, 8 pp.

D117. ''Discrimination in Employment in Defense Industries: selected sources of information.'' *Employment Review* 3 (June 1941), 309–11.

D118. *Discrimination in Housing: a selected bibliography.* Chicago, Ill.: American Council on Race Relations, 1948, 4 pp.

D119. ''Division of Negro Literature and History, 135th St. Branch, The New York Public Library.'' *Dunbar News* (July 30, 1930).

D120. Dixon, Elizabeth. *Afro-American Resources of the El Camino College Library.* Via Torrance, Cal.: El Camino College Library, 1969. A second edition was published in 1970.

D121. Dixon, J. ''Book Selection, Racism, and the Law of the Land.'' *Assistant Librarian* 72 (July-Aug. 1979), 94+.

D122. Dixon, Johanne C. *A Selected Annotated Bibliography on Black Families.* New York: National Urban League, Project Thrive, 1977.

D122A. Dixon, Robert M.W., and John Godrich. *Blues and Gospel Records, 1902–42.* Hatch End, England: Rust, 1963, 765 pp. Reprinted by

Scholarly in 1977. Second edition, London: Storyville, 1969, 912 pp. Additions in *John Edwards Memorial Foundation Quarterly* 7:3 (1971), 142; 8:1 (1972), 7.

D123. Dixon, Robert M.W., and John Godrich. *Recording the Blues*. New York: Stein and Day, 1970, 109 pp.

* Dixon, Robert M.W. See also G48.

D124. *Documents Relating to the Kansas-Nebraska Act, 1854*. New York: Lovell, 1894, 20 pp.

D125. Dodd, Don, and Alma D. Steading. *The History of Black Politics in Alabama: a preliminary bibliography*. Public Administration Series No. 347. Monticello, Ill.: Vance Bibliographies, 1979, 10 pp.

D126. Dodds, Barbara. *Negro Literature for High School Students*. Champaign, Ill.: National Council of Teachers of English, 1968, 157 pp.

* Dodds, Barbara. See also Stanford, Barbara Dodds.

* Dolce, Peter. See H28.

D127. Dollard, Peter. *Brief Guide to Black Studies*. Providence, R.I.: Brown University, John D. Rockefeller, Jr., Library, 1970.

* Dolphy, Eric. See E31.

D128. Donahue, Margaret M., et al. *A Selected List of Black Materials in the McKeldin Library, University of Maryland*. College Park, Md.: University of Maryland, McKeldin Library.

D129. Donald, David. *The Nation in Crisis, 1861–1877*. New York: Appleton-Century-Crofts, Goldentree Bibliographies, 1969, 92 pp.

D130. Dooley, John B., and Lynn Mackin. *Black Studies: a selected bibliography*. San Mateo, Cal.: College of San Mateo Library, 1969, 43 pp.

D131. Doran, James M. "Erroll Garner: a discography update." *Journal of Jazz Studies* 6:1 (Fall/Winter 1979), 64–88.

D132. Dorsey, Leonia Lamier. "Negro Poetry Since 1916: a selective bibliography." M.S. thesis, Columbia University School of Library Service, 1935.

D133. Dorton, Eleanor, and Lenwood G. Davis. *Juvenile Delinquency in the Black Community*. Exchange Bibliography no. 804. Monticello, Ill.: Council of Planning Librarians, 1975, 16 pp.

D134. Doyle, J. "Million Selling 'Race' Records." *Alley Music* 2 (1968), 14; 3 (1968), 11.

* Drake, St Clair. See N37.

D135. Drew, Margaret. "The Black Experience in Books." *Parents Choice* 2:3 (1979), 11.

D136. Drewal, Margaret Thompson, and Glorianne Jackson. *Sources on African and African-Related Dance*. New York: American Dance Guild, 1974, 38 pp.

D137. Driskell, David C. "Bibliographies in Afro-American Art." *American Quarterly* 30:3 (1978), 374–94.

D138. Driscoll, Patricia. *Black Authors in Major Periodicals, 1950–1960*. Niagara, N.Y.: Niagara University Library, 12 pp.

D139. Drowne, Lawrence, Ted Kumatz, and Janyce Wolf. *The Black Experience: a bibliography of books on black studies in the academic libraries of Brooklyn, N.Y.* Brooklyn, N.Y.: Academic Libraries of Brooklyn, 1971, 235 pp.

D140. Drzick, Kathleen, John Murphy, and Constance Weaver. *Annotated Bibliography of Works Relating to the Negro in Literature and to Negro Dialects*. Kalamazoo, Mich.: Authors, 1969, 36 pp.

D141. DuBois, W.E.B. "Bibliography of Negro Health and Physique." *The Health and Physique of the Negro American. Report of a Social Study Made Under the Direction of Atlanta University; Together with the Proceedings of the Eleventh Conference for the Study of the Negro Problems, Held at Atlanta University, on May the 29th, 1906*. Atlanta, Ga.: Atlanta University Press, 1906, pp. 6–13.

D142. Du Bois, W.E.B. "A Bibliography of the Negro Artisan and the Industrial Training of Negroes." *The Negro Artisan. Report of a Social Study Made Under the Direction of Atlanta University; Together with the Proceedings of the Seventh Conference for the Study of Negro Problems, Held at Atlanta University, on May 27th 1902*. Atlanta, Ga.: Atlanta University Press, 1902, pp. v-vii.

D143. Du Bois, W.E.B. "Select Bibliography of Negro Churches." *The Negro Church. Report of a Social Study Made Under the Direction of Atlanta University; Together with the Proceedings of the 8th Conference for the Study of Negro Problems, Held at Atlanta University, May 26th, 1903*. Atlanta, Ga.: Atlanta University Press, 1903, pp. vi-viii.

D144. Du Bois, W.E.B. "A Select Bibliography of Negro Crime." *Some Notes on Negro Crime Particularly in Georgia. Report of a Social Study Made Under the Direction of Atlanta University; Together with the Proceedings of the Ninth Conference for the Study of Negro Problems, Held at Atlanta University, May 24, 1904*. Atlanta, Ga.: Atlanta University Press, 1904, pp. vi-viii.

D145. Du Bois, W.E.B. "A Select Bibliography of the American Negro for General Readers." *The College-Bred Negro. Report of a Social Study Made Under the Direction of Atlanta University; Together with the Proceedings of the Fifth Conference for the Study of the Negro Problems, Held at Atlanta University, May 29–30, 1900*. Atlanta, Ga.: Atlanta University Press, 1900, pp. 6–9. Reprinted in Betty Kaplan Gubert. *Early Black Bibliographies, 1863–1918*. New York: Garland, 1982, pp. 93–7.

D146. Du Bois, W.E.B. "A Select Bibliography of the American Negro for General Readers." *The Negro Common School. Report of a Social Study Made Under the Direction of Atlanta University; Together with the Pro-*

ceedings of the Sixth Conference for the Study of the Negro Problems, Held at Atlanta University, on May 28th, 1901. Atlanta, Ga.: Atlanta University Press, 1901, pp 4–13.

D147. Du Bois, W.E.B. *A Selected Bibliography of the Negro American. A Compilation Made Under the Direction of Atlanta University; Together with the Proceedings of the Tenth Conference for the Study of the Negro Problems, Held at Atlanta University, on May 30, 1905.* Atlanta, Ga.: Atlanta University Press, 1905, 71 pp. Reprinted in Betty Kaplan Gubert. *Early Black Bibliographies, 1863–1918.* New York: Garland, 1982, pp. 99–163.

D148. Du Bois, W.E.B. "A Select Bibliography of the Negro American Family." *The Negro American Family. Report of a Social Study Made Principally by the College Classes of 1909 and 1910 of Atlanta University, under the Patronage of the Trustees of the John F. Slater Fund; Together with the Proceedings of the 13th Annual Conference for the Study of the Negro Problem, Held at Atlanta University on Tuesday, May the 26th, 1908.* Atlanta, Ga.: Atlanta University Press, 1908, pp. 6–8.

D149. Du Bois, W.E.B. "Selected Bibliography of Economic Co-operation among Negro Americans." *Economic Co-operation among Negro Americans. Report of a Social Study Made by Atlanta University, under the patronage of the Carnegie Institution of Washington, D.C., Together with the Proceedings of the 12th Conference for the Study of the Negro Problems, Held at Atlanta University, on Tuesday, May the 28th, 1907.* Atlanta, Ga.: Atlanta University Press, 1907, pp. 6–9.

D150. Du Bois, W.E.B. "A Selected Bibliography of Efforts for Social Betterment among Negro Americans." *Efforts for Social Betterment among Negro Americans. Report of a Social Study Made by Atlanta University under the Patronage of the Trustees of the John F. Slater Fund; Together with the Proceedings of the 14th Annual Conference for the Study of the Negro Problems Held at Atlanta University on Tuesday, May the 24th, 1909.* Atlanta, Ga.: Atlanta University Press, 1909, pp. 7–8.

D150A. Du Bois, W.E.B., and Augustus Granville Dill. "Publications [of Negro Authors]." *The College-Bred Negro American. Report of a Social Study Made by Atlanta University under the Patronage of the Trustees of the John F. Slater Fund; with the Proceedings of the 15th Annual Conference for the Study of the Negro Problems, Held at Atlanta University, on Tuesday, May 24, 1910.* Atlanta, Ga.: Atlanta University Press, 1910, pp. 75–78. Reprinted in Betty Kaplan Gubert. *Early Black Bibliographies, 1863–1918.* New York: Garland, 1982, pp. 166–9.

D151. Du Bois, W.E.B., and Augustus Granville Dill. "A Select Bibliography." *Morals and Manners among Negro Americans. Report of a Social Study Made by Atlanta University under the Patronage of the Trustees of the John F. Slater Fund; with the Proceedings of the 18th Annual Conference for the Study of the Negro Problems, Held at Atlanta Uni-*

versity, on Monday, May 26, 1913. Atlanta, Ga.: Atlanta University Press, 1914, pp. 9–10.

D152. Du Bois, W.E.B., and Augustus Granville Dill. "A Select Bibliography of Common School Education for Negro Americans." *The Common School and the Negro American. Report of a Social Study Made by Atlanta University under Patronage of the Trustees of the John F. Slater Fund; with the Proceedings of the 16th Annual Conference for the Study of the Negro Problems, Held at Atlanta University, on Tuesday, May 30th, 1911*. Atlanta, Ga.: Atlanta University Press, 1911, pp. 9–12.

D153. Du Bois, W.E.B., and Augustus Granville Dill. "A Select Bibliography of Higher Education for Negro Americans." *The College-Bred Negro American. Report of a Social Study Made by Atlanta University under the Patronage of the Trustees of the John F. Slater Fund; with the Proceedings of the 15th Annual Conference for the Study of the Negro Problems, Held at Atlanta University, on Tuesday, May 24th, 1910*. Atlanta, Ga.: Atlanta University Press, 1910, pp. 8–10.

D154. Du Bois, W.E.B., and Augustus Granville Dill. "A Select Bibliography of the Negro American Artisan." *The Negro American Artisan. Report of a Social Study Made by Atlanta University under the Patronage of the Trustees of the John F. Slater Fund; with the Proceedings of the 17th Annual Conference for the Study of the Negro Problems, Held at Atlanta University, on Monday, May 27, 1912*. Atlanta, Ga.: Atlanta University Press, 1912, pp. 9–12.

D155. Du Bois, W.E.B., and Guy B. Johnson. *Encyclopedia of the Negro: preparatory volume with reference lists and reports*. New York: Phelps-Stokes Fund, 1945, 207 pp. A revised and enlarged edition of 215 pp. was published in 1946.

* Du Bois, W.E.B. See also L144, R51.

D156. Duffert, Gorman L., and Dawn McGaghy. *A Bibliography of Items in the Libraries of Cuyahoga Community College on African and Afro-American Subjects*. Cleveland, Ohio: Cuyahoga Community College, Metropolitan Campus Library.

* Duffy, David. See F84.

D157. Duffy, Lillian. *Bibliography of Black Studies Books in the Santa Ana College Library*. Santa Ana, Cal.: Santa Ana College, Neally Library, 35 pp.

* Dufour, Joël. See M116, M117.

D158. Duignan, Peter. "Pan-Africanism: a bibliographic essay." *African Forum* 1:1 (1965), 105–7.

* Duigan, Peter. See also C137.

* Duke, Dennis. See K95A.

D158A. Duke, James O. "Disciples of Christ Historical Society and Its Black Materials Project." *Discipliana* 31 (Winter 1971).

* Duke, Maurice. See D1, D10, G36, I16, K80, M83, M84, R66, T110A.

D159. Duker, Abraham G. "Selected Bibliography [on Negro-Jewish Relations]." *Negro-Jewish Relations in the U.S.: papers and proceedings of a conference convened by the Conference on Jewish Social Studies, New York City.* New York: Citadel Press, 1966, pp. 67–71.

D160. Dumond, Dwight Lowell. *A Bibliography of Antislavery in America.* Ann Arbor, Mich.: University of Michigan Press, 1961, 119 pp.

D161. Duncan, Margaret. *Changing the African Image through History.* Tacoma Park, Md.: Columbia Union College Library.

D162. Duncan, Margaret. *The Negro in American History and Culture.* Tacoma Park, Md.: Columbia Union College Library.

* Dunlap, Irene E. See W23.

D163. Dunlap, Mollie E. "Bibliographical Notes." *Journal of Human Relations* 1 (Spring 1952), 77–80; 1 (Autumn 1952), 83–8. "Selected Readings in Human Relations." 1 (Spring 1953), 112–20; 1 (Winter 1953), 94–100; 2 (Spring 1954), 102–11; 3 (Autumn 1954), 120–8; 2 (Winter 1954), 90–5; 3 (Spring 1955), 104–19; 3 (Summer 1955), 108–16; 4 (Autumn 1955), 88–101; 4 (Spring 1956), 126–47; 4 (Summer 1956), 106–21; 4 (Winter 1956), 137–54.

D164. Dunlap, Mollie E. *A Partial Bibliography of the Publications of the Faculty of College of Education and Industrial Arts, Wilberforce, Ohio.* Yellow Springs, Ohio: The Antioch Press, 1949, 15 pp.

D165. Dunlap, Mollie E. "A Selected Annotated List of Books by and about the Negro." *Negro College Quarterly* 3 (March 1945), 40–5; (June 1945), 94–6; (Sept. 1945), 153–8.

D166. Dunlap, Mollie E. "Special Collections of Negro Literature in the U.S." *Journal of Negro Education* 4 (Oct. 1935), 482–9.

* Dunlap, Sarah. See B80.

D167. Dunmore, Charlotte. *Black Children and Their Families.* San Francisco, Cal.: R and E Research Associates, 1976, 103 pp.

D168. Dunmore, Charlotte. *Poverty, Participation, Protest, Power and Black Americans: a selected bibliography for use in social work education.* New York: Council on Social Work Education, 1970, 67 pp.

D169. Durden, Robert F. "Primary Sources for the Study of Afro-American History [at Duke University]." *Gnomon* (1970), 39–42.

* Dutilh, Alex. See B351.

* Dutton, F. See C26.

D170. Dutton, Frank. "Brunswick Modern Rhythm Series." *Matrix* 50 (Dec. 1963), 3–12.

D171. Dvorkin, Bettifae E. *Blacks and Mental Health in the U.S., 1963–1973: a selected annotated bibliography of journal articles.* Washington, D.C.: Howard University, Medical-Dental Library, 1974, 34 pp.

D172. Dworaczek, Marian. *Human Rights: a bibliography of government documents held in the library.* Toronto, Ont.: Ontario Ministry of Labour Research Library, 1973, 34 pp.

* Dworaczek, Marian. See also A102, B291.
D173. Dybek, Caren. "Black Literature for Adolescents." *English Journal* 63 (Jan. 1974), 63–7.
D174. Dyke, C.B. "Professional Library for Teachers." *The Hampton Leaflets* (May 1900), 302.
D175. Dykes, DeWitt S. *Black Genealogy: a select list of books*. Rochester, Mich.: Oakland University, 1977, 3 pp.
* Dykes, E.B. See C192.
D176. Dzwonkoski, Peter. "Langston Hughes, 1902–1967." *In* Matthew J. Bruccoli, ed. *First Printings of American Authors: contributions toward descriptive checklists*, Vol. 3. Detroit, Mich.: Gale Research, 1978, pp. 157–81.

E

E1. [Earl "Bud" Powell Discography]. *Swing Journal* 31 (Nov. 1977), 298–303.
E2. Eason, V.T. "Annotated Bibliography of Black Theology." *In* Gayraud S. Wilmore and James H. Cone, eds. *Black Theology, A Documentary History*. New York: Orbis Books, 1979, pp. 624–37.
E2A. Eaton, Elsie M., Sally Chang, Louise M. Gordon, and Chang-Chien Lee. *A Classified Catalogue of the Negro Collection in the Samuel H. Coleman Library, Florida Agricultural and Mechanical University*. Tallahassee, Fla.: Florida Agricultural and Mechanical University, 1969, 269 pp.
E3. *Educating the Disadvantaged Child: annotated bibliography*. ERIC Document no. ED 030–682. Albany, N.Y.: New York State Education Department, 1968. Supplemented by ERIC Documents nos. ED 030–705 and ED 045–754.
E4. *Education of Negroes in Ante-bellum America: a guide to an exhibition in the William L. Clements Library*. Bulletin no. 76. Ann Arbor, Mich.: University of Michigan, William L. Clements Library, 1969, 18 pp.
E4A. *[Edward] Duke Ellington Discography*. Carnegie, Pa.: Pope's Records, 1967(?), 24 pp.
E5. Edwards, Ernie, George Hall, and Bill Korst. *Charlie Parker*. Whittier, Cal.: Erngeobil, 1965.
E6. Edwards, Ernie, George Hall, and Bill Korst. *Erskine Hawkins—Horace Henderson Discography* Whittier, Cal.: Erngeobil, 1965, 10 pp.
E7. Edwards, Ernie, George Hall, and Bill Korst. *The Jimmy Lunceford Band*. Whittier, Cal.: Erngeobil, 1965, 12 pp. A revised edition with the same number of pages was published the same year.
E8. Edwards, Ernie, George Hall, and Bill Korst. *[John] Dizzy Gillespie: big bands, 1945–1950, 1955–1957*. Whittier, Cal.: Erngeobil, 1966, 10 pp.

A revised edition with the same number of pages was published the same year.

* Eichholz, Alice. See R110.

E9. Eichman, Barbara. *A Selective Bibliography of Civil Liberties Books*. New York: American Civil Liberties Union, 1979(?), 85 pp.

E9A. *1860–1919: a selected bibliography by Negro American Authors*. New York: The New York Public Library, Schomburg Library, 1956, 7 pp.

E10. *Elementary Library Books about the Negroes in the U.S.* Oakland, Cal.: Oakland Public Schools, Office of the Coordinator of Library Services, 1964. With title changed to "Afro-Americans," an edition of 9 pp. was issued in 1969.

E11. El-Khawas, Mohamed A., and Francis A. Kornegay, Jr., *American-Southern African Relations: bibliographic essays*. Westport, Conn.: Greenwood Press, 1975, 188 pp.

E12. Ellis, Ethel M. Vaughan. *The American Negro: a selected checklist of books, including a list of periodicals, films and filmstrips, recordings and agencies that distribute free and inexpensive material*. Washington, D.C.: Howard University Library, 1968, 46 pp.

* Ellis, Ethel M. Vaughan. See also P112.

E13. Ellison, Curtis W., and E.W. Metcalf, Jr. *Charles W. Chesnutt: a reference guide*. Boston, Mass.: G.K. Hall, 1977, 150 pp.

E14. Ellison, Curtis W., and E.W. Metcalf, Jr. *William Wells Brown and Martin R. Delany: a reference guide*. Boston, Mass.: G.K. Hall, 1978, 276 pp.

* Ellison, Virginia H. See B305.

E15. Elmenhorst, Gernot W., and Walter von Bebenburg. *Die Jazz-Diskothek*. Reinbek bei Hamburg, Germany: Rowohlt, 1961, 362 pp.

E16. Emanuel, James A. "The Invisible Men of American Literature." *Books Abroad* 37 (Autumn 1963), 391–4.

E17. Emmer, Pieter C. "The History of the Dutch Slave Trade: a bibliographic survey." *Journal of Economic History* 32 (Sept. 1972), 728–47.

E18. *Employment of Minorities*. Newark, N.J.: Newark Public Library, 1972, 2 pp.

E19. Enabulele, Arlene B., and Dionne J. Jones. *A Resource Guide on Black Women in the U.S.* Washington, D.C.: Howard University, Institute for Urban Affairs and Research, 1978, 107 pp.

E20. The Enforcement of the Slave Trade Laws." In *Annual Report of the American Historical Association, 1891*. Washington, D.C.: Government Printing Office, 1892, pp. 161–75.

E21. Engel, Margritt A. *Working Bibliography on Black Literature*. Anchorage, Alaska: Alaska Methodist University Library.

* Engeldinger, Eugene A. See F7.

E22. Englund, Bjorn. "Discography of Recordings from 'Chocolate Kiddies.'" *Storyville* 62 (Dec. 1975/Jan. 1976), 50.

E23. Englund, Bjorn. "A Louis Armstrong Filmography." *Coda* (Jan. 1975), 5–6. Additions and corrections by Klaus Strateman, *Coda* (Mar. 1976), 32–3.

E24. Epstein, Dena J. "African Music in British and French America." *Musical Quarterly* 59 (Jan. 1973), 61–91.

E24A. Epstein, Dena J. "Documenting the History of Black Folk Music in the U.S.: a librarian views interdisciplinary research." *In* P.S. Bayne, ed. *Library Lectures*. Knoxville, Tenn.: University of Tennessee, 1979, pp. 32–43.

E25. Epstein, Dena J. "The Search for Black Music's African Roots." *The University of Chicago Magazine* 66:1 (1973), 18–24.

E26. Epstein, Dena J. "Slave Music in the U.S. before 1860: a survey of sources." *Music Library Association Notes* 20 (Spring 1973), 195–212; 20 (Summer 1963), 377–90.

E27. Epstein, Irene. *A Bibliography on the Negro Woman in the U.S.* New York: Jefferson School of Social Science, 1949(?), 5 pp.

E28. *Equal Opportunity: a bibliography of research on equal opportunity in housing*. Washington, D.C.: U.S. Department of Housing and Urban Development Library, 1969, 24 pp. A second edition of 34 pp. was published in 1974.

E29. *Equal Opportunity in Employment: personnel bibliography*. Washington, D.C.: U.S. Civil Service Commission Library, Series no. 29, 1968, 122 pp.; Series no. 38, 1972, 135 pp.; Series no. 49, 1973, 170 pp.; Series no. 65, 1975, 170 pp.

E30. Ereman, Sevino. *Bibliographie concernant la Convention européenne des droits de l'homme*. Strasbourg(?): Conseil de l'Europe, 1973, 129 pp.

E31. [Eric Dolphy Discography]. *Swing Journal* (June 1974), 250–5.

E32. Erikson, Conrad. *Black Studies Books*. St. Louis, Mo.: Harris Teachers College Library.

* Erikson, Marlene J. See A98.

E33. *The Ernest R. Alexander Collection of Negroana*. Nashville, Tenn.: Fisk University, 1945.

E34. Ernst, Robert T. "Geographic Literature of Black America, 1949–1972: a selected bibliography of journal articles, serial publications, theses and dissertations." *In* Robert T. Ernst and Lawrence Hugg, eds. *Black America: geographic perspectives*. New York: Doubleday, 1976, pp. 405–25.

E35. Ernst, Robert T. *The Geographical Literature of Black America, 1949–1972: a selected bibliography of journal articles, serial publications, theses, and dissertations*. Exchange Bibliography no. 492. Monticello, Ill.: Council of Planning Librarians, 1973, 29 pp.

E36. Ernst, Robert T. "Negro Migration: a review of the literature." M.A. thesis, St. Louis University, 1969.

E37. Eshelman, Sylvia N., and Dianna A. Femley. *On Being Black Bibliog-*

raphy. Cleveland, Ohio: Cleveland Public Library, Mt. Pleasant Branch, 1970, 54 pp.

* Espin, Olivia M. See C29.

E38. *Ethnic and Cultural Studies: a bibliography*. Baltimore, Md.: Maryland School Media Office, 1978, 24 pp.

E39. *Ethnic and Racial Groups in the U.S.: a selected bibliography*. New York: American Jewish Committee, Institute of Human Relations, 1968, 9 pp.

E40. *Ethnic and Racial Minorities in North America: a selected bibliography of the geographical literature*. Exchange Bibliography no. 359–360. Monticello, Ill.: Council of Planning Librarians, 1973, 71 pp.

E41. "Ethel Waters: her radio bow, 1922." *Record Research* 1:2 (Apr. 1955), 10.

E42. [Eubie Blake Discographies]. *Record Research* 1:1 (Feb. 1955), 7–10; 1:3 (June 1955), 1; 1:4 (Aug. 1955), 11; 2:1 (Feb. 1956), 14; 2:2 (May-June 1956), 23.

E43. [Eubie Blake Discography]. *Stereo Review* (Nov. 1972).

* Evans, Dorothy. See B41, R112.

E44. Evans, Lola. "An Annotated Bibliography of the Dated Manuscripts in the Countee Cullen Memorial Collection at Atlanta University." Thesis, Atlanta University, 1959.

E45. Evensmo, Jan. *The Tenor Saxophone of Coleman Hawkins, 1929–1942: with a critical assessment of all his known recordings and broadcasts*. Hosle, Norway: Author, 1975(?), 33 pp.

E46. Everett, Thomas G. "An Annotated List of English-Language Jazz Periodicals." *Journal of Jazz Studies* 3:2, 47–57. Addenda appeared in 4:1, 110–1; 4:2, 94–7; 5:2, 99–103.

E47. Everett, Thomas. "Concert Band Music by Black-American Composers: a select bibliography." *The Black Perspective in Music* 6:2 (Fall 1978), 143–50.

E48. Everly, Elaine C. *Records of Superintendent of Education for State of Georgia Bureau of Refugees, Freedmen and Abandoned Lands, 1865–1870*. Washington, D.C.: U.S. National Archives, 1969, 8 pp.

E49. Everly, Elaine C. *Selected Series of Records Issued by Commissioner of Bureau of Refugees, Freedmen, and Abandoned Lands, 1865–1872*. Washington, D.C.: U.S. National Archives, 1969, 8 pp.

E50. *Exercises Marking the Opening of the James Weldon Johnson Memorial Collection of Negro Arts and Letters, founded by Carl Van Vechten. Sprague Memorial Hall, 7 January 1950*. New Haven, Conn.: Yale University, 1950, 19 pp.

E51. Ezell, Martha, and Bernice Lawson. *Northwest Association of Private Colleges and Universities: bibliography-black and other ethnic groups studies*. McMinnville, Ore.: Linfield College, Northup Library, 124 pp.

F

F1. Fabre, Genevieve E. "Afro-American Theatre: a bibliographic survey." *American Quarterly* 30:3 (1978), 358–73.

F2. Fabre, Genevieve E. "A Checklist of Original Plays, Pageants, Rituals, and Musicals by Afro-American Authors Performed in the U.S. from 1960 to 1973." *Black World* 23 (Apr. 1974), 81–97.

* Fabre, Genevieve E. See also F79.

F3. Fabre, Michel. "A Selected Bibliography of Chester Himes' Work." *Black World* 21 (Mar. 1972), 76–8.

F4. Fabre, Michel, and Charles T. Davis. *Richard Wright: a primary bibliography*. Boston, Mass.: G.K. Hall, 1982, 320 pp.

F5. Fabre, Michel, and Edward Margolies. "Richard Wright (1908–1960: a bibliography." *Bulletin of Bibliography* 24 (Jan.-Apr. 1965), 131+. Reprinted in Constance Webb. *Richard Wright: a biography*. New York: G.P. Putnam's Sons, 1968, pp. 423–9. Reprinted in *Negro Digest* 18 (Jan. 1969), 86–92. Reprinted, revised and enlarged, in *New Letters* 38:2 (Winter 1971), 155–69. Reprinted in David Ray and Robert M. Farnsworth. *Richard Wright: impressions and perspectives*. Ann Arbor, Mich.: University of Michigan Press, 1973, pp. 191–205. Reprinted in Michel Fabre. *The Unfinished Quest of Richard Wright*. New York: William Morrow, 1973, pp. 625–38.

* Fabre, Michel. See also B71, F79.

F6. *Fair Employment Practices Act and Selection Tests for Negroes*. Committee of University Industrial Relations Librarians. Exchange Bibliography no. 1486. Chicago, Ill.: University of Chicago, Industrial Relations Center, A.G. Bush Library, 1966, 2 pp.

F7. Fairbanks, Carol, and Eugene A. Engeldinger. *Black American Fiction: a bibliography*. Metuchen, N.J.: Scarecrow Press, 1978, 359 pp.

F8. Fairbanks, Helen. *Black Workers and the Unions: selected references*. Princeton, N.J.: Princeton University, Industrial Relations Section, 1970, 4 pp.

F9. Fairchild, Rolph. "Pete Johnson Discography." *Jazz Report* 2:12 (Aug. 1962), and following issues.

* Falk, Charlotte. See S229.

F10. Farber, Evan. *Afro-American Studies: reference materials in the Lilly Library*. Richmond, Ind.: Earlham College, Lilly Library, 1969, 4 pp.

F11. "Farewell [Julian] Cannonball [Adderley]." *Swing Journal* 29 (Oct. 1975), 348–55.

F11A. Farmer, George L. *A Panorama of the Afro-American*. Culver City, Cal., 1971, 58 pp.

* Farnsley, Charles. See F12.

F12. Farnsley, Nancy, and Charles Farnsley. *Lost Cause Press Microcard Collection: anti-slavery propaganda in the Oberlin College Library*. Louisville, Ky.: Lost Cause Press, 1968, 101 pp.

F13. Farrison, W. Edward. "What American Negro Literature Exists and Who Should Teach It?" *College Language Association Journal* 13 (June 1970), 374–81.

F14. [Fats Waller Discography]. *Record Research* 1:1 (Aug. 1955), 11; 1:5 (Oct. 1955), 8+; 1:6 (Dec. 1955), 13–4; 2:1 (Feb. 1956), 13.

F15. Faucett, Melba. *Books by, about and relating to Afro-Americans in the Byrne Memorial Library, St. Xavier College: a bibliography*. Chicago, Ill.: St. Xavier College, Byrne Memorial Library, 20 pp.

F16. Fauset, Arthur Huff. "Negro Folk Lore." *In* Alain Locke, ed. *The New Negro: an interpretation*. New York: Albert and Charles Boni, 1925, pp. 438–43. Reprinted by Arno in 1968 and Atheneum in 1969.

* Favors, Gail. See Mc31.

F17. Fayenz, Franco. *Il Jazz dal mito all'avanguardia*. Milan, Italy: Sapere Ed., 1970, 510 pp.

F18. Feather, Leonard. "Jazz per le biblioteche." *Musica Jazz* 19 (July-Aug. 1963), 39–40.

F19. Featherstonhaugh, Thomas. "A Bibliography of John Brown." *Southern History Association Publications*. 1:3 (1897), 196–202; 3:4 (1899), 302–6. Also published separately.

F20. Fedink, Simon. *Bibliography of Publications by and about New York State Division of Human Rights, 1945–1970*. New York: New York State Division of Human Rights, 1971, 41 pp.

F21. Fedricci, Glenda. "Ishmael Reed, 1938- ." *In* Matthew J. Brucolli, ed. *First Printings of American Authors: contributions toward descriptive checklists*, Vol. 2. Detroit, Mich.: Gale Research, 1977, pp. 315–6.

* Femley, Dianna A. See E37.

F22. Fenf, Yi. *Relevance in the Novel: "Native Son" bibliography*. Orangeburg, S.C.: South Carolina State College, Miller F. Whittaker Library.

* Fennell, Janice. See B216.

F22A. Fergusson, Isaac. "[Bob Marley] LP Discography." *The Village Voice* 27:20 (May 18, 1982), 41.

F22B. Ferm, D.W. "Contemporary Black Theology: a historical sketch." *Choice* 16 (Feb. 1980), 1539–50.

F23. Ferris, William R., Jr. "A Discography of Mississippi Negro Folk Song Music." *Mississippi Folklore Register* 2:2 (1968), 51–4.

F24. Ferris, William R., Jr. *Mississippi Black Folklore: a research bibliography and discography*. Hattiesburg, Miss.: University and College Press of Mississippi, 1971, 61 pp.

* Fershleiser, Steven. See J27A.

F25. *Fifteen Topics on Afroamericana: an annotated bibliography*. Stockton, Cal.: Relevant Instructional Materials, 1973.

* Fikes, Robert, Jr. See W47.

F26. Filler, Louis. "Negro Material of the 1960's." *Choice* 5:2 (Apr. 1968), 161–9.

F26A. "Filmstrips about Blackness: a descriptive listing." *Film News* (Dec. 1969), 42–4.

F27. Finney, Frederick. *Aaron's Index: Afro-American, Third World and alternative literature*. Dayton, Ohio: Challenge Press, 1978, 335 pp.

F28. Finney, James E. *The Long Road to Now: a bibliography of materials relating to the American black man*. Farmingdale, N.Y.: Charles W. Clark Co., 1969, 54 pp.

F29. *The Fire This Time: selected reviews of the most significant books on the Negro in the U.S.* New York: United Presbyterian Church in the U.S.A., Board of National Missions, General Department of Mission Strategy and Evangelism, 1967.

F30. Fischer, Russell G. "James Baldwin: a bibliography, 1947–1962." *Bulletin of Bibliography* 24 (Jan.-Apr. 1965), 127–30.

F31. Fisher, Barbara, and James McCabe. *Black Literature and Films*. Rensselaer, Ind.: St. Joseph's College Library.

F32. Fisher, Edith Maureen. *Focusing on Afro/Black American Research: a guide and annotated bibliography to selected resources in the University of California, San Diego, Libraries*. San Diego, Cal.: University of California at San Diego Libraries, 1975, 45 pp.

* Fisher, Lorette. See G110.

* Fisher, Mary L. See M79.

F33. Fisher, R.A. "Manuscript Materials Bearing on the Negro in British Archives." *Journal of Negro History* 27 (Jan. 1942), 83–93.

F34. Fisher, William H. *Free at Last: a bibliography of Martin Luther King, Jr.* Metuchen, N.J.: Scarecrow Press, 1977, 169 pp.

F35. Fisher, William H. *The Invisible Empire: a bibliography of the Ku Klux Klan*. Metuchen, N.J.: Scarecrow Press, 1980, 202 pp.

F36. Fishman, Diane, and Barbara Alden. "A Selected Bibliography of Books by and about American Negro Writers." *Trinkle Little Star* [newsletter of the E.L. Trinkle Library, Mary Washington College, University of Virginia] (Apr. 1970), 9–21.

F37. *Fisk University Theses, 1917–1942*. Nashville, Tenn.: Fisk University Library, 1942, 29 pp. An earlier publication covered the years 1917–1939.

F38. Fitzgerald, Mae Isom. *Sweeny Collection*. Memphis, Tenn.: LeMoyne-Owen College, Hollis F. Price Library, 65 pp. An 11 pp. supplement was also issued.

F39. Flanagan, James, and Margaret Parker. "Taking the Oreo out of Colored: materials for the black experience." *Media and Methods—Exploration in Education* 7 (Dec. 1970), 24 + .

F40. Flanders, Teresa. "Equal Employment Opportunity: a selected bibliography." *ALA Library Service to Labor Newsletter* 17:1 (Fall 1964), 1–5.

F41. Fleischman, Al. *Merritt College Library Guide for Afro-American Studies*. Oakland, Cal.: Merritt College Library.

F42. Fleming, Robert E. *James Weldon Johnson and Arna Wendell Bontemps: a reference guide*. Boston, Mass.: G.K. Hall, 1978, 149 pp.

* Fleming, Robert E. See also B31, B32, Q3, Q7.

F43. Flesher, Lorna. *American Minorities: a checklist of bibliographies published by government agencies, 1960–1970*. Sacramento, Cal.: California State Library, Government Publications Section, 1970, 7 pp.

F44. [Fletcher Henderson Discography]. *Record Research* 1:4 (Aug. 1955), 11.

F45. [Fletcher Henderson Discography]. *Record Research* 72 (Nov. 1965), 5.

F46. Fletcher, Marvin E. "Famulus: a bibliographic servant." *Historical Methods Newsletter* 7:2 (1974), 83–6.

F47. Fletcher, Ruth, and Beverly Hall. *The Black American: a selected checklist of books and periodicals*. Norton, Mass.: Wheaton College Library.

F48. Floyd, Samuel A., Jr. "Black Music in the Driscoll Collection." *The Black Perspective in Music* 2:2 (Fall 1974), 158–71.

F49. Flückiger, Otto. "Cab Calloway Discography and Solography [*sic*]." *Jazz Journal* 14:5 (May 1961), 1–4; 14:6 (June 1961), 13–4; 14:7 (July 1961), 11–2.

F50. Flückiger, Otto. *Discography of Lionel Hampton Orchestra, 1951–1953*. Reinach: Jazz Publications, 1961, 22 pp.

* Flückinger, Otto. See also D79, D80, D81.

F51. *Focus Black: a selected list of books about current black problems by black writers*. Omaha, Neb.: Omaha Public Library, 1970(?).

F52. *Focus on Minorities*. Washington, D.C.: U.S. Department of Defense, Army, Library Branch, Special Services Division, 1973, 93 pp.

F53. *Folklore*. The Black Culture Series for Young Readers. Chicago, Ill.: Chicago Public Library, 1972, 3 pp.

F54. Fonteyne, Andre. "Brian Rust: quelques corrections et une bonne nouvelle." *Le Point du Jazz* 6 (Mar. 1972), 106–10; 9 (Dec. 1973), 129–30; 11 (June 1975), 100–10.

F55. Forbes, George W. "Mr. A. A. Schomburg's Race Library." *A.M.E. Church Review* 31 (Oct. 1914), 212–4.

F56. Forbes, Jack D. *Afro-Americans in the Far West: a handbook for educators*. Berkeley, Cal.: Far West Laboratory for Educational Research and Development, 1967(?), 106 pp.

F57. [Ford Dabney]. *Record Research* 1:2 (Apr. 1955), 7–8; 1:4 (Aug. 1955), 11.

F58. Ford, Nick Aaron. "Battle of the Books: a critical survey of significant books by and about Negroes published in 1960." *Phylon* 22 (1961), 119–24.

F59. Ford, Nick Aaron, "The Fire Next Time: a survey of belles lettres by and about Negroes published in 1963." *Phylon* 25 (1964), 123–34.

F60. Ford, Nick Aaron, "I Teach Negro Literature." *College English* 2 (Mar. 1941), 530–41.

F61. Ford, Nick Aaron. "Search for Identity: a critical survey of significant belles lettres by and about Negroes published in 1961." *Phylon* 22 (1962), 128–38.

F62. Ford, Nick Aaron. "Walls Do a Prison Make: a critical survey of significant belles lettres by and about Negroes published in 1962." *Phylon* 24 (1963), 123–34.

F63. Foreman, Paul B., and Mozell C. Hill. *The Negro in the United States: a bibliography; a select reference and minimum college library resources list.* Stillwater, Ok.: Oklahoma A. and M. College, 1947, 24 pp.

* Foreman, Paul B. See also H69, T88.

* Fortenberry, George. See Mc29.

F64. Foster, Frederick L., and G. Smith. *The Human Crisis in America.* New Haven, Conn.: Yale Coop and the New Haven Public Library.

F65. Foster, Joanna. "Books on the American Negro." *Senior Scholastic* 90 (Feb. 17, 1967), 29.

F66. Foster, William E. "The Harris Collection on Civil War and Slavery [in the Providence, R.I., Public Library]." *In* Stuart C. Sherman, et al., eds. *The Special Collections of the Providence Public Library.* Providence, R.I.: Providence Public Library, 1968, pp. 12–8.

F67. Fouch, Deborah Smith. *Everett LeRoi Jones (Imamu Amiri Baraka).* Atlanta, Ga.: Atlanta University, Center for African and African American Studies, 1977(?), 11 pp.

F68. *14,000,000 of Your Fellow-Americans Need Your Understanding.* New York: City-Wide Citizens' Committee on Harlem, 6 pp.

F68A. Fowler, Carolyn. *Black Arts and Black Aesthetics: a bibliography.* Atlanta, Ga.: First World Foundation, 1981.

* Fowler, Julian S. See H111.

F69. Fox, Charles, Peter Gammond, Alun Morgan, and Alexis Korner. *Jazz on Record: a critical guide.* London, England: Hutchinson, 1960, 352 pp. Reprinted by Greenwood Press.

F70. Fralken, Laurie. *The Negro Experience in the U.S.* Trenton, N.J.: Trenton State College Library, 1969.

F71. Frank, Ilona, and Marquita Breit. *A Bibliography of Black Studies.* Louisville, Ky.: Bellarmine College Library.

F72. "Frank J. Klingberg: a select list of publications." *Negro History Bulletin* 21:3 (1957), 52–7.

F73. Frase, Bill. "Assorted Additions, Corrections and Other Junk Concerning Recordings in Brian Rust's Compilation, 'Jazz Records 1897–1942'." *Record Research* 144–5 (Mar. 1975), 10; 153–4 (Apr. 1978), 14.

F74. Fraser, James H. "Black Publishing for Black Children: the experience of the sixties and the seventies." *Library Journal* 98 (Nov. 15, 1973), 3421–6; *Scholastic Library Journal* 20:3 (Nov. 1973), 19–24.

F75. Fraser, Lyn. *Bibliography of Publications Relative to Afro-American Studies.* Miscellaneous Series no. 10. Greeley, Col.: Colorado State College, Museum of Anthropology, 1969, 93 pp.

F76. Frazier, E. Franklin. "The Booker T. Washington Papers." *The Library of Congress Quarterly Journal of Current Acquisitions* 2:2 (Feb. 1945), 23–31.

F77. Freeman, Leah. *The Black Man in America: a bibliography.* Bibliographic Series no. 4. Sacramento, Cal.: Sacramento State College Library, 1969, 13 pp.

* Freeman, Walter E. See T34.

F78. Freeney, Mildred, and Mary T. Henry. *A List of the Manuscripts, Published Works and Related Items in the Charles Waddell Chesnutt Collection of the Erastus Milo Cravath Memorial Library, Fisk University.* Nashville, Tenn.: Fisk University, 1954, 32 pp. A revised edition by Beth M. Howse was issued in 1973.

F79. French, William P., Michel J. Fabre, Amritjt Singh, and Genevieve Fabre. *Afro-American Poetry and Drama, 1760–1975: a guide to information sources.* Detroit, Mich.: Gale Research, 1979, 493 pp.

* French, William P. See also D88, D89.

F80. Fresia, E. "Discografia [Edward (Duke) Ellington]." *Musica Jazz* 19 (Oct. 1963), 50–1.

F81. Fresia, E. "Discografia [Jimmie Lunceford]." *Musica Jazz* 18 (July-Aug. 1962), 28–31.

F82. Fresia, E. "Discografia [John Coltrane and Oscar Peterson, 1961–63]." *Musica Jazz* 20 (Feb. 1964), 42–3.

F83. Freund, Roberta B. "The American Negro: a bibliography of background material." *Read, See and Hear* [Newark, N.J., Board of Education, Department of Libraries and Audiovisual Education] 17:2 (Feb. 9, 1968), 1–4.

F84. Frey, Mitsue, and David Duffy. *Directory of African and Afro-American Studies in the U.S.* Waltham, Mass.: Crossroads Press, 1979, 306 pp.

F85. Friend, Bruce I. *Guide to the Microfilm Record of Selected Documents of Records of the Committee on Fair Employment Practice in the Custody of the National Archives.* Glen Rock, N.J.: Microfilming Corporation of America, 1970.

F86. Not used.

F87. *From Bondage to Black Power: a reading and film list.* Mid-Hudson Libraries, System Service Center for Member Community Libraries, 9 pp.

F88. *From Negro Protest to Black Revolt: a selected working bibliography of Negro writings, 1940–1968, in the U.S.* Chicago, Ill.: Chicago Public Library, George Cleveland Hall Branch.

F89. *From Slavery to Protest: a bibliography of Afro-American resources for Pennsylvania schools.* Harrisburg, Pa.: Bureau of General and Academic Education, Social Studies Division, Division of School Libraries, 1968.

F90. Fuller, Juanita B. "An Annotated Bibliography of Biographies and Autobiographies of Negroes, 1839–1961." Thesis, M.S. in L.S., Atlanta

University, 1963. Published in 1964 by the University of Rochester Press for the Association of College and Research Libraries.

F91. Fuller, Sara, Edie Hedlin, and David Larson. *Ohio Black History Guide*. Columbus, Ohio: Ohio Historical Society, Archives-Library, 1975, 221 pp.

F92. Fuller, Willie J. *Blacks in Alabama, 1528–1865*. Exchange Bibliography no. 1033. Monticello, Ill.: Council of Planning Librarians, 1976, 30 pp.

F93. Funkhouser, Myrtle. "Folk-Lore of the American Negro: a bibliography." *Bulletin of Bibliography* 16:2 (Jan.–Apr. 1937), 28–9; 16:3 (May-Aug. 1937), 49–51; 16:4 (Sept.-Dec. 1937), 72–3; 16:6 (May-Aug. 1938), 108–10; 16:7 (Sept.-Dec. 1938), 136–7; 16:8 (Jan.-Apr. 1938), 159–60.

F94. Furniss, W. Todd. *Colleges and Minority/Poverty Issues: bibliography and other resources*. Washington, D.C.: American Council on Education, 1969.

F95. "Further Reading on Student Movement: a selected bibliography." *New South* 15:10 (Oct. 1960), 13–4.

G

G1. Gagala, Kenneth L. *Economics of Minorities: a guide to information sources*. Detroit, Mich.: Gale Research, 1976, 212 pp.

G2. Gaidoz, H., and Paul Sébillot. *Bibliographies des Traditions et de la Littérature Populaire des Frances d'Outre-Mer* [Creole Language and Customs]. Paris, France: Maisonneuve Frères et C. Leclerc, 1886.

G3. Galbreath, C.B. "John Brown: bibliography." *Ohio Archaeological Quarterly* 30 (July 1921), 180–289.

* Gammond, Peter. See F69.

G3A. Ganfield, Jane. "Books and Periodical Articles on Jazz in America from 1926–1934." Paper, School of Library Service, Columbia University, 1933, 13 pp.

G4. Garcia, William Burres. "Church Music by Black Composers: a bibliography of choral music." *The Black Perspective in Music* 2:2 (Fall 1974), 145–57.

G5. Gardiner, George L. *A Bibliography of Charles S. Johnson's Published Writings*. Nashville, Tenn.: Fisk University Library, 1960, 41 pp.

G6. Gardiner, George L. *CSU Library Notes; Black Literature 1971*. Wilberforce, Ohio: Central State University, 1971, 14 pp.

G7. Gardner, Henry L. *Readings in Contemporary Black Politics: an annotated bibliography*. Carbondale, Ill.: Southern Illinois University, Public Affairs Research Bureau, 1970, 12 pp.

G7A. Gardner, Jane. "Pro-Slavery Propaganda in Fiction Written in Answer to 'Uncle Tom's Cabin,' 1852–1861." *Resources for American Literary Study* 7 (1977), 201–9.

G8. Gardner, M. "Bargain Bird [Charlie Parker on cut-price labels]." *Jazz Journal* 20 (June 1967), 8–11.

G9. Gardner, M. "A Desirable Dozen: some recent American reissues." *Jazz Journal* 21 (June 1968), 31–3.

G10. Gardner, M. "[Earl] Bud Powell on Record, 1956–1966." *Jazz Monthly* 13 (July 1967), 28–30.

G11. Gardner, M., and F. Gibson. "A Discography of the 'Live' Recordings of Charlie Parker." *Jazz Journal* 17 (June 1964), 29; (July 1964), 25.

G12. Gardner, M., and F. Gibson. "A Discography of the Studio Recordings of Charlie Parker." *Jazz Journal* 17 (May 1964), 26–7.

G13. Gardner, Mark. *Horace Silver Discography with a Brief Biography.* Droitwick, Worcestershire, England: Author, 1967, 22 pp.

G14. Garodkin, John. *Little Richard [Richard W. Penniman] Special: king of rock 'n' roll.* Copenhagen, Denmark: C.P. Wulff, 1975, 71 pp.

* Garodkin, John. See also M117.

G15. Garoogian, Andrew. *School Desegregation and "White Flight": a selected bibliography.* Monticello, Ill.: Vance Bibliographies, 1980.

G16. Gary, D.S. "Bibliographical Essay: black views on Reconstruction." *Journal of Negro History* 58 (Jan. 1973), 73–85.

G17. Gaudio, R., et al. *Ghetto: a bibliography.* Rochester, N.Y.: St. John Fisher College Library, 1969, 73 pp.

* Gault, James. See H89, W104.

G18. Gay, B.S. "Representation of Books by and about the American Negro in the Central Library of the Atlanta Library System." M.S. in L.S. thesis, Atlanta University, 1962, 41 pp.

* Gayle, Addison. See K15.

G19. Gelly, D. "The [William] Count Basie Octet." *Jazz Monthly* 9 (July 1963), 9–11.

G20. Genovese, E.D. "Cities Within Our Cities." *Nation* 207 (Aug. 5, 1968), 86–8.

G21. George, Melvin. *The City, with a special bibliography about Chicago.* Elmhurst, Ill.: Elmhurst College, Memorial Library, 1969. A supplement of 44 pp. was issued in 1970.

G22. George, Zelma. *Bibliographical Index to Negro Music. Master catalogue of 9,592 titles in the Moorland Collection, Howard University.* Washington, D.C.: Howard University, 1944.

G23. George, Zelma Watson. "A Guide to Negro Music: an annotated bibliography of Negro folk music, and art music by Negro composers or based on Negro thematic material." Ph.D. dissertation, N.Y.U., 1953, 302 pp.

G24. Gerstenberger, Donna, and George Hendrick. "Harriet Beecher Stowe." *The American Novel, 1789–1959: a checklist of twentieth century criticism.* Denver, Col.: Alan Swallow, 1961, pp. 231–2.

G25. Gerstenberger, Donna, and George Hendrick. "Ralph Ellison." *The*

American Novel, 1789–1959: a checklist of twentieth century criticism. Denver, Col.: Alan Swallow, 1961, pp. 67–8.

G26. Gerstenberger, Donna, and George Hendrick. "Richard Wright." *The American Novel, 1789–1959: a checklist of twentieth century criticism.* Denver, Col.: Alan Swallow, 1961, pp. 270–1.

G27. Gheusi, Jacques. "Discographie [Leontyne Price]." *Diapason* 124 (Mar. 1968), 15.

G28. Gibson, Donald B. "Afro-American Fiction: contemporary research and criticism, 1965–1978." *American Quarterly* 30:3 (1978), 395–409.

G29. Gibson, Donald B. "Richard Wright: a bibliographic essay." *College Language Association Journal* 12 (June 1969), 360–5.

* Gibson, Donald B. See also C177.

* Gibson, F. See G11, G12.

G30. Gibson, Mary Jane, and Sylvia Lyons Render. "Afro-American Experience: a selected list of references by Afro-Americans." *Library of Congress Information Bulletin* 38 (Feb. 2–16, 1979), 39–44, 49–52, 56–60. Reprinted in *Readers Advisory Service: selected topical booklists* 8:1 (1981), 547–1—547–10.

G30A. Gilbert, Abby L., and Thomas H. Countee, Jr. "Black Banks: a bibliographic survey." *Bulletin of Bibliography* 28:2 (Apr.-June 1972), 60–72.

* Gilchrist, V.D. See T75.

G31. Gilenson, Boris. "Afro-American Literature in the Soviet Union." *Negro American Literature Forum* 9:1 (Spring 1975), 25+. Reprinted from *Soviet Life* (Aug. 1973), 60–1.

G32. Gillis, Frank, and Alan P. Merriam. *Ethnomusicology and Folk Music: an international bibliography of dissertations and theses.* Middletown, Conn.: Wesleyan University Press, 1966, 148 pp.

G33. Ginger, Ann Fagan. *Angela Davis Case Collection: annotated procedural guide and index.* Meiklejohn Civil Liberties Institute. Berkeley, Cal.: Oceana Publications, 1974, 162 pp.

* Giordano, Grace Pineiro. See G34.

G34. Giordano, Joseph, and Grace Pineiro Giordano. *The Ethno-Cultural Factors in Mental Health: a literature review and bibliography.* New York: Institute on Pluralism and Group Identity of the American Jewish Committee, 1979.

* Gitter, Ira. See M141.

G35. Gittleman, J. *The Black Experience in America.* South Fallsburg, N.Y.: Sullivan County Community College Library.

G36. Giza, Joanne. "Ralph Ellison." *In* M. Thomas Inge, Jackson R. Bryer, and Maurice Duke, eds. *Black American Writers: bibliographic essays,* Vol. 2. New York: St. Martin's Press, 1978, pp. 47–71.

G37. Glancy, Barbara J. "Annotated Bibliography of Integrated and Black Books for Children." *In* Jean Dresden Grambs, John C. Carr, et al. *Black Im-*

age. Education Copes wth Color: essays on the black experience. Dubuque, Iowa: William C. Brown, 1972, pp. 155–76.

G38. Glancy, Barbara J. "The Beautiful People in Children's Books." *Childhood Education* 46 (Apr. 1970), 365–70.

G39. Glancy, Barbara J. "Black Barbeque: an essay review." *The Record* (Apr. 1969), 661–84.

G40. Glancy, Barbara J. *Children's Interracial Fiction: an unselective bibliography.* Curricular Viewpoints Series no. 4. Washington, D.C.: American Federation of Teachers, 1969, 124 pp.

G41. Not used.

G42. Glenn, Robert W. *Black Rhetoric: a guide to Afro-American Communication.* Metuchen, N.J.: Scarecrow Press, 1976, 386 pp.

G43. Glicksberg, C.I. "Science and the Race Problem." *Phylon* 12:4 (1951), 319–27.

G44. Gloster, H.M. "Negro Writer and the Southern Scene." *Southern Packet* 4 (Jan. 1948), 1–3.

G45. Glover, T. "The Groovy Boom in R & B." *Sing Out* 16:3 (1966), 37–43.

* Goddet, Laurent.See R147.

G46. Godrich, John "Jazz Information: a listing of the reissues." *Matrix* 82 (Apr. 1969), 3.

G47. Godrich, John. *John Godrich's Survey of Pre-war Artists Reissued on EP and LP, 1951–1964.* Bexhill-on-Sea, England: Blues Unlimited, 1965, 16 pp.

G48. Godrich, John, and R.M.W. Dixon. *Blues and Gospel Records, 1902–1942.* London: Author, 1963. A second edition of 912 pp. was issued by Storyville Publications, Chigwell, Essex, England, in 1971.

* Godrich, John. See also D122A, D123.

G49. Goetz, Vera C. *Afro-American Bibliography.* Chicago, Ill.: Malcolm X College Library, 10 pp.

* Gold, Steven C. See I9.

G50. Goldberg, M.A. "Design for Reading: six bibliographies for intercultural understanding." *English Journal* 34 (Nov. 1945), 494.

G51. Goldman, Elliott. *Clarence Williams Discography.* London, England: Jazz Music Books, 1947, 28 pp.

G52. Goldman, R.J., and F.M. Taylor. "Coloured Immigrant Children: a survey of research, studies and literature on their educational problems and potentials in the U.S.A." *Educational Research* 9 (Nov. 1966), 39–43.

G53. Goldstein, Samuel. *Journals of Negro Interest: a bibliographic list.* Amherst, Mass.: University of Massachusetts Library, 1968, 18 pp.

G54. Goldwater, Walter. *Radical Periodicals in America, 1890–1950: a bibliography with brief notes.* New Haven, Conn.: Yale University Library, 1966, 51 pp.

G55. Gonzales, Alex S. *Minorities and the U.S. Economy.* Santa Barbara, Cal.: University of California at Santa Barbara, Library, 1974, 112 pp.

* Goon, Susan. See K38.

G56. Gordon, John D. "Carl Van Vechten: notes for an exhibition in honor of his seventy-fifth birthday." *Bulletin of The New York Public Library* 59 (July 1955), 331–66.

G57. Gordon, Carolyn. *Lorraine Hansberry*. CAAS Bibliography no. 1. Atlanta, Ga.: Atlanta University, Center for African and African American Studies.

G58. Gordon, Edmund W. *An Annotated Bibliography on Higher Education of the Disadvantaged*. ERIC Document no. Ed 038–478. New York: Columbia University, Teachers College, The Study of Collegiate Compensatory Programs for Minority Group Youth, 1970.

G59. Gordon, Edmund W., and Derek Green. *An Affluent Society's Excuses for Inequality: developmental, economic, and educational*. ERIC Document no. ED 087–823. New York: ERIC Clearinghouse on the Urban Disadvantaged. Also appears in *American Journal of Orthopsychiatry* 44:1 (Jan. 1974), 4–18.

G60. Gordon, Elizabeth DeLouis. *Afro-Americans in [Government] Documents: an annotated bibliography*. La Jolla, Cal.: University of California at La Jolla, Central University Library, Documents Department, 1974.

G61. Gordon, Eugene. "The Negro Press." *The Annals of the American Academy of Political and Social Science* 140 229 (Nov. 1928), 248–56.

* Gordon, Louise M. See E2A.

G62. Graham, Hugh Davis. "Bibliographic Essay: political tendencies in Louisiana and the South." *Journal of Negro History* 57 (Jan. 1972), 40–4.

G63. Graham, Hugh Davis. *A Selected Bibliography of Twentieth Century Southern History with Special Emphasis on Racial Relations especially since 1954*. Palo Alto, Cal.: Stanford University, Department of History, 1967, 16 pp.

G64. Graham, James D. "Negro Protest in America, 1900–1955: a bibliographic guide." *South Atlantic Quarterly* 67 (Winter 1968), 94–107.

G65. Grambs, Jean Dresden. *Intergroup Education: methods and materials*. Sponsored by the Anti-Defamation League of B'nai B'rith. Englewood Cliffs, N.J.: Prentice-Hall, 1968, pp. 87–199.

G66. Grambs, Jean Dresden. "What People Read: a bibliography of research and commentary on the contents of textbooks and literary media." *In* Jean Dresden Grambs, John C. Carr, et al. *Black Image. Education Copes with Color: essays on the black experience*. Dubuque, Iowa: William C. Brown, 1972, pp. 177–88.

* Grambs, Jean Dresden. See also G37.

G67. Grandorge, Richard. *Jazz Records A-Z, 1897–1931: index [to Rust's second edition]*. Hatch End, Middlesex, England: Rust's Rare Records, 1963, 62 pp.

G68. Grant, Edmonia White. "American Negroes." *American Minority People During World War II*. Rev. ed. New York: American Missionary Association, 1945, pp. 9–11.

* Gray, Alma L. See C119, J25.
G69. Gray, Daniel Savage. "Bibliographical Essay: black views on Reconstruction." *Journal of Negro History* 58:1 (1973), 73–85.
G70. Grayshon, Matthew C., and Vincent P. Houghton. *Initial Bibliography
of Immigration and Race*. Nottingham, England: Nottingham Univer-
sity, Institute of Education, 1966, 38 pp.
G71. *Great Black Americans as Reported in "The New York Times": program
guide*. Sanford, N.C.: Microfilming Corporation of America, 1980.
G72. Green, Dan S. "Bibliography of Writing about W.E.B. Du Bois." *College Language Association Journal* 20:3 (Mar. 1977), 410–21.
G73. Green, Dan S. "Resurrection of the Writings of an American Scholar
[W.E.B. Du Bois]." *Crisis* 79:9 (1972), 311–3.
G74. Green, Dan S. "W.E.B. Du Bois: his journalistic career." *Negro His-
tory Bulletin* 40:2 (Mar.-Apr. 1977), 672–77.
* Green, Derek. See G59.
G75. Green, Elizabeth Lay. *The Negro in Contemporary American Literature:
an outline for individual and group study*. Chapel Hill, N.C.: University
of North Carolina Press, 1928, pp. 76–94.
* Greenblat, Cathy S. See T102.
* Greene, Ethyl Graham. See C8, C9.
* Greene, F.F. See W7.
G76. Greene, Harry W. *Two Decades [1921–1939] of Research and Creative
Writings at West Virginia State College*. Institute, W. Va.: West Vir-
ginia State College, 1939, 24 pp. A supplement covering 1939–1945
was issued in 1946. See also "Publications of the Faculty and Staff of
West Virginia State College, Jan. 1, 1946-Dec. 31, 1959." *West Vir-
ginia State College Bulletin* 47:5 (Aug. 1960), 23 pp.
G77. Greene, Lorenzo J. "Negro Manuscript Collections in Libraries." *Negro
History Bulletin* 30 (Mar. 1967), 20; (Oct. 1967), 14–5; (Dec. 1967),
14–7.
G78. Gregorovich, Andrew. *Canadian Ethnic Groups Bibliography: a selected
bibliography of ethnocultural groups in Canada and the Province of
Ontario*. Toronto, Ont., Canada: Ontario Department of the Provincial
Secretary and Citizenship, 1972, 208 pp.
G79. Grendysa, Peter. "The Buddy Johnson Story." *Record Exchanger* 6:1
[issue no. 28] (1979?), 18–23.
G80. Grendysa, Peter. "The Mills Brothers: four boys and a guitar." *Record
Exchanger* 5:2 [issue no. 24] (Oct. ? 1977), 4–12.
G81. Griffen, Louise. *Multi-Ethnic Books for Young Children: annotated bib-
liography for parents and teachers*. Washington, D.C.: National Asso-
ciation for the Education of Young Children, 1970, 74 pp.
G82. Not used.
G83. Not used.
G84. Griffin, John C. "Jean Toomer: a bibliography." *South Carolina Review*
7 (Apr. 1975), 61–4.

G85. Griffin, R.G. "Research Source: Heartman Negro Collection at Texas Southern University." *Negro History Bulletin* 20 (Feb. 1957), 118.

G86. Griffin, Richard G. *To Study Black*. Old Westbury, N.Y.: SUNY, 1971, 14 pp.

G87. Griffith, George. *Bibliography for Race and Ethnic Relations*. Bellevue, Neb.: Bellevue College Library.

* Grindon, Mimi. See B311.

G88. Grinstead, Scott E. *A Select, Classified and Briefly Annotated List of Two Hundred Fifty Books by or about the Negro Published during the Past Ten Years*. Nashville, Tenn.: Fisk University Library, 1939, 42 pp.

G89. Gross, James A. "Historians and the Literature of the Negro Worker." *Labor History* 10:3 (Summer 1969), 536–46.

G90. Gross, Seymour. "The Negro in American Literature: a checklist of criticism and scholarship." *In his Images of the Negro in American Literature*. Chicago, Ill.: University of Chicago Press, 1966, pp. 289–315.

G91. Gross, Seymour. "The Negro in Southern Literature." *In Louis D. Rubin, Jr., ed. A Bibliographical Guide to the Study of Southern Literature*. Baton Rouge, La.: Louisiana State University Press, 1969, pp. 58–66.

G92. Grossack, Martin M., Elias Blake, Jr., Antonio F. Chaves, and Joseph S. Roucek. "Current Literature on Negro Education." *Journal of Negro Education* 34:1 (1965), 78–83.

* Grove, Pearce. See R89.
* Grustas, Carol. See B138.

G93. Gubert, Betty Kaplan. *Early Black Bibliographies, 1863–1918*. New York: Garland, 1982, 380 pp.

G93A. Gubert, Betty Kaplan. *Suggestions and Selected Resources to Begin a Search for Family History*. New York: Schomburg Center, The New York Public Library, 1977, 2 pp.

* Gubert, Betty Kaplan. See also A15, A16, B233, D145, D147, D154A, L80, L84, L87A, L90, L108, Mc27, M44, M159, R69A, S43, S58, S59, S140.

G94. *A Guide for Teaching the Contribution of the Negro Author to American Literature*. San Diego, Cal.: San Diego City Schools, 1969.

G95. Not used.

G96. *A Guide to Facts about the Negro*. New York: NAACP Training Department, 1970, 68 pp.

G97. *Guide to Manuscripts and Archives in the Negro Collection of the Trevor Arnett Library*. Atlanta, Ga.: Atlanta University Libraries, 1971, 45 pp.

G98. *Guide to Manuscripts and Source Material Relating to the Negro in Massachusetts [from 1827 to 1865 in the Boston Public Library]*. Boston, Mass.: U.S. Works Progress Administration, Historical Records Survey, Division of Community Service Programs, 1942, 129 pp.

G99. "Guide to Periodical Literature." *Interracial Review* 33:5 (May 1960), 132.

G100. *A Guide to Publications by and about Negro Americans.* Minneapolis, Minn.: Youth Development Project, 1965, 28 pp.

G101. *Guide to Research on Afro-American History and Culture.* Northampton, Mass.: Smith College Library, 1972–7, 3 vols.

G102. *A Guide to Resources for Anti-Poverty Programs: a selected bibliography.* New York: Federation Employment and Guidance Service, Richard J. Bernhardt Memorial Library, 1965, 24 pp.

G102A. *Guide to Resources in Afro-American History.* Cambridge, Mass.: MIT Humanities Library, 1977, 2 pp.

G103. *Guide to the Literature for Black Studies: sources in the Vassar College Library.* Poughkeepsie, N.Y.: Vassar College Library, 1972, 41 pp.

G104. *Guide to the Microfilm Edition of the Countee Cullen Papers, 1921–1969.* New Orleans, La.: Amistad Research Center, 1975, 49 pp.

G105. *Guide to the Microfilm Edition of the New England Emigrant Aid Company Papers, 1854–1909, in the Kansas State Historical Society.* Topeka, Kan.: Kansas State Historical Society, 1967, 22 pp.

G106. *Guide to the Microfilm Edition of the Peter Smith Papers, 1763–1850, and Gerrit Smith Papers, 1775–1924.* Glen Rock, N.J.: Microfilming Corporation of America, 1974, 88 pp.

G107. *A Guide to the Microfilm Publication of The Pennsylvania Abolition Society at The Historical Society of Pennsylvania.* Sanford, N.C.: Microfilming Corporation of America.

G108. Gumby, L.S. Alexander. "The Gumby Scrapbook Collection of Negroana." *Columbia Library World* (Jan. 1951), 1–8.

G109. Guralnick, P. "Records, Blues: a survey of recent releases." *Rolling Stone* 77 (Mar. 4, 1971), 56.

* Gurwich, A. See S49A.

G110. Guss, Margery, Pia Tollo, and Loretta Fisher. *Basic Indexing, Bibliographic and Periodical Services Useful to Students Interested in Ethnic and Minority Groups.* Corvallis, Ore.: Oregon State University, William Jasper Kerr Library, 4 pp.

G111. Guzman, Jessie P. "An Annotated List of Books by or concerning Negroes in the United States, in Africa and in Latin America, 1938–1946." *Negro Year Book: a review of events affecting Negro life 1941–1946.* Tuskegee, Ala.: Tuskegee Institute, Department of Records and Research, 1947, pp. 635–84.

G112. Guzman, Jessie P. *Civil Rights and the Negro: a list of references relating to present day discussions.* Rev. ed. Tuskegee, Ala.: Tuskegee Institute, Department of Records and Research, 1950, 28 pp. The first edition, in 1949, had 19 pp.

G113. Guzman, Jessie P. *George Washington Carver: a classified bibliography.* Tuskegee, Ala.: Tuskegee Institute, Department of Records and Research, 1954, 26 pp.

G114. Guzman, Jessie P. "George Washington Carver: a classified bibliography." *Bulletin of Bibliography* 21:1 (May-Aug. 1953), 13–16; 21:2 (Sept.-Dec. 1953), 34–8.

G115. Guzman, Jessie P., and Woodrow W. Hall. *Desegregation and the Southern States, 1957. Legal action and voluntary group action.* Tuskegee, Ala.: Tuskegee Institute, Department of Records and Research, 1958.

H

* Haas, Edward F. See J95, S279.

H1. Hackman, Martha. *A Library Guide to Afro-American Studies.* Los Angeles, Cal.: California State College, John F. Kennedy Memorial Library, 1969, 13 pp.

H1A. Hadley, Richard T. "The Published Choral Music of Ulysses Kay, 1943–1968." Ph.D. thesis, University of Iowa, 1972, 337 pp.

* Hady, Maureen C. See S265.

H2. Haggerty, Brian A. "Martin Luther King, Jr.: a chronological bibliography." *Journal of Negro History* 66:1 (Spring 1981), 64–9.

H3. Hague, Aba Saeed Zahurul. "A Bibliography of Mississippi Folklore, 1968." *Mississippi Folklore Register* 4 (1970), 28–36.

H4. Haigler, Mrs. Virgie Biggins, Mrs. Walter T. Wittman, and Ethel R. Wood. *Bibliographies for Negro History and Culture and Teacher Resources and Teaching Materials.* Englewood, N.J.: Urban League for Bergen County, Education Committee.

H5. Hall, George. *Nat "King" Cole Trio.* Whittier, Cal.: Erngeobil, 1965, 18 pp.

* Hall, George. See also E5, E6, E7, E8.

H6. Hall, Jo Anne. "Busing Bibliography: a preliminary survey." *RQ* 11:4 (Summer 1972), 320–7.

H7. Hall, Woodrow Wadsworth. *A Bibliography of the Tuskegee Gerrymander Protest: pamphlets, magazine and newspaper articles chronologically arranged.* Tuskegee, Ala.: Tuskegee Institute, Department of Records and Research, 1960, 54 pp.

* Hall, Woodrow Wadsworth. See also G115.

H8. Haller, Elizabeth S. *American Diversity: a bibliography of resources on racial and ethnic minorities for Pennsylvania schools.* Harrisburg, Pa.: Pennsylvania Department of Education, Bureau of General and Academic Education, 1969, 236 pp.

H9. Halliday, Thelma Y. *The Negro in Business: annotated bibliography.* Washington, D.C.: Howard University, Small Business and Development Center, 1969, 23 pp.

H10. Halliday, Thelma Y. *The Negro in the Field of Business: an annotated bibliography.* Washington, D.C.: Howard University, Institute for Minority Business Education, 1970, 42 pp. A second edition of 85 pp. was issued in 1972, and a third edition of 131 pp. in 1975.

H11. Hamilton, C.V., and T.F. Pettigrew. "Blacks on Campus: IQ's and Uncle Toms." *Commonweal* 99 (Oct. 5, 1973), 14+.

H12. Hamilton, Dave. *A Guide to Negro Newspapers on Microfilm: a selected list*. ERIC Document no. 062–240. DeKalb, Ill.: Northern Illinois University.

* Hammond, Agnes. See S171, S172.

H13. Handler, June. "Books for Loving." *Elementary English* 47 (May 1970), 687–92.

* Haner, Lucy. See M45A.

H14. Not used.

H15. Hannerz, Ulf. "Research in the Black Ghetto: a review of the sixties." *Journal of Asian and African Studies* [Netherlands] 9:3/4 (1974), 139–59.

H16. Hansen, Anne. *A Select Bibliography on Negro History: books in the Brazoport College Library*. Brazoport, Tex.: Brazoport Junior College Library, 1970.

* Hansen, Carol. See C98.

H17. Hansen, Chadwick. "The 54th Massachusetts Volunteer Black Infantry as a Subject for American Artists." *Massachusetts Review* 16 (Autumn 1975), 745–59.

H18. Harber, Jean R., and Jane N. Beatty. *Reading and the Black English-Speaking Child: an annotated bibliography*. Newark, Del.: International Reading Association, 1978, 47 pp.

H19. Harber, Jean R., and D.N. Bryen. "Black English and the Task of Reading." *Review of Educational Research* 46 (Summer 1976), 387–405.

H20. Hargrave, Victoria. *Dr. Martin Luther King, Jr., Memorial Collection*. Jacksonville, Ill.: Henry Pfeiffer Library, 9 pp.

H21. Harlan, Louis R. "The Booker T. Washington Papers." *Maryland Historian* 6:1 (1975), 55–9.

H22. *Harlem on Review: exhibition of printed material from the Harold Jackman collection*. Atlanta, Ga.: Atlanta University Library, 1943, 7 pp.

H23. Harley, Ralph L., Jr. "A Check List of Afro-American Art and Artists." *The Serif* 7:4 (Dec. 1970), 3–63.

H24. Haro, Robert P. *Affirmative Action in Higher Education: a selected and annotated bibliography*. Exchange Bibliography no. 1229. Monticello, Ill.: Council of Planning Librarians, 1977.

* Harper, Harriett. See B297.

* Harrington, Bryce. See S7.

H25. Harris, Abram L. "Problems of Economic Research." *ACLS Bulletin* 32 (Sept. 1941), 46–67.

H26. Harris, Addie. *Afro-American Politicians: a selected bibliography*. Chicago, Ill.: Association for the Study of Afro-American Life and History, 1981, 9 pp.

* Harris, H. Meunier. See D20.

H27. Harris, Helen Y., Lanetta Parks, and Lillie Story. *The Blacklist*. Baltimore, Md.: Enoch Pratt Free Library, 1969.

* Harris, Lois. See Mc16.

H28. Harris, Mal James, Dorothy Lake, Peter Dolce, and Mary Ann O'Laughlin. "Separate But Unequal: the education of blacks in the U.S.: a selected list." *Race Relations Information Center Library* 2 (Oct. 1970), 2–6.

* Harris, Marcia. See M166.

* Harris, Mrs. R.D. See B220.

H29. Harris, Rex, and Brian Rust. *Recorded Jazz: a critical guide*. Harmondsworth, England: Penguin Books, 1958.

H30. Harris, Robert L., Jr. "Daniel Murray and the 'Encyclopedia of the Colored Race'." *Phylon* 37:3 (Fall 1976), 270–82.

H31. Harrison, Max, Alun Morgan, Ronald Atkins, Michael James, and Jack Cooke. *Modern Jazz: the essential records*. London, England: Aquarius Books, 1975.

* Harrison, Max. See also Mc15.

* Harrison-Stewart, E. See M112.

H32. Hartel, Harold H. "The H^3 Chrono-matrix File!" [Index to Brian Rust, *Jazz Records, 1897–1942*]. *Record Research* (Sept. 1980), 4–10.

* Harvey, Cecil. See S47.

* Harvey, Michael G. See B43.

* Harwell, Richard B. See C85.

H33. Haselgrove, J.R., and D. Kennington. *Readers' Guide to Books on Jazz*. 2nd ed. London, England: Library Association, County Libraries Section, 1965, 16 pp.

H34. Hatch, James V. *Black Image on the American Stage: a bibliography of plays and musicals, 1770–1970*. New York: D.B.S. Publications [Drama Book Specialists], 1970, 162 pp.

H35. Hatch, James V. "A White Folks Guide to 200 Years of Black and White Drama." *The Drama Review* 16:4 (Dec. 1972), 5–24.

H35A. Hatch, James V., and OMANii (*sic*) Abdullah. *Black Playwrights, 1823–1977: an annotated bibliography*. New York: R.R. Bowker, 1977, 319 pp.

H35B. Hatch, James V., Douglas A.M. Ward, and Joe Weixlmann. "The Rungs of a Powerful Long Ladder: an Owen Dodson bibliography." *Black American Literature Forum* 14, pp. 60–8.

H36. Haugen, Einar. *Bilingualism in the Americas: a bibliography and research guide*. Gainesville, Fla.: American Dialect Society, 1965, 159 pp.

H37. Havrilesky, Catherine, and Preston Wilcox. *A Selected Bibliography on White Institutional Racism.* New York: Afram Associates, 1969, 7 pp.

* Hawes, Richard. See C171.

H38. Hayes, C.J. "Mahalia Jackson: a discography." *Matrix* 62 (Dec. 1965), 3–5.

H39. Hayes, C.J. "Sister Rosetta Tharpe [Nubin]: a discography." *Matrix* 77 (June 1968), 3–14.

H40. Hayes, Floyd W., III. "The African Presence in America before Columbus: a bibliographic essay." *Black World* 22:9 (1973), 4–22.

H41. Hayes, Mary. *The Black Experience in America.* Washington, D.C.: Trinity College Library, 20 pp.

H42. Hayward, Olga Hines. "A Bibliography of Literature by and about Whitney M. Young, Jr., 1921–1971: an annotated checklist." *Bulletin of Bibliography* 31:3 (1974), 122–5.

H43. Haywood, Charles. *A Bibliography of North American Folklore and Folksong.* 2nd ed. New York: Dover Publications, 1961. The section on blacks is pp. 430–560.

H44. Haywood, Terry S. *Bibliography of Doctoral Dissertations on Blacks Accepted in the Ohio State University, 1932–1974.* Author, 1976, 28 pp.

H45. Hazelton, Louise. "Negro: a bibliography." *North Country Libraries* 10 (Nov. 1967), 192–4.

H46. Healy, Thomas. *A List of Titles in Black Studies.* Publication no. 69. Potsdam, N.Y.: SUNY, College at Potsdam, F.W. Crumb Memorial Library, 1969, 23 pp.

H47. Heartman, Charles F. "Bibliography of the Poetical Works of Phillis Wheatley." *In* Arthur A. Schomburg. *A Bibliographical Checklist of American Negro Poetry.* New York: Charles F. Heartman, 1916, pp. 47–57.

H48. Heartman, Charles F. *Phillis Wheatley (Phillis Peters): a critical attempt and a bibliography of her writings.* New York: Author, 1915, 44 pp.

* Heath, Robert. See O22.

H49. Heath, Trudy. *Slavery and Anti-Slavery Pamphlets: an index to the microfilm collection.* Ann Arbor, Mich.: University Microfilms, 1979, 30 pp.

H50. Heaton, Margaret M. "Books to Break the Stereotype." *Education* 66 (Jan. 1946), 321–5.

* Hedlin, Edie. See F91.

H51. Hefele, Bernhard. *Jazz Bibliography, International Literature on Jazz: blues, spirituals, gospel and ragtime (with a selected list of works on the social and cultural background).* Hamden, Conn.: K.G. Saur, distributed by Shoe String Press, 1981, 368 pp.

H52. Heffron, Paul T. "Manuscript Sources in the Library of Congress for a Study of Labor History." *Labor History* 10 (Fall 1969), 630–8.

* Heggerman, Ruth. See B132.

H53. Heider, Wally. *Transcography: a discography of jazz and popular music issued on 16" transcriptions*. San Francisco, Cal.: Author, 1970, 96 pp.

H53A. Heinig, Christine M. *Integration and the Public Schools: a selected and annotated bibliography for education and social studies chairmen*. American Association of University Women, 1955, 4 pp.

H54. Heins, P. "The Ecstasy Which Comes from Knowing That One is a Human Being: books on Negro life received during 1968 by the 'Horn Book' Magazine." *Horn Book* 45 (Apr. 1969), 141.

H55. Heller, Paul. *An Annotated Bibliography of Black History*. San Francisco, Cal.: Human Rights Commission, 1969(?), 12 pp.

* Helliwell, Geoffrey. See T18.

H56. Helmreich, William B. "Afro-Americans and Africa: anthropological and sociological investigations." *Current Bibliography of African Affairs* 8:3 (1975), 232–44.

H57. Helmreich, William B. *Afro-Americans and Africa: black nationalism at the crossroads*. Westport, Conn.: Greenwood Press, 1977, 74 pp.

H58. Henderson, L.J. "Black Political Life in the U.S.: a bibliographic essay." *In* Lenneal J. Henderson, Jr., ed. *Black Political Life in the U.S.: a fist as the pendulum*. San Francisco, Cal.: Chandler Publications, 1972, pp. 253–69.

* Henderson, Mae G. See B214.

* Henderson, Mary. See H130.

H59. Henderson, Rose. "The Schomburg Collection of Negro History and Literature." *Southern Workman* 63 (1934), 327–34.

* Hendrick, George. See G24, G25, G26.

* Henrichsen, Barge P. See S13.

* Henry, Lorraine. See B41, R112.

* Henry, Mary T. See F78.

H60. *The Heritage of the Negro in America: a bibliography; books, records, tapes, filmstrips, film, pictures*. Rev. ed. Lansing, Mich.: Michigan Department of Education, Joint Committee for Media Center Development, 1970, 100 pp. An earlier edition, 1969, consisted of 48 pp.

H61. Hershaw, L.M. "The Negro Press in America." *Charities* 15:1 (Oct. 7, 1905), 66–8.

H62. Herskovits, Melville J., ed. "The Interdisciplinary Aspects of Negro Studies." *American Council of Learned Societies Bulletin* 32 (Sept. 1941), 111 pp.

H63. Herskovits, Melville J. "Les Noirs du Nouveau Monde: bibliographie." *Soc. Africanistes Journal* 8 (1938), 1–2.

H64. Herzog, George. "Research in Primitive and Folk Music in the U.S.: a survey." *American Council of Learned Societies Bulletin* 24 (Apr. 1936), 1–97.

H65. Not used.

* Hicks, Richard. See S292.

H66. Hildebrand, Lorraine, and Richard S. Aiken. *A Bibliography of Afro-American Print and Non-Print Resources in Libraries of Pierce County, Washington.* Area Urban Coalition, Education Task Force in cooperation with Pierce County Libraries. Tacoma, Wash.: Tacoma Community College, Pearl A. Wanamaker Library, 1969, 116 pp.

H67. Hildreth, Margaret Holbrook. *Harriet Beecher Stowe: a bibliography.* Hamden, Conn.: Archon Books, 1976, 257 pp.

H68. Hill, James Lee. "Bibliography of Works by Chester Himes, Ann Petry and Frank Yerby." *Black Books Bulletin* 3 (1975), 60–72.

H69. Hill, M.C., and P.B. Foreman. "The Negro in the U.S.: a bibliography." *Southwestern Journal* 2 (Summer 1946), 225–30.

H70. Hill, Marnesta D. *A Bibliography of Black History and Literature.* New York: Herbert H. Lehman College of the City University of New York, Library, 1971, 42 pp. A revised edition of 84 pp. was issued in 1974.

H71. Hill, Mozell C. "Negroes in the U.S.: a critique of the periodical literature." *Social Forces* 26 (Dec. 1947), 218–23.

* Hill, Mozell C. See also F63.

H72. Hillman, J.C. [Tommy Ladnier Discography]. *Jazz Journal* 18 (Aug. 1965), 9–10.

* Hindle, Mary. See D86.

H73. Hippenmeyer, Jean Roland. *Jazz sur films; ou, 55 années de rapports jazz-cinéma vus á travers plus de 800 films tournés entre 1917 et 1972.* Yverdon, France: Editions de la Thièle, 1973.

H74. Hirabayashi, Joanne, and Barbara Dillon. *"And the Dark-faced Child, Listening": books about Negroes for children, 1969.* Marin Co., Cal.: School Librarians' Association of Marin County, 1969, 57 pp.

H75. *His House Below: books from a black struggle.* Oakland, Cal.: Oakland Public Library, 1969, 6 pp.

H76. *History of the Word "Jazz" as a Musical Term: a bibliography.* New York (?): New York Public Library. Schomburg Collection (?), 1965, 1 p.

H77. Hite, Roger. "Racial Rhetoric: a bibliography." *In* James E. Roever, ed. *Proceedings: Speech Association of America Summer Conference V.* New York: Speech Association of America, 1969, pp. 88–124.

H78. Hodara, Morris. "The Duke [Edward Kennedy Ellington] on Discs: a key to all currently available recordings." *High Fidelity* 24:11 (Nov. 1974), 79–85.

H79. Hoefer, G. "Basic Library of Long-playing Jazz Classics." *Jazz* 3 (July-Aug. 1964), 48–9.

H80. Hoefer, G. "Hot Box [Jimmy Blanton Discography]." *Down Beat* 29 (Feb. 1, 1962), 36–7.

H81. Hoefer, G. "John Kirby." *Down Beat* 29 (Oct. 11, 1962), 27.

* Hoefer, George, Jr. See L156.

* Hoellstrom, Carl A. See J74, S34.

H82. Hoerder, Dirk. *Protest, Direct Action, Repression; dissent in American society from colonial times to the present: a bibliography*. Munich, Germany: Verlag Dokumentation, 1977, 434 pp.

H83. Hoerder, Dirk. *Violence in the U.S.: riots, strikes, protest and suppression: a working bibliography for teachers and students*. Berlin, Germany: John F. Kennedy Institut für Nordamerikastudiern, Freie Universität Berlin, 1973, 151 pp.

H84. Hoffman, Daniel G. "From Blues to Jazz: recent bibliographies and discographies." *Midwest Folklore* 5:2 (Summer 1955), 107–14.

H85. Hoffman, Elizabeth P. *Exposure; Media Evaluations: Afro-American non-book resources*. Harrisburg, Pa.: Pennsylvania Department of Education, Bureau of General and Academic Education, Division of School Libraries, 22 pp.

* Hogan, Tim. See T80.

H86. Hogg, Peter C. *The African Slave Trade and Its Suppression: a classified and annotated bibliography of books, pamphlets and periodical articles*. London, England: Frank Cass, 1973, 409 pp. Based on his 1970 thesis.

* Holcomb, Helen E. See B132.

H87. *Holdings on Black Americans*. Troy, N.Y.: Russell Sage College, James Wheelock Clark Library.

H88. Holland, Bernard. "A Discography of Joe Lee Williams, Blues Singer." *Matrix* 34, pp. 9–17.

* Holland, Laurence B. See Mc39.

H89. Holland, Mary K., James Gault, et al. *For My People: a bibliography*. Berkeley, Cal.: University of California at Berkeley, General Library, 111 pp.

H90. Holley, Sharon Jordan. *Black List No. 5: for the children*. Buffalo, N.Y.: Buffalo and Erie County Public Library, 1979, 5 pp.

H91. Holmes, Oakley N., Jr. *The Complete Annotated Resource Guide to Black American Art: books, doctoral dissertations, exhibition catalogues, periodicals, films, slides, large prints, speakers, filmstrips, video tapes, black museums, art galleries and much more*. Spring Valley, N.Y.: Black Artists in America, 1978, 275 pp.

H92. Homer, Dorothy R. "A Selected Book List on Negro Life and History." *Senior Scholastic* 91:14 (Jan. 18, 1968).

H93. Homer, Dorothy R., and Evelyn B. Robinson. "The Negro: a selected bibliography." *New York Public Library Bulletin* 59 (Mar. 1955), 133–53. Reprinted as a pamphlet. A publication of 25 pp. with the same title was issued in 1960 with the note "8th revised edition."

H94. Homer, Dorothy R., and Ann M. Swartout. *Books About the Negro: an annotated bibliography*. In cooperation with the Anti-Defamation League of B'nai B'rith. New York: Praeger, 1966, 148 pp.

H95. Hopkins, Lee Bennett. "For and about Afro-Americans: selected paperbacks for children." *The Instructor* 78 (Nov. 1968), 126–8.

H96. Hopkins, Lee Bennett. "1965 and 1966: happy new years for non-fiction

books about the Negro.'' *Negro History Bulletin* 30 (Nov. 1967), 15–
7.

H97. Hopkins, Lee Bennett, and Misha Arenstein. ''Pages of History: a bibliography of great Negro Americans.'' *Elementary English* 46 (Feb. 1969),
204–6.

H98. *Horace Mann Bond*. CAAS Bibliography no. 10. Atlanta, Ga.: Center
for African and African-American Studies.

H99. Horn, Zoia. ''Workshop for the Study of the American Negro.'' *Wilson
Library Bulletin* 43:4 (1968), 354–9.

* Horowitz, Benjamin. See K27.

H100. *Hot Jazz*. London, England: Discographical Society, 1947, 20 pp.

* Houghton, Vincent P. See G70.

H101. Houston, Helen Ruth. *The Afro-American Novel: a descriptive bibliography of primary and secondary materials*. Troy, N.Y.: Whitson Publishing Co., 1977, 214 pp. Based on her D.A. dissertation, Middle Tennessee State University, 1976.

H102. Houston, Helen Ruth. ''Contributions of the American Negro to American Culture: a selected checklist.'' *Bulletin of Bibliography* 26:3 (July-
Sept. 1969), 71–9.

H103. Howard, John M. ''Sickle Cell Anemia: a selected bibliography.'' RAS
1. *Readers Advisory Service* (1974), 3 pp.

H104. Howard, Sharon M. ''Black Reference Books: a select bibliography of
retrospective sources.'' *Bibliography of Sources by and about Blacks
Compiled by the Interns in the Interrship in Black Studies Librarianship
Program*. Nashville, Tenn.: Fisk University Library, 1974(?), pp. 26–
32.

H105. ''Howard University Acquires the Most Comprehensive Collection of
Works by Negro Authors in the World [The Spingarn Collection].''
Howard University Bulletin 28 (Jan.-Feb. 1949), 3–5.

H106. Howe, Mentor A., and Roscoe E. Lewis. *A Classified Catalogue of the
Negro Collection in the Collis P. Huntington Library, Hampton Insti-
tute*. Compiled by Workers of the Writers' Program of the Works Prog-
ress Administration in the State of Virginia. Hampton, Va.: Hampton
Normal and Agricultural Institute, 1940, 255 pp. The Negro History Press,
Detroit, Mich., reprinted this catalogue in 1971.

H107. Howerton, Joseph B. *Some Sources of Federal Documentation of Minority Groups in Chicago*. Preliminary draft prepared for the Conference on the National Archives and Urban Research, June 1970. Washington, D.C.: National Archives and Records Service, 1970, 24 pp.

H108. Howie, Marguerite. *Interdisciplinary Seminar: an annotated bibliography of the Negro in American history*. Orangeburg, S.C.: South Carolina State College, Miller F. Whittaker Library.

* Howison, Beulah. See W85.

H109. Howse, Beth M. "The Aaron Douglas Collection." *BANC!* 4:2/5:1 (Sept. 1974/June 1975), 16–21.

* Howse, Beth M. See F78.

H110. Hubbard, Edward E., and Lenwood G. Davis. *Suicides in the Black Community: a preliminary survey.* Exchange Bibliography no. 887. Monticello, Ill.: Council of Planning Librarians, 1975, 8 pp.

H111. Hubbard, Geraldine Hopkins, and Julian S. Fowler. "A Classified Catalogue of the Collection of Anti-Slavery Propaganda in the Oberlin College Library." *Oberlin College Library Bulletin* 2:3 (1932), 84 pp.

H112. Hudson, Gossie Harold. *Directory of Black Historians, Ph.D.'s and Others, 1975–1976: essays, commentaries, and publications.* Exchange Bibliography no. 870/1/2. Monticello, Ill.: Council of Planning Librarians, 1975, 196 pp.

H113. Hudson, Theodore R. *A LeRoi Jones (Amiri Baraka) Bibliography: a keyed research guide to works by LeRoi Jones and to writing about him and his works.* Washington, D.C.: Author, 1971, 18 pp.

* Hugg, Lawrence. See E34.

H114. Huggins, Kathryn. "Aframerican Fiction." *Southern Literary Messenger* 3:6 (June 1941), 315–20.

H115. Hughley, Sadie, and Pennie E. Perry. *The Martin Collection.* Durham, N.C.: North Carolina Central University, James E. Shepard Memorial Library, 1968, 46 pp.

* Hulbert, J.A. See C22.

H116. Hull, Doris M., and Dolores C. Leffall. "Bibliography: periodical references." *Journal of Negro Education* 28 (Fall 1959), 458–66.

H117. Hull, Doris M., and Dolores C. Leffall. "Bibliography: periodical references." *Journal of Negro Education* 29 (Winter 1960), 63–9.

* Hull, Gloria. See B316, D12, M80, S51, S130, S170, S251, W123, Y2.

H117A. Hull, W. Frank, IV. "The Black Student in Higher Education: a bibliography." *Journal of College Student Personnel* (Nov. 1970), 423–5.

H118. Hull, W. Frank, IV, and Marshall W. Davies. "The Black Student in Higher Education: a second bibliography." *Journal of College Student Personnel* 14 (July 1973), 309–12.

* Hulme, G. See H119.

H119. *Human Relations: a basic booklist.* Madison, Wis.: Madison Public Schools, 1965.

H120. *Human Relations Guide to Intergroup Education in Schools.* Harrisburg, Pa.: Pennsylvania Committee on Human Relations, Department of Public Instruction.

H121. *Human Rights: a list of books for boys and girls.* Rev. ed. Detroit, Mich.: Detroit Public Library, Children's Service, 1966, 16 pp.

H122. *Human Rights: a selected bibliography.* Brooklyn, N.Y.: Brooklyn Public Library, 3 pp.

H123. *Human Rights: guide to good human relations.* Mt. Vernon, N.Y.: Westchester County Library System, 1964.

* Humbertson, Jane. See S225.

H124. Hume, Mildred, and Gayle Marko. *Orodha Ya Vitabu: a bibliography of Afro-American Life.* Rev. ed. Minneapolis, Minn.: Minneapolis Public Schools, Board of Education Library.

H125. Hunt-Bryan, Barbara, Jacqueline McGirt, and Emily Page. *Afro and Afro-American Materials.* Greensboro, N.C.: Bennett College, Thomas F. Halgate Library.

H126. Hunterton, C. Stanley, et al. *Busing; Ground Zero in School Desegregation: a literature review with policy recommendations.* ERIC Document no. ED 085–451. Syracuse, N.Y.: Syracuse University Research Corporation, 1972.

H127. Hunton, Margaret R., Ethel Williams, and Dorothy B. Porter. *A Catalogue of Books in the Moorland Foundation.* Compiled by Workers on Projects 271 and 328, Works Progress Administration. Part I: "Printed Titles Dating from 1682–1849," 94 pp.; Part II: "Printed Titles Dating from 1850–1899," 166 pp.; Part III: "Printed Titles Dating from 1900–1938," 159 pp.; Part IV: "Undated Titles," 23 pp.; Part V: "Selected List of Uncatalogued Pamphlets, " 38 pp.; Part VI: "Unpublished Howard University Master's Theses," 19 pp. Washington, D.C.: Howard University, 1939.

H128. Hurley, R.J. "Negro Books in the Library." *Catholic Library World* 37 (Oct. 1965), 120–1.

H129. Hurwitz, H.L. "New Books on the American Negro." *Senior Scholastic* 83 (Nov. 15, 1963), 8T–10T.

H130. Hussey, Edith, Mary Henderson, and Barbara Marx. *The Negro American: a reading list.* New York: National Council of Churches of Christ in the U.S.A., Department of Racial and Cultural Relations, 1957, 40 pp.

H131. Hutson, Jean Blackwell. "Harlem, a Cultural History: selected bibliography." *The Metropolitan Museum of Art Bulletin* 27 (Jan. 1969), 280–8. Reprinted as a pamphlet.

H132. Hutson, Jean Blackwell."The Schomburg Collection." *Freedomways* 3:3 (Summer 1963), 431–5.

* Hutson, Jean Blackwell. See also Blackwell, Jean.

H133. Huus, Helen. *Children's Books to Enrich the Social Studies.* Washington, D.C.: National Council for the Social Studies, 1966.

H133A. Hyatt, Marshall. *The Afro-American Cinematic Experience.* Wilmington, Del.: Scholarly Resources, 1983, 260 pp.

H134. Hymon, Mary Watson, et al. *Bibliography of Resources in the Afro-American Collection.* Grambling, La.: Grambling College, A.C. Lewis Memorial Library.

I

I1. *I, Too, Am America: a selective list of available books about Negroes.* Rev. ed. Pittsburgh, Pa.: Carnegie Library, 1950, 10 pp.

* Iarusso, Marilyn Berg. See D93.

I2. [Identification of Gene Ammons' Aristocrat and Chess Recordings]. *Record Research* 1:1 (Feb. 1955), 3.

* Igoe, James Thomas. See I3.

I3. Igoe, Lynn Moody, and James Thomas Igoe. *250 Years of Afro-American Art: an annotated bibliography.* New York: R.R. Bowker Co., 1981, 1296 pp.

* Ihde, H. See D95.

I4. Ikegami, Teizo. *New Orleans Renaissance on Record.* Tokyo, Japan: Alligator Jazz Club, 1980.

I5. Iliff, John G. *Where to Read Up on Racism and Human Rights.* San Francisco, Cal.: Northern California Branch, ACLU, 2nd West Coast Regional Office, NAACP, 1954, 79 pp.

I6. *Immigration.* Includes publications relating to naturalization, citizenship, Europeans, Japanese, Chinese, Negroes. Washington, D.C.: Superintendent of Documents, 1916, 18 pp.

I7. *Immigration, Naturalization, Citizenship, Aliens, Races: list of publications relating to above subjects for sale by the Superintendent of Documents.* Price List 67. Washington, D.C.: U.S. Superintendent of Documents, 1943–1945, 3 vols.

I8. *Index of the Alfred H. Stone Collection on the Negro and Cognate Subjects.* Jackson, Miss.: Mississippi Department of Archives and History, 516 pp.

I9. *An Index to Minority Group Employment Information.* Document and Reference Text (DART). Produced under the sponsorship of the Equal Employment Opportunity Commission. Ann Arbor, Mich.: University of Michigan-Wayne State University, Institute of Labor and Industrial Relations, 1967, 602 pp. A supplement of 447 pp. by Joe A. Miller and Steven C. Gold was issued in 1971.

I10. *An Index to Multi-Ethnic Teaching Materials and Teacher Resources.* Washington, D.C.: National Education Association, National Commission on Professional Rights and Responsibilities, Committee on Civil and Human Rights of Educators, 1967, 18 pp.

I10A. *Index to Negro Spirituals.* Cleveland, Ohio: Cleveland Public Library, 1937.

I11. *Index to Periodical Articles by and about Blacks.* Boston, Mass.: G.K. Hall, 1973, 410 pp.; 1974, 438 pp.; 1975, 532 pp.; 1976, 527 pp.; 1977,

471 pp.; 1978, 357 pp.; 1979, 416 pp.; 1980, 173 pp. This was previously *Index to Selected Periodicals* and *Index to Selected Periodicals by and about Negroes.*

I12. *Index to Periodical Articles by and about Negroes.* Boston, Mass.: G.K. Hall, 1971, 543 pp.; 1972, 828 pp. This was previously *Index to Selected Periodicals* and became *Index to Selected Periodicals by and about Blacks.*

I13. *Index to Periodical Articles by and about Negroes, Cumulated 1960–1970.* Compiled by the staffs of the Hallie Q. Brown Library, Central State University, Ohio, and the Schomburg Collection, The New York Public Library. Boston, Mass.: G.K. Hall, 1971, 606 pp. This was formerly *Index to Selected Periodicals* and became *Index to Periodical Articles by and about Blacks.*

I14. *Index to Selected Periodicals. Decennial Cumulation, 1950–1959.* Received in the Hallie Q. Brown Library, Central State University, Ohio. Boston, Mass.: G.K. Hall, 1962, 501 pp. This became *Index to Periodical Articles by and about Negroes,* and then *Index to Periodical Articles by and about Blacks.*

I15. Inge, M. Thomas. "Contemporary Southern Black Writers." *Mississippi Quarterly* 31:2 (Spring 1976), 185–90.

I16. Inge, M. Thomas, Jackson R. Bryer, and Maurice Duke. *Black American Writers: bibliographic essays.* New York: St. Martin's Press, 1978, 2 vols.

* Inge, M. Thomas. See also D1, D10, G36, K80, M83, M84, M85, R66, T110A.

* Ingram, Helen. See P140.

I17. *Insight; the Negro in the United States: a selected bibliography.* Terre Haute, Ind.: Indiana State University, Cunningham Memorial Library, 1970, 45 pp.

I18. *Integrated Book List.* Memphis, Tenn.: Memphis Public Library.

I19. *Integrated School Books: a descriptive bibliography of 399 pre-school and elementary school texts and story books prepared by the NAACP Education Department.* New York: NAACP Education Department, 1967, 55 pp.

I20. *Intercultural Educational Literature: pamphlets, leaflets, bibliographies, manuals, 1943–1944, for school and community.* New York: Bureau for Intercultural Education, 7 pp.

I21. *Interracial Relationships in the U.S.: a selected list of references.* Washington, D.C.: Library of Congress, 1945, 21 pp.

I22. *An Introduction to Materials for Ethnic Studies in the University of Southern California Library.* Los Angeles, Cal.: University of Southern California Library, 1970, 198 pp.

I23. *Inventory and Calendar of the John Brown, Jr., Papers.* Columbus, Ohio: Ohio Historical Society, 1962, 32 pp.

I24. *Inventory of Research in Racial and Cultural Relations*. Committee on Education, Training and Research in Race Relations at the University of Chicago. 1:1 (June 1948)–5:4 (Summer 1953).

I25. Irby, Charles. *Fifteen Topics on Afro-Americana: an annotated bibliography*. Relevant Instructional Materials, 1973, 86 pp.

I26. Not used.

I27. Irvine, Betty Jo, and Jane A. McCabe. *Fine Arts and the Black American/Music and the Black American*. Focus: Black American Bibliography Series. Urbana, Ill.: University of Illinois Libraries, 1969, 33 pp.

I28. Irwin, Leonard Bertram. *Black Studies: a bibliography for the use of schools, libraries, and the general reader*. Brooklawn, N.J.: McKinley Publishing Co., 1973, 122 pp.

I29. Isani, Mukhtar Ali. "Early Versions of Some Works of Phillis Wheatley." *Early American Literature* 14:2 (Fall 1979), 149–55.

I30. Ishimatsu, Chiz, and Annie Laurie Bezrry. *Black Bibliography: a selected listing*. Salt Lake City, Utah: University of Utah Libraries.

I31. Ivory, Mrs. Edrice. *Black Fiction: a select list for children*. Cleveland, Ohio: Cleveland Public Library, Walz Branch, 1970, 7 pp.

J

J1. *J.C. Higginbotham*. London, England: Discographical Society, 1947, 24 pp.

J2. "The J.E. Moorland Foundation of the University Library." *Howard University Record* 10 (Jan. 1916), 1–15.

J3. Jablonsky, Adelaide. *Curriculum and Instruction for Minority Groups: an annotated bibliography of doctoral dissertations*. ERIC Document no. 086–748. Revised as ERIC Document no. 110–587. New York: ERIC Clearinghouse on the Urban Disadvantaged, 1973.

J4. Jablonsky, Adelaide. "Media for Teaching Afro-American Studies." *Information Retrieval Center on the Disabled Bulletin* 5:1–2 (Spring-Summer, 1970).

J5. Jablonsky, Adelaide. *School Desegregation: an annotated bibliography of doctoral dissertations*. ERIC Document no. 078–098. New York: ERIC Clearinghouse on the Urban Disadvantaged, 1973.

J6. Jablonsky, Adelaide. *Social and Psychological Studies of Minority Children and Youth: an annotated bibliography of doctoral dissertations*. ERIC Document no. ED 110–589. New York: ERIC Clearinghouse on the Urban Disadvantaged, 1975.

J7. Jacchetti, Renato. "Discografia Archie Shepp." *Musica Jazz* (May 1975), 47–8; (June 1975), 46–8.

J8. Jacchetti, Renato. "Discografia Cecil Taylor." *Musica Jazz* 22 (May 1976), 47–8.

J9. Jack, C. "Library of Black People's Literature." *Ontario Library Review* 58 (Mar. 1974), 20–3.

J10. Jackson, Albert. "American First Editions of Paul Laurence Dunbar." *Publishers Weekly* 120:17 (Oct. 24, 1931), 1958.

J11. Jackson, Anne. *Ethnic Groups: their cultures and contributions*. Little Rock, Ark.: Arkansas State Department of Education, 1970, 152 pp.

J12. Jackson, B. "Survey Course in Negro Literature." *North Carolina Librarian* 3 (Spring 1974), 7–11.

J13. Jackson, Blyden. "The Blithe Newcomers: resume of Negro literature in 1954." *Phylon* 16 (1955), 5–12.

J14. Jackson, Blyden. "The Continuing Strain: resume of Negro literature, 1955." *Phylon* 17 (1956), 35–40.

J15. Jackson, Bruce. "Further Reading." In *The Negro and His Folklore in Nineteenth Century Periodicals*. Austin, Tex.: Printed for the American Folklore Society by the University of Texas Press, 1967, pp. 353–67.

J16. Jackson, Clara O. *A Bibliography of Afro-American and Other American Minorities Represented in Library and Library-Related Listings*. New York: American Institute of Marxist Studies, 1970, 32 pp. A supplement of 51 pp. was published in 1972.

J17. Jackson, Clara O. *Library Listings of Multi-Ethnic Materials during the Sixties*. Author, 1970(?), 18 pp.

J18. Jackson, Giovanna R. *Afro-American Religion and Church and Race Relations*. Focus: Black American Bibliography Series. Bloomington, Ind.: Indiana University Libraries, 1969, 18 pp.

J19. Jackson, Giovanna R., and Charles E. Sweet. *Black Nationalism; The Negro and the Establishment: law, politics and the courts*. Focus: Black American Bibliography Series. Bloomington, Ind.: Indiana University Libraries, 1969, 28 pp.

 *   Jackson, Giovanna R. See also S289.

 *   Jackson, Glorianne. See D136.

J20. Jackson, Irene V. *Afro-American Religious Music: a bibliography and a catalogue of gospel music*. Westport, Conn.: Greenwood Press, 1979, 210 pp.

J21. Jackson, Jacqueline Johnson. "A Partial Bibliography on or related to Black Women." *Journal of Social and Behavioral Sciences* 21:1 (Winter 1975), 90–135.

J22. Jackson, John W. *Afro-American Resources*. Vallejo, Cal.: Solano Community College Library, 1969.

J23. Jackson, Miles M. *A Bibliography of Materials by and about Negro Americans for Young Readers*. Washington, D.C.: U.S. Office of Education, 1967, 92 pp.

J24. Jackson, Miles M. "Significant Belles Lettres by and about Negroes Published in 1964." *Phylon* 26 (1965), 216–27.

J25. Jackson, Miles M., Mary W. Cleaves, and Alma L. Gray. *A Bibliography of Negro History and Culture for Young Readers.* Pittsburgh, Pa.: University of Pittsburgh Press, 1969, 134 pp. Published for Atlanta University.

* Jackson, Miles M. See also C119.

J26. Jackson, Wallace Van. "The Countee Cullen Memorial Collection at Atlanta University." *Crisis* 51:5 (May 1947), 140–2.

* Jacobs, Alma Smith. See T48.

J27. Jacobs, Donald M. *Antebellum Black Newspapers: indices to "Freedom's Journal" (1827–1829), "The Rights of All" (1829), "The Weekly Advocate" (1837), and the "Colored American" (1837–1841).* Westport, Conn.: Greenwood Press, 1976, 587 pp.

J27A. Jacobs, Donald, and Steven Fershleiser. *Index to the "American Slave."* Westport, Conn.: Greenwood Press, 1981, 274 pp.

J28. Jacobs, Sylvia M. "Black American Missionaries in Africa: a selected bibliography." *Current Bibliography of African Affairs* 13:2 (1980/1981), 167–72.

J29. Jaffe, Harry Joe. "American Negro Folklore: a check list of scarce items." *Southern Folklore Quarterly* 36:1 (Mar. 1972), 68–70.

J30. Jahn, Janheinz. *A Bibliography of Neo-African Literature from Africa, America, and the Caribbean.* New York: Praeger, 1965, 359 pp. The British edition was published by Andre Deutsch.

J31. Jahn, Janheinz. *Die neoAfrikanische literatur: gesambibliographie von dem anfangen bis zur gegenwart.* Dusseldorf, Germany: Diederichs Verlag, 1965.

* Jahn, Janheinz. See also P13.

J32. Jain, Sushil Kumar. *The Negro in Canada: a select list of primary and secondary sources for the study of [the] Negro community in Canada from the earliest times to the present days.* Unexplored Fields of Canadiana, vol. 3. Minorities in Canada Series, no. 1. Regina, Saskatchewan, Canada: Regina Campus, University of Saskatchewan, 1967, 30 pp.

* Jakle, Cynthia A. See J33.

J33. Jakle, John A., and Cynthia A. Jakle. *Ethnic and Racial Minorities in North America: a selected bibliography of the geographical literature.* Exchange Bibliography no. 459/460. Monticello, Ill.: Council of Planning Librarians, 1973.

J34. [Jamaica Jazzers]. *Record Research* 1:1 (Feb. 1955), 11.

J35. Jambro, Thomas. *Black Art and Afro-American Art: sources for visual materials.* Albany, N.Y.: New York State Education Department, Division of the Humanities and the Arts, Bureau of Art Education, 22 pp.

J36. James, A. "Twenty Basic Books on Race." *Community* 21 (Feb. 1962), 4–5.

J37. James, Michael. "Kenny Dorham: soloist extraordinary." *Jazz and Blues* 2 (Jan. 1972), 9.

* James, Michael. See also H31.
J38. James, Milton M. "Biographical Approach to the Study of Negro History." *Negro History Bulletin* 23:4 (Jan. 1960), 74+.
* Jamieson, A. Leland. See B342.
J39. Jarrett, Thomas D. "Recent Fiction by Negroes." *College English* 16 (Nov. 1954), 85–91.
J40. Jasen, David A. *Recorded Ragtime, 1897–1958*. Hamden, Conn.: Archon Books, 1973, 155 pp.
J41. Jayatilleke, Raja. *The Law, the Courts, and Minority Group Education: an ERIC/CUE capsule bibliography*. ERIC Document no. ED 128–497. New York: Columbia University, Teachers College, Institute for Urban and Minority Education, 1976.
J42. *Jazz in New York*. London, England: Discographical Society, 1947, 24 pp.
J43. *Jazz on LP's: a collector's guide to jazz by Decca, Brunswick, Capitol, London and Felsted Long Playing Records*. London, England: Decca Record Co., 1955. A revised edition appeared in 1956.
J44. *Jazz on 78s: a guide to the many examples of classic jazz on Decca, Brunswick and London 78 R.P.M. Records*. London, England: Decca Record Co., 1954.
J45. "Jazz Sounds of the Twenties." *Jazz Monthly* 8 (June 1962), 22–5.
J46. Jefferson, Karen L., and Brigette M. Rouson. *The Glenn Carrington Collection: a guide to the books, manuscripts, music and recordings*. Washington, D.C.: Howard University, Moorland-Spingarn Research Center, 1977, 119 pp.
J47. Jenkins, Betty Lanier, and Susan Phillis. *Black Separatism: a bibliography*. Westport, Conn.: Greenwood Press, 1976, 163 pp.
J48. Jenkins, Betty, Lorna Kent, and Jeanne Perry. *Kenneth B. Clark: a bibliography*. New York: Metropolitan Applied Research Center, 1970, 69 pp.
J49. Jenkins, John Julian. *Some Contributions of the American Negro Church to the Process of Race Integration: a bibliography*. 1951, 5 pp.
* Jenkins, M. See C44.
* Jenkins, Mildred. See T42.
J50. Jepsen, Jorgen Grunnet. *Art Tatum: a discography*. Copenhagen, Denmark: Author, 1957, 10 pp.
J51. Jepsen, Jorgen Grunnet. "Cecil Taylor Diskografi." *Orkester Journalen* 30 (Dec. 1962), 48.
J52. Jepsen, Jorgen Grunnet. *Charlie Christian*. Copenhagen, Denmark: Author, 1957, 9 pp.
J53. Jepsen, Jorgen Grunnet. *Clifford Brown: a discography*. Copenhagen, Denmark: Author, 1957, 9 pp.
J54. Jepsen, Jorgen Grunnet. *Coleman Hawkins, 1947–1957*. Copenhagen, Denmark: Author, 1957, 12 pp.

J55. Jepsen, Jorgen Grunnet. "Discographie d'Art Tatum." *Les Cahiers du Jazz* 5, pp. 76–84.

J56. Jepsen, Jorgen Grunnet. "Discographie l'oeuvre de Lester Young." *Les Cahiers du Jazz* 1, pp. 128–44.

J57. Jepsen, Jorgen Grunnet. *Discography of Art Tatum/[Earl] Bud Powell.* Brande, Denmark: Debut Records, 1961, 28 pp.

J58. Jepsen, Jorgen Grunnet. *A Discography of Billie Holliday.* Rev. ed. Copenhagen, Denmark: Karl E. Knudsen, 1969, 37 pp.

J59. Jepsen, Jorgen Grunnet. *Discography of Charlie Parker.* Brande, Denmark: Debut Records, 1959, 23 pp. A second edition of 30 pp. was published in 1960.

J60. Jepsen, Jorgen Grunnet. *A Discography of Charlie Parker.* Copenhagen, Denmark: Karl E. Knudsen, 1969, 38 pp.

J61. Jepsen, Jorgen Grunnet. *Discography of [Edward] Duke Ellington. Vol. 1, 1925–1936*, 24 pp.; *Vol. 2, 1937–1946*, 25 pp.; *Vol. 3, 1947–1960*, 27 pp. Brande, Denmark: Debut Records, 1959–60.

J62. Jepsen, Jorgen Grunnet. *Discography of [Ferdinand] Jelly Roll Morton. Vol. 1, 1922–1929*, 18 pp.; *Vol. 2, 1930–1940*, 21 pp. Brande, Denmark: Debut Records, 1959.

J63. Jepsen, Jorgen Grunnet. *A Discography of John Coltrane.* Rev. ed. Copenhagen, Denmark: Karl E. Knudsen, 1969, 35 pp.

J64. Jepsen, Jorgen Grunnet. *A Discography of [John] Dizzy Gillespie. Vol. 1, 1937–1952*, 39 pp.; *Vol. 2, 1953–1968*, 30 pp. Copenhagen, Denmark: Karl E. Knudsen, 1969.

J65. Jepsen, Jorgen Grunnet. *Discography of [Julian] Cannonball Adderley/John Coltrane.* Brande, Denmark: Debut Records, 1959, 32 pp.

J66. Jepsen, Jorgen Grunnet. *Discography of Lester Young.* Brande, Denmark: Debut Records, 1959, 26 pp. A second edition with the same number of pages was issued in 1960.

J67. Jepsen, Jorgen Grunnet. *A Discography of Lester Young.* Copenhagen, Denmark: Karl E. Knudsen, 1968, 45 pp.

J68. Jepsen, Jorgen Grunnet. *Discography of Louis Armstrong. Vol. 1, 1923–1931*, 26 pp; *Vol. 2, 1932–1946*, 19 pp.; *Vol. 3, 1947–1960*, 24 pp. Brande, Denmark: Debut Records, 1959. A second and revised edition of 27, 20, and 25 pp. was issued in 1960.

J69. Jepsen, Jorgen Grunnet. *A Discography of Louis Armstrong, 1923–1971.* Rugsted Vyst, Denmark: Karl E. Knudsen, 1973, 102 pp.

J70. Jepsen, Jorgen Grunnet. *A Discography of Miles Davis.* Rev. ed. Copenhagen, Denmark: Karl E. Knudsen, 1969, 40 pp.

J71. Jepsen, Jorgen Grunnet, *A Discography of Thelonius Monk and [Earl] Bud Powell.* Rev. ed. Copenhagen, Denmark: Karl E. Knudsen, 1969, 44 pp.

J72. Jepsen, Jorgen Grunnet. *A Discography of Thelonius Monk and [Theodore] Sonny Rollins.* Brande, Denmark: Debut Records, 1960, 27 pp.

J73. Jepsen, Jorgen Grunnet. *Discography of [Theodore] Fats Navarro/Clifford Brown*. Brande, Denmark: Debut Records, 1960, 14 pp.

J74. Jepsen, Jorgen Grunnet. *A Discography of [William] Count Basie, Vol. 2, 1951–1968*. Copenhagen, Denmark: Karl E. Knudsen, 1969, 44 pp. For *Vol. 1, 1929–1950*, see Bo Scherman and Carl A. Hoellstrom (S34).

J75. Jepsen, Jorgen Grunnet. *Donald Byrd: a discography*. Copenhagen, Denmark: Author, 1957, 13 pp.

J76. Jepsen, Jorgen Grunnet. *Edmond Hall*. Copenhagen, Denmark: Author, 1957.

J77. Jepsen, Jorgen Grunnet. *[Edward] Kid Ory*. Copenhagen, Denmark: Author, 1957.

J78. Jepsen, Jorgen Grunnet. *Jazz Records: a discography*. Holte, Denmark: Karl E. Knudsen, 1963–. A multi-volume series.

J79. Jepsen, Jorgen Grunnet. *Johnny Hodges without Ellington*. Copenhagen, Denmark: Author, 1957, 14 pp.

J80. Jepsen, Jorgen Grunnet. *Lionel Hampton, 1947–1957*. Copenhagen, Denmark: Author, 1957, 16 pp.

J81. Jepsen, Jorgen Grunnet. *Sidney Bechet Discography*. Lubeck, Germany: Uhle and Kleimann, 1962, 38 pp.

J82. Jepsen, Jorgen Grunnet. "Sidney Bechet, 1921–1939." *Les Cahiers du Jazz* 10, pp. 103–11.

J82A. Jepsen, Jorgen Grunnet. *[Theodore] Fats Navarro: a discography*. Copenhagen, Denmark: Author, 1957, 11 pp.

J83. Jepsen, Jorgen Grunnet. *[Theodore] Sonny Rollins: a discography*. Copenhagen, Denmark: Author, 1957, 11 pp.

J84. Jepsen, Jorgen Grunnet. *[Wilbur] Buck Clayton, 1949–1957*. Copenhagen, Denmark: Author, 15 pp.

* Jepsen, Jorgen Grunnet. See also C27, D81, M142.

J85. Jeter, M.H. *Presentation of the Negro in Children's Books Published between 1951 and 1961*. M.S. in L.S. thesis, Atlanta University, 1962, 115 pp.

J86. [Jimmy Yancey Discography]. *Matrix* 95 (Dec. 1971); 105 (Nov. 1974), 17.

J87. [Jimmy Yancey Discography]. *Record Research* 2:1 (Feb. 1956), 3–6.

J88. [Joe Williams Discography]. *The Discophile* 47 (Apr. 1956), 16.

J88a. [John Lee (Sonny Boy) Williamson Discography]. *Record Research* 2:3 (July-Aug. 1956), 11.

J89. "Johnny Dodds Discography." *Jazz* 1:9, pp. 23–6.

J89A. [Johnny Dunn]. *Record Research* 1:6 (Dec. 1955), 12.

J90. Johnson, Charles S. "The Negro Enters Literature." *The Carolina Magazine* 57:7 (May 1927), 3+.

J91. Johnson, Clifton H. *A.M.A. [American Missionary Association] Archives as a Source for the Study of American History*. New York: AMA of the United Church Board for Homeland Ministries, 32 pp.

J92. Johnson, Clifton H. *The Amistad Research Center*. New Orleans, La.: Amistad Research Center.

J93. Johnson, Clifton H. "Some Archival Sources on Negro History in Tennessee." *Tennessee Historical Quarterly* 28 (Winter 1969), 297 + .

J94. Johnson, Clifton H. "Some Archival Sources on Negro History in Tennessee." *Tennessee Librarian* 22 (Winter 1970), 80–90.

J95. Johnson, Clifton H. "Some Manuscript Sources in Louisiana Archival Repositories for Study of the History of Louisiana Blacks." *In* Robert R. MacDonald, John R. Kemp, Edward F. Haag, eds. *Louisiana Black Heritage*. New Orleans, La.: Louisiana State Museum, 1979, pp. 209–30.

J96. Johnson, Clifton H., and Carroll G. Barber. *The Negro American: a selected and annotated bibliography for high schools and junior colleges*. Nashville, Tenn.: Amistad Research Center, 1968, 113 pp.

J97. Johnson, Earl, Jr. *African Americans in the Protestant Episcopal Church: a comprehensive bibliography*, 1975. An unpublished typescript of 150 items.

J98. Johnson, Edwina. "Black History: the early childhood vacuum." *School Library Journal* (May 1969), 43–4. *Library Journal* 94 (May 15, 1969), 205–6.

J99. Johnson, G.B. "Books on Race and Race Relations." *Social Forces* 15 (May 1937), 580.

* Johnson, Guy B. See D155, L144, R51.

J100. Johnson, Harry Alleyn. "Developing a Current Awareness of Non-Print Media: implications for Afro-American collections." *In* Herman L. Totten, ed. *Bibliographic Control of Afro-American Literature*. Eugene, Ore.: University of Oregon, School of Librarianship, 1976, pp. 33–68.

J101. Johnson, Harry Alleyn. *Ethnic American Minorities: a guide to media and materials*. New York: R.R. Bowker Co., 1976, 304 pp.

J102. Johnson, Harry Alleyn. *Multimedia Materials for Afro-American Studies: a curriculum orientation and annotated bibliography of resources*. New York: R.R. Bowker Co., 1971, 353 pp.

J103. Johnson, James, and Frances O. Churchill. "Black and Bibliographical." *Wilson Library Bulletin* 47 (Nov. 1972), 248–50; (Dec. 1972), 374–7; (Jan. 1973), 415–7; (Feb. 1973), 529–31; (June 1973), 877–81.

J104. Johnson, James Peter. *Bibliographical Guide to the Study of Afro-American Music*. Washington, D.C.: Howard University Libraries, 1973, 24 pp.

* Johnson, James Peter. See also L55.

J105. Johnson, Jerome W. *The Afro-American Experience: a bibliography of printed materials held by the Andersen Library, Wisconsin State University, Whitewater*. Whitewater, Wisc.: Wisconsin State University, Harold Andersen Library, 1969. Two supplements were issued.

J106. Johnson, Merle. "Carl Van Vechten, 1880– [bibliographic check-list]." *Publishers Weekly* 105 (1924), 524.

* Johnson, Michele. See S196.
* Johnson, Nancy. See W85.
* Johnson, Pat. See M156.

J107. Johnson, Pat Taylor. *Black Authors File*. Newark, Del.: University of Delaware, Hugh M. Morris Library, 1970.

J108. Johnson, Pat Taylor. *Black Studies Acquisitions File*. Newark, Del.: University of Delaware, Hugh M. Morris Library.

J109. Johnson, Preston C., and Julia O. Saunders. "The Education of Negroes in Virginia: an annotated bibliography." *Virginia State College Gazette* 50:1 (Feb. 1944), 1–16.

J110. Johnson, T.L. "Bookman's Journal [Collections for Negro genealogical research]." *South Carolina Librarian* 21 (Spring 1977), 12–22; (Fall 1977), 30–3.

J111. Johnson, Vivian R. *A Selected Bibliography of the Black Experience*. Roxbury, Mass.: Afro-American Studies Resource Center, Circle Associates, 1971, 107 pp.

J112. Johnston, Bob. *Black Literature*. Santa Maria, Cal.: Allan Hancock College Library.

J113. Johnston, Bob. *Ethnic Studies*. Santa Maria, Cal.: Allan Hancock College Library.

J114. Jolly, David. *Master's Theses, 1932–1945; an annotated bibliography*. Hampton, Va.: Hampton Institute, 1946, 34 pp.

J115. Jonas, Carol. *Bibliography for Afro-American Studies*. Rev. ed. Elmhurst, Ill.: Elmhurst College, Memorial Library, 1970, 34 pp.

J116. Jonas, Klaus W. "Additions to the Bibliography of Carl Van Vechten." *Papers of the Bibliographical Society of America* 55 (First Quarter 1961), 42–5.

J117. Jonas, Klaus W. *Carl Van Vechten: a bibliography*. New York: Alfred A. Knopf, 1955, 94 pp.

J118. Jones, Betty, and Joyce Lacey. *Bibliography of Resources: Afro-American studies*. Norwalk, Conn.: Cerritos College Library.

* Jones, Dionne J. See E19.

J119. Jones, G.L. "Books about Negro Children." *Illinois Librarian* 25 (Feb. 1943), 94–9.

* Jones, Iris. See P120.

J120. Jones, J. Alvin. *A Selected Bibliography of Current Literature and Visual Aids on Employment of Minority Group Workers*. Washington, D.C.: Minority Groups Conference, 1956, 16 pp.

J121. Jones, Leon. *From Brown to Boston: desegregation in education, 1954–1974*. Metuchen, N.J.: Scarecrow Press, 1979, 2 vols.

* Jones, LeRoi. See Baraka, Imamu Amiri.

J122. Jones, Mary E. *James Baldwin*. Atlanta, Ga.: Atlanta University, Center for African and African American Studies, 1977(?), 18 pp.

J123. Jones, Paulette Pennington. *Amiri Baraka: bibliography, biography, playography*. London, England: Theatre Quarterly Publications, 21 pp.

J124. Jones, Valerie A., and John Stalker. *Interpreting the Black Experience in America to Foreign Students: a guide to materials*. Atlanta, Ga., and Washington, D.C.: Atlanta University, Trevor Arnett Library and National Association for Foreign Student Affairs, 1976, 76 pp.

J125. Jordan, Casper LeRoy. "Afro-American Indexes: a descriptive analysis." *In* Herman L. Totten, ed. *Bibliographical Control of Afro-American Literature*. Eugene, Ore.: University of Oregon, School of Librarianship, 1976, pp. 228–54.

J126. Jordan, Casper LeRoy. *The Benjamin William Arnett Papers at Carnegie Library, Wilberforce University, Wilberforce, Ohio*. Wilberforce, Ohio: Wilberforce University, 1958.

J127. Jordan, Casper LeRoy. "Black Academic Libraries: state of affairs and selected annotated bibliography of black academe and its libraries." In *Library and Information Services for Special Groups*. New York: Science Associates, 1974, pp. 146–201.

J128. Jordan, Casper LeRoy. *Black Materials Bibliography: a state of the art*. Paper delivered at ASALH, Atlanta, Ga., 1975.

J129. Jordan, Casper LeRoy. *Consortium List of Afro-American Materials*. ERIC Document no. 089–781. Durham, N.C.: North Carolina Central, School of Library Science, 1974.

J130. Jordan, Casper LeRoy. "A Content Analysis and Cumulative Index, Annotated of *Phylon*, 1940–49." M.S.L.S. thesis, Atlanta University, 1951, 220 pp.

J131. Jordan, Casper LeRoy. *The Levi Jenkins Coppin Collection at Carnegie Library, Wilberforce University, Wilberforce, Ohio*. Wilberforce, Ohio: Wilberforce University, 1957, 17 pp.

* Jordan, Jennifer. See B41, R112.

* Jorgensen, John. See S13.

J132. Jorgensen, Venita McPherson. *American Literature: Black voices [Afro–American Literature, 1940–1968 in the University of California, Riverside, Library]*. Riverside, Cal.: University of California, Riverside, General Library, 1969.

J133. Jorgensen, Venita McPherson. *Books on Negro Religion in the University of California, Riverside, Library*. Riverside, Cal.: University of California, Riverside, General Library, 1969.

J134. Jorgensen, Venita McPherson. *Negro History: a selected bibliography of the Afro-American experience*. Riverside, Cal.: University of California, Riverside, General Library, 1969.

J135. Jorgenson, Chester E. *"Uncle Tom's Cabin" as Book and Legend: a guide to an exhibition (at the Main Library, Oct. 8 through Nov. 15, 1952)*. Detroit, Mich.: Friends of the Detroit Public Library, 1952, 51 pp.

* Josey, E.J. See C72, C109, K14, L9, S136.

J136. Joyce, Donald F. *Journey into Black History*. Chicago, Ill.: Chicago Public Library, Hall Branch, 1969, 13 pp.

J137. Joyce, Donald F., and Ron Blazek. "Arthur Alonzo Schomburg: pioneering black bibliophile." *Journal of Library History* 10:2 (Apr. 1975), 169–82.

J138. *The Julia Davis Collection; Negro and African life and culture: a bibliography*. St. Louis, Mo.: St. Louis Public Library, 1971, 46 pp.

J139. Jurges, Oda. "Selected Bibliography: black plays, books, and articles related to black theatre published from January 1960 to February 1968." *Drama Review* 12 (Summer 1968), 176–80.

J140. Juris, Gail, and Ronald Krash. *Afro-American Research Bibliography*. St. Louis, Mo.: St. Louis University, Pius XII Memorial Library, 1970, 90 pp.

J141. Juris, Gail, Margaret Krash, and Ronald Krash. *Survey of Bibliographic Activities of U.S. Colleges and Universities on Black Studies*. St. Louis, Mo.: St. Louis University, Pius XII Memorial Library, 1971, 60 pp.

* Juris, Gail. See also K95A.

J142. Justice, J. "American Negro History: a bibliography of black studies material." *California School Libraries* 41 (Jan. 1970), 58 + .

K

K1. K., L. [Len Kunstadt]. "The Legendary Recordings of Bessie Smith." *Record Research* 1:3 (June 1955), 5.

K2. Kailin, Clarence S. *Black Chronicle*. Madison, Wis., 1974, 36 pp.

K3. Kain, Mary Ann. *Books about the Afro-American*. Marshalltown, Iowa: Marshalltown Community College, 1968. A revised edition was issued in 1969.

K4. Kaiser, Ernest. "Annotated Bibliography." *In* Floyd B. Barbour, ed. *The Black Seventies*. Boston, Mass.: Porter Sargent, 1970, pp. 315–25.

K5. Kaiser, Ernest. "Bibliography by and about Franz Fanon." In *International Tribute to Franz Fanon*. New York: United Nations Centre Against Apartheid, 1979, pp. 76–7.

K6. Kaiser, Ernest. "A Bibliography by and about Paul Robeson." *Freedomways* 11 (First Quarter 1971), 125–33.

K7. Kaiser, Ernest. "Bibliography on Black Education." *Freedomways* 17:4 (Fourth Quarter 1977), 239–55.

K8. Kaiser, Ernest. "Black History Reference." *New York Amsterdam News*, Feb. 23, 1974, p. D7.

K9. Kaiser, Ernest. "Black Images in the Mass Media: a bibliography." *Freedomways* 14:3 (1974), 274–87.

K10. Kaiser, Ernest. "Black Youth: a bibliography." *Freedomways* 15:3 (Third Quarter 1975), 226–41.

K11. Kaiser, Ernest. "A Critical Look at [Ralph] Ellison's Fiction and at Social and Literary Criticism by and about the Author." *Black World* 20:2
(Dec. 1970), 53 + .

K12. Kaiser, Ernest. "The History of Negro History." *Negro Digest* 17:4 (Feb.
1968), 10 + . Reprinted in Werner Sollors, ed. *A Bibliographic Guide
to Afro-American Studies*. Berlin, Federal Republic of Germany: Free
University, John F. Kennedy Institute for North American Studies, 1972,
pp. 20–31.

K13. Kaiser, Ernest. "In Defense of the People's Black and White History and
Culture." *Freedomways* 10:1 (First Quarter 1970), 48–62; 10:2 (Second
Quarter 1970), 157–77; 10:3 (Third Quarter 1970), 198–225. Later published as a pamphlet. Reprinted in Werner Sollors, ed. *A Bibliographic
Guide to Afro-American Studies*. Berlin, Federal Republic of Germany:
Free University, John F. Kennedy Institute for North American Studies,
1972, pp. 1–12.

K14. Kaiser, Ernest. "Library Holdings on Afro-Americans." *In* E.J. Josey
and Ann Allen Shockley, eds. *Handbook of Black Librarianship*. Littleton, Col.: Libraries Unlimited, 1977, pp. 228–45.

K15. Kaiser, Ernest. "The Literature of Harlem." *Freedomways* 3:3 (Summer
1963), 276–91. Reprinted in John Henrik Clarke, ed. *Harlem: a community in transition*. New York: Citadel Press, 1964, pp. 26–41. Reprinted in Addison Gayle, ed. *Black Expression: essays by and about
Black Americans in the creative arts*. New York: Weybright and Tolley,
1969, pp. 239–55. Reprinted in R. Baird Shuman, ed. *A Galaxy of Black
Writing*, Durham, N.C.: Moore Publishing Co., 1970, pp. 6–27.

K16. Kaiser, Ernest. "The Literature of the Negro Revolt." *Freedomways* 3:1
(Winter 1963), 36–47.

K17. Kaiser, Ernest. "Literature on the South." *Freedomways* 4:1 (Winter
1964), 149–67.

K18. Kaiser, Ernest. "Myrdal Revisited." *Freedomways* 5 (Fourth Quarter
1964), 525–31.

K19. Kaiser, Ernest. "Negro History: a bibliographical survey." *Freedomways* 7:4 (Fall 1967), 335–45.

K20. Kaiser, Ernest. "Public, University, and Private American Library Holdings on the Negro." *In* Patricia Romero, ed. *Black America 1968: the
year of awakening*. Washington, D.C.: United Publishing Corp., 1969,
pp. 333–53.

K21. Kaiser, Ernest. "Recent Literature on Black Liberation Struggles and the
Ghetto Crisis: a bibliographic survey." *Science and Society* 33:2 (Spring
1969), 168–96.

K22. Kaiser, Ernest. "Recently Published Negro Reference and Research
Tools." *Freedomways* 6:4 (Fall 1966), 358–81.

K23. Kaiser, Ernest. "A Selected Bibliography of the Published Writings by
and about Paul Robeson." *In* John Henrik Clarke, ed. *Dimensions of*

the Struggle Against Apartheid: a tribute to Paul Robeson. New York: United Nations Centre Against Apartheid, 1979, pp. 85–90.

K24. Kaiser, Ernest. "Selected Bibliography of the Published Writings of Langston Hughes." *Freedomways* 8 (Spring 1968), 185–91.

K25. Kaiser, Ernest. "A Selected Bibliography of the Published Writings of W.E.B. Du Bois." *Freedomways* 5:1 (Winter 1965), 207–13. Enlarged and reprinted in John Henrik Clarke, ed. *Black Titan: an anthology by the editors of "Freedomways."* Boston, Mass.: Beacon Press, 1970, pp. 309–30. An abridged version appeared in John Henrik Clarke, ed. *Pan-Africanism and the Liberation of Southern Africa: a tribute to W.E.B. Du Bois.* New York: United Nations Centre Against Apartheid, 1978, pp. 75–9.

K26. Kaiser, Ernest. "Trends in American Negro Historiography." *Journal of Negro Education* 31:4 (Fall 1962), 468–79.

K27. Kaiser, Ernest, and Benjamin Horowitz. "A Charles White Bibliography." *Freedomways* 20:3 (Third Quarter 1980), 206–27.

K28. Kaiser, Ernest, and Robert Nemiroff. "A Lorraine Hansberry Bibliography." *Freedomways* 19:4 (Fourth Quarter 1979), 285–304.

K29. Kallenbach, Jessamine S. *Index to Black American Literary Anthologies.* Sponsored by the Center of Educational Resources, Eastern Michigan University. Boston, Mass.: G.K. Hall, 1978, 219 pp.

K30. Kaplan, Emma N. *Guide to Research in Afro-American History and Culture: a selected and annotated bibliography of materials in the Smith College Library.* Northampton, Mass.: Smith College, 1972, 3 vols. Revised and enlarged in 1975.

K31. Kariger, Marie. "Suggested Readings in Negro Biography." *Hoosier School Librarian* (May 1970), 37–41.

K32. *Katherine Mary Dunham Papers, 1919–1968; inventory.* Carbondale, Ill.: Southern Illinois University Library, 1970, 22 pp.

* Katopes, Peter J. See M83, M84, M85.

* Katz, W.A. See S134.

K33. Kaufman, M. "Recent Books on Human Relations." *Wilson Library Bulletin* 25 (Nov. 1950), 251 + .

K34. Kaurouma, Patricia. "Resources for Researching Afro-American Genealogy." *Afro-Americans in New York Life and History* 1:2 (1977), 217–24.

K35. Kazin, A. "Brothers Crying Out for More Access to Life." *Saturday Review* 54 (Oct. 2, 1972), 33–5.

K36. Keating, Charlotte M. *Building Bridges of Understanding Between Cultures.* Tucson, Ariz.: The Palo Verde Publishing Co., 1967, 134 pp. An edition issued in 1971 has 233 pp.

* Keeler, Florine. See P140.

K37. Keller, Dean H. "Charles Waddell Chesnutt, 1858–1932." *In* Matthew

J. Bruccoli, ed. *First Printings of American Authors: contributions toward descriptive checklists*, Vol. 3. Detroit, Mich.: Gale Research, 1978, pp. 47–9.

K38. Keller, Dean H. "Charles Waddell Chesnutt (1858–1932)." *American Literary Realism* 3 (Summer 1968), 1–4.

K39. Kelley, Estelle F. *Negro Literature*. Project 1–Fl–44. Los Angeles, Cal.: Office of the County Superintendent of Schools, Curriculum Division, 1935, 106 pp.

K40. Kellner, Bruce. *A Bibliography of the Works of Carl Van Vechten*. Westport, Conn.: Greenwood Press, 1980, 258 pp.

K41. Kellogg, Jefferson B. "Selected Secondary Sources [on Afro-American Studies]" *American Studies International*. Supplement to *American Quarterly* 17:4 (Summer 1979), 25–8.

* Kelly, F.M. See L156.

K42. Kelly, Sara. *Blacks in America: selected holdings of the University of Michigan*. Dearborn, Mich.: The Library, 1973, 62 pp.

* Kemler, Doris M. See S50.

K43. Kemp, Charles H. *Blacks in America*. Forest Grove, Ore.: Pacific University, Harvey W. Scott Memorial Library.

* Kemp, John R. See J95, S279.

K44. Kendoziora, Carl. "Behind the Cobwebs [Corrections and additions to Rust's 1962 second edition]." *Record Research* 70 (Aug. 1965), 5; 72 (Nov. 1965), 6+.

* Kennedy, Louise Venable. See R116.

K45. Not used.

K46. Kennicott, Patrick. "The Black Revolution in America: a selected bibliography." *In* James E. Roever, ed. *Proceedings: Speech Association of America Summer Conference V*. New York: Speech Association of America, 1969, pp. 125–50.

K47. Kennicott, Patrick C. "The Study of Black American Rhetoric: an annotated bibliography." RAS 39. *Readers Advisory Service*, 1974(?), 39–1—39–3.

* Kennicutt, H. See T104.

K48. Kennington, Donald. *The Literature of Jazz: a critical guide*. Chicago, Ill.: American Library Association, 1971, 142 pp. Published in London by the Library Association in 1970. A second, revised edition of 236 pp. with Danny L. Read as co-author was issued by ALA in 1981.

K49. Kent, George E. "Notes on the 1974 Black Library Scene." *Phylon* 36:2 (June 1975), 182–203.

K50. Kent, George E. "Outstanding Works in Black Literature during 1972." *Phylon* 34:4 (1973), 307–29.

K51. Kent, George E. "Struggle for the Image: selected books by or about blacks during 1971." *Phylon* 33:4 (Winter 1972), 304–23.

* Kent, Lorna. See J48.

K52. Kerlin, Robert. "A Decade of Negro Literature." *Southern Workman* 59 (May 1930), 226–9.

K53. Kerr, Jeanette. *The Story of Black America.* Orange, Cal.: Chapman College Library, 1969.

K54. Kerri, James N., and Anthony Layng. *Bibliography of Afro-American (Black) Studies.* Exchange Bibliography no. 657/658. Monticello, Ill.: Council of Planning Librarians, 1974, 82 pp.

K55. Kessler, Sidney H. "American Negro Literature: a bibliographical guide." *Bulletin of Bibliography* 21 (Sept. 1955), 181–5.

K56. Kessler, Sidney H. "Collectors, Scholars, and Negro Literature." *The Midwest Journal* 7 (Fall 1955), 222–34.

K57. Kessler, Sidney H. "Studying Negro Life Through American Negro Literature: a bibliographic guide for college students." M.S. thesis, Pratt Institute, School of Library Science, 1953.

K58. Keyssar-Franke, Helene. "Afro-American Drama and Its Criticism, 1960–1972: an annotated check list with appendices." *New York Public Library Bulletin* 78 (Spring 1975), 276–364.

K59. Kimball, Mark Dennis. *A Bibliography of Slavery in the U.S.* Salt Lake City, Utah, 1965.

K60. Kindt, Kathleen. "James Baldwin: a checklist, 1947–1962 " *Bulletin of Bibliography* 24 (Jan.-Apr. 1965), 123–6.

K60A. King, Gertrude E.N. *World Friendships, a Bibliography: sources of educational material.* Boston, Mass.: Chapman and Grimes, 1935, 81 pp.

K61. King, William M. *Black Labor in the Cities: a selected bibliography.* Exchange Bibliography no. 548. Monticello, Ill.: Council of Planning Librarians, 1974, 19 pp.

K62. King, William M. *Blacks, Crime, and Criminal Justice: an introductory bibliography.* Exchange Bibliography no. 570. Monticello, Ill.: Council of Planning Librarians, 1974, 19 pp.

K63. King, William M. *Health, Health Care and the Black Community: an exploratory bibliography.* Exchange Bibliography no. 555. Monticello, Ill.: Council of Planning Librarians, 1974, 16 pp.

K64. King, William M. *Urban Racial Violence in the U.S.: an historical and comparative bibliography.* Exchange Bibliography no. 591. Monticello, Ill.: Council of Planning Librarians, 1974, 20 pp.

K65. Kinton, Jack F. *American Ethnic Groups: a sourcebook.* 3d ed. Mt. Pleasant, Iowa: Social Science and Sociological Resources, 1973, 173 pp.

K66. Kinton, Jack F. *American Ethnic Groups and the Revival of Cultural Pluralism: evaluative sourcebook for the 1970's.* 4th ed. Aurora, Ill.: Social Science and Sociological Resources, 1974, 206 pp.

K67. Kirby, David K. "Charles W. Chesnutt." *American Fiction to 1900: a guide to information sources.* Detroit, Mich.: Gale Research, 1975, pp. 51–3.

K68. Kirk, Diana H., and Susan Goon. "Desegregation and the Cultural Deficit Model: an examination of the literature." *Review of Educational Research* 45 (Fall 1975), 599–611.

K69. Kirk, Sherri, and Glenda Peace. *Black Sojourn: a bibliography.* Davis, Cal.: University of California at Davis Library, Collection Development Section, Ethnic Studies Unit, 1969, 95 pp.

K70. Kirkham, E. Bruce. "The First Edition of 'Uncle Tom's Cabin': a bibliographical study." *Papers of the Bibliographic Society of America* 65 (Fourth Quarter 1971), 365–82.

K71. Kirkley, A. Roy, Jr. *Labor Unions and the Black Experience: a selected bibliography.* New Brunswick, N.J.: Rutgers University, Labor Education Center and Library, Institute of Management and Labor Relations, University Extension Division, 1972, 16 pp.

K72. Kirshner, A. "Teachers' Bibliography for a Scientific Approach to the Development of Tolerance." *High Points* 23 (Nov. 1941), 80.

K72A. Kitchens, John W. *Guide to the Microfilm Edition of the Tuskegee Institute News Clipping File.* Tuskegee, Ala.: Tuskegee Institute, 1978.

K73. Kitchens, John W., Lynne B. Kitchens, Catherine Buchanan, and Jonell Chisholm. *Guide to the Microfilm Edition of the George Washington Carver Papers at Tuskegee Institute.* Tuskegee, Ala.: Tuskegee Institute, Carver Research Foundation, Division of Behavioral Science Research, 1975, 50 pp.

* Kitchens, Lynne B. See K73.

K74. Klaphaak, Esther W. *Author Bibliography of Paul Laurence Dunbar,* 22 pp.

* Klein, Barry. See C51.
* Klein, Carol. See B311A.
* Klein, Thomas A. See W143.

K75. Kleinhans, Robert G. *Bibliography on Afro-American Pentecostalism.* Chicago, Ill.: Author, 1982, 4 pp. A revised version appears in *Newsletter of the Afro-American Religious History Group of the American Academy of Religion* 7:2 (Spring 1983), 4–8.

K76. Klinge, Norma, and Georg-Anna Tod. "The American Negro: a selected list of books." *St. Louis Public Library Monthly Bulletin* 20:12 (n.s.) (Dec. 1922), 282–93. A revised list by Margaret McDonald appeared on pp. 239–54 of the August 1929 *Bulletin.*

K77. Klotman, Phyllis Rauch. *Frame by Frame: a black filmography.* Bloomington, Ind.: Indiana University Press, 1979, 700 pp.

K78. Klotman, Phyllis Rauch, and Wilmer H. Baatz. *The Black Family and the Black Woman: a bibliography.* New York: Arno Press, 1978, 231 pp.

K79. Klotman, Phyllis Rauch, et al. *Black Family and the Black Woman: a* bibliography prepared by the library staff and the Afro-American Studies Department. Bloomington, Ind.: Indiana University Library, 1972, 107 pp.

K80. Klunkowitz, Jerome. "Early Writers: Jupiter Hammon, Phillis Wheatley, and Benjamin Banneker." *In* M. Thomas Inge, Jackson R. Bryer, and Maurice Duke, eds. *Black American Writers: bibliographic essays*, Vol. 1. New York: St. Martin's Press, 1978, pp. 1–20.

* Knapp, Marjorie. See B130.

* Knight, Brian. See C88.

K81. Knight, E.W., and L.V. Norman. "Negroes." *Review of Educational Research* 11 (June 1941), 337–9.

* Knight, Kate B. See A80.

K82. Knipp, Thomas. *Richard Wright: letters to Joe C. Brown*. Kent, Ohio: Kent State University Libraries, 1968, 16 pp.

K83. Knox, Ellis O. "Bibliography [of dissertations by Negroes]." *Journal of Negro Education* 15 (Spring 1946), 220–30.

K84. Knox, Ellis O., and Mary A. Mortin. "Selected Bibliography [on race relations]." *Journal of Negro Education* 4 (July 1935), 456–64.

K85. Koblitz, Minnie W. *The Negro in Schoolroom Literature: resource materials for the teacher of kindergarten through the sixth grade*. New York: Center for Urban Education, 1967, 67 pp.

K86. Koch, Lawrence O. "A Discography of [Joseph] King Oliver's 1923 Okeh Recordings." *Journal of Jazz Studies* 3:2, p. 46.

K87. Koch, Lawrence O. "A Numerical Listing of Charlie Parker's Recordings." *Journal of Jazz Studies* 2:2 (June 1975), 86–93.

* Koepke, Carol-Lou. See L161.

K88. Kolm, Richard. *Bibliography of Ethnicity and Ethnic Groups*. ERIC Document no. ED 090–340. Rockville, Md.: National Institute of Mental Health, Center for Studies of Metropolitan Problems, 1973, 250 pp.

K89. Kopkin, T.J. "Representation of Books by and about American Negroes in Georgia Regional Libraries." M.A. thesis, Emory University, 1957, 64 pp.

K90. Korey, R.A. "Children's Literature for Integrated Classes." *Elementary English* 43 (Jan. 1966), 39–42.

K91. Kornegay, F.A. "Southern Africa and the Emerging Constituency for Africa in the U.S.: a selected survey of periodical literature." *Current Bibliography of African Affairs* 5 (Jan. 1972), 29–40.

* Kornegay, Francis A., Jr. See E11.

* Korner, Alexis. See F69.

* Korst, Bill. See E5, E6, E7, E8.

K92. Koster, Piet, and Dick M. Bakker. *Charlie Parker, 1940–1947*. Alphen aan de Rijn, Netherlands: Micrography, 1974, 34 pp.; *1948–1950*, 1975, 36 pp.; *1940–1955*, 1976, 62 pp.

K93. Kotei, S.I.A. *Dr. W.E.B. Du Bois, 1868–1963: a bibliography*. Accra,

Ghana: Ghana Library Board, Padmore Research Library on African Affairs, 1964, 39 pp.

K94. Kraner, Dietrich Heinz. "[Charles] Mingus in Europe, 1964: a listing of private recordings." *Discographical Forum* 10 (Jan. 1969), 11.

K95. Kraner, Dietrich Heinz. *The Eric Dolphy Discography, 1958–1964.* Graz, Austria: Author, 1967, 14 pp.

* Krash, Margaret. See J141.

K95A. Krash, Ronald, Gail Juris, and Dennis Duke. *Black America: a research bibliography.* Rev. and enlarged. St. Louis, Mo.: St. Louis University, Pius XII Library, 1972, 114 pp.

* Krash, Ronald. See also J140, J141.

K96. Krestensen, K. *The Negro in Canada: material held in the library; a bibliography prepared for the Human Rights Commission by the Ontario Department of Labour Library.* Toronto, Ont., Canada, 1972, 5 pp.

* Kristensen, Sven M. See S13.

K97. Krogman, W.M., et al. "Bibliography in Physical Anthropology." *American Journal of Physical Anthropology* n.s. 1 (Dec. 1943); 2 (Dec. 1944), 386; 3 (Dec. 1945), 372.

K98. Krutchkoff, Sonya. *The New Negro: a bibliography for the general reader.* New York: Harlem Adult Education Committee, 9 pp.

K99. Kugler, Reuben F. "Bibliography for Afro-American History." *Social Studies* 60:5 (Oct. 1969), 211–7.

K100. Kugler, Reuben F. *Bibliography for Afro-American History.* 2nd ed. Los Angeles, Cal.: California State College at Los Angeles, John F. Kennedy Memorial Library, 1970.

K101. Kühn, Gerhard. "Jazz Porträt Louis Armstrong." *HiFi-Stereophonie* 19:7 (July 1980), 804 + .

* Kumatz, Tad. See D139.

K102. Kuncio, Robert A. *Negro History 1553–1903: an exhibition of books, prints, and manuscripts from the shelves of the Library Company and the Historical Society of Pennsylvania, April 17-July 17, 1969.* Philadelphia, Pa.: The Library Company of Philadelphia, 1969, 83 pp.

K103. Kunstadt, Len. "Bessie Smith Says She Will Retire in 1960." *Record Research* 2:2 (May–June 1956), 2.

* Kunstadt, Len. See also K1, S126.

K104. Kuvlesky, William P., and Michael F. Lever. *Occupational Status Orientations of Negro Youth: annotated abstracts of the research literature.* College Station, Tex.: Texas A. and M., Department of Agricultural Economics and Sociology, 1967.

L

L1. "LC Receives [Roy] Wilkins Papers." *Wilson Library Bulletin* 55 (Feb. 1981), 406–7.

L2. "Label Discography [Blues]." *Billboard* 79 (June 24, 1969), 90.

L3. *Labor Education Materials on Minority Problems: an annotated list*. New York: American Labor Education Service, 1948.

L4. Labrew, Arthur. *Black Musicians of the Colonial Period: preliminary index*. Detroit, Mich.: Author, 1977.

L5. LaBrie, Henry G. *The Black Press: a bibliography*. Kennebunkport, Me.: Mercer House Press, 1973, 39 pp.

L6. LaBrie, Henry G. *A Survey of Black Newspapers*. Kennebunkport, Me.: Mercer House, 1980, 72 pp. Updates 1970 and 1973 editions.

* Lacey, Joyce. See J118.

L7. Lachatanere, Diana. "Blacks in California: an annotated guide to the manuscript sources in the California Historical Society Library." *California History* 57:3 (Fall 1978).

* Lacy, Helen. See W18.

L8. LaFarge, John. "Past and Present on Race." *America* 100 (Dec. 20, 1958), 378–9.

L9. Lake, Dorothy. "Best Selling Books by Black Authors." *In* E.J. Josey and Ann Allen Shockley, eds. *Handbook of Black Librarianship*. Littleton, Col.: Libraries Unlimited, 1977, pp. 154–5.

L10. Lake, Dorothy G. *Images in Black Artifacts: negative and positive*. Nashville, Tenn.: Fisk University Library, 1981, 6 pp.

* Lake, Dorothy. See also H28.

L11. Lambert, G.E. "Microgroove Re-issues of Rare Early [Edward (Duke)] Ellington Recordings." *Jazz Monthly* 12 (Nov. 1967), 29–30.

L12. Lambert, G.E. "Some Foreign Blues Re-issues." *Jazz Monthly* 8 (Feb. 1963), 26–7.

* Lamont, Sylvia. See B53.

L13. Lancaster, Emmet M. *A Guide to Negro Marketing Information*. Washington, D.C.: Department of Commerce, Business and Defense Services Administration, 1966, 50 pp.

L14. Landis, Benson Y. "Race: a reading list on employment, education, and housing." *Information Service* 43 (Mar. 1964), 58.

L15. Landra, Guido, and Giulio Cogni. *Piccola bibliografia razziale*, vol. 4. Ragguagli bibliografici. Rome, Italy, 1939, 80 pp.

L16. Lange, Horst H. *Die deutsche Jazz-Discographie. Eine Geschichte des Jazz auf Schallplatten von 1902 bis 1955*. Berlin, Germany: Bote and Bock, 1955.

L17. Lange, Horst H. *The Fabulous Fives* [Small jazz bands of the 1920's]. Chigwell, Essex, England: Storyville Publications, 1978, 150 pp.

L18. Langhorne, Joseph L. "The Use of Audio-visual Aids with Negro Themes." *Journal of Negro Education* 20 (Sept. 1951), 223–7.

L19. "Langston Hughes Manuscripts." *Bancroftiana* 56, pp. 6–7.

L20. *Language Development in Disadvantaged Children: an annotated bibliography*. ERIC Document no. ED 026 414. Washington, D.C.: ERIC Clearinghouse for Urban Disadvantaged, 1968, 86 pp.

* Lanier, Betty Jo. See P111.

L21. Lannon, Maria Mercedes. *The Black Man in America: an overview of Negro history with bibliography and basic book list for K–12*. New York: Joseph F. Wagner, Inc., 1969, 43 pp.

L21A. Lapsansky, Phil. *Black Voices, 1709–1863: a selection of twenty-one examples of Afroamerican expression and opinion, from the shelves of the Library Company of Philadelphia. Prepared for the visit of the Black Studies Librarians' Discussion Group, July 12, 1982, by Phil Lapsansky*. Philadelphia, Pa.: Library Company of Philadelphia, 1982, 15 pp.

* Larson, David. See F91.

* Larson, Verena. See R82.

L22. Lash, John S. "The American Negro and American Literature: a check list of significant commentaries." *Bulletin of Bibliography* 19:1 (Sept.-Dec. 1946), 12–5; 19:2 (Jan.-Apr. 1947), 33–6.

L23. Lash, John S. "The American Negro in American Literature: a selected bibliography of critical materials." *Journal of Negro Education* 15:4 (Fall 1946), 722–30.

L24. Lash, John S. "The Anthropologist and the Negro Author." *Phylon* 8:2 (1947), 105–16.

L25. Lash, John S. "The Conditioning of Servitude: a critical summary of literature by and about Negroes in 1957." *Phylon* 19 (1958), 143 + .

L26. Lash, John S. "Dimension in Racial Experience: a critical summary of literature by and about Negroes in 1958." *Phylon* 20 (1959), 115–31.

L27. Lash, John S. "Expostulation and Reply: a critical summary of literature by and about Negroes in 1959." *Phylon* 21 (1960), 111–23.

L28. Lash, John S. "A Long Hard Look at the Ghetto: a critical summary of literature by and about Negroes in 1956." *Phylon* 18 (1957), 7–24.

L29. Latimer, Catherine A. *The Negro: a selected bibliography (1942–1943)*. New York: New York Vocational High School for Boys, Intercultural Education, 7 pp.

L30. Latimer, Catherine A. "Where Can I Get Material on the Negro?" *Crisis* 41 (June 1934), 164–5.

* Latimer, Catherine A. See also B99.

L30A. "A Latter-day Discography of Sidney Bechet." *Melody Maker* 28 (Jan. 26, 1952), 9.

* Lavin, David E. See S138.

* Lawrence, Laeta. See R112.

L31. Lawrenz, Marguerite Martha. *Bibliography and Index of Negro Music*. Detroit, Mich.: The Board of Education of the City of Detroit, Department of Music Education, 1968, 52 pp.

* Lawson, Bernice. See E51, N113.

L32. Lawson, Hilda J. "The Negro in American Drama (Bibliography of Contemporary Negro Drama)." *Bulletin of Bibliography* 17:1 (Jan.-Apr. 1940), 7–8; 17:2 (May-Aug. 1940), 27–30. Based on her 1939 University of Illinois Ph.D. thesis.

L33. Layer, Harold A. *Ethnic Studies and Audiovisual Media: a listing and discussion*. Stanford, Cal.: Stanford University, Institute for Communication Research, ERIC Clearinghouse on Educational Media and Technology, 1969, 11 pp.

* Layng, Anthony. See K54.

L34. Leadbitter, Mike, and Eddie Shuler. *From the Bayou: the story of Goldband records*. Bexhill-on-Sea, England: Blues Unlimited, 1969, 62 pp.

L35. Leadbitter, Mike, and Neil Slaven. *Blues Records: January 1943 to December 1966*. London, England: Hanover Books; New York: Oak Publications, 1968, 381 pp.

L36. Leary, Lewis. "Carl Van Vechten." *Articles on American Literature, 1900–1950*. Durham, N.C.: Duke University Press, 1954, p. 297.

L37. Leary, Lewis. "Charles Waddell Chesnutt." *Articles on American Literature, 1900–1950*. Durham, N.C.: Duke University Press, 1954, p. 42.

L38. Leary, Lewis. "Countee Cullen." *Articles on American Literature, 1900–1950*. Durham, N.C.: Duke University Press, 1954, p. 65.

L39. Leary, Lewis. "Harriet Beecher Stowe." *Articles on American Literature, 1900–1950*. Durham, N.C.: Duke University Press, 1954, pp. 282–3.

L40. Leary, Lewis. "Langston Hughes." *Articles on American Literature, 1900–1950*. Durham, N.C.: Duke University Press, 1954, p. 150.

L41. Leary, Lewis. "Paul Laurence Dunbar." *Articles on American Literature, 1900–1950*. Durham, N.C.: Duke University Press, 1954, pp. 75–6.

L41A. Leary, Lewis. "Phillis Wheatley." *Articles on American Literature, 1900–1950*. Durham, N.C.: Duke University Press, 1954, p. 302.

L42. Leary, Lewis. "Richard Wright." *Articles on American Literature, 1900–1950*. Durham, N.C.: Duke University Press, 1954, p. 329.

L42A. Leary, Lewis. "Sutton E. Griggs." *Articles on American Literature, 1900–1950*. Durham, N.C.: Duke University Press, 1954, p. 123.

L43. Leary, Lewis. "W.E.B. Du Bois." *Articles on American Literature, 1900–1950*. Durham, N.C.: Duke University Press, 1954, p. 75.

L44. Leary, Lewis. "Wendell Phillips." *Articles on American Literature, 1900–1950*. Durham, N.C.: Duke University Press, 1954, p. 235.

L45. Leary, Lewis. "William Stanley Braithwaite." *Articles on American Literature, 1900–1950*. Durham, N.C.: Duke University Press, 1954, p. 26.

L46. Not used.

L47. Not used.

L48. Leary, Lewis. "Zora Neale Hurston." *Articles on American Literature, 1900–1950*. Durham, N.C.: Duke University Press, 1954, p. 151.

L49. "[Ledbetter, Huddie (Leadbelly)] Allegro-Elite 4027; Royale 18131." *Record Research* 1:6 (Dec. 1955), 12.

* Lee, Chang-Chien. See E2A.

* Leeper, Dennis P. See D68.

L50. Leffall, Dolores C. *Bibliographic Survey: the Negro in print; five-year subject index (1965–1970)*. Washington, D.C.: Negro Bibliographic and Research Center, 1971, 166 pp.

L51. Leffall, Dolores C. "Bibliography: books, bulletins, pamphlets." *Journal of Negro Education* 28 (Fall 1959), 454–8.

L52. Leffall, Dolores C. "Bibliography: books, bulletins, pamphlets." *Journal of Negro Education* 29 (Winter 1960), 59–63.

L53. Leffall, Dolores C. "The Bicentennial and the Afro-American: a selected bibliography." *Negro History Bulletin* 38 (Feb. 1975), 358–61.

L54. Leffall, Dolores C. *Black Church: an annotated bibliography*. Washington, D.C.: Minority Research Center, 1973, 93 pp.

L55. Leffall, Dolores C., and James Peter Johnson. *Black English: an annotated bibliography*. Washington, D.C.: Minority Research Center, 1973, 75 pp.

L56. Leffall, Dolores C., and Janet L. Sims. "Mary McLeod Bethune—the Educator; also including a selected annotated bibliography." *Journal of Negro Education* 45:3 (Summer 1976), 342–59.

* Leffall, Dolores C. See also H116, H117, P111A.

L57. *Legislation Affecting Minority Groups: a selected bibliography*. Chicago, Ill.: American Council on Race Relations, 3 pp.

* Legler, April. See D66.

L58. Leigh, Audrey. *Marcus Mosiah Garvey, 1887–1940: a reading list of printed material in the West India Reference Library*. Kingston, Jamaica: Institute of Jamaica, West India Reference Library, 1973, 13 pp.

* LeMay, J.A. Leo. See R140.

L58A. Lemmon, Alfred E. "Report from Tulane University: the William Ransom Hogan jazz archive." *Current Musicology* 19 (1975), 13–5.

L59. Lepper, Gary M. "James Baldwin." *A Bibliographic Introduction to 75 Modern American Authors*. Berkeley, Cal.: Serendipity Books, 1976, pp. 17–9.

L60. Lerner, Gerda. "Bibliographic Notes." *Black Women in White America: a documentary history*. New York: Random House, 1972, pp. 615–30.

L60A. Lerou, Marion. "Division of Negro Literature, History and Prints, 135th St. Branch, New York Public Library." *Mission Fields at Home* 6 (Feb. 1934), 71–3.

* LeRoy, Nelson L. See B29.

L61. "Les soli di piano enregistres par Thelonius Monk." *Jazz hot* 306 (June 1974), 11.

L62. Lesser, Alexander. "American Negro." *In* "Bibliography of American Folklore, 1915–1928." *Journal of American Folk-lore* 41 (Jan.-Mar. 1928), 47–52.

L63. Lesser, Saal D. "Bibliography on Human Relations Education." *Bulletin* of the National Association of Secondary School Principals 39 (Mar. 1955), 101–9.

L64. *Lesson Plans on Black Literature: the short story.* Niagara, N.Y.: Niagara University Library, 1970, 45 pp.

L65. Lester, Julius. "The Black Experience [reprint publishing]." *New York Times Book Review*, Feb. 15, 1970, pp. 2 + .

L66. [Lester Young Discography]. *HiFi Stereophonie*, (Dec. 1974), 1486.

L67. "Lester Young on Record, 1945–1949." *Jazz Monthly* 7 (April 1962), 23–4.

* Lever, Michael F. See K104.

* Levidova, I.M. See P12.

L68. Levtow, Patricia. *Black-Jewish Relations in the U.S.: a selected annotated list of books, pamphlets and articles.* New York: American Jewish Committee, 1978, 26 pp.

L69. Lewinson, Paul. *A Guide to Documents in the National Archives for Negro Studies.* Washington, D.C.: American Council of Learned Societies, 1947, 28 pp.

L70. Lewis, Alvin. *Bibliography on the Black American.* Manhattan, Kan.: Kansas State University, Farrell Library, Minorities Resources and Research Center, 1975, 19 pp.

L71. Lewis, Ellistine P. *The E. Azalia Hackley Memorial Collection of Negro Music, Dance and Drama: a catalogue of selected Afro-American materials.* Ph.D. thesis, University of Michigan, 1978.

* Lewis, Roscoe E. See H106.

L72. *Library Materials Written by or about Negroes, including Africa and Island History.* Ravenswood, Cal.: Ravenswood City School District Instructional Materials Center, 1968, 6 pp.

L73. "The Life and Work of Richard Wright Including Haiku and Unpublished Prose." *New Letters* 38:2 (Winter 1971).

L74. Light, I. "Disadvantaged Minorities in Self-Employment." *International Journal of Comparative Sociology* 20 (Mar./June 1979), 42–5.

* Lilje, Pauline. See P114.

L75. Lillard, R. Stewart. "A Ralph Waldo Ellison Bibliography (1914–1967)." *The American Book Collector* 19 (Nov. 1968), 18–22. See Carol Polsgrove (P80) for addenda.

L76. Limbacher, James L. "Blacks on Film: a selected list of film available for 16mm rental (and some which are not but should be)." *Journal of Popular Film* 4:4 (1975), 358–78.

L77. Lindgren, William. *Afro-American Bibliography.* East Peoria, Ill.: Illinois Central College, Sandburg Library, 17 pp.

L78. Lindsay, A.G. "Manuscript Materials Bearing on the Negro in America." *Journal of Negro History* 27 (Jan. 1942), 94–101.

L79. Lindsay, Crawford Bernard. "The Cornell University Special Collection on Slavery: American publications through 1840." Ph.D. thesis, Cornell University, 1949.

L80. Lindsay, Samuel McCune. "A Partial List of Books and Pamphlets on the Negro Question in the United States." In *Race Problems of the South, report of the proceedings of the first annual conference held under the auspices of the Southern Society for the Promotion of the Study of Race Conditions and Problems in the South, Montgomery, Alabama, May 8, 9, 10, A.D. 1900*. Richmond, Va.: Published for the Southern Society by the B.F. Johnson Publishing Co., 1900, pp. 224–40. Reprinted in Betty Kaplan Gubert. *Early Black Bibliographies, 1863–1918*. New York: Garland, 1982, pp. 183–202.

* Link, Arthur S. See W17A.

L81. Lipscombe, Mildred. *The Education of the Afro-American: a selected bibliography*. Newark, N.J.: Newark Public Library, Education Division, 1968, 7 pp.

L82. Lissner, John. "The Genius of [Edward (Duke)] Ellington." *Pulsebeat* (Summer 1970), 27–8.

L83. Lissner, John. "Pop/Folk/Jazz: guideposts to a basic record library, with discography." *Library Journal* 94 (Jan. 15, 1969), 158–61.

L84. *List of Additional References on the Anthropology and Ethnography of the Negro Race*. Washington, D.C.: Library of Congress, Division of Bibliography, 1916, 3 pp. A supplement to L108. Reprinted in Betty Kaplan Gubert. *Early Black Bibliographies, 1863–1918*. New York: Garland, 1982, pp. 261–3.

L85. "List of Anti-Slavery Periodicals in the May Anti-Slavery Collection." *Cornell Library Bulletin* 1 (Jan. 1884), 229–32.

L86. *List of Books about the Negro for Young Adults*. New York: The New York Public Library, Countee Cullen Branch, 1965, 6 pp.

L87. *List of Books in the Library of Congress Relating to John Brown*. Washington, D.C.: Library of Congress, 1910, 8 pp. A supplement of 5 pp. was issued in 1921.

L87A. *List of Books on the History of Slavery*. Washington, D.C.: Library of Congress, 1917, 6 pp. Reprinted in Betty Kaplan Gubert. *Early Black Bibliographies, 1863–1918*. New York: Garland, 1982, pp. 265–70.

L88. *List of Books on the Negro Question, 1915–1926*. Select List of References no. 956. Washington, D.C.: Library of Congress, 1926, 10 pp.

L89. *A List of Books Owned by, or from the Library of, the Reverend Lemuel Haynes (1753–1833) One-time Pastor of the West Parish, Rutland, Vermont*. Rutland, Vt.: Rutland Historical Society, 1980(?), 3 pp.

L90. *List of Discussions of the 14th and 15th Amendments with Special Reference to Negro Suffrage*. Washington, D.C.: Library of Congress, Division of Bibliography, 1906, 18 pp. Reprinted in Betty Kaplan Gubert. *Early Black Bibliographies, 1863–1918*. New York: Garland, 1982, pp. 237–52.

L91. *A List of Intercultural Textbooks and Readers Available as of Spring 1966 in the Subject Areas of English and Social Studies*. Richmond, Va.: Virginia Council on Human Relations, 1966.

L92. *A List of Negro Newspapers, Magazines, Trade Journals and Press Services in the U.S.* Washington, D.C.: U.S. Department of Commerce, Bureau of Foreign and Domestic Commerce, Negro Affairs Division, 1930–1937. Irregularly issued directories.

L93. *A List of Negro Plays.* National Services Bureau Publication no. 24. Washington, D.C.: U.S. Works Progress Administration. Federal Theatre Project, 1938.

L94. "List of Publications Containing Important Information on the General Subject of Slavery." In *Substance of the Debate in the House of Commons on the 15th May 1823 on a Motion for a Mitigation and Gradual Abolition of Slavery Throughout the British Dominions . . . .* London, England: Printed by Ellerton and Henderson for the Society for the Mitigation and Gradual Abolition of Slavery Throughout the British Empire, 1823, p. xxiv.

L96. *A List of Published Books by Members of the Fisk Faculty and Alumni Since 1955.* Nashville, Tenn.: Fisk University, Erastus Milo Cravath Memorial Library, 1962.

L97. *List of Recent References on the Negro, with Special Reference to Economic and Industrial Conditions.* Washington, D.C.: Library of Congress, Division of Bibliography, 1935, 20 pp.

L98. *List of References on Alexander Crummell.* Washington, D.C.: Library of Congress, 1917, 3 pp.

L99. *List of References on Frederick Douglass.* Washington, D.C.: Library of Congress, 1916, 3 pp.

L100. *List of References on Intermarriage of Races with Special Emphasis on Immigration.* Washington, D.C.: Library of Congress, 1920, 4 pp.

L101. *List of References on Knights of the Ku Klux Klan (exclusive of the original KKK, but including Night Riders, etc.).* Washington, D.C.: Library of Congress, Division of Bibliography, 1923, 6 pp.

L102. *List of References on Lynch Law.* Washington, D.C.: Library of Congress, 1921, 15 pp. An edition of 25 pp. was issued in 1934. An edition of 16 pp. by Ann Duncan Brown was issued in 1940.

L103. *List of References on Negro Education.* Washington, D.C.: Library of Congress, 1906, 5 pp.

L104. *List of References on Negro Segregation in the U.S.* Washington, D.C.: Library of Congress, Division of Bibliography, 7 pp.

L105. *List of References on Poor Whites of the South.* Washington, D.C.: Library of Congress, 1919, 2 pp.

L106. *List of References on Racial Migration.* Select List of References no. 793. Washington, D.C.: Library of Congress, 1923, 7 pp.

L107. *List of References on Thaddeus Stevens.* Washington, D.C.: Library of Congress, 1916, 5 pp.

L108. *List of References on the Anthropology and Ethnography of the Negro Race.* Washington, D.C.: Library of Congress, 1905, 5 pp. Reprinted in Betty Kaplan Gubert. *Early Black Bibliographies, 1863–1918*. New York: Garland, 1982, pp. 231–5.

L109. *A List of References on the Ku Klux Klan*. Washington, D.C.: Library of Congress, 1924, 10 pp.

L110. *List of References on the (Old) Ku Klux Klan*. Washington, D.C.: Library of Congress, 1924, 8 pp.

L111. *List of References on White Cap Raids and Night-Riders (supplementary list on KKK)*. Washington, D.C.: Library of Congress, 1921, 4 pp. A 1 p. supplement was issued in 1922.

L112. Not used.

L113. *List of References Relating to Harriet Beecher Stowe (excluding periodical articles)*. Washington, D.C.: Library of Congress, 1921, 4 pp.

L114. "A List of Significant Books." *The Ebony Handbook*. Chicago, Ill.: Johnson Publishing Co., 1974, pp. 188–90.

L115. "List of Works relating to the American Colonization Society, Liberia, Negro Colonization, etc., in the New York Public Library." *New York City (sic) Public Library Bulletin* 6 (1902), 265–9.

L116. *List of Writings on the Negro in the U.S. (a selection of books published 1915–1929)*. Washington, D.C.: Library of Congress, Division of Bibliography, 1929, 11 pp.

L117. *Lists of Books by and about Negroes Available in the Libraries of the University of North Carolina and Duke University*. Chapel Hill, N.C.: University of North Carolina, 88 pp.

L118. *Literature List*. New York: National Committee Against Discrimination in Housing, 1956, 4 pp.

L119. "Literature of Slavery." *New Englander* 10 (Nov. 1852), 588–613.

L120. *Literature of the Civil War and Reconstruction Period: a list of selected readings*. Minneapolis, Minn.: Minneapolis Board of Education, 1939, 28 pp.

L120A. "Little Mt. Zion Baptist Church of Harlem. [Thomas] Fats Waller, accompanist." *Record Research* 1:4 (Aug. 1955), 11.

L121. Little, Patricia Anne. "A Selected Bio-bibliography of W.E.B. Du Bois." Paper, School of Library Service, Atlanta University, Jan. 7, 1971.

L122. Litweiler, John B. "[Archie] Shepp: an old schoolmaster in a brown suit." *Downbeat* 41 (Nov. 7, 1974), 17.

L123. Lockard, D. "Black Books: 14 books covering the range of problems on the subject of race." *Trans-Action* 6 (July 1969), 53–8.

L124. Locke, Alain. "Best Books on the Negro." *Publishers Weekly* 124 (July 22, 1933), 228.

L125. Locke, Alain. "A Critical Retrospect of the Literature of the Negro for 1947." *Phylon* 9 (1948), 3–12.

L126. Locke, Alain. "Dawn Patrol: a review of the literature of the Negro for 1948." *Phylon* 10 (1949), 5–13.

L127. Locke, Alain. *A Decade of Negro Self-Expression* [*1914–1928*]. Occasional Papers no. 26. Charlottesville, Va.: Trustees of the John F. Slater Fund, 1928, 20 pp.

L128. Locke, Alain. "Deep River, Deeper Sea." *Opportunity* 14 (Jan. 1936), 6.

L129. Locke, Alain. "From 'Native Son' to 'Invisible Man': a review of the literature of the Negro in 1952." *Phylon* 14 (1953), 34–44.

L130. Locke, Alain. "The High Price of Integration: a review of the literature of the Negro for 1951." *Phylon* 13 (1952), 7–18.

L131. Locke, Alain. "Inventory at Mid-Century: a review of the literature of the Negro for 1950." *Phylon* 12 (1951), 5–12.

L132. Locke, Alain. "Negro Drama: a selected list of plays of Negro life." *In* Alain Locke, ed. *The New Negro: an interpretation*. New York: Albert and Charles Boni, 1925, pp. 430–1. Reprinted by Arno in 1968 and Atheneum in 1969.

L133. Locke, Alain. *The Negro in America*. Chicago, Ill.: American Library Association, 1933, 64 pp.

L134. Locke, Alain. "The Negro in Literature." *In* Alain Locke, ed. *The New Negro: an interpretation*. New York: Albert and Charles Boni, 1925, pp. 426–9. Reprinted by Arno in 1968 and Atheneum in 1969.

L135. Locke, Alain. "Negro Music: a bibliography." *In* Alain Locke, ed. *The New Negro: an interpretation*. New York: Albert and Charles Boni, 1925, pp. 432–5. Reprinted by Arno in 1968 and Atheneum in 1969.

L136. Locke, Alain. "The Negro Race Problems." *In* Alain Locke, ed. *The New Negro: an interpretation*. New York: Albert and Charles Boni, 1925, pp. 444–6. Reprinted by Arno in 1968 and Atheneum in 1969.

L137. Locke, Alain, "The Negro's Contribution to American Art and Literature." *The Annals of the American Academy of Political and Social Science*. 40 (Nov. 1928), 234–47.

L138. Locke, Alain. "Of Native Sons, Real and Otherwise." *Opportunity* 19 (Feb. 1941), 48–52.

L139. Locke, Alain. "A Selected List of American Music, Influenced by American Negro Themes or Idioms." *In* Alain Locke, ed. *The New Negro: an interpretation*. New York: Albert and Charles Boni, 1925, pp. 436–7. Reprinted by Arno in 1968 and Atheneum in 1969.

L140. Locke, Alain. "Wisdom *de Profundis*: the literature of the Negro, 1949." *Phylon* 11 (1950), 5–14.

L141. Locke, Alain. *World View on Race and Democracy: a study guide in human group relations*. Chicago, Ill.: American Library Association, 1943, 19 pp.

L142. Locke, Don. "[Ferdinand] Jelly Roll Morton: the Library of Congress recordings." *Jazz Journal* 13 (Jan. 1960), 15–8.

L143. Loff, Jon N. "Gwendolyn Brooks: a bibliography." *College Language Association Journal* 17 (Sept. 1973), 21–32.

L144. Logan, Rayford W. "Bibliography of Bibliographies Dealing Directly or Indirectly with the Negro." *In* W.E.B. Du Bois and Guy B.

Johnson, eds. *Encyclopedia of the Negro: preparatory volume with reference lists and reports*. New York: Phelps-Stokes Fund, 1946, pp. 191–8.

* Logan, Rayford, W. See also M23.

L145. Lohmann, Jan, and Nils Winther. "Discographie des enregistrements inédits de Miles Davis." *Jazz Hot* 39 (Jan. 1973), 20–1; 29 (July 1973), 6+.

* Long, Catherine. See A108.

L146. Long, Charles. *African and Afro-American Religions: a bibliography*. Chicago, Ill.: University of Chicago Divinity School.

L147. Long, Margaret. *The Book Explosion of 1964: authors assess Negro protest, poverty and personality; a year's books*. Atlanta, Ga.: Southern Regional Council, 1964, 24 pp.

L148. Long, Richard A. *A Select Chronology of Afro-American Prose and Poetry, 1760–1970*. CAAS Bibliographies no. 9. Atlanta, Ga.: Center for African and African-American Studies, 17 pp.

L149. Lopez, Manuel D. "Claude McKay." *Bulletin of Bibliography* 29 (Oct.-Dec. 1972), 128–33.

L150. Lord, Tom, et al. "Clarence Williams Discography." *Storyville* 13 (Oct.-Nov. 1967) 8–13; and following issues.

L151. Lornell, Kip. "Black Material Folk Culture." *Southern Folklore Quarterly* 42:2–3 (1978), 287–94.

L152. [Louis Armstrong]. *Record Research* 1:4 (Aug. 1955), 11.

L153. "Louis Armstrong Discography." *Down Beat* 17 (June 14, 1950), 14–5.

L154. "Louis Armstrong: his greatest years." *Jazz Monthly* 8 (June 1962), 26–7.

L155. "Louis [Armstrong], 1925–1947." *Metronome* 67 (Aug. 1951), 18–9.

L156. Love, William C., Dick Rieber, George Hoefer, Jr., F.M. Kelly, and Charles Payne Rogers. "Ma Rainey Discography." *Jazz Information* 2:4 (Sept. 6, 1940), 9–14.

L157. Loveman, Amy. "Clearing House: writers on the Negro, Negro writers." *Saturday Review of Literature* 10:45 (May, 1934), 719; 11:1 (July 21, 1934), 15. See also 12:17 (Aug. 24, 1935), 24.

* Loventhal, Milton. See Mc28.

L158. Lover, William C. "Louis Armstrong Discography." *Jazz* 1:12 (Dec. 1943), 18–22.

L159. Lowenfels, Doris B. *Selected Reference Materials: the black man in America*. Purchase, N.Y.: Manhattanville College, Brady Memorial Library.

L160. Lowry, P. "Blues Bleachings." *Blues Unlimited* 84 (Sept. 1971), 23.

L161. Luebbert, Mrs. Jack, and Carol-Lou Koepke. *Black Studies Bibliography*. St. Louis, Mo.: Webster College, Eden-Webster Libraries.

L162. Lutsky, Irving, and John Norris. "The Billie Holliday Story." *Coda* 11:1 (May–June 1973), 12–14.

L163. Lutton, Helen. *Thinking Together in Intergroup Living: an annotated bibliography for adults and young people*. Chicago, Ill.: American Council on Education, Project on Intergroup Education in Cooperating Schools, 1945, 26 pp.

L164. Luttrell, Squire. *Afro-American Audio-Visual Materials Held by the Learning Materials Center of Wisconsin State University—Whitewater*. Whitewater, Wis.: Wisconsin State University, Harold Anderson Library.

L165. Luzzi, Mario. "Discografia Booker Little." *Musica Jazz* 31 (Nov. 1975), 52–4.

L166. Luzzi, Mario. "Discografia Keith Jarrett." *Musica Jazz* 30 (May 1974), 54–6.

L167. Luzzi, Mario. "Discografia Pharaoh Sanders." *Musica Jazz* 30 (Oct. 1974), 45–7.

L168. Lyells, Ruby E. Stutts. *Understanding the Negro: a short list of recent books by and about the Negro, selected to give a background for understanding what the Negro thinks in the present crisis*. Prepared for the Mississippi Council on Interracial Cooperation. Alcorn, Miss.: Alcorn A and M College Library, 1942, 16 pp. A revised edition of 28 pp. was issued in 1945.

L169. Lytle, E. E. *The Geography of Black America*. Public Administration Series No. 924. Monticello, Ill.: Vance Bibliographies.

Mc

Mc1. McAllister, Dorothy M. "Library Resources for Graduate Study in Southern Universities for Negroes." *Journal of Negro Education* 23 (Winter 1959), 51–9.

Mc2. McBride, David. *The Afro-American in Pennsylvania: a critical guide to sources in the Pennsylvania State Archives*. Harrisburg, Pa.: Pennsylvania Historical and Museum Commission, 36 pp.

* McBride, David. See also Mc3.

Mc3. McBride, Rebecca, and David McBride. "Corrections of a Richard Wright Bibliography." *College Language Association Journal* 20:3 (Mar. 1977), 422–3.

Mc4. McBrown, Gertrude Parthenia. "The Countee Cullen Memorial Collection of Atlanta University." *Negro History Bulletin* 17 (Oct. 1953), 11–6.

* McCabe, James. See F31.

Mc5. McCabe, Jane A. *Education and the Afro-American*. Focus: Black American Bibliography Series. Bloomington, Ind.: Indiana University Libraries, 1969, 26 pp.

Mc6. McCabe, Jane A., Robert S. Wood, and Wilmer A. Baatz. *Black Americans and the Entertainment Industry/Black American Athletes*. Focus:

Black American Bibliography Series. Bloomington, Ind.: Indiana University Libraries, 1969, 23 pp.

* McCabe, Jane A. See also I27.

Mc7. McCabe, William J. *Materials Available for Black Studies*. South Orange, N.J.: Seton Hall University, McLaughlin Library.

Mc8. McCain, Sara B., and Angela Poulos. *Negro Culture: a selected bibliography*. Bowling Green, Ohio: Bowling Green State University Libraries, Bibliographic Research Center, 1968, 23 pp. A second edition was issued in 1970.

Mc9. McCall, Emmanuel L. "Select Annotated Bibliography on the Black Church." *Review and Expositor* 70 (1973), 371–6.

Mc9A. MacCann, Donnarae, and Gloria Woodard. *The Black American in Books for Children: readings in racism*. Metuchen, N.J.: Scarecrow Press, 1972, 223 pp.

* McCarroll, Jean. See B75.

Mc10. McCarthy, Albert J. [Discography of Big Bill Broonzy]. *Jazz Forum* 4, pp. 25–30.

Mc11. McCarthy, Albert J. *Jazz Discography I: an international discography of recorded jazz, including blues, gospel and rhythm and blues for the year January-December 1958*. London, England: Cassell, 1960.

Mc12. McCarthy, Albert J. "Jelly Roll Morton Discography." *Jazz Music* 11:2–3 (Feb.-Mar. 1944), 102–6.

Mc13. McCarthy, Albert J. "Louis Armstrong Discography." *The Record Changer* 9:7–8 (June-Aug. 1950), 37–42.

Mc14. McCarthy, Albert J. "Recent Reissues." *Jazz Monthly* 13 (Feb. 1968), 2–4; 14 (June 1968), 22–6; 14 (Aug. 1968), 19–21.

Mc15. McCarthy, Albert J., Alun Morgan, Paul Oliver, and Max Harrison. *Jazz on Record: a critical guide to the first 50 years, 1917–1967*. London, England: Hanover Books, 1968; New York: Oak Publications, 1968, 416 pp.

* McCarthy, Albert J. See also C27.

Mc16. McClure, Daisy D., Mary Scarborough, and Lois Harris. *Black Heritage and Horizons: a booklist*. Kokomo, Ind.: Kokomo Public Library, 1969, 45 pp.

Mc17. McConnell, J. Michael. *Bibliography of Books and Other Materials on Negro History and Culture in the Park College Library*. Parkville, Mo.: Park College, Carnegie Library, 1970, 69 pp.

Mc18. McConnell, Ray M. "The Negro Problem." In *A Guide to Reading in Social Ethics and Allied Subjects: lists of books and articles selected and described for the use of general readers; by teachers in Harvard University*. Cambridge, Mass.: Harvard University Press, 1910, pp. 90–9.

Mc19. McConnell, Roland C. "The Importance of Records in the National Archives on the History of the Negro." *Journal of Negro History* 34 (1949), 135–52.

Mc20. McConnell, Roland C. *Preliminary Inventory of the Papers of the Emmett J. Scott Collection in Morgan State College, 1916–1951*. Baltimore, Md.: Morgan State College, Soper Library, 1959, 8 pp.

Mc21. McCrum, Blanche Prichard. *Negroes in the Armed Services of the U.S. from the Earliest Times to the Present: a select list of references*. Washington, D.C.: Library of Congress, General Reference and Bibliography Division.

* McCulloch, Margaret C. See B127.

* McDonald, Deborah A. See B312.

Mc22. McDonald, Denise, and Kathy White. *King Memorial Library—Booklist*. Syracuse, N.Y.: Syracuse University, King Memorial Library.

* McDonald, Margaret. See K76.

* McDonald, Robert R. See J95, S279.

Mc23. McDonnell, Robert W. *The Papers of W.E.B. Du Bois: a guide to the microfilm edition*. Sanford, N.C.: Microfilming Corporation of America, 1981, 275 pp.

Mc24. McDonnell, Robert W. "Selection Sources of Afro-American History: a bibliographic discussion." *Current Studies in Librarianship* (Spring/Fall 1978), 59–70.

Mc25. McDonnell, Robert W. "The W.E.B. Du Bois Papers." *The Library Newsletter* 11:3 (May 1980), 5–15. Also in *Crisis* 87:9 (Nov. 1980), 359–64. Also published as a pamphlet by University of Massachusetts Library Associates.

Mc26. McDonough, John. "Manuscript Resources for the Study of Negro Life and History." *Quarterly Journal of the Library of Congress* 26 (July 1969), 126–48.

Mc27. McDougall, Marion Gleason. "Bibliography of Fugitive Slave Cases and Fugitive Slave Legislation." *In* her *Fugitive Slaves (1619–1865)*. Publications of the Society for the Collegiate Instruction of Women. Fay House Monographs no. 3. Boston, Mass.: Ginn and Co., 1891, pp. 129–37. Reprinted in Betty Kaplan Gubert. *Early Black Bibliographies, 1863–1918*. New York: Garland, 1982, pp. 27–39.

Mc28. McDowell, Jennifer, and Milton Loventhal. *Black Politics: a study and annotated bibliography of the Mississippi Freedom Democratic Party*. Occasional Papers Series no. 3. San Jose, Cal.: Bibliographic Information Center for the Study of Political Science, 1971, 96 pp.

Mc29. McDowell, Robert E., and George Fortenberry. "A Checklist of Books and Essays about American Negro Novelists." *Studies in the Novel* 3:2 (Summer 1971), 219–36.

* McElroy, Hilda. See W132.

* McGaghy, Dawn. See D156.

Mc36. McGarney, Robert. "[Sidney] Bechet's Records." *Playback* 2:9 (Sept. 1949), 5–15.

* McGill, Michael E. See B43.

Mc31. McGirt, Jacqueline, Gail Favors, and Pauline Wyetch. *A Bibliography on Performing and Visual Arts*. Greensboro, N.C.: Bennett College, Thomas F. Holgate Library.

* McGirt, Jacqueline. See also H125.

* McGuire, Laura. See R89.

Mc32. McIlvaine, Eileen. *Selected Reference Materials: black American studies*. New York: Columbia University Libraries.

* McKay, Eleanor. See W149.

Mc33. MacKay, M.B., and T.M. Maher. "Selected Bibliography on the American Negro." *South Dakota Library Bulletin* 55 (July 1969), 154–66.

* McKinney, Frances M. See B216.

Mc34. MacLean, Grace Edith. " 'Uncle Tom's Cabin' in Germany." *Americana Germanica* 10 (1910), 101.

Mc35. McLin, Velma E. *The Charles Eaton Burch Collection in Founders Library, Howard University*. Washington, D.C.: Howard University, 1962, 67 pp.

* McMickle, Marion. See S229.

Mc36. McNaspy, C.J. "Reading for a Hot Summer." *America* 110 (June 20, 1964), 851–2.

Mc37. McPheeters, Annie L. *Negro Progress in Atlanta, Georgia, 1950–1960: a selective bibliography on human relations from four Atlanta newspapers*. Atlanta, Ga.: Atlanta Public Library, West Hunter Branch, 1964, 55 pp.

Mc38. McPherson, Dorothy. "Black Power in Print." *California Librarian* 30 (Apr. 1969), 93–103.

Mc39. McPherson, James M., Laurence B. Holland, James M. Banner, Jr., Nancy J. Weiss, and Michael D. Bell. *Blacks in America: bibliographic essays*. Garden City, N.Y.: Doubleday, 1971, 430 pp.

Mc40. McWhirter, Mary Esther. *Books for Friendship: a list of recent books recommended for children*. Philadelphia, Pa., and New York: American Friends Service Committee and Anti-Defamation League of B'nai B'rith, 1968.

Mc41. McWhorter, Gerald A. *The Political Sociology of the Negro: a selected review of the literature*. New York: Anti-Defamation League of B'nai B'rith, 1967, 31 pp.

M

M1. Mack, Molly A. *Black Students and Standard English: an annotated bibliography for teachers*. Burlington, Vt.: University of Vermont, Department of English.

* Mackin, Lynn. See D130.

M2. Maddrell, Jane G. *Bibliography of Negro Books Published from January 1, 1948 through July 31, 1949*. Kansas City, Kan.: Bibliographical Publishing Co., 1949, 10 pp.

M3. Madison, B.Q., and M. Schapiro. "Black Adoption, Issues and Policies: review of the literature." *Social Service Review* 47 (Dec. 1973), 531–60.

M4. Magnusson, Tor. *An Almost Complete [Thomas] "Fats" Waller Discography*. Stockholm, Sweden: Author, 1964.

M5. Magnusson, Tor. "[Thomas] Fats Waller Piano Rolls Discography." *Matrix* 106 (Feb. 1975), 3–8.

M6. Magnusson, Tor. "[Thomas] Fats Waller with Gene Austin on the Record." *Journal of Jazz Studies* 4:1 (Fall 1976), 82.

M7. [Mahalia Jackson Discography]. *Matrix* 61 (Oct. 1965), 3–8.

* Maher, T.M. See Mc33.

M8. Mahoney, Heidi L. "Selected Checklist of Material by and about Gwendolyn Brooks." *Negro American Literature Forum* 8 (Summer 1974), 210–1.

* Mahony, Dan. See D20.

M9. Mahony, Daniel. *Columbia 13/14000–D Series* [Race records, 1923–1933]. Stanhope, N.J.: Walter C. Allen, 1961, 80 pp.

* Maire, Xavier. See M116, M117.

* Major, Clarence. See W46.

M10. *Malcolm X*. Bibliographies in Black Studies no. 1. Chicago, Ill.: Chicago Center for Afro-American Studies and Research, 16 pp.

M11. Malkoc, Anna Maria, and A. Hood Roberts. "Bidialectism: a special report from CAL/ERIC." *Elementary English* 48 (Jan. 1971), 125–36. Also in *English Journal* 60 (Feb. 1971), 279–88.

M12. Mandelik, Peter, and Stanley Schatt. *A Concordance to the Poetry of Langston Hughes*. Detroit, Mich.: Gale Research, 1975, 295 pp.

* Manny, Elsie S. See B29.

M13. Mansfield, Stephen. *Collections in the Manuscript Division, Alderman Library, the University of Virginia, Containing References to Slavery for the Period from 1820 to 1865*. Charlottesville, Va.: University of Virginia, Alderman Library, 1967, 178 pp.

M13A. *MARC: a selected bibliography, 1967–1971*. New York: Metropolitan Applied Research Center, 1972, 58 pp.

* Marco, Guy A. See C165.

M14. Margolies, Edward, and David Bakish. *Afro-American Fiction, 1853–1976: a guide to information sources*. Detroit, Mich.: Gale Research, 1979, 161 pp.

M14A. Margolies, Edward, and David Bakish. "Black American Short Fiction: a comprehensive bibliography of collections." *Studies in Short Fiction* 16 (Fall 1979), 371–5.

* Margolies, Edward. See also F5.

M15. "Marion Brown." *Swing Journal* 29 (Sept. 1975), 238–41.

M16. Markenwich, Reese. *Bibliography of Jazz and Pop Tunes Sharing the Chord Progressions of Other Compositions.* Riverdale, N.Y.: Author, 1970, 58 pp. A "new, expanded" bibliography was issued in 1974.

M17. Markewich, Reese. *Jazz Publicity: bibliography of names and addresses of hundreds of international jazz critics and magazines.* New York: Author, 1974(?), 25 pp.

* Marko, Gayle. See H124.

M18. Marr, Warren. "The Many Shades of History [Amistad and Schomburg Collections]." *Crisis* 77:2 (Feb. 1970), 43–7.

M19. Marshall, Albert P. *A Guide to Negro Periodical Literature* 1:1 (Feb. 1941)/3:4 (Feb. 1943). Irregular index.

* Marshall, Arnell J. See B312.

M20. Martin, C.T. *The Civil Rights Movement and Publications relating to the Negro and Race Relations.* M.A. thesis, University of Chicago, 1969, 56 pp.

M21. Martin, Olivia J. *Guide to the Microfilm Edition of the Charles Waddell Chesnutt Papers in the Library of the Western Reserve Historical Society.* Cleveland, Ohio: Western Reserve Historical Society, 1972.

M22. Martin, Olivia J. *The John A. Green Papers in the Library of the Western Reserve Historical Society: a microfilm edition.* Cleveland, Ohio: Western Reserve Historical Society, 1972, 8 pp.

* Martin, R. Lawrence. See B286.

M23. Martin, Robert E. "Bibliography of the Writings of Alain LeRoy Locke." *In* Rayford W. Logan, et al., eds. *The New Negro Thirty Years Afterward: papers contributed to the 16th annual spring conference of the Division of the Social Sciences, April 20, 21, and 22, 1955.* Washington, D.C.: Howard University Press, 1955, pp. 89–96.

M24. Martin, T.L. "The Plastic Muse [Ornette Coleman]." *Jazz Monthly* 10 (May 1964), 13–5; 10 (June 1964), 14–8; 10 (August 1964).

* Martin, Tony. See A15, B25.

M25. *The Martin Luther King, Jr., Memorial Collection.* San Anselmo, Cal.: San Francisco Theological Seminary Library, 1969.

M26. Martson, Alexandra. *A Bibliography of the Negro and the Arts.* San Francisco, Cal.: San Francisco State College Library, 1969.

* Marx, Barbara. See H130.

M27. Mary Helen, Sister. "The Negro in Books." *Catholic Library World* 35 (Nov. 1963), 149+.

M28. Mason, Julian D., Jr. "Charles W. Chesnutt." *In* Louis D. Rubin, ed. *A Bibliographical Guide to the Study of Southern Literature.* Baton Rouge, La.: Louisiana State University Press, 1969, pp. 171–3.

M29. Massagli, Luciano, Liborio Pusateri, and Giovanni M. Volonte. [*Edward*] *Duke Ellington's Story on Records, 1923–1931.* Milan, Italy: Musica Jazz, 1961.

M30. Massagli, Luciano, Liborio Pusateri, and Giovanni M. Volonte. [*Edward*] *Duke Ellington's Story on Records, 1939–1955*. Milan, Italy: Musica Jazz, 1967–72, 9 vols.

M31. Massey, James Earl. "Bibliographic Essay: Howard Thurman and Rufus M. Jones, Two Mystics." *Journal of Negro History* 57 (Apr. 1972), 190–5.

M32. Masters, Deborah C. *A Guide to Research in Black Studies Prepared for the Exhibition on the Black Experience, Feb. 28-Mar. 25, 1977*. University Park, Pa.: Pennsylvania State University Libraries.

M33. Masters, Deborah C. *A Guide to Sources in Black Studies in the Pennsylvania State University Libraries*. University Park, Pa.: Pennsylvania State University, University Libraries and the Black Studies Program, 1978, 88 pp.

M34. *Masters' Theses at Fisk University, 1912–1963*. Nashville, Tenn.: Fisk University Press, 1964.

M35. "Materials Specially Selected for Workshop on Black Studies." *Read, See and Hear* 20:1 (Nov. 8, 1971), 3 pp. Issued by the Newark, N.J., Board of Education, Department of Libraries and Audiovisual Education.

M36. Mathieson, Moira B., and Rita M. Tatis. *Understanding Disadvantaged Youth, Their Problems and Potentials: an annotated bibliography*. ERIC Document no. ED 044–380. Washington, D.C.: ERIC Clearinghouse on Teacher Education, 1970.

* Mattern, Margaret. See T14.

M36A. Matthews, Geraldine O. "Bibliographic Control of Afro-American Literature: an analysis of selected items." *In* Herman L. Totten, ed. *Bibliographic Control of Afro-American Literature*. Eugene, Ore.: University of Oregon, School of Librarianship, 1976, pp. 199–227.

M37. Matthews, Geraldine O., and the African-American Materials Project Staff, School of Library Science, North Carolina Central University. *Black American Writers, 1773–1949: a bibliography and union list*. Boston, Mass.: G.K. Hall, 1975, 222 pp.

M38. Matthews, Miriam. "The Negro in California from 1781–1810: an annotated bibliography." Paper prepared for LS 290ab, University of Southern California, 1944, 52 pp. Expanded to a Master's thesis.

M39. Matthews, Miriam. "Selected Bibliography [on Race Relations]." *Journal of Educational Sociology* 19:3 (Nov. 1945), 198–206.

* Matthewson, Ramona. See W123.

M40. Mauerer, Hans J. *A Discography of Sidney Bechet*. Copenhagen, Denmark: Karl E. Knudsen, 1969, 86 pp. A revised edition was published in 1970.

M41. Maultsby, Portia K. "Selected Bibliography: U.S. black music." *Ethnomusicology* 29:3 (Sept. 1975), 422–49.

M42. Maultsby, Portia K. "Sources of Films, Video-tapes, Dissertations, and

Field Recordings for Afro-American Music." *Music Library Association Newsletter* 14 (Sept.-Oct. 1973), 4–5.

M43. [Max Roach Discography]. *Swing Journal* 31 (Sept. 1977), 288–93.

M44. May, Samuel, Jr. "Catalogue of Anti-Slavery Publications in America." In *Proceedings of the American Anti-Slavery Society, at its Third Decade, held in the city of Philadelphia, Dec. 3d and 4th, 1863. With an Appendix and a Catalogue of the Anti-Slavery Publications in America, from 1750–1863*. New York: American Anti-Slavery Society, 1864, pp. 157–75. Reprinted in Betty Kaplan Gubert. *Early Black Bibliographies, 1863–1918*. New York: Garland, 1982, pp. 3–25.

M45. Maycock, Wiloughby. "Prefaces to 'Uncle Tom's Cabin.' " *Notes and Queries* (July 17, 1915), 58.

M45A. Meade, Mary Jo, Lucy Haner, and Susan Cromer. *Black and Brown Bibliography*. San Bernardino, Cal.: Library, California State College at San Bernardino.

M46. Meadows, Eddie S. *Jazz Reference and Research Materials: a bibliography*. New York: Garland, 1981, 300 pp.

M47. Meadows, Eddie S. *Theses and Dissertations on Black American Music*. Beverly Hills, Cal.: Theodore Front Musical Literature, 1980, 19 pp.

M48. "A Medical Bibliography [of W. Montague Cobb]." *Negro History Bulletin* 36 (Nov. 1973), 162–4.

M49. Meier, August. "Black America as a Research Field: some comments." *American Historical Association Newsletter* (Apr. 1968).

M50. Melamud, Ruth. *A Bibliography of Books by Negro Authors*. Jamaica, N.Y.: Queensborough Public Library, Department of Reference, 11 pp.

M51. Melamud, Ruth. *Books on the Negro by White Authors*. Jamaica, N.Y.: Queensborough Public Library, Department of Reference, 7 pp.

M52. Melton, J. Gordon. *A (First Working) Bibliography of Black Methodism*. Evanston, Ill.: Institute for the Study of American Religion, 1970, 45 pp.

* Menon, Anila Bhatt. See C16.

M53. Merriam, Alan P., and Robert J. Brenford. *A Bibliography of Jazz*. Philadelphia, Pa.: American Folklore Society, 1954, 145 pp. Reprinted in 1970 by DaCapo.

M54. Merriam, Alan P., and Robert J. Brenford. "Louis Armstrong: bibliography." *Record Changer* 9:7–8 (June-Aug. 1950), 33–5.

M55. Merriam, Alan P. "A Short Bibliography of Jazz." *Notes* 10:2 (Mar. 1953), 202–10.

* Merriam, Alan P. See also G32.

M56. *Merritt College Library Guide for Afro-American Studies*. Oakland, Cal.: Merritt College Library, 1969, 33 pp.

M57. Merritt, Nancy Gertrude. "Negro Spirituals in American Collections: a handbook for students studying Negro spirituals." Master's thesis, Howard University, 1940.

M58. Messner, Stephen D. *Minority Groups and Housing: a selected bibliography, 1950–1967*. Storrs, Conn.: University of Connecticut, Center for Real Estate and Urban Economic Studies, 1969, 60 pp. For the second edition, see Byrl N. Boyce (B280).

M59. Metcalf, E.W., Jr. *Paul Laurence Dunbar: a bibliography*. Metuchen, N.J.: Scarecrow Press, 1975, 193 pp.

* Metcalf, E.W., Jr. See also E13, E14.

M60. Not used.

M61. Meyer, F. "Four Books on Race." *Commonweal* 80 (July 10, 1964), 490–1.

M62. Meyer, H.N. "Book Marks." *Nation* 206 (June 3, 1968), 737 + .

M63. Meyer, Jon K. *Bibliography on the Urban Crisis: the behavioral, psychological and sociological aspects of the urban crisis*. A publication of the U.S. National Clearinghouse for Mental Health Information. Washington, D.C.: National Institute of Mental Health, 1969, 452 pp.

M64. Meyer, Robert. "New Orleans Jazz Research Center." *New York Times*, May 6, 1962.

M65. Meyers, A. "Keeping Up: a checklist of black reference books." *American Libraries* 8 (Feb. 1977), 77.

M66. Michalak, Thomas J. *Economic Status and Condition of the Negro*. Focus: Black American Bibliography Series. Bloomington, Ind.: Indiana University Libraries, 1969, 21 pp.

M67. Midgette, Lillian Avon. "A Bio-Bibliography of Alain LeRoy Locke." M.S.L.S. thesis, Atlanta University School of Library Science, 1963, 48 pp.

M68. Mignon, Molly R. *Racism in America: a bibliography of government documents and pamphlets in the Wilson Library, West Washington State College*. Bellingham, Wash.: West Washington State College, Mabel Z. Wilson Library, 9 pp.

M69. Miles, Louella. *One World in School: a bibliography*. Montgomery, Ala.: American Teachers Association, 1946, 58 pp.

M70. Miles, William A. *Black List No. 1: Black Mother [Africa]*. Buffalo, N.Y.: Buffalo and Erie County Library, 1969, 5 pp.

M71. Miles, William A. *Black List No. 2: the inhuman institution [slavery]*. Buffalo, N.Y.: Buffalo and Erie County Library, 1970, 5 pp.

M72. Miles, William A. *Black List No. 3: the many shades of black*. Buffalo, N.Y.: Buffalo and Erie County Library, 1970, 3 pp.

M73. Miles, William A. *Black List No. 4: the shadow that scares*. Buffalo, N.Y.: Buffalo and Erie County Library, 1970, 5 pp.

M74. Millar, Jack. "A Selected Discography of Air-Shots, Concert Recordings and Film Soundtracks Featuring Vocals by Billie Holliday." *Discographical Forum* 32 (1974), 3–6; and subsequent issues.

M75. Millar, Jack. "Take Two: a preliminary listing of the alternative masters made by Billie Holliday." *Matrix* 96 (Apr. 1972), 14–5; 97 (Sept. 1972), 12–4; 98 (Nov. 1972), 9–12.

M76. Millender, Dharathula H. *Real Negroes/Honest Settings: children's and young people's books about Negro life and history*. Chicago, Ill.: American Federation of Teachers, AFL-CIO, 1967, 28 pp.

M77. Millender, Dharathula H. "Through a Glass Darkly: the representation of the Negro in books for children." *Library Journal* 92 (Dec. 15, 1967), 4571–6; *School Library Journal* 14 (Dec. 1967), 28–34.

M78. Miller, Albert Jay. *Confrontation, Conflict, and Dissent: a bibliography of a decade of controversy, 1960–1970*. Metuchen, N.J.: Scarecrow Press, 1972, 567 pp.

* Miller, C.L. See P59.

* Miller, Edward B. See B37.

M79. Miller, Elizabeth W. *The Negro in America: a bibliography*. Compiled for the American Academy of Arts and Sciences. Cambridge, Mass.: Harvard University Press, 1966, 190 pp. A second edition of 351 pp. compiled by Mary L. Fisher was published in 1970.

M80. Miller, Jeanne-Marie A. "Black Women Playwrights from Grimke to Shange: selected synopses of their work." *In* Gloria T. Hull, Patricia Bell Scott, and Barbara Smith, eds. *But Some of Us Are Brave: black women's studies*. Old Westbury, N.Y.: Feminist Press, 1982, pp. 280–96.

* Miller, Joe A. See I9.

M81. Miller, Joseph C. *Slavery: a comparative teaching bibliography*. Waltham, Mass.: Crossroads Press, 1978, 123 pp.

M82. Miller, R. Baxter. *Langston Hughes and Gwendolyn Brooks: a reference guide*. Boston, Mass.: G.K. Hall, 1978, 149 pp.

M83. Miller, Ruth, and Peter J. Katopes. "The Harlem Renaissance: Arna W. Bontemps, Countee Cullen, James Weldon Johnson, Claude McKay and Jean Toomer." *In* M. Thomas Inge, Jackson R. Bryer, and Maurice Duke, eds. *Black American Writers: bibliographic essays*, Vol. 1. New York: St. Martin's Press, 1978, pp. 161–206.

M84. Miller, Ruth, and Peter J. Katopes. "Modern Beginnings: William Wells Brown, Charles Waddell Chesnutt, Martin R. Delany, Paul Laurence Dunbar, Sutton E. Griggs, Frances Ellen Watkins Harper, and Frank J. Webb." *In* M. Thomas Inge, Jackson R. Bryer, and Maurice Duke, eds. *Black American Writers: bibliographic essays*, Vol. 1. New York: St. Martin's Press, 1978, pp. 133–217.

M85. Miller, Ruth, and Peter J. Katopes. "Slave Narratives." *In* M. Thomas Inge, Jackson R. Bryer, and Maurice Duke, eds. *Black American Writers: bibliographic essays*, Vol. 1. New York: St. Martin's Press, 1978.

M86. Miller, Wayne, et al. *A Comprehensive Bibliography for the Study of American Minorities*. New York: New York University Press, 1976, 2 vols.

M87. Miller, William H. *A Discography of the "Little" Recording Companies [Commodore, Hot Record Society, Solo Art, Jazz Man, General, Etc.]*. Melbourne, Australia: Author, 1943, 20 pp.

M88. Millett, Fred Benjamin. "Carl Van Vechten." *Contemporary American Authors: a critical survey and 219 bio-bibliographies.* New York: Harcourt, Brace and World, 1940, pp. 626–8.

M89. Millett, Fred Benjamin. "Langston Hughes." *Contemporary American Authors: a critical survey and 219 bio-bibliographies.* New York: Harcourt, Brace and World, 1940, pp. 403–4.

M90. Mills, Annie B., and Mary Lu Yavenditti. *The Negro in America: a selected bibliography of books available in Monteith Library.* Alma, Mich.: Alma College, Monteith Library, 1969, 12 pp.

M91. Mills, Clarence Harvey. "Selective Annotated Bibliography on the Negro and Foreign Languages." *Journal of Negro Education* 8 (April 1939), 170–6.

M92. Mills, Gladys H. *Bibliography: equal educational opportunity, myth or reality?* ERIC Document no. 110–538. Denver, Col.: Education Commission of the State, 1975.

M93. Mills, Hazel E., and Nancy B. Prior. *The Negro in the State of Washington, 1788–1969: a bibliography of published works and of unpublished source materials on the life and achievements of the Negro in the Evergreen State.* Rev. ed. Olympia, Wash.: Washington State Library, 1970, 21 pp.

M94. Mills, Joyce White. *The Black World in Literature for Children: a bibliography of print and non-print materials.* Atlanta, Ga.: Atlanta University, School of Library Service, 1975, 42 pp. A 1977 edition contained 56 pp.

M95. Mims, A. Grace. "Nervous Nellies on Race Relations." *Library Journal* 92 (Mar. 15, 1967), 1291 + ; *School Library Journal* 14 (Mar. 1967), 101 + .

M96. Min, Tae H. *The Black in America.* Pocatello, Id.: Idaho State University Library, 1970, 32 pp.

M97. "Minimum Reference Shelf [on Race]." *Propaganda Analysis* 2 (Jan. 1939), 16.

M97A. *Minorities and Allied Health: an annotated bibliography.* Southwest Program Development Corp., 1973, 65 pp.

M98. *Minorities and Discrimination in the U.S. with Particular Reference to Employment Practices: a selected list of books in the Washington State Library.* Olympia, Wash.: Washington State Library, 1967(?), 8 pp. A revised edition of 21 pp. was published in 1970.

M99. *Minorities and Intergroup Relations: a selected bibliography.* Chicago, Ill.: American Council on Race Relations, 1948, 3 pp.

M100. *Minority Business Enterprise: a bibliography.* Washington, D.C.: U.S. Department of Commerce, Office of Minority Business Enterprise, 1973, 231 pp.

M101. *Minority Group Performance under Various Conditions of School, Ethnic, and Economic Influence.* ERIC Document no. ED 021–945. New York: ERIC Clearinghouse for Urban Disadvantaged, 1963.

M102. *Minority Groups: a bibliography*. Salt Lake City, Utah: Utah Board of Education, Office of the State Superintendent of Public Instruction, 1968, 20 pp.

M103. *Minority Groups Bibliography*. St. Paul, Minn.: Minnesota Department of Education, Division of Instruction, 1968, 25 pp.

M104. *Minority Groups/Disadvantaged Youth: a selected bibliography*. ERIC Document no. ED 074–685. Arlington, Va.: Council for Exceptional Children, 1972.

M105. *Minority Groups: exceptional child bibliographic series*. ERIC Document no. 054–575. Arlington, Va.: Council for Exceptional Children, 1971.

M106. *Minority Groups in Medicine: selected bibliography*. DHEW Publication no. (NIH) 72–33. Bethesda, Md.: U.S. National Institute of Health, Division of Physician and Health Professions Education, 1972, 15 pp.

M107. *Minority Groups: selected bibliographies and references of materials for children and young adults*. Chicago, Ill.: American Library Association, Children's Services and Young Adult Services Division, 1969, 4 pp. A supplement of 4 pp. was issued in 1970.

M108. Mitchell, Henry S., and Darryl M. Smaw. *A Bibliography of Afro-American History, Ambrose Swasey Library, Colgate Rochester/Bexley Hall/Crozer Seminary, Rochester, N.Y.* Rochester, N.Y.: Colgate Rochester/Bexley Hall/Crozer Seminary, Black Church Studies Program, 1971, 40 pp.

M109. Mitchell, James J.R. "Paperbacks on Anthropology Allied to Human Relations: a bibliography." *Journal of Human Relations* 9 (Summer 1961), 514–7.

M110. Mock, James R. "The National Archives with respect to the Records of the Negro." *Journal of Negro History* 23 (1938), 49–56.

M111. Mode, Peter G. "The Christianization and Emancipation of the Negro: Colonial Period to the Civil War." *Source Book and Bibliographical Guide for American Church History*. Menasha, Wis.: George Banta Publishing, 1921, pp. 538–48. Reprinted by J.S. Canner of Boston in 1964.

M112. Moe, Christian, and E. Stewart-Harrison. "A Bibliography of Theatrical Craftsmanship, 1976, part VIIG, Production Reports: black theatre." *Theatre Quarterly* 8, 72–89.

M113. Mohr, C.L. "Southern Blacks in the Civil War, a Century of Historiography: bibliographic essay." *Journal of Negro History* 59 (Apr. 1974), 177–95.

M114. Mohr, Kurt. "Charlie Mingus Discography: some additions." *Jazz Monthly* 6 (June 1960), 24.

M114A. Mohr, Kurt. *Discographie du jazz*. Geneva, Switzerland: Vuagnat, 1945, 84 pp.

M115. Mohr, Kurt, and M. Chauvard. "Discographie complète de Ray Charles."

Jazz Hot 176 (May 1962), 8–9; 177 (June 1962), 37; 178 (July-Aug. 1962), 44.

M116. Mohr, Kurt, Joël Dufour, Xavier Maire, and Jacques Périn. "Bo Diddley discographie." *Soul Bag* 61 (June 1977), 11–5.

M117. Mohr, Kurt, Xavier Maire, Joël Dufour, Jacques Périn, Daniel Bellemain, Terence Courtney, and John Garodkin. "Little Richard Discography." *Soul Bag* 61 (June 1977), 18–23.

* Mohr, Kurt. See also D4, D81, M142.

M118. Moneypenney, Anne, and Barrie Thorne. "A Bibliography of Melville Jean Herskovits." *American Anthropologist* 66:1 (1964), 91–109.

M119. Montalbana, Pierre. *Biographie discographie Clifford Brown*. Marseilles, France: Jazz Club Aix-Marseille, 1969, 13 pp.

M120. Montesano, Philip M. *San Francisco Black People, 1860–1865: a bibliographical essay*. San Francisco, 8 pp.

M121. Montgomery, Michael. "Eubie Blake Piano Rollography (revised)." *Record Research* 159/160 (Dec. 1978), 4–5.

M122. Montgomery, Michael. "Eubie Blake Rollography." *Record Research* 27 (Mar.-Apr. 1960), 19; 30 (Oct. 1960), 2.

M123. Montgomery, Michael. "James P. Johnson Rollography." *Record Research* 20 (Nov.-Dec. 1959), 16.

M124. Montgomery, Michael. "More Rolls by [Ferdinand (Jelly Roll)] Morton." *Record Research* 49 (Mar. 1963), 6–7.

M125. Montgomery, Michael. "Revised Eubie Blake Rollography." *Record Research* 33 (Mar. 1961), 16.

M126. Montgomery, Michael. "Scott Joplin Rollography." *Record Research* 22 (Apr.-May 1959), 2.

M127. Moon, Pete. *A Bibliography of Jazz Discographies* [*1960–1969*]. London, England: British Institute of Jazz Studies, 1970, 24 pp. A second edition of 32 pages was published in 1972.

M128. Moon, Pete, and Don Tarrant. "Sonny Rollins: a discography." *Discographical Forum* 39 (1977), 3–6; and following issues.

M129. Moorachian, Rose. *Negro Voices*. Boston, Mass.: Boston Public Library, Young Adult Section, 1967.

M130. Moorer, Frank E., and Lugene Baily. "A Selected Check List of Materials by and about Ralph Ellison." *Black World* 20 (Dec. 1970), 126–7.

* Moorer, Frank E. See also B9.

M131. Morehouse, Jean, et al. *Bibliography of the Black*. Oswego, N.Y.: SUNY-Oswego, Penfield Library, 85 pp.

M132. Morgan, Alun. "[Charlie] Bird [Parker] and the Lover Man Session." *Jazz Monthly* 8 (Aug. 1962), 3–6.

M133. Morgan, Alun. "Discography [Howard McGhee]." *Jazz Journal* 19 (Jan. 1966), 14; 19 (Feb. 1966), 29.

M134. Morgan, Alun. "George Wallington: a name discography." *Jazz Monthly* 9 (Nov. 1963), 25.

M135. Morgan, Alun. "John Williams: the pianist from Vermont." *Jazz Monthly* 8 (Oct. 1962), 2–5.

M136. Morgan, Alun. "Talking of [Thomas] Fats [Waller] and [Walter] Brownie [McGhee]." *Melody Maker* 30 (July 10, 1954), 9.

M137. Morgan, Alun. "White Christmas, from [Charlie] Bird [Parker] in the Roost: Parker's better-known transcription." *Melody Maker* 27 (Dec. 15, 1951), 4.

* Morgan, Alun. See also F69, H31, Mc15.

M138. Morgenstern, Dan. "Basic Louis [Armstrong]." *Down Beat* 37:13 (July 9, 1970), 28–9.

M139. Morgenstern, Dan. "Reissues: jazz's rich legacy." *Down Beat* 36 (Jan. 23, 1969), 16+.

M140. Morgenstern, Dan. *Thelonious Monk Discography*. New York: Soundscape (?), 1981, 19 pp.

M141. Morgenstern, Dan, Ira Gitter, and Jack Bradley. *[Charles] Bird [Parker] and [John Birks] Diz [Gillespie]: a bibliography*. New York: New York Jazz Museum, 1973.

M142. Morgenstern, Dan, Kurt Mohr, Jorgen Grunnet Jepsen, and Michael Shera. "[Oran] Hot Lips Page on Record." *Jazz Journal* 15:12 (1962), 17+. See also previous issue.

M143. Morris, Effie Lee. "Blowing in the Wind: books on black history and life in America." *Library Journal* 94 (Mar. 15, 1969), 1298–1300; *School Library Journal* 16 (Mar. 1969), 122–4.

M144. Morris, Effie Lee. *Minority Groups: a bibliography of books and pamphlets*. San Francisco, Cal.: San Francisco Public Library, Office of Children's Services, 1969, 2 pp.

M145. Morris, Milton Donald. *The Politics of Black America: an annotated bibliography*. Carbondale, Ill.: Southern Illinois University, Public Affairs Research Bureau, 1971, 84 pp.

* Mortin, Mary A. See K84.

M146. Mosby, Elizabeth. *Bibliography of the Black Studies Collection*. Concord, N.C.: Barber-Scotia College Library.

M147. Moshburn, S. *Afro-American History and Culture*. Mt. Vernon, Wash.: Skagit Valley College Library, 11 pp.

M148. Moss, Josephine. *Basic Books for Black Studies in Denison University*. Granville, Ohio: Denison University, William Howard Doane Library, 1970, 8 pp.

* Mowery, Robert. See W97.

M149. "Muddy Waters Discography." *Jazz Report* 1 (June 1961), 31–2.

M150. Mulhauser, Roland. "Library Services for Negroes." *Bulletin of Bibliography* 13:8 (Jan.-Apr. 1929), 155–7; 13:9 (May-Aug. 1929), 177–80.

M151. Mullen, Patrick B. *Black American Folklore: a bibliography*. Columbus, Ohio: Ohio State University, Department of English, 1970.

M152. Muller, Robert E. *Negroes in Children's Books: comparative bibliog-

raphy of children's books on American history and culture. Daly City, Cal.: Jefferson Elementary School District, 1970, 37 pp.

M153. *Multi-Ethnic Bibliography: grade 9 through grade 12.* Philadelphia, Pa.: School District of Philadelphia, Office of Integration and Intergroup Education, 1967, 6 pp.

M154. *Multi-Ethnic Bibliography: kindergarten through 8th grade.* Philadelphia, Pa.: School District of Philadelphia, Office of Integration and Intergroup Education, 1967, 7 pp.

M155. *Multi-Ethnic Media: selected bibliographies.* Chicago, Ill.: American Library Association, American Association of School Libraries, Treatment of Minorities in Library Books and Other Instructional Materials Committee, 1969(?), 12 pp. This was published under the same title in *School Libraries* 19 (Winter 1970), 49–57. A supplement appeared in Spring 1970 on pp. 44–7. D. Cohen prepared an additional supplement which appeared in *Library Journal* 98 (Apr. 15, 1973), 1352–8, and in *School Library Journal* 19 (Apr. 1973), 32–8.

* Munos, Doris. See C29.

M156. Murphy, Jane, and Pat Johnson. *Current Acquisitions in Black Studies.* Newark, Del.: University of Delaware, Hugh M. Morris Library.

* Murphy, John. See D140.

M157. Murphy, Lucile L. *Books by and about the Negro.* Clarksville, Ark.: College of the Ozarks, Dobson Memorial Library.

M158. Murray, Daniel. "Bibliographia—Africana." *Voice of the Negro* 1 (May 1904), 186–91.

M159. Murray, Daniel. *Preliminary List of Books and Pamphlets by Negro Authors for Paris Exposition and Library of Congress.* Washington, D.C.: U.S. Commission to the Paris Exposition, 1900, 8 pp. Reprinted in Betty Kaplan Gubert. *Early Black Bibliographies, 1863–1918.* New York: Garland, 1982, pp. 170–82.

* Murray, Florence. See R55.

M160. Muse, Daphne P. "Black Children's Literature: rebirth of a neglected genre." *Black Scholar* 7 (Dec. 1975), 11–5.

M161. *Music Composed by Negroes.* New York: National Recreational Association, 192?, 7 pp.

M162. "My Best on Wax: Billy Eckstein." *Down Beat* 18 (May 4, 1951), 6.

M163. Myers, Arthur E. *The Black Man in Films: African heritage and American history.* Baltimore, Md.: Enoch Pratt Free Library, Community Action Program, 1968, 6 pp.; 1969, 12 pp. Part II is listed in *Film News* 26:5 (1969), 6–8.

M164. Myers, Carol. "A Selected Bibliography of Recent Afro-American Writers." *College Language Association Journal* 16 (1972), 377–82.

M165. Myers, Carol. "Supplement to 'A Bibliographical Introduction to the American Literature of the 1930's and the Background': black American literature." *Bulletin of Bibliography* 34:2 (Apr. 1977), 68–72.

* Myers, Carol. See also R148.
M166. Myers, Hector F., Phyllis G. Rana, and Marcia Harris. *Black Child Development in America, 1927–1977: an annotated bibliography.* Westport, Conn.: Greenwood Press, 1979, 470 pp.
M167. Mylne, David. "[Sidney] Bechet Discography." *Melody Maker* 28 (Feb. 9, 1952), 9; 28 (Feb. 16, 1952), 9; 28 (Feb. 23, 1952), 9; 28 (Mar. 8, 1952), 9; 28 (Mar. 15, 1952), 9.

N

N1. *The NAACP: a register of its records in the Library of Congress.* Washington, D.C.: Library of Congress, Manuscript Division, 1972.
N2. *NAACP: a selected bibliography.* New York: The New York Public Library, Schomburg Collection, 1955, 2 pp.
N3. *National Negro History Week.* Houston, Tex.: Houston Public Library, 1967.
N4. Neff, Wesley M. "Discography of Jimmie Noone." *Jazz Information* 2:8 (Nov. 8, 1940), 15–22.
N5. "The Negro." Compiled by the Staff of the Countee Cullen Branch. First Annual Supplement to the Oct. 1950 List. *Branch Library Book News* [The New York Public Library] 28:9 (Nov. 1951), 129–30.
N6. *The Negro.* Jamestown, N.Y.: Chautauqua-Cattaraugus Public Library, 1964, 4 pp.
N7. *The Negro.* Milwaukee, Wis.: Milwaukee Public Library, 1960. A 24 pp. supplement was issued in 1965.
N8. "The Negro—A Selected Bibliography." *Branch Library Book News— Supplement to the Bulletin of The New York Public Library* 17:9 (Nov. 1940), 138–56. Reprinted as a pamphlet.
N9. "The Negro: a selected bibliography." *Bulletin of The New York Public Library* 54 (Oct. 1950), 471–85. A selection from this list was published under the title "The Negro" in *Branch Library Book News* [The New York Public Library] 27:8 (Oct. 1950), 111.
N10. "The Negro—a Selected Bibliography." *Bulletin of The New York Public Library; Branch Library Book News* 7:2 (Feb. 1930), 18–30.
N11. "The Negro: a selected bibliography including supplements for 1951–1953." *Branch Library Book News* [The New York Public Library] 31:2 (Feb. 1954).
N12. "The Negro—a Selected Bibliography (Part 1)." *Branch Library Book News—Supplement to the Bulletin of The New York Public Library* 12:4 (Apr. 1935), 66–74. Part 2 appeared in 12:5 (May 1935), 82–92. Both parts were reprinted as a single 22 pp. pamphlet.
N13. *The Negro: a selected list for school libraries of books by or about the Negro in Africa and America.* Rev. ed. Nashville, Tenn.: Tennessee Department of Education, Division of School Libraries, 1935, 22 pp. In

1941, an edition of 48 pp. was issued, "revised and reprinted through the courtesy of the Julius Rosenwald Fund."

N14. "The Negro, A Selected Reading List." First Annual Supplement to the 1945 Edition. Compiled by the Staff of the 135th Street Branch. *Branch Library Book News* [The New York Public Library] 23:9 (Nov. 1946), 129–30.

N15. "The Negro—A Selected Reading List." *Branch Library Book News* [The New York Public Library] 22:2 (Feb. 1945), 39–45.

N16. "The Negro, A Selected Reading List." Compiled by the Staff of the 135th Street Branch. *Branch Library Book News* [The New York Public Library] 24:9 (Nov. 1947), 129–30.

N17. *The Negro: a selected reading list.* Compiled by the staff of the 135th Street Branch Library, [The New York Public Library]. 1949(?), 1 p. The fourth supplement to the 1945 list.

N18. *The Negro American: a reading list.* New York: National Council of Churches of Christ in the U.S.A., Department of Racial and Cultural Relations, 1957.

N19. *The Negro American: a selected list of books, magazines and recordings for school libraries.* Nashville, Tenn.: Tennessee Department of Education, Equal Educational Opportunities Program, 1969, 14 pp.

N20. *Negro-American Life and History.* Atlanta, Ga.: Georgia Department of Education, Office of Instructional Services, Curriculum Development Division, School Library Services Unit, 1970, 42 pp.

N21. *The Negro and His Achievements in America: a list of books compiled for the American Negro Exposition.* Chicago, Ill.: Chicago Public Library, 1940, 15 pp.

N22. *The Negro and the War: a brief list of books selected by the staff of the Schomburg Collection of Negro Literature.* New York: The New York Public Library, 1943, 4 pp.

N23. *Negro Bibliography.* Tacoma, Wash.: Tacoma Public Library.

N24. *Negro Book Club's Guide to African American Books, Records, Visual Aids, Maps, Film Strips, and Art.* New York: Negro Book Club, 1969, 38 pp.

N25. *The Negro: books for boys and girls.* Pasadena, Cal.: Pasadena Public Library, 1969.

N26. *The Negro: books for boys and girls.* San Diego, Cal.: San Diego Public Library, 1968.

N27. *The Negro; Books for Young People: bibliographies compiled by the Secondary School Librarians of the Oakland Public Schools.* Oakland, Cal.: Oakland Public Schools, 1963.

N28. "Negro Education." *School and Society.* 63 (1946), 303.

N29. *The Negro Freedom Movement, Past and Present: an annotated bibliography.* Detroit, Mich.: Wayne County Intermediate School District, Desegregation Advisory Project, 1967, 101 pp.

N30. *Negro Heritage*. Booklist for Grades 4–6. Denver, Col.: Denver Public Library, 1970(?), 33 pp.

N31. *Negro Heritage*. Booklist for Grades 1–3. Denver, Col.: Denver Public Library, 1970(?), 5 pp.

N32. *Negro Heritage in Children's Books*. Toledo, Ohio: Toledo Public Library, 1968.

N33. *Negro Heritage Resource Guide: a bibliography of the Negro in contemporary America*. New York: National Council of Churches of Christ in the U.S.A., Division of Christian Education, 1967, 31 pp.

N34. *Negro History and Culture*. Wayne, Mich.: Wayne County Intermediate School District, Assist Center-Information Service, 31 pp.

N35. *Negro History and Culture: a selected list of books for boys and girls*. Los Angeles, Cal.: Los Angeles Public Library, 1969, 11 pp.

N36. *Negro History and Culture in America*. Rochester, N.Y.: Monroe County Library System, 5 pp.

N37. *Negro History and Literature: a selected annotated bibliography*. New York: American Jewish Committee, Anti-Defamation League of B'nai B'rith, National Federation of Settlements and Neighborhood Centers, 1968, 29 pp.

N38. *Negro History: 1553–1903*. Exhibition April 16-July 17, 1969. Philadelphia, Pa.: Library Company of Philadelphia and the Historical Society of Pennsylvania, 1969, 83 pp.

N39. *Negro History Project at Crouse School*. Akron, Ohio: Akron Public Schools.

N40. "Negro History Week, Feb. 9–15, 1969." *Paperbound Books in Print* (Feb. 1969), 4–9.

N41. *Negro Housing in Town and Cities, 1927–1937*. New York: Russell Sage Foundation Library, 1937, 3 pp.

N42. *The Negro in Agriculture: a partial list*, 2 pp.

N43. *The Negro in America*. Detroit, Mich.: Detroit Public Library.

N44. *The Negro in America*. Oakland, Cal.: Oakland Public Library, Young Adult Division, 1968, 9 pp. An edition of 10 pp. was issued in 1969.

N45. "The Negro in America." *Scholastic Teacher* (Jan. 18, 1968), 17.

N46. *The Negro in America: recent books for adults*. Boston, Mass.: Boston Public Library, 1969.

N47. *The Negro in American Civilization: outline and selected bibliography*, 5 pp.

N48. *The Negro in American History*. Negro History Week, Feb. 14–20. Cincinnati, Ohio: Public Library of Cincinnati and Hamilton County, 1971.

N49. *The Negro in American History*. New York: New York City Board of Education.

N50. *The Negro in American History*. Raleigh, N.C.: North Carolina Department of Public Instruction, 196?, 31 pp.

N51. *The Negro in American History: a guide for teachers, 1965*. Detroit, Mich.: Detroit Public Schools, Department of Social Studies, 1965.

N52. *The Negro in American History and Culture: a bibliography of sources for teaching*. New York: Union Theological Seminary, Auburn Library, Urban Education Collection, 1965.

N53. *The Negro in American Life*. Baltimore, Md.: Baltimore Public Schools.

N54. *The Negro in American Life*. Cincinnati, Ohio: Public Library of Cincinnati and Hamilton County, 1969. Revises 1966 edition of the same title.

N55. *The Negro in American Life: a selected bibliography, 1960–1963*. Boston, Mass.: Massachusetts Department of Education, Division of Library Extension, 1963.

N56. *The Negro in American Life and History: a resource book for teachers*. (Preliminary edition). San Francisco, Cal.: San Francisco Unified School District, 1965, 367 pp. A subsequent edition was published in 1967.

N57. *The Negro in Books for Children*. Washington, D.C.: District of Columbia Public Library, Children's Service, 1968, 32 pp. A revised edition of 71 pp. entitled *The Afro-American in Books for Children* was published by the library in 1974.

N58. *The Negro in Business: a bibliography, 1935*. Washington, D.C.: U.S. Department of Commerce, Negro Affairs Division, 1935, 9 pp.

N59. *The Negro in Industry*. Bulletin no. 66. New York: Russell Sage Foundation Library, 1924, 4 pp.

N60. *The Negro in Life and Literature*. Chicago, Ill.: Chicago Public Schools, Division of Libraries, 1965.

N61. "The Negro in Literature." *Crisis* 36:11 (Nov. 1929), 376–7. See also 37:2 (Feb. 1930), 51.

N62. "The Negro in Print: a selected list of magazines and books by and about Negroes." *Survey Graphic* 53 (Mar. 1, 1925), 703–7.

N63. *The Negro in Science: a selected bibliography prepared in the Schomburg Collection, New York Public Library*, 9 pp.

N64. *The Negro in Social Work*, 1932, 2 pp.

N65. *The Negro in the State of Washington; 1788–1967: a bibliography of published works and unpublished source materials on the life and achievements of the Negro in the Evergreen State*. Olympia, Wash.: Washington State Library, 1968, 14 pp.

N66. "The Negro in the U.S.: a list of significant books." A Supplement to the 9th rev. ed. [1965]. *Branch Library Book News* [The New York Public Library] 45 (Apr. 1968), 39–46. Reprinted as a pamphlet.

N67. *The Negro in the U.S.: a list of significant books*. 9th rev. ed. New York: The New York Public Library, Office of Adult Services, 1965, 24 pp.

N68. *Negro Interest List*. San Francisco, Cal.: San Francisco Public Library, 1969, 20 pp.

N69. *Negro-Jewish Relations: a selected bibliography*. New York: American Jewish Committee, 1963, 4 pp. An addendum of 3 pp. was published in 1967, and another of 3 pp. in 1970. Other pamphlets of the same title were issued in 1969 and 1976.

N70. *Negro Life: a selected booklist.* Mt. Vernon, N.Y.: Westchester County Library System, 1965, 4 pp.

N71. *Negro Life and History: a booklist for children.* Boston, Mass.: Boston Public Library, 1969, 21 pp.

N72. *The Negro Literature Collection: books of Negro authorship to be found in the Oakland Free Library.* Rev. ed. Oakland, Cal.: Oakland Free Library, 1937, 11 pp.

N73. *Negro Materials in the Manuscript Section.* Nashville, Tenn.: Tennessee State Library and Archives, 1969, 2 pp.

N74. *The Negro Movement: past and present.* Detroit, Mich.: Wayne County Intermediate School District, Desegregation Advisory Project, 1967.

N75. *Negro Newspapers and Periodicals in the U.S.: 1939.* Washington, D.C.: U.S. Department of Commerce, Bureau of the Census, 1940. A directory for 1940 was published in 1941.

N76. *Negro Newspapers on Microfilm: a selected list.* Washington, D.C.: Library of Congress, Photoduplication Service, 1953, 8 pp.

N77. *The Negro Past and Present: an annotated bibliography.* Mt. Clemens, Mich.: Mt. Clemens Public Library, 1968, 50 pp.

N78. *The Negro Spiritual.* Washington, D.C.: Library of Congress, 1970, 3 pp.

N79. *The Negro: to improve his self-image.* Gary, Ind.: Gary Public Library, Adult Education Department, 1967.

N80. *The Negro Today: a selected reading list.* New York: Congregational Church, 1936, 2 pp.

N81. *Negroes First and Foremost.* Boston, Mass.: Boston Public Library, 1964.

N82. *Negroes in American Life: an annotated bibliography of books for elementary school.* Rockville, Md.: Montgomery County Public Schools, Department of Educational Media and Technology, 1968, 74 pp.

N83. *Negroes in Michigan: a selected bibliography.* 2nd ed. rev. Lansing, Mich.: Michigan Bureau of Library Services, 1969, 5 pp. A 4 pp. list was published in 1968.

N83A. *Negroes—Labor Unions: recent references.* Cornell List No. 168. Committee of University Industrial Relations Librarians Exchange Bibliography no. 1192. Ithaca, N.Y.: Cornell University, New York State School of Industrial and Labor Relations, 1959, 2 pp.

N84. *Negroes—Stories.* Detroit, Mich.: Detroit Public Library, 1966.

N85. Nelson, A'Lelia. *Black Spectrum: a bibliography.* New York: The City College Library, 1973, 187 pp.

N86. Nelson, John. "Ethel Waters on Record." *Coda* 10:1 (May-June 1971), 2–4.

N87. Nelson, John. "Louis Armstrong on Record: big band era." *Coda* 11:2 (July-Aug. 1973), 19–23.

N88. Nelson, Robert N. *The Negro in Literature*. New York: Service Bureau for Intercultural Education, 1939, 8 pp.

N89. Nelson, Rose K. *Bibliography of the Negro*. New York: Service Bureau for Intercultural Education, 23 pp.

* Nemiroff, Robert. See K28.

N90. Nevard, M. "[Theodore] Fats Navarro on Record." *Melody Maker* 28 (July 12, 1952), 4.

N91. Nevers, Daniel. "Discographie de [Joseph] King Oliver." *Jazz Hot* 312 (Jan. 1975), 18–9; 333 (Dec. 1976), 36–9.

N92. Nevers, Daniel. "Discographie de [Theodore] Fats Navarro." *Jazz Hot* 328 (June 1976), 26–9.

N93. Nevin, David. "Afro-American Disc Recordings." *Audiovisual Instruction* 17 (Nov. 1972), 30–42.

N94. Nevin, David. *The Black Record: a selected discography of Afro-America on audio discs*. St. Louis, Mo.: Washington University Libraries, Audio Visual Department, 1969, 11 pp. A revised edition in 1973 contained 19 pp.

* Nevin, David. See also D5.

N95. "New Acquisitions in the Board Library." *Read, See and Hear* 19:5 (Jan. 15, 1971), 3 pp. Issued by the Newark, N.J., Board of Education, Department of Libraries and Audiovisual Education. This supplements 17:2 and 18:4.

N96. "New Negro Libraries." *Crisis* 39 (Sept. 1932), 284–5.

N97. *New Orleans and Chicago Jazz*. London, England: Discographical Society, 1947, 24 pp.

N98. "New Orleans Jazz Band." *Record Research* 1:1 (Feb. 1955), 11; 1:4 (Aug. 1955), 10.

N99. Newby, Corene. *Black America: past-present-future*. Lima, Ohio: Lima Public Library, 18 pp.

N100. Newby, James E. "Black Authors: an annotated bibliography of autobiographies and biographies." *Black Books Bulletin* 6 (1980), 90–6.

N101. Newby, James E. *Black Authors and Education: an annotated bibliography of books*. Washington, D.C.: University Press of America, 1980, 113 pp.

N102. Newby, James E. "Black Authors in Philosophy, Psychology and Religion: an annotated bibliography of selected books." *Journal of Religious Thought* 36 (Spring-Summer 1979), 61–5.

N103. Newman, Debra L. *Selected Documents Pertaining to Black Workers among the Records of the Department of Labor and Its Component Bureaus 1902–1969*. Special List 40. Washington, D.C.: National Archives and Records Service, 1977, 55 pp.

N104. Newman, Richard. "Bibliography: periodical readings [on Black Power]." *In* Floyd B. Barbour, ed. *The Black Power Revolt*. Boston: Porter Sargent, 1968, pp. 273–7. Published also by Collier Books.

N105. Newman, Richard. "Bishop James A. Healy: a bibliography of secondary sources." *Newsletter of the Afro-American Religious History Group of the American Academy of Religion* 4:2 (Spring 1980), 3–4.

N106. Newman, Richard. *Black Index: Afro-Americana in selected periodicals, 1907–1949.* New York: Garland Publishing, 1981, 266 pp.

N107. Newman, Richard. *Black Power: a bibliography.* Wakefield, Mass.: Community Change, Inc., 1969, 20 pp.

N108. Newman, Richard. "A Preliminary List of Bibliographies on Afro-American Religion." *Newsletter of the Afro-American Religious History Group of the American Academy of Religion* 5:2 (Spring 1981), 8–12.

N109. Newman, Richard. "Sermons of Lemuel Haynes." *Newsletter of the Afro-American Religious History Group of the American Academy of Religion* 4:1 (Fall 1979), 7–8.

N110. Newman, Richard. "Some Recent Bibliographic Resources for Black Religion." *Newsletter of the Afro-American Religious History Group of the American Academy of Religion* 2:1 (Fall 1977), 3.

* Newman, Richard. See also S187.

N111. *Newspapers and Periodicals by and about Black People: Southeastern library holdings.* African-American Materials Project Staff, School of Library Science, North Carolina Central University. Boston, Mass.: G.K. Hall, 1978, 180 pp.

N112. *Niagara University Library Holdings in Black Literature.* Niagara, N.Y.: Niagara University Library, 1970, 57 pp.

N113. Niccols, Barbara, and Bernice Lawson. *List of Materials Purchased Cooperatively with Other NAPCU [Northwest Association of Private Colleges and Universities] Libraries.* McMinnville, Ore.: Linfield College, Northrup Library.

N114. Nichols, Margaret S. *Multicultural Educational Materials: bibliography of a demonstration collection assembled for all ages and reading abilities largely in the areas of black and Mexican-American culture.* Menlo Park, Cal.: Menlo Park Public Library, 1970, 53 pp.

N115. Nichols, Margaret S., and Peggy O'Neill. *Multicultural Materials: a selected bibliography of adult materials concerning human relations and the history, culture and current social issues of Black, Chicano, Asian-American and Native American peoples.* Stanford, Cal.: Multicultural Resources, 1974.

N116. Nicolosi, Anthony S. *Slavery in America: manuscripts and other items, 1660–1865, selected from the collection of Philip D. and Elsie O. Sang.* New Brunswick, N.J.: Rutgers University Library, 1963, 16 pp.

N117. *948 Titles on Negro History and Culture.* Dayton, Ohio: Dayton and Montgomery County Public Library, 1969.

N117A. *1968–1969 Books about the Black Experience in America.* Subject Bibliography no. 7/69. Washington, D.C.: U.S. Information Agency, 1969, 18 pp. See also Subject Bibliographies no. 11/68 and 11/68A.

N117B. "1965 and 1966: happy new years for non-fiction books about the Negro, for young people and children." *Negro History Bulletin* 30 (Nov. 1967), 15–7.

N118. Niquet, Bernard. "Chambers Brothers." *Jazz Hot* 246 (Jan. 1969), 38–9.

N119. Niquet, Bernard. "Deux Pionniers Méconnus: Ike et Tina Turner." *Jazz Hot* 243 (Oct. 1968), 14–6.

N120. Niquet, Bernard. "Ethel Waters Discography." *Le Point du Jazz* 6 (Mar. 1972), 5–18.

N121. Niquet, Bernard. "Jay McShann ou la légende de K.C." *Jazz Hot* 235 (Oct. 1967), 23–5.

N122. Niquet, Bernard. "Otto Hardwick, 1904–1970." *Le Point du Jazz* 10 (Oct. 1974), 44 + .

N123. Niquet, Bernard. "Une valeur sûre du blues: Muddy Waters." *Jazz Hot* 243 (Oct. 1968), 25.

N124. *No Crystal Stair: a bibliography of black literature.* New York: The New York Public Library, Office of Adult Services, 1971, 63 pp. This is called the 10th edition of "The Negro in the U.S."

N125. [Noble Sissle Discography]. *Record Research* 1:1 (Feb. 1955), 7 + .

N126. Noel, D.C. "The Black and the Library." *Catholic Library World* 43 (Dec. 1971), 183–6.

* Noone, George. See C213.

N127. Nordholt, J.W. Schulte. "Beredeneerde Bibliografie Over de Geschiedenis van de Neger in de V.S. [Critical bibliography of the history of the Negro in the U.S.]." *Kleio* [Netherlands] 7:2 (1966), 4–11.

N128. Nordlie, Margaret. *Guide to Afro-American Material in the Carl B. Ylvisaker Library.* Moorhead, Minn.: Concordia College, Carl B. Ylvisaker Library, 62 pp.

N129. Norgen, Paul A. *Racial Discrimination in Employment.* Princeton, N.J.: Princeton University, Industrial Relations Section, 1962, 4 pp.

* Norman, L.V. See K81.

N130. Norris, John. "Collector's Classics: a survey of recent blues reissues." *Coda* 7:12 (Feb.-Mar. 1967), 6–10.

N131. Norris, John. "The Listening Dog Bites Back [Louis Armstrong]." *Coda* 10:6 (Mar.-Apr. 1972), 6–8.

N132. Norris, John. "Louis Armstrong on Record: Ambassador Satch." *Coda* 11:2 (July-Aug. 1973), 34 + .

N133. Norris, John. "A Musical Autobiography of Louis Armstrong." *Jazz Journal* 11 (Feb. 1958), 24–6.

N134. Norris, John. "The Other Side of Louis Armstrong: a discography of privately recorded film sound tracks, concerts, and broadcasts." *Coda* 11:2 (July-Aug. 1973), 40–6.

N135. Norris, John. "Sound of Harlem." *Coda* 7:8 (June-July 1966).

* Norris, John. See also B4, L162.

* Norwitch, Susan. See B67.

N136. *Not Just Some of Us: a limited bibliography on minority group relations*. Washington, D.C.: U.S. Department of Health, Education, and Welfare, Social Security Administration, Office of Administration, Special Staff for Employee Management Relations and Equal Employment Opportunity, 1963, 29 pp. Issues of 1968 contained 29 pp. and of 1969, 42 pp.

N137. "Notable Children's Trade Books in the Field of Social Studies." *Social Education* 37:8 (Dec. 1973), 784–92.

N138. *Novels by Black Authors*. Cleveland, Ohio: Cleveland Public Library, 1970, 3 pp.

N139. "Now on Hand at Your Jazz Museum." *The Second Line* 22 (Sept.-Oct. 1970), 398–410.

N140. Nutter, David L. *A List of Black History and Literature [Ludgood-Walker Afro-American Collection]*. Winfield, Kan.: Southwestern College, Memorial Library.

N141. Nyang, Suleyman S. "Islam in the U.S.: a review of the sources." *Search: Journal for Arab and Islamic Studies* 1:2 (1980), 164–82.

O

O1. Oaks, Priscilla S. *Minority Studies: a selective annotated bibliography*. Boston, Mass.: G.K. Hall, 1976, 304 pp.

O2. O'Brien, Gail. *Bibliography on Black American Studies*. Plattsburgh, N.Y.: SUNY at Plattsburgh, Benjamin F. Feinburg Library.

O3. Obudho, Constance E. *Black-White Racial Attitudes: an annotated bibliography*. Westport, Conn.: Greenwood Press, 1976, 180 pp.

O4. O'Daniel, Therman B. "Langston Hughes: a selected classified bibliography." *College Language Association Journal* 11:4 (June 1968), 349–66.

O5. Odum, Howard W. "Brief Bibliography of Negro Folk Songs." *Journal of American Folklore* 24 (Oct.-Dec. 1911), 393–4.

O6. Odum, Howard W. "Regional Portraiture in Bibliography." *Saturday Review* 6 (July 27, 1929), 1–2.

* Ogman, M. Kay. See D8.

O7. O'Hara, Minna. *Employment Problems and Opportunities of Minority Groups: the past, present and future of Negroes and Puerto Ricans in the world of work*. New York: Board of Education of the City of New York, Office of the Assistant Superintendent, 1965, 4 pp.

* Okpaku, Joseph. See P13.

* O'Laughlin, Mary Ann. See H28.

O8. Oliver, Paul. "Blues on the 'Southern Folk Heritage' LPs." *Jazz Monthly* 7 (Feb. 1962), 21–5.

O9. Oliver, Paul. "Blues '65." *Jazz* 4:7 (1965), 26–9.

* Oliver, Paul. See also Mc15.

O10. Olsson, Martin. *A Selected Bibliography of Black Literature: the Harlem Renaissance.* American Arts Pamphlet no. 2. Exeter, England: University of Exeter, American Arts Documentation Center, 1973, 24 pp.

* OMANii(*sic*), Abdullah. See H35A.

O11. O'Meally, Robert G. "An Annotated Bibliography of Works by Sterling A. Brown." *College Language Association Journal* 19 (Dec. 1975), 268–79.

O12. *On Being Black.* Youngstown, Ohio: Public Library of Youngstown and Mahoning County, 1968, 4 pp.

O13. *One Hundred Years of Freedom: a selected bibliography of books about the American Negro.* Washington, D.C.: Association for the Study of Negro Life and History.

O14. *One Step Forward.* Canton, Ohio: Canton Public Library, Children's Department, 1968.

O15. Not used.

O16. Not used.

O17. Not used.

* O'Neill, Mora. See C13, C17.

* O'Neill, Peggy. See N115.

O18. *The Opening Day Collection.* Atlanta, Ga.: Martin Luther King, Jr., Memorial Center Library, Documentation Project, 1969, 32 pp.

O19. Opperman, Harry Earl III. "A Bibliography and 'Stemma Codicum' for British Editions of 'Uncle Tom's Cabin,' 1852–1853." Ph.D. dissertation, Kansas State University, 1971.

O20. Opperman, Harry Earl III. "Two Ghost Editions of 'Uncle Tom's Cabin.' " *Papers of the Bibliographic Society of America* 65 (1971), 295–6.

O21. O'Quinlivan, Michael, and Benjamin F. Speller, Jr. "An Index to Obituary Sketches in the 'Journal of Negro History,' 1926–1958." *Journal of Negro History* 57 (Oct. 1972), 447–54.

O22. O'Rourke, Martha, and Robert Heath. *Guide to Stillman College Archives.* Tuscaloosa, Ala.: Stillman College, William H. Sheppard Library, 4 pp.

O23. Osborn, Francis H., Jr. *Resource Handbook in Human Relations.* Cleveland, Ohio: Council on Human Relations, 1959, 75 pp.

O24. "Otis Redding: a singles discography." *Music World and Record Digest Weekly News* 63 (Sept. 19, 1974), 6. Reprinted from *Stak-O-Wax.*

O25. Ottaway, L.M. "Read, Baby, Read: a first step to action." *Christianity Today* 14 (Dec. 19, 1969), 6–8.

O26. *Our American Heritage: a suggested book list.* San Mateo, Cal.: San Mateo School District, 5 pp.

O27. Overton, Holda, and James Poole. *Bibliography on the History of the Negro*. Tougaloo, Miss.: Tougaloo College, Eastman Library.

O28. Ovington, Mary White. "Certain Books on the Negro [in the American Library in Paris]." *Ex Libris* 2:9 (June 1925), 263–4.

O29. Owen, F., and L. Wright. "The Country Blues: a survey of currently available LPs and EPs." *Storyville* 9 (Feb. 1967), 14–6.

O30. Owens, Irene. "Black World Religious Resources at the Howard University School of Religion Library." *Journal of Religious Thought* 32 (Fall-Winter 1975), 113–23.

O31. Oxley, Lawrence A. *Bibliography on Negro Labor*. Washington, D.C.: U.S. Bureau of Labor Statistics, 1937, 34 pp. A 5 pp. supplement was issued in 1938.

P

P1. Page, James A. *Selected Black American Authors: an illustrated bio-bibliography*. Boston, Mass.: G.K. Hall, 1977, 398 pp.

P2. Pagenstecher, Ann. "Martin Luther King, Jr.: an annotated checklist." *Bulletin of Bibliography* 24 (Jan.-Apr. 1965), 201–7.

P3. Paige, Earl. *Black Music: a genealogy of sound*. Billboard, 197?, 40 pp.

P4. Pailhe, Joel. "My Favorite Things [John Coltrane]." *Jazz Hot* 38 (Dec. 1972), 14–6.

P5. Palmer, B. "Jazz: the classic on record." *Rolling Stone* 76 (Feb. 18, 1971), 54+.

P6. Palmer, Pamela, and R.D. Bohanan. *The Robert R. Church Family of Memphis: guide to the papers with selected facsimiles of documents and photos*. Memphis, Tenn.: Memphis State University Press, 1979, 87 pp.

P7. Panassié, Hugues. *Discographie critique des meilleurs disques de jazz*. Paris, France: Laffont, 1958, 621 pp.

P8. Panassié, Hugues. *Histoires des disques swing, enregistrés à New York par Tommy Ladnier, Mezz Mezzrow, Frank Newton, etc*. Geneva, Switzerland: Ch. Grasset, 1944, 117 pp.

P9. Panassié, Hugues. *Quand Mezzrow enregistre: histoire des disques de Milton Mezzrow et Tommy Ladnier*. Paris, France: Robert Laffont, 1952.

P10. *Paperbacks on Intergroup Relations, 1964*. New York: National Conference of Christians and Jews, 1964.

P11. *The Papers of the Congress of Racial Equality, 1941–1967; a guide to the microfilm edition*. Sanford, N.C.: Microfilming Corporation of America, 1980.

P11A. Paramoure, Ann F. *Understanding One Another: a selected list of books on interracial and intercultural relations*. White Plains, N.Y.: Westchester Library Association, 1946, 9 pp.

P12. Parchevskaia, B.M. *Langston Hughes: a bibliographical guide*. All-Union State Library of Foreign Literature. Moscow, U.S.S.R.: Kniga, 1964, 90 pp.

P13. Paricsy, P. "Supplement to Janheinz Jahn's Bibliography of Neo-African Literature: Africa, America, and the Caribbean." *In* Joseph Okpaku, ed. *New African Literature and the Arts*, Vol. 2. New York: Crowell, 1970, pp. 231–45.

P14. Parker, Charlie. "My Best on Wax." *Down Beat* 18 (June 29, 1951), 15.

P15. Parker, Franklin. *Negro Education in the USA: a bibliography of doctoral dissertations*. Austin, Tex.: Author(?), 1960, 9 pp.

P15A. Parker, Franklin. "Negro Education in the USA: a partial bibliography of doctoral dissertations." *Negro History Bulletin* 24:8 (May 1961), 192 + ; 25 (Oct. 1961), 24 + .

P16. Parker, Franklin. "Public School Desegregation: a partial bibliography of 113 doctoral dissertations." *Negro History Bulletin* 26:7 (Apr. 1963), 225–8.

P17. Parker, Franklin. "School Desegregation: a partial list of 94 doctoral dissertations." *Journal of Human Relations* 10 (Autumn 1961), 118–24.

P18. Parker, Franklin. "Teaching for World Understanding: a bibliographical essay on international and multicultural education." *Phi Delta Kappan* 51 (Jan. 1970), 276–81.

P19. Parker, James E. *Media Relating to the Black Man*. Durham, N.C.: North Carolina College, 1969, 74 pp.

P20. Parker, John W. "A Bibliography of the Published Writings of Benjamin Griffith Brawley." *North Carolina Historical Review* 34:2 (Apr. 1957), 165–78.

* Parker, Margaret. See F39.

P21. Parker, W.J. "Famous Melodies, Own Negro Authorship: rare manuscripts collected by Maud Cuney Hare reveal musical inheritance of race from sixth century when Mahet was favorite singer." *Musical America* (Aug. 9, 1924).

* Parks, Lanetta. See H27.

P22. Parks, Martha. *The Negro: a selected list for school librarians of books by or about the Negroes in Africa and America*. Rev. ed. Nashville, Tenn.: Tennessee Department of Education, 1941, 48 pp.

P23. Parry, W.H., and D. Stewart-Baxter. "Lil Green Discography." *Playback* 3 (Feb. 1950), 13–4.

P24. Parsons, Elsie Clews. "Tales from Guilford County, North Carolina." *Journal of American Folk-Lore* 30 (Apr.-June 1917), 170.

P25. *A Partial List of Community Studies on the Social and Economic Conditions of Minority Population in Various Cities, 1940–1967*. New York: National Urban League, 8 pp.

P25A. Partington, Paul G. *An Annotated Index to the Collected Short Works of W.E.B. Du Bois, 1883–1922*. Whittier, Cal.: Author.

P25B. Partington, Paul G. *A Bibliography of the Contributions of Dr. W.E.B. Du Bois to "Freedom,"* vols. *1–5.* Whittier, Cal.: Author, 1 p.

P25C. Partington, Paul G. *Bibliography of W.E.B. Du Bois's Contributions to the "National Guardian."* Whittier, Cal.: Author, 5 pp.

P26. Partington, Paul G. "A Checklist of the Creative Writings of W.E.B. Du Bois." *Black American Literature Forum* 13:3 (Fall 1979), 110–1.

P27. Partington, Paul G. *An Index to Biographical Sketches in the Published Writings of W.E.B. Du Bois.* Whittier, Cal.: Author, 13 pp.

P27A. Partington, Paul G. *An Index to the "Brownies' Book."* Whittier, Cal.: Author.

P28. Partington, Paul G. *W.E.B. Du Bois: a bibliography of his published writings.* Whittier, Cal.: Author, 1977, 202 pp.

P29. Partridge, Dorothy. *The Negro/Black/Afro-American: yesterday, today, tomorrow.* Farmingdale, N.Y.: Farmingdale High School, 1969, 14 pp.

P30. Pastorette, Tomma N. *Race Relations: selected references.* Rev. ed. Special Bibliography no. 200. Maxwell Air Force Base, Ala.: U.S. Department of Defense, Air Force, Air University Library, 1975, 38 pp.

P31. Patrick, James S. "Discography as a Tool for Musical Research." *Journal of Jazz Studies* 1:1 (Oct. 1973), 65–81.

* Patrick, Reinhart W. See W17A.

P32. Patterson, Cecil L. "A Different Drum: the image of the Negro in the Nineteenth Century Songster." *College Language Association Journal* 8 (Sept. 1944), 44–50.

P33. Patterson, John S. *William Stanley Braithwaite: a register of his papers in the Syracuse University Library.* Syracuse, N.Y.: Syracuse University Library, 1964, 18 pp.

P34. Pawley, James A. *The American Negro: a select reading list.* Hackensack, N.J.: Works Progress Administration, 1937, 32 pp.

* Pawley, Thomas D. See R34.

P35. *Peabody Collection of Works by and about Negroes.* Hampton, Va.: Hampton Institute, 1945.

P36. Peabody, Ina. *Chester Himes.* CAAS Bibliography no. 3. Atlanta, Ga.: Center for African and African American Studies, 17 pp.

* Peabody, Patricia. See R160.

P37. Peabody, Ruth. *The Afro-Americans: their heritage and contributions; education: a guide to black education materials, a selected bibliography.* Albany, N.Y.: SUNY at Albany, University Libraries, 1977, 70 pp.

P38. Peabody, Ruth. *The Afro-Americans: their heritage and contributions; reference.* Albany, N.Y.: SUNY at Albany, University Libraries, 1975, 44 pp.

* Peace, Glenda. See K69.

* Pearlmutter, Jane. See C17.

P39. Pearson, Bill. "Country Muddy Waters: a survey of Muddy's early recordings." *Jazz Journal* 27:6 (June 1974), 12 + .

P40. Peavy, Charles D. *Afro-American Literature and Culture Since World War II: a guide to information sources*. Detroit, Mich.: Gale Research, 1979, 302 pp.

P40A. Peavy, Charles D. "Black Journals at the University of Houston." *ALDUS* (Apr. 1970).

P41. Peck, I. "New Books on Negro History." *Senior Scholastic* 91 (Jan. 18, 1968).

P42. Peebles, Joan. *Black Studies: a dissertation bibliography; doctoral research on the Negro, 1966–1977*. Ann Arbor, Mich.: University Microfilms, 1978(?), 65 pp. A supplement to Earle H. West (W55).

* Peebles, Joan. See also W55.

P43. Peek, Phillip M. *Catalog of Afro-American Music and Oral Data Holdings in the Archives of Traditional Music*. Bloomington, Ind.: Indiana University Folklore Institute, 1970.

P44. *The Pen is Mightier: a catalogue of publications in the field of human relations*. New York: American Jewish Committee. 5 volumes were issued from 1950 to 1956.

* Pendell, Lucille. See B80.

P45. Pendergrass, Margaret E., and Catherine E. Roth. "Selected List of Books by and about the Negro." *Illinois Libraries* 51 (Jan. 1969), 62–82. A supplement appeared in 52 (Feb. 1970), 211–33.

P46. Penn, Joseph E., Elaine C. Brooks, and Mollie L. Beech. *The Negro American in Paperback: a selected list of paperbound books compiled and annotated for secondary school students*. Washington, D.C.: National Education Association, National Committee on Professional Rights and Responsibilities, Committee on Civil and Human Rights of Educators, 1967, 28 pp. An edition of 45 pp. was issued in 1968.

P46A. Pensoneault, Ken, and Carl Sarles. *Jazz Discography*. New York: The Needle, 1944, 145 pp.

P47. Peplow, Michael W., and Robert S. Bravard. *Samuel R. Delany: a primary and secondary bibliography*. Boston, Mass.: G.K. Hall, 1980, 112 pp.

P48. Perin, Jacques. "Les Albums de Bo Diddley [Ellas McDaniel]." *Soul Bag* 61 (June 1977), 10.

P49. Perin, Jacques. "[Antoine (Fats)] Domino Walking to New Orleans." *Jazz Magazine* 200 (May 1972), 18–9.

* Perin, Jacques. See also D4, M116, M117.

* Perry, Jeanne. See J48.

P50. Perry, Margaret. *A Bio-Bibliography of Countee P. Cullen, 1903–1946*. Westport, Conn.: Greenwood Press, 1971, 134 pp. Based on M.A. thesis, Catholic University of America, 1959.

P51. Perry, Margaret. *The Harlem Renaissance: an annotated bibliography and commentary*. New York: Garland Publishing, 1982, 272 pp.

P52. Perry, Margaret. *Silence to the Drums: a survey of the literature of the*

Harlem Renaissance. Westport, Conn.: Greenwood Press, 1976, 194 pp.

P52A. Perry, Patricia H. *Charlemae Hill Rollins: a bibliography*. Durham, N.C.: North Carolina Central University School of Library Science, 1980, 7 pp. Plus a list of contributors to the Black Librarians Collection, 1978–1982, and a list of contributors (1975–1982) to the William Tucker Collection of the works of black authors and illustrators of children's materials.

* Perry, Pennie. See H115, S253.

P53. Peters, Martha. *Where Do We Go from Here? A Question for Memphis and the Nation: a selected bibliography on the changing role of the Negro*. Memphis, Tenn.: Memphis Public Library, Adult Services Department, 1968, 14 pp.

P54. Peters, S. "Black Experience in Books." *Top of the News* 25 (June 1969), 384–7.

* Pettigrew, T.F. See H11.

P55. Pfeiffer, John. "Black American Speculative Literature: a checklist." *Extrapolation* 17 (Dec. 1975), 35–43.

P56. Pflieger, E.F. "Bibliography on Afro-American History and Culture." *Social Education* 33 (Apr. 1969), 447–61.

P57. *Phelps-Stokes Fellowship Papers, University of Virginia*. Charlottesville, Va.: University of Virginia, Alderman Library, 2 pp.

P58. Phillips, Linda N. "Piano Music by Black Composers: a computer-based bibliography." D.M.A. thesis, Ohio State University, 1977.

P59. Phillips, Myrtle R., and C.L. Miller. "A Selected Annotated Bibliography on the Relationship of the Federal Government to Negro Education." *Journal of Negro Education* 7:3 (July 1938), 468–74.

P60. Phillips, Robert Ethel. *Folk Literature Reflecting the Unity of Races: a bibliography*. Los Angeles, Cal.: Office of the County Superintendent of Schools, 1943, 10 pp.

P61. Phillips, Romeo E. "A Selected, Annotated Discography: [Thomas A.] Dorsey Songs on Record." *Black World* 23 (July 1974), 29–32.

* Phillis, Susan. See J47.

P62. Phinazee, Annette Hoage. *The Georgia Child's Access to Materials Pertaining to American Negroes*. Presented at a conference sponsored by the Atlanta University School of Library Service and the Georgia Council on Human Relations. Atlanta, Ga.: Atlanta University School of Library Service, 1968, 79 pp.

P63. Phinazee, Annette Hoage. *Materials by and about Negroes*. Institute on Materials by and about American Negroes, 1965. Atlanta, Ga.: Atlanta University School of Library Service, 1967, 111 pp.

P64. Phipps, Claire A. *Afro-Americana in the Library of Chico State College*. Chico, Cal.: Chico State College Library, 1969, 66 pp.

P65. "Piano Roll-ography [James P. Johnson]." *Record Research* 1 (Apr. 1955), 19.

P65A. Piccinato, Stefania. "La letteratura afro-americana in Italia. Nota bibliografica a cura di Stefania Piccinato." *Studi americani* 17 (1971), 473–505.

P66. Piccolo, Vincent, and Daniel Dick. *Black Studies Library*. Worcester, Mass.: Worcester State College Library.

P67. Pier, Helen Louis, and Mary Louisa Spalding. "The Negro: a selected bibliography." *Monthly Labor Review* 22:1 (Jan. 1926), 216–44.

P68. Piker, Jeffrey. *Entry into the Labor Force: a survey of literature on the experience of Negro and white youths*. Ann Arbor, Mich.: University of Michigan-Wayne State University, Institute of Labor and Industrial Relations, 1969, 282 pp.

P69. Pinkett, Harold T. "Recent Federal Archives as Sources for Negro History." *Negro History Bulletin* 30 (Dec. 1967), 14–7.

P70. Pinto, Patrick R., and J.O. Buchmier. *Problems and Issues in the Employment of Minority, Disadvantaged, and Female Groups: an annotated bibliography*. Minneapolis, Minn.: University of Minnesota, Industrial Relations Center, 1973, 62 pp.

P71. Plank, Marietta. *The New Revolution: a selected reading list*. Washington, D.C.: Georgetown University Library, 1968, 6 pp.

P72. Pleasants, Henry. "Gladys Knight and the Pips: 25 years!" *Stereo Review* 38:4 (Apr. 1977), 92–3.

P73. Podlish, Phillip, Alice Weaver, Kathleen Voight, and Patricia Barringer. *The Black Experience: the Negro in America, Africa, and the world; a comprehensive, annotated subject bibliography of works in the University of Toledo libraries*. Toledo, Ohio: University of Toledo, 1969, 74 pp. An edition of 1970 contained 83 pp.

P74. Poehlman, Dorothy. *Equal Employment Opportunity: selected references*. Washington, D.C.: U.S. Department of Transportation, Federal Aviation Administration, Library Services Division, 1968, 7 pp.

P75. *Poetry, Music and Art*. The Black Culture Series for Young Readers. Chicago, Ill.: Chicago Public Library, 1972, 4 pp.

* Pointer, W. Donald. See W149A.

P76. *The Police and Race Relations: a selected bibliography*. New York: American Jewish Committee, Institute of Human Relations, 1966, 14 pp.

P77. Polk, Alma Forrest. "Recent Books on Intercultural Education." *Social Science* 22 (Jan. 1947), 40–3.

P78. Pollak-Eltz, Angelina. "Afro-American Studies." *Review of Ethnology* [Vienna] 8 (Apr. 1969), 1–8; 9 (May 1969), 1–4.

* Pollard, Richard. See D87.

P79. Pollard, William Robert. *Black Literature: a classified bibliography of newspapers, periodicals, and books by and about the Negro in the D.H. Hill Library, North Carolina State University at Raleigh*. Raleigh, N.C.: North Carolina State University at Raleigh, 1969, 77 pp. A supplement was issued in 1970.

P80. Polsgrove, Carol. "Addenda to 'A Ralph Waldo Ellison Bibliography, 1914–1968.' " *American Book Collector* 20 (Nov.-Dec. 1969), 11–2. Supplements R. Stewart Lillard's article of Nov. 1968 (L75).

* Polsgrove, Carol. See also L75.

P81. Polts, Alfred M. *Knowing and Educating the Disadvantaged: an annotated bibliography.* ERIC Document no. ED 012–189. Alamoso, Cal.: Adams State College, 1965, 462 pp.

* Poole, James. See O27.

P82. "Pops Foster's Early Records." *Record Research* 34 (Apr. 1961), 13.

P83. Porter, B. "One Sweet Letter from You: bebopdiscography." *Jazz Journal* 22 (Jan. 1969), 16.

P84. Porter, Bob. "Great Chicago Jazz! Gene Ammons." *Different Drummer* 1 (Oct./Nov. 1974), 14.

P85. Porter, Dorothy B. "Afro-American Writings Published before 1835, with an Alphabetical List (Tentative) of Imprints Written by American Negroes, 1760–1835." M.A. thesis, Columbia University, 1932.

P86. Porter, Dorothy B. *American Negro Collections: a list of references.* 4 pp.

P87. Porter, Dorothy B. "A Bibliographical Checklist of American Negro Writers about Africa." *In* "Africa Seen by American Negroes." *Présence Africaine* (1958), 379–99.

P88. Porter, Dorothy B. "Bibliography and Research in Afro-American Scholarship." *Journal of Academic Librarianship* 2 (May 1976), 77–81.

P89. Porter, Dorothy B. "Bibliography: books, bulletins, pamphlets." *Journal of Negro Education* 29:4 (Fall 1960), 470–80.

P90. Porter, Dorothy B., ed. *A Catalogue of the African Collection in the Moorland Foundation, Howard University Library.* Compiled by Students in the Program of African Studies. Washington, D.C.: Howard University Press, 1958, 398 pp.

P91. Porter, Dorothy B. "Documentation on the Afro-American: familiar and less familiar sources." *African Studies Bulletin* 12 (Dec. 1969), 293–303.

P92. Porter, Dorothy B. "Early American Negro Writings: a bibliographical study with a preliminary checklist of the published writings of American Negroes, 1760–1835." *Papers of the Bibliographic Society of America* 39:3 (Third Quarter 1945), 192–268.

P92A. Porter, Dorothy B. "Early Manuscript Letters Written by Negroes." *Journal of Negro History* 5 (Apr. 1939), 199–210.

P93. Porter, Dorothy B. "Family Records, a Major Source for Documenting the Black Experience in New England." *Old-Time New England* 63:3 (1973), 69–72.

P94. Porter, Dorothy B. *Howard University Masters' Theses Submitted in Partial Fulfillment of the Requirements for the Master's Degree at Howard University, 1918–1945.* Washington, D.C.: Howard University, Graduate School, 1946.

P95. Porter, Dorothy B. "A Library on the Negro." *American Scholar* 7 (Winter 1938), 115–7.

P96. Porter, Dorothy B. "Library Resources for the Study of Negro Life and History." *Journal of Negro Education* 5 (Apr. 1936), 232–44; 11 (Oct. 1942), 527–8.

P97. Porter, Dorothy B. "Luther P. Jackson, Bibliographical Notes." *Negro History Bulletin* 13 (June 1950), 213–5.

P98. Porter, Dorothy B. *The Negro in American Cities: a selected and annotated bibliography*. Prepared for the National Advisory Commission on Civil Disorders. Washington, D.C.: Howard University Library, 1967, 206 pp.

P99. Porter, Dorothy B. *The Negro in the U.S.: a selected bibliography*. Washington, D.C.: Library of Congress, 1970, 313 pp.

P100. Porter, Dorothy B. *The Negro in the United States: a working bibliography*. Ann Arbor, Mich.: University Microfilms, 1969, 128 pp.

P101. Porter, Dorothy B. *North American Negro Poets: a bibliographical checklist of their writings, 1760–1944*. Hattiesburg, Miss.: Book Farm, 1945, 90 pp.

P102. Porter, Dorothy B. "The Preservation of University Documents with Special Reference to Negro Colleges and Universities." *Journal of Negro Education* 11 (Oct. 1942), 527–8.

P103. Porter, Dorothy B. *Reading List on the Negro in the U.S. and Other Countries*. Washington, D.C.: Howard University, Moorland Foundation, 1944, 17 pp.

P104. Porter, Dorothy B. "Recent Literature on the Negro." *Quarterly Review of Higher Education Among Negroes* 8:3 (July 1940), 118–23.

P105. Porter, Dorothy B. *A Selected Bibliography of Bibliographies on the Negro*, 10 pp.

P106. Porter, Dorothy B. *A Selected List of Books by and about the Negro*. Washington, D.C.: U.S. Department of Commerce, Bureau of Foreign and Domestic Commerce, 1936, 9 pp.

P107. Porter, Dorothy B. "A Selected List of Books with Negro Characters for Young Children." *National Educational Outlook among Negroes* 1 (Dec. 1937), 33–5; (Jan. 1938), 27–9.

P108. Porter, Dorothy B. "Selected References on the American Negro in World War I and World War II." *Journal of Negro Education* 12 (Summer 1943), 579–85.

P109. Porter, Dorothy B. "Selected Writings by Negro Women." *Women's Education* 7 (Dec. 1968), 4–5.

P109A. Porter, Dorothy B. "Some Books Featuring Negro Characters for Young Children." *National Educational Outlook among Negroes* 1 (Sept. 1937), 14–5.

P110. Porter, Dorothy B. "Some Recent Literature Pertaining to the American Negro." *The Wilson Bulletin for Librarians* 9 (June 1935), 569–70.

P111. Porter, Dorothy B., and Ethel M.V. Ellis. *"The Journal of Negro Education": index to vols. 1–31, 1932–1962.* Washington, D.C.: Howard University Press, 1963, 82 pp.

P112. Porter, Dorothy B., and Betty Jo Lanier. *Howard University: a selected list of references.* Washington, D.C.: Howard University Library, 1965, 9 pp.

P112A. Porter, Dorothy B., and Dolores C. Leffall. "Bibliography." *Journal of Negro Education* 29:2 (Spring 1960), 168–73.

* Porter, Dorothy. See also H127.

P113. Porter, Jack N. "Black-Jewish Relations: some notes on cross-cultural research plus a selected annotated bibliography." *International Review of Sociology* (Sept. 1971), 1–9.

P114. Porter, Nancy, and Pauline Lilje. *A Guide to Washington State University Library Materials for the Black Studies Program.* Pullman, Wash.: Washington State University Library.

P115. *Portraits: literature of minorities, an annotated bibliography of literature by and about four ethnic groups in the U.S. [Black, Mexican-American, North American Indian, Asian-American] for grades 7–12.* Los Angeles, Cal.: Superintendent of Schools, Los Angeles County Office, 1970, 70 pp.

P116. Posselt, Jane. *Bibliography of Books and Pamphlets in the Middlesex County College Library Which Deal with the Negro in the U.S.* Edison, N.J.: Middlesex County College Library, 1969.

P117. Postif, François. "Ike and Tina [Turner]." *Jazz Hot* 270 (Mar. 1971), 6–11.

P118. Potter, R. Ancil. *A Bibliography on Minority Contributions to United States Aviation.* Washington, D.C.: U.S. Department of Transportation, Federal Aviation Administration, 1971, 8 pp.

P119. Potts, Alfred M. *Knowing and Educating the Disadvantaged: an annotated bibliography.* Alamosa, Cal.: Adams State College, Center for Cultural Studies, 1965, 460 pp.

P120. Poulos, Angela, and Iris Jones. *Black Culture: a selective bibliography.* 3d ed. Bowling Green, Ohio: Bowling Green State University Libraries, Reference Department, 1974, 134 pp. An edition of 32 pp. had been published in 1970.

* Poulos, Angela. See also Mc8.

P121. Pouncy, Mitchell L. "An Annotated Cumulated Index to 'Phylon Quarterly' from 1950 through 1959." M.A. thesis, Atlanta University School of Library Science, 1961, 205 pp.

P122. *Poverty, Rural Poverty, and Minority Groups Living in Rural Poverty: an annotated bibliography.* ERIC Document no. 041–679. Institute for Rural America. Lexington, Ky.: Spindletop Research Center, 1969, 159 pp.

P123. Powell, Ronald H. *Bibliography for Afro-American Studies.* Largo, Md.: Prince George's Community College Library.

P124. Powers, Anne. *Blacks in American Movies: a selected bibliography.* Metuchen, N.J.: Scarecrow Press, 1974, 167 pp.

P125. *Prejudice and the Child.* New York: American Jewish Committee, 1960, 10 pp. An edition in 1961 also had 10 pp., while one in 1965 contained 14 pp.

P126. "Prejudice in America: optimistic views." *Current History* 32 (May 1957), 301 + .

P127. *Preliminary Author List of Black Literature.* Rosemont, Pa.: Rosemont College Library.

P128. *Preliminary Guide to Black Materials in the Disciples of Christ Historical Society.* Nashville, Tenn.: Disciples of Christ Historical Society, 1971, 32 pp.

P129. *Preliminary List of Resource Materials on Minority Groups.* Olympia, Wash.: Washington Department of Education, 1968, 36 pp.

P130. *The Presence of the Negro in America as Expressed in Films, Filmstrips.* Akron, Ohio: Akron Public Library, 1967, 8 pp.

P131. Pressley, Milton M. *Selected Bibliography of Readings and References Regarding Marketing to Black America.* Exchange Bibliography no. 671. Monticello, Ill.: Council of Planning Librarians, 1974, 36 pp.

P132. Preston, Clarence Johnson, and Julia O. Saunders. *The Education of Negroes in Virginia: an annotated bibliography*, 1944, 16 pp.

P133. Preston, M.B. "Blacks and Public Policy: a selected bibliography." *Policy Studies Journal* 9 (Spring 1981), 775–84.

P134. *The Prevention and Control of Race Riots: a bibliography for police officers.* Social Adjustment Bibliography no. 1. Los Angeles, Cal.: Los Angeles Public Library, Municipal Reference Library, 1944, 12 pp.

P135. Price, Leontyne. "Speaking of Records." *High Fidelity* 19 (May 1969), 28.

P136. Pride, Armistead Scott. *The Black Press: a bibliography.* Madison, Wis.: Association for Education in Journalism, 1968, 37 pp.

P137. Pride, Armistead Scott. *Negro Newspapers on Microfilm: a selected list.* Washington, D.C.: Library of Congress, Photoduplication Service, 1953, 8 pp.

P137A. Pride, Armistead Scott. "A Register and History of Negro Newspapers in the United States, 1827–1950." Ph.D. thesis, Northwestern University, 1950, 426 pp.

P138. Priestley, Brian. "Collectors' [Louis] Armstrong." *Jazz and Blues* 2:3 (June 1972), 29.

P139. Primeau, Ronald. "Bibliography No. 3: Black Literature of the Midwest." *Great Lakes Review* 2:1 (Summer 1975), 51–9.

P140. Prince, Mary, Florine Keeler, and Helen Ingram. *Books by or about Negroes.* Itta Bena, Miss.: Mississippi Valley State College Library.

* Prior, Nancy B. See M93.

P141. *Proud Heritage of the Afro-American.* Rev. ed. Jamaica, N.Y.: Queensborough Public Library, 1968, 10 pp. A third edition of 20 pp. was issued in 1970.

P142. *Proud Heritage: the Negro in America*. Washington, D.C.: District of Columbia Public Library, 1968.

P143. *Provisional Bibliography on Slavery*. Prepared for the UN Library and UN Ad Hoc Committee on Slavery according to an outline supplied by the sponsors. Washington, D.C.: Library of Congress, General Reference and Bibliography Division, 1950, 157 pp.

P144. Psencik, Leroy F. "Teaching about the Negro in Social Studies: a guide to sources." *Social Studies* 61:5 (1970), 195–200.

P145. *Psychological Perspectives on Black Women: a selected bibliography of recent citations*. Washington, D.C.: Committee on Black Women's Concerns, American Psychological Association, 1977, 10 pp.

P146. *Public School Desegregation in the North and West*. Washington, D.C.: U.S. Department of Health, Education, and Welfare, 1966.

P147. *Publications for Brotherhood*. New York: Anti-Defamation League of B'nai B'rith.

P148. "Publications of the Faculty and Staff of West Virginia State College, Jan. 1, 1946-Dec. 31, 1959." *West Virginia State College Bulletin* 47:5 (Aug. 1960), 23 pp.

P149. "Publications of William Stuart Nelson." *Journal of Religious Thought* 35:2 (Fall-Winter 1978–1979), 69.

P150. *Published Negro Material*. Columbia, Mo.: Missouri State Historical Society, 1969(?), 12 pp.

P151. Pusateri, Liborio. "[Joseph] King Oliver on LP: a listing of microgroove reissues. Part 1: 1923–1924." *Collector* 2:3–6 (Mar. 1967), 52–4.

* Pusateri, Liborio. See also M29, M30.

P152. Pyne, Charlynn Spencer. "Books to Share with the Youngest: a selected bibliography of picture books and easy readers for black children." *Black Books Bulletin* 6:3 (1979), 78–81.

Q

Q1. Quarles, Benjamin. "Black History's Ante-bellum Origins." *Proceedings of the American Antiquarian Society* 89:1 (1979), 89–122.

Q2. "Quelques enregistrements marquants de [George] Pops Foster actuellement disponible." *Jazz Hot* (May 1975), 29.

Q3. Querry, Ronald, and Robert E. Fleming. "A Working Bibliography of Black Periodicals." *Studies in Black Literature* 3 (Summer 1972), 31–6.

Q4. Quigless, Helen, et al. *Black Information Index*. Washington, D.C.: Federal City College, Media Center.

Q5. Quintana, Helena. *A Guide to Ethnic Studies at Zimmerman Library*. Albuquerque, N.M.: University of New Mexico, Zimmerman Library.

Q6. Quintana, Helena, Chris Carson, and Charles Becknell. *Afro-American Bibliography*. Albuquerque, N.M.: University of New Mexico, Zimmerman Library.

Q7. Quirk, Tom, and Robert E. Fleming. "Jean Toomer's Contributions to the New Mexico Sentinel." *College Language Association Journal* 19:4 (June 1976), 524–32.

R

R1. "RCA to Cut Long-Lost [Thomas (Fats)] Waller Solos." *Billboard* 63 (Nov. 10, 1951).

R2. Raben, Erik. "Albert Ayler pa skiva." *Orkester Journalen* 35 (May 1967), 8–9.

R3. Raben, Erik. "Discografia di George Russell." *Musica Jazz* 21 (May 1965), 19–21.

R4. Raben, Erik. *A Discography of Free Jazz* [Albert Ayler, Don Cherry, Ornette Coleman, Pharaoh Sanders, Archie Shepp, Cecil Taylor]. Copenhagen, Denmark: Karl E. Knudsen, 1969, 38 pp.

R5. Raben, Erik. "Erich Dolphy." *Musica Jazz* 21 (Nov. 1965), 36–7.

R6. Raben, Erik. "Lester Young Discography." *Jazz Journal* 21 (Jan. 1968), 28–9; 21 (Feb. 1968), 21–2; 21 (Mar. 1968), 17–9.

R7. Raben, Erik. "Quincy Jones Discografi." *Orkester Journelen* 34 (Nov. 1966), 32; 35 (Jan. 1967), 31; 35 (Feb. 1967), 28; 35 (Mar. 1967), 28.

* Raben, Eric. See also W16.

R8. "Race Problem in the U.S." *Chautauquan* 32 (Feb. 1901), 549–50.

R9. *The Race Problem in the U.S.: a brief bibliographical list*. Washington, D.C.: Library of Congress, 1929, 5 pp.

R10. *Race Relations Issues in 1961: a bibliography*. New York: NAACP, 1961(?), 6 pp.

R11. *Race Relations: recordings suggested for use with young adults*. Catskill, N.Y.: Ramapo Catskill Library System, 1968.

R12. *Race Relations: selected references for the study of the integration of minorities in American labor*. Washington, D.C.: Library of Congress, 1944, 38 pp.

R13. *Race Relations, with Special Reference to Employment*. Bibliographic Reference List no. 102. Geneva, Switzerland: International Labour Office, Library, 1963, 8 pp.

R14. *Race Restrictive Covenants: a selected list of references*. Detroit, Mich.: Detroit Public Library. Distributed by the National Association for the Advancement of Colored People, 1946, 8 pp.

R15. Race, S. "[Edward (Duke)] Ellington's Best." *Melody Maker* 34 (Jan. 10, 1959), 5.

R16. *Racism and Education: a review of selected literature relating to segregation, discrimination, and other aspects of racism in education.* ERIC Document no. 034–836. Detroit, Mich.: Michigan-Ohio Regional Education Laboratory, 1969, 93 pp.

R17. *Racism and Reconstruction: a selected, annotated bibliography of periodical articles, 1966–Sept. 1969.* Bibliography Series no. 3. Ithaca, N.Y.: Cornell University, John M. Olin Library, Reference Department, 31 pp.

R18. Rader, Hannelore. *Black American Literature in Eastern Michigan University Library.* Ypsilanti, Mich.: Eastern Michigan University Library, 13 pp.

R19. Ragan, Pauline K., and Mary Simonin. *Black and Mexican American Aging: a selected bibliography.* Los Angeles, Cal.: Ethel Percy Andrus Gerontology Center, University of Southern California, 1977, 32 pp.

R20. Ragatz, Lowell J. *A Guide for the Study of British Caribbean History, 1763–1834, including the Abolition and Emancipation Movements.* Washington, D.C.: Government Printing Office, 1932, 725 pp.

R21. Ralph, George. *The American Theatre, the Negro, and the Freedom Movement: a bibliography.* Chicago, Ill.: City Missionary Society, 1964, 33 pp.

R22. Ramsey, Frederic. *A Guide to Longplay Jazz Records.* New York: Long Player Publications, 1954, 282 pp. Reprinted in 1977 by DaCapo.

* Ramsey, Frederic. See also S176.

* Rana, Phyllis G. See M166.

R23. Randall, A.K. "African American Resources in American Libraries: collection development, reader services and administrative factors." D.L.S. thesis, Columbia University, 1977, 480 pp.

R24. Randall, D. "New Books for Black Readers." *Publishers Weekly* 204 (Oct. 22, 1973), 48–51.

R25. Randall, David A., and John T. Winterich. "One Hundred Good Novels: Stowe, Harriet Beecher: 'Uncle Tom's Cabin.' " *Publishers Weekly* 137 (May 8, 1940), 1931–2.

R26. Randall, Dudley. "Black Emotion and Experience: the literature for understanding." *American Libraries* 4 (Feb. 1973), 86–90.

R27. Randolph, H. Helen. *Urban Education Bibliography: an annotated listing.* New York: Center for Urban Education, 1968, 97 pp.

R28. "A Rare Collection of Negro Literary Works [Julia Davis Collection, St. Louis, Mo., Public Library]." *Negro History Bulletin* 27 (Apr. 1964), 162–3.

R29. "Ray Charles Discography." *Billboard* 78 (Oct. 15, 1966), 10.

R30. Raynham, Warner R. *Bibliographies Relating Various Areas of Theological Study to the Black Experience in America.* Boston, Mass.: Boston Theological Institute, 1973.

* Read, Danny L. See K48.

R31. Reader, Dave. "Early [William] Count Basie on Decca 78's." *Record Collector's Journal* (Apr. 1976), 24.

R32. *Reading for Action: a guide for parish libraries, organizations, and lay apostles.* San Francisco, Cal.: Catholic Interracial Council of the Archdiocese of San Francisco, 26 pp.

R33. *Readings and References in Intergroup Relations.* Washington, D.C.: National Association of Intergroup Relations Officials, 1966.

R34. Reardon, William R., and Thomas D. Pawley. *The Black Teacher and the Dramatic Arts: a dialogue, bibliography, and anthology.* Westport, Conn.: Negro Universities Press, 1970, pp. 70–121.

R35. Reason, J.H. "Librarian Selects Books for This Generation." *Library Service Review* 1 (June 1948), 9–13.

R36. Reason, J.H. "Veterans in College: a bibliography." *Negro College Quarterly* 5 (Mar. 1947), 27–30.

* Rebman, Elizabeth. See D87.

R37. *Recent Books in the Field of Negro Life and Culture, 1966.* Detroit, Mich.: Detroit Public Library, 1966.

R38. "Recent Books on Race and the South." *New South* 21 (Winter 1966), 91–2.

R39. "Recent Contributions to the Study of Negro Songs." *Social Forces* 4 (June 1926), 788–92.

R40. *Recent Klapper Library Acquisitions in Black Studies.* Flushing, N.Y.: Queens College, Paul Klapper Library, 1970, 22 pp.

R41. "Recent Publications by and about Negroes." *Quarterly Review of Higher Education among Negroes* 11 (July 1943), 43.

R42. *Recommended Books.* New York: Council on Interracial Books for Children, 1965.

R43. *Record Albums of Charles Mingus.* New York: Jazz Workshop, 8 pp.

R44. "Records Made by Sleepy John Estes." *Jazz Journal* 3 (Jan. 1950), 3.

R45. "The Records of Muddy Waters." *Jazz Report* 1 (June 1961), 31–2.

R46. Redd, Jan. *The American Negro: his history and literature.* Cupertino, Cal.: DeAnza College Library.

R47. Redden, Carolyn L. "The American Negro: an annotated list of educational films and film strips." *Journal of Negro Education* 33:1 (Winter 1964), 79–82.

* Redden, Carolyn L. See also W101A.

R48. Reddick, Lawrence D. "Bibliographical Problems in Negro Research." *American Council of Learned Societies Bulletin* 32 (Sept. 1941), 26–30.

R49. Reddick, Lawrence D. *Bibliography: the Afro-American experience.* Nashville, Tenn.: Fisk University, Workshop on Negro Culture, 1969, 5 pp.

R50. Reddick, Lawrence D. "Library Facilities for Research in Negro Colleges." *Quarterly Review of Higher Education among Negroes* 8:3 (July 1940), 127–9.

R51. Reddick, Lawrence D. "Library Resources for Negro Studies in the U.S.

and Abroad." *In* W.E.B. Du Bois and Guy B. Johnson, eds. *Encyclopedia of the Negro: preparatory volume with reference lists and reports.* New York: Phelps-Stokes Fund, 1946, pp. 171–90.

R52. Reddick, Lawrence D. "The Negro and the War." *Branch Library Book News* [The New York Public Library] 20:3 (Mar. 1943), 56–7.

R53. Reddick, Lawrence D. "Select Bibliography" [of studies on Negro colleges]. *Journal of Educational Sociology* 19 (Apr. 1946), 512–6.

R54. Reddick, Lawrence D. "A Selected Bibliography for the Exhibit of 'The Contribution of Negro Women to American Civilization.' " *Journal of the National Association of College Women* 19 (1941), 61–3.

R55. Reddick, Lawrence D. "Special Libraries on the Negro." *In* Florence Murray, ed. *The Negro Handbook 1946–1947.* New York: Current Books, 1947, pp. 236–7.

R56. Redding, Saunders. "James Weldon Johnson." *In* Louis D. Rubin. *A Bibliographical Guide to the Study of Southern Literature.* Baton Rouge, La.: Louisiana State University Press, 1969, pp. 228–9.

* Reed, Ishmael. See W47.

R57. Reed, Rex. "The Essential Mabel Mercer." *Stereo Review* 34:2 (Feb. 1975), 90–1.

* Reeder, Barbara. See S235.

R58. Reedy, S.J. "Selected Annotated Bibliography of the Negro Novel, 1954–1964." M.S. in L.S., thesis, Catholic University of America, 1965, 73 pp.

R59. "References on Slavery in the U.S." *Tamiment Institute Library Bulletin* 39 (Nov. 1963), 2–5.

R60. *References Relating to Mixed and Separate Schools, and Legal Aspects of Education in the U.S.* Washington, D.C.: U.S. Office of Education, 2 pp.

R61. Reichard, Max. *The Black Man in St. Louis: a preliminary bibliography.* Exchange Bibliography no. 574. Monticello, Ill.: Council of Planning Librarians, 1974, 36 pp.

R62. Reid, Ira De Augustine. *Negro Youth, Their Social and Economic Backgrounds: a selected bibliography of unpublished studies, 1900–1938.* Washington, D.C.: American Youth Commission of the American Council on Education, 1939, 71 pp.

R63. Reid, John D. "A Discography of Sidney Bechet." *Jazz Information* 2:9 (Nov. 22, 1940), 11–20.

R64. Reid, John D. [*Edward*] *Duke Ellington Discography on Victor and Bluebird Records,* 23 pp.

R64A. Reilly, John M. "Black Literature." *American Literary Scholarship; an annual/1980.* Durham, N.C.: Duke University Press, 1982, pp. 437–68.

R65. Reilly, John M. "Jean Toomer: an annotated checklist of criticism." *Resources for American Literary Study* 4:1 (Spring 1974), 27–56.

R66. Reilly, John M. "Richard Wright." *In* Thomas M. Inge, Jackson R. Bryer, and Maurice Duke, eds. *Black American Writers*, Vol. 2. New York: St. Martin's Press, 1978, pp. 1–46.

R67. Reilly, John M. "Richard Wright: an essay in bibliography." *Resources for American Literary Study* 1 (Autumn 1971), 131–80.

* Reiner, Ethel L. See T82.

R68. Reisner, Robert George. "Bibliography [on Jazz]." *In* Marshall W. Stearns. *The Story of Jazz*. New York: Oxford University Press, 1956, pp. 343–56.

R69. Reisner, Robert George. *The Literature of Jazz: a preliminary bibliography*. New York: The New York Public Library, 1954, 53 pp. Reprinted from the *Bulletin of The New York Public Library* (Mar.-May 1954).

* Render, Sylvia Lyons. See G30.

R70. *Report of Reading List Sub-committee, Young Adult Service Division, Library Service to Disadvantaged Youth*. Chicago, Ill.: American Library Association, 1967.

R70A. *Report of the Commissioner of Education for the Year 1893–1894*. Vol. I. "Bibliography." Part I. "Education of the Colored Race," pp. 1038–47; Part II. "Negroes in America," pp. 1048–56; Part III. "Works by Negro Authors," pp. 1056–61. Washington, D.C.: U.S. Bureau of Education, 1896. Reprinted in Betty Kaplan Gubert. *Early Black Bibliographies, 1863–1918*. New York: Garland, 1982, pp. 41–65.

R71. *Report on Creative Activities, Research and Publications of the Fisk University Faculty*. Nashville, Tenn.: Fisk University, 1951, 49 pp.

R72. *Research on Racial Relations*. Amsterdam, Netherlands: United Nations, UNESCO, 1966, 265 pp.

R73. *Research on the Disadvantaged: an annotated list of relevant E.T.S. studies, 1951–1969*. ERIC Document no. ED 037–392. Princeton, N.J.: Educational Testing Service, 1969.

R74. *Resource Guide for Teaching Contributions of Minorities to American Culture (for Use with Secondary School Students)*. Oakland, Cal.: Oakland Public Schools, 1966, 121 pp.

R75. *Resource Materials relating to Minority Groups, 1969–1970*. Los Angeles, Cal.: Los Angeles City Unified School District, Library Section. Instructional Services Branch. Division of Instructional Planning and Services, 1969, 131 pp.

R76. "Resources: black studies." *Educate* 3 (Mar. 1970), 40–5.

R77. *Resources for Race Relations: work, study, involvement*. Atlanta, Ga.: U.S. National Student Association, Southern Student Human Relations Project, 1964, 7 pp.

R78. *Resources for Reading about the Negro*. Madison, Wis.: Cooperative Children's Book Center, 1968. A 3 pp. supplement was issued in 1969.

R79. "Retour aux sources [traditional jazz]." *Jazz Magazine* 9 (June 1963), 18–9.

R80. "A Return to Schomburg: Richard Wright's papers acquired." *Bulletin of The New York Public Library* 74 (May 1970), 284.

R81. Revitt, Paul Joseph. *The George Pullen Jackson Collection of Southern Hymnology: a bibliography*. Los Angeles, Cal.: University of California at Los Angeles Library, 1964, 26 pp.

* Reynolds, Florence E. See C159.

* Reynolds, Luisa J. See W150.

R82. Rhodes, Barbara, and Verena Larson. *A Selected Listing of Materials Held by the Texas A and M University Library relative to the Black Man in America*. College Station, Tex.: Texas A and M University Library, 1969, 17 pp.

R83. Rhodes, Lelia G., et al. *Classified Bibliography of the Afro-American Collection and Selected Works on Africa in the Library*. Compiled for the National Evaluative Conference in Black Studies. Sponsored by the Institute for the Study of the History, Life and Culture of Black People. Jackson, Miss.: Jackson State College, 1971, 304 pp.

R84. Rhodes, Marion E. "The Black Man and His Black Heritage." *The Bookmark* (Jan. 1971), 150–5.

R85. "Rhythm and Blues Discography." *Billboard* 79 (June 24, 1967), 83–8.

* Richard, David. See R147.

R85A. Richard, Roger. "The Baltimore Sides [Ferdinand (Jelly Roll) Morton]." *Point du Jazz* 13 (June 1977), 133–4.

R86. Richards, Marion, and Robert Dees. *Black and Brown: bibliography*. San Jose, Cal.: Spartan Bookstore, 1969, 67 pp.

R87. Richardson, J. "Black Children's Books: an overview." *Journal of Negro Education* 43 (Summer 1974), 380–400.

R88. Richardson, Marilyn. *Black Women and Religion: a bibliography*. Boston, Mass.: G.K. Hall, 1980, 139 pp. See also Marilyn P. Truesdell (T91).

R89. Richter, Edward, Laura McGuire, and Pearce Grove. *An Introductory Bibliography of Black Studies Resources in the Eastern New Mexico University Library*. Portales, N.M.: Eastern New Mexico University, 1970, 69 pp.

* Rieber, Dick. See L156.

R90. Rieder, Thomas J. *The George A. Myers Papers, 1890–1929: an inventory of the microfilm edition*. Columbus, Ohio: Ohio Historical Society, Archives-Library, 1974, 32 pp.

R91. Riley, Anne. *History of the Negro in California*. Fullerton, Cal.: Fullerton Junior College, William T. Boyce Library, 3 pp.

R92. Rinchon, Dieudonné. "Bibliographie Générale de la Traité et de l'Esclavage." *La Traité et l'Esclavage des Congolais par les Européens: histoire de la déportation de 13 millions 250,000 noirs en Amérique*. Brussels, Belgium, 1929, pp. 239–80.

* Rinder, Irwin D. See S271.

* Ripley, C. Peter. See C47.
R93. "The Rise of the American Negro (Saluting a Century of Negro Progress. 100th anniversary of the Emancipation Proclamation, Jan. 1, 1863–Jan. 1, 1963)." *The Open Shelf* 9–12 (Sept.-Dec. 1962), 36–53. A publication of the Cleveland, Ohio, Public Library.
R94. Rissi, Mathias. *Archie Shepp Discography*. Adliswil, Switzerland, 1977, 21 pp.
* Rivoir, Farah E. See D108.
* Roberts, A. Hood. See M11.
R95. Roberts, J.R. *Black Lesbians: an annotated bibliography*. Tallahassee, Fla.: Naiad Press, 1981, 112 pp.
R96. Robinson, Carrie. "Media for the Black Curriculum." *ALA Bulletin* 63:2 (Feb. 1969), 242–6.
R97. Robinson, Carrie. "Negro History Week, Feb. 9–15, 1959, Bibliography." *Library Journal* 93 (Jan. 15, 1968), 268–9; *School Library Journal* 15 (Feb. 1968), 48–9. Reprinted as an 8 pp. pamphlet in 1969 by *Paperback Books in Print* as *Negro History in Paperbound Books*.
* Robinson, Corienne K. See C28.
* Robinson, Evelyn B. See H93.
R98. Robinson, Gertrude. "Resources for Afro-American Music." *Music Library Association Newsletter* 14 (Sept.-Oct. 1973), 5–6.
R99. Robinson, Harry, Jr. "Afro-American Collections: a status report." *In* Herman L. Totten, ed. *Bibliographical Control of Afro-American Literature*. Eugene, Ore.: University of Oregon, School of Librarianship, 1976, pp. 105–21.
R99A. Robinson, Sharon, et al. "Desegregation: a bibliographic review of teacher attitudes and black students." *Negro Educational Review* 23 (April 1980), 48–59.
R100. Robinson, William H. *Phillis Wheatley: a bio-bibliography*. Boston, Mass.: G.K. Hall, 1981, 192 pp.
* Roever, James E. See H77, K46.
* Rogers, Charles Payne. See L156, S176.
* Roland, Andrew. See D64.
R101. "Roland Hayes Discography." *Record Collector* 10 (July 1955), 38–45.
R102. *The Role of Afro- [sic] and Afro-Americans in American History*. Philadelphia, Pa.: School District of Philadelphia, Office of Integration and Intergroup Education, 1967, 4 pp.
* Rollins, Adine McClarty. See D12A.
R103. Rollins, Charlemae. "Books about Negroes for Children." *ALA Bulletin* 53 (Apr. 1959), 306–8.
R104. Rollins, Charlemae. "Children's Books on the Negro: to help build a better world." *Elementary English Review* 20 (Oct. 1943), 219–33.
R105. Rollins, Charlemae. "Children's Literature in 1943 dealing with Negro Life." *Negro College Quarterly* 2 (Mar. 1944), 19–23.

R106. Rollins, Charlemae. *We Build Together: a reader's guide to Negro life and literature for elementary and high school use.* Champaign, Ill.: National Council of Teachers of English, 1941. A revised edition appeared in 1948, and a third edition, of 71 pp., in 1967.

R107. Rollock, Barbara. *The Black Experience in Children's Books.* New York: The New York Public Library, Office of Branch Libraries, 1974, 122 pp.

* Romero, Patricia. See K20.

R108. Rose, Ernestine. "Books and the Negro. 135th St. Branch of the New York Public Library." *Library Journal* 52 (Nov. 1, 1927), 1012–4.

R109. Rose, Ernestine. "A Librarian in Harlem." *Opportunity* 1 (July 1923), 206.

R110. Rose, James, and Alice Eichholz. *Black Genesis* [*genealogy*]. Detroit, Mich.: Gale Research, 1978, 326 pp.

R111. Rose, Peter I. *Research Bulletin on Intergroup Relations.* New York: Anti-Defamation League of B'nai B'rith, 1962, 30 pp. A 1963 edition contained 48 pp.

R112. Rose, Vattel T., Virginia Barret, Enid Bogle, Dorothy Evans, Lorraine Henry, Jennifer Jordan, and Loeta Lawrence. "An Annotated Bibliography of Afro-American, African, Caribbean Literature for the Year 1976." *College Language Association Journal* 21 (Sept. 1977), 100–57.

* Rose, Vattel T. See also B41.

R113. Rosenberg, Arnold S. *Bibliography for a Black Studies Minor.* Danbury, Conn.: Western Connecticut State College Library, 1971.

R114. Rosenfeld, Harriet. *Books to Enhance the Self-Image of Negro Children.* New York: Yeshiva University, 15 pp.

R115. Rosenfield, Geraldine, and Howard Yagerman. *The New Environmental-Heredity Controversy: a selected annotated bibliography.* ERIC Document no. ED 087–825. New York: American Jewish Committee.

R116. Ross, Frank Alexander, and Louise Venable Kennedy. *A Bibliography of Negro Migration.* New York: Columbia University Press, 1934, 251 pp. Reprinted by Burt Franklin in 1969.

R117. Ross, Stewart L. "Selected Bibliography of Jazz Improvisation Books." *The Instrumentalist* (Nov. 1974), 64.

* Rossi, Peter H. See B224, B225, B282.

R118. Rotante, Anthony. "Big Maybelle: a discography of Big Maybelle Smith." *Record Research* 60 (May-June 1964), 8–9.

R119. Rotante, Anthony. [Dinah Washington Discography]. *Record Research* 1:1 (Feb. 1955), 3.

R120. Rotante, Anthony. "Jimmy Witherspoon Discography." *Record Research* 62 (Aug. 1964), 5–6; 63 (Sept. 1964), 7–8; 66 (Feb. 1965), 8–9; 67 (Apr. 1965), 10; 68 (May 1965), 7.

R121. Rotante, Anthony. "The Recordings of Billy Mitchell." *Record Research* 30 (July 1961), 10.

R122. Rotante, Anthony. "The Records of Junior Wells." *Record Research* 37 (Aug. 1961), 11.

R123. Rotante, Anthony. "Sam 'Lightning' Hopkins Discography." *The Discophile* 45 (Dec. 1955), 3–7; 47 (Apr. 1956), 11.

* Rotberg, Robert. See T103.
* Roth, Catherina E. See P44.
* Rotoli, Nicholas John. See A97.
* Roucek, Joseph S. See G92.

R124. Rountree, Louise. *American Negro and African Studies: a bibliography on the special collections in Carnegie Library.* Salisbury, N.C.: Livingstone College, 1968, 80 pp.

R125. Rountree, Louise. *An Annotated Bibliography on Joseph Charles Price (1882–1893), Founder of Livingstone College.* Salisbury, N.C.: Livingstone College, Carnegie Library, 1956, 10 pp. A revised edition of 15 pp. was published in 1963.

R126. Rountree, Louise. *An Annotated Bibliography on Livingstone College Including the Presidents and College-Church History.* Salisbury, N.C.: Livingstone College, 1963, 15 pp.

R127. Rountree, Louise. *Collector's Itemized Bibliography on Slavery, the Anti-Slavery Movement, and Emancipation.* Salisbury, N.C.: Livingstone College, Carnegie Library, 1966.

R128. Rountree, Louise. *An Index to Biographical Sketches and Publications of the Bishops of the A.M.E. Zion Church.* Salisbury, N.C.: Livingstone College, Carnegie Library, 1960, 28 pp. An edition in 1963 contained 39 pp.

R129. Rountree, Louise. *Multi-Cultures: a multi-ethnic bibliography for the young reader.* Salisbury, N.C.: Livingstone College, Carnegie Library, 1969.

R130. Rowell, Charles Henry. "Afro-American Literary Bibliographies: an annotated list to bibliographic guides for the study of Afro-American literature, folklore and related areas." Ph.D. dissertation, Ohio State University, 1972, 208 pp.

R131. Rowell, Charles Henry. "A Bibliography of Bibliographies for the Study of Black American Literature and Folklore." *Black Experience: a southern university journal* 55 (June 1969), 95–111.

R132. Rowell, Charles Henry. "A Checklist for Building Black Collections." *Louisiana Library Association Bulletin* 35 (Winter 1973), 129–33.

R133. Rowell, Charles Henry. "Ernest J. Gaines: a checklist, 1964–1978." *Callaloo* 1:3 (1978), 125–31.

R134. Rowell, Charles Henry. "On Teaching Works by and about Black Americans: a review of articles." *Negro American Literature Forum* 3 (Summer 1969), 64–7.

R135. Rowell, Charles Henry. "Studies in Afro-American Literature: an annual annotated bibliography, 1974." *Obsidian* 1:3 (Winter 1975), 100–27.

R136. Rowell, Charles Henry. "Studies in Afro-American Literature: an annual annotated bibliography, 1975." *Obsidian* 2:3 (Winter 1976), 96–123.

R137. Rowell, Charles H. "Studies in Afro-American Literature: an annual annotated bibliography, 1976." *Obsidian* 3:3 (Winter 1977), 80–104.

R138. Rowell, Gordon A. *Bibliography of Books on the Black Experience in the USA Available in Manhattan Beach and Mid-Brooklyn Libraries.* New York: Kingsborough Community College of CUNY, 1969, 35 pp.

R138A. "Roy Wilkins Papers." *Library of Congress, Acquisitions, Manuscript Division, 1980.* Washington, D.C.: Library of Congress, 1982, pp. 14–9.

R139. Rubin, Leonard. *An Annotated Bibliography on the Employment of Disadvantaged Youth, 1960–1966.* ERIC Document no. ED 035–732. Washington, D.C.: Bureau of Social Science Research, 1969.

R140. Rubin, Louis D., and J.A. Leo Lemay. *A Bibliographical Guide to the Study of Southern Literature.* Baton Rouge, La.: Louisiana State University Press, 1969, 368 pp.

* Rubin, Louis D. See also B325, M28, R56, T63, T106.

R141. Ruecker, Norbert. *Jazz Index: bibliography of jazz literature in periodicals.* Frankfurt, Germany: Author, 1978.

R142. Ruppli, Michel. *Atlantic Records: a discography.* Westport, Conn.: Greenwood Press, 1979, 4 vols.

R143. Ruppli, Michel. "Discographie de Charles Mingus." *Jazz Hot* 337 (May 1977); 338 (June 1977), 20–3; 342 (Oct. 1977), 30.

R144. Ruppli, Michel. *The Prestige Label: a discography.* Westport, Conn.: Greenwood Press, 1980, 377 pp.

R145. Ruppli, Michel. *The Savoy Label: a discography.* Westport, Conn.: Greenwood Press, 1980, 442 pp.

R146. Ruppli, Michel. "[Theodore] Fats Navarro: a discography." *Discographical Forum* 42 (1979), 4–6; 43 (1979), 7–8.

R147. Ruppli, Michel, Gerald Arnaud, Daniel Richard, and Laurent Goddet. "Discographie Thelonius Monk." *Jazz Hot* 131 (Oct. 1976), 22+.

R148. Rush, Theressa Gunnels, Carol Fairbanks Myers, and Esther Spring Arata. *Black American Writers Past and Present: a biographical and bibliographical dictionary.* Metuchen, N.J.: Scarecrow Press, 1975, 865 pp.

R149. Rushing, A.B. "Annotated Bibliography of Images of Black Women in Black Literature." *College Language Association Journal* 21 (Mar. 1978), 435–42.

R150. Russell, P. "Buck Clayton: an introduction and discography." *Jazz Journal* 12 (Sept. 1959), 3–9.

R151. Russell, Tony. "Blind Pete." *Jazz and Blues* 1:10 (Feb. 1972), 25.

R152. Russell, Tony. "Bypassed Blues." *Jazz and Blues* 3:1 (Apr. 1973), 10.

* Russell, William. See S176.

R153. Rust, Brian. *Brian Rust's Guide to Discography.* Westport, Conn.: Greenwood Press, 1980, 133 pp.

R154. Rust, Brian. *Discography of Historical Records on Cylinders and 78's.* Westport, Conn.: Greenwood Press, 1979, 327 pp.

R155. Rust, Brian. "Ferdinand Jelly Roll Morton: a discography." *Jazz Journal* 2 (Aug. 1949), 6; 2 (Sept. 1949), 12; 2 (Oct. 1949), 12 + .

R156. Rust, Brian. "The [Ferdinand] Jelly Roll Morton Discography." *Melody Maker* 28 (Aug. 16, 1952), 9.

R157. Rust, Brian. [*George*] *Pops Foster, 1892–1969.* Berkeley, Cal., 1971, 208 pp.

R158. Rust, Brian. *Jazz Records. A-Z, 1897–1931.* Hatch End, England: Author, 1961, 884 pp. A second edition was published in 1963. A volume covering 1932–1942 was published by the author in 1965. In 1970 Storyville of London issued a revised edition in two volumes covering 1897–1942. Arlington House of New Rochelle, N.Y., issued a 4th ed., revised and enlarged, in 2 volumes and 1996 pp. in 1978.

R159. Rust, Brian. "More Sounds of Silence." *Storyville* 21 (Feb.-Mar. 1969), 96–9.

* Rust, Brian. See also G67, H29, R153.

R160. Rutstein, Joel, and Patricia Peabody. *Black Studies on Campus: a bibliographic approach.* Durham, N.C.: University of New Hampshire, Ezekiel W. Dimond Library, 1969, 20 pp.

R161. Ryan, Pat M. *Black Writing in the U.S.A.: a bibliographic guide.* Brockport, N.Y.: SUNY-Brockport, Drake Memorial Library, 1969, 48 pp.

R162. Ryder, Sarah. "Holdings in Black Literature at Hempstead High School." *Negro American Literature Forum* 3 (Winter 1969), 122–38.

S

S1. *SRC Publications: a listing of current materials relating to race relations and allied subjects available from the Southern Regional Council.* Atlanta, Ga.: Southern Regional Council, 1962(?), 8 pp.

S2. Sabin, Joseph W.E., and R.W.G. Vail. "Harriet Beecher Stowe." *Bibliotheca Americana.* New York: Bibliographical Society of America, 1933, pp. 33–73.

S3. Sachs, Tom. "Erroll Garner Discography." *Jazz Monthly* 4:9 (Nov. 1958), 7 + ; 4:10 (Dec. 1958), 29–32; 4:11 (Jan. 1959), 24–5.

S4. Sagawe, Harm. "[Charlie] Elgar's Creole Orchestra." *Storyville* 52 (Apr.-May 1974), 150–1.

S5. St. Clair, Diane. "Bibliography on Repression." *Black Scholar* 12:1 (Jan./Feb. 1981), 85–90.

S6. St. John, Nancy Hoyt, and Nancy Smith. *Annotated Bibliography on School Racial Mix and the Self Concept: aspirations, academic achievement and interracial attitudes and behavior of Negro children.* ERIC Document no. ED 011–331. Cambridge, Mass.: Harvard Research and Development Center on Educational Differences, 1967, 81 pp.

S7. Saleem, Betty, and Bryce Harrington. *School Dropouts: a commentary and annotated bibliography*. Syracuse, N.Y.: Syracuse University, Youth Development Center, 1963.

S8. Salk, Erwin A. *Du Bois/Robeson, Two Giants of the Twentieth Century: the story of an exhibition and a bibliography*. Chicago, Ill.: Columbia College Press, 1977, 20 pp.

S9. Salk, Erwin A. *A Layman's Guide to Negro History*. Rev. ed. New York: McGraw-Hill Book Co., 1967, 196 pp.

S10. Salzman, Eric. "The Second Annual Ragtime Roundup." *Stereo Review* 32:6 (June 1974), 126–7.

S11. [Sam Cooke Discography]. *Record Exchanger* 4:1 (1974), 14.

S12. Sampson, F.A., and W.C. Breckenridge. "Bibliography of Slavery in Missouri." *Missouri Historical Review* 2 (Apr. 1908), 233–44.

S13. Sandegren, Kare, Sven M. Kristensen, John Jorgensen, Erik Wiedemann, and Barge R. Henrichsen. *Boken om Jazz*. Stavanger, Norway: Dreyer, 1954, 392 pp.

S14. Sanders, E.G. "Presence of the Black Person in American History, Eighteenth to Twentieth Centuries: a bicentennial bibliography." *Unabashed Librarian* 23 (1977), 26–7.

S15. Sanders, Jean B. "Black Literature for Young Children and Young Adults Published in 1971." *Negro American Literature Forum* 7:1 (Spring 1973), 3–15.

S15A. Sandhu, Manmohan Singh. *Race Relations and Group Relations: a selected research bibliography*. Jackson, Miss.: Jackson State University, 1977, 62 pp.

S16. Sandoval, Valerie. "The Bran of History: an historiographic account of the work of J.A. Rogers." *The Schomburg Center for Research in Black Culture Journal* 1:4 (Spring 1978), 5 + .

S17. Sanfilippo, Luigi. *General Catalog of [Edward] Duke Ellington's Recorded Music*. Palermo, Italy: New Jazz Society, 1964, 70 pp. A second edition in 1966 contained 112 pp.

S18. Sanford, Marvin. *A Bibliography on the Revolutionary Approach to the Negro Question in America*. Mena, Ark.: Commonwealth College Library, 1937, 16 pp.

* Sarles, Carl. See P46A.

* Saunders, Julia O. See J109, P132.

S19. S[avage], N[oel]. "Black History: an Afro-American resource guide." *Paperbound Books in Print* 15:4 (Apr. 1970), 4–32.

S20. S[avage], N[oel]. "Black Literature." *Paperbound Books in Print* 14:11 (Nov. 1969), 4–33. Reprinted in pamphlet form by R.R. Bowker Co.

S21. Savage, Noel. "Black Literature: a supplement." *Paperbound Books in Print* 15 (Nov. 1970), 4–28.

S22. S[avage], N[oel]. "Blacks Today: a modern Afro-American library." *Paperbound Books in Print* 15:5 (May 1970), 4–56.

* Sax, Dave. See W103.

S23. Say, Dave. "Early [John Lee] Hooker Discography." *The Blues* 9, pp. 50–2.

S24. *Say It Loud: I'm Black and I'm Proud*. Philadelphia, Pa.: Free Library of Philadelphia, Reader Development Program, 1969.

S25. *Say It Loud: I'm Black and I'm Proud: children's stories for the older set*. Los Angeles, Cal.: Los Angeles Public Library, Venice Branch.

S26. Scally, Mary Anthony. "The Carter Woodson Letters in the Library of Congress: sidelights on research in black history." *Negro History Bulletin* 38:5 (1975), 419–21.

S27. Scally, Mary Anthony. *Negro Catholic Writers, 1900–1943: a bio-bibliography*. Detroit, Mich.: Walter Romig & Co., 1945, 152 pp.

S28. Schaefer, H.J. "Dean Dixon: ein Schallplattenportrat." *Musica* 24:2 (1970), 301.

* Schapiro, M. See M3.

S29. Schatt, Stanley. "LeRoi Jones: a checklist to primary and secondary sources." *Bulletin of Bibliography* 28:2 (Apr.-June 1972), 55–7.

* Schatt, Stanley. See also M12.

S30. Schatz, Walter. *Directory of Afro-American Resources*. New York: R.R. Bowker Co., 1970, 485 pp.

S31. Scheffner, Manfred. *Katalog der Jazzschallplatten*. Bielefeld, Germany: Bielefelder Verlagsanstalt, 1967, 207 pp.

S32. Scherer, Lester. "Bibliography: dissertations in Afro-American religion." *Newsletter of the Afro-American Religious History Group of the American Academy of Religion* 2:2 (Spring 1978), 4–16.

S33. Scherer, Lester B. "Bibliography: 'The National Baptist Magazine,' 1894–1901." *Newsletter of the Afro-American Religious History Group of the American Academy of Religion* 6:2 (Spring 1982), 4–9.

S34. Scherman, Bo, and Carl A. Hoellstrom. *A Discography of [William] Count Basie, 1929–1950*. Copenhagen, Denmark: Karl E. Knudsen, 1969, 52 pp.

* Scherman, Bo. See also J74.

S35. Schlachter, Gail, and Donna Belli. *Blacks in an Urban Environment: a selected annotated bibliography of reference sources*. Exchange Bibliography no. 819. Monticello, Ill.: Council of Planning Librarians, 1975, 45 pp.

S36. Schlachter, Gail, and Donna Belli. *Minorities and Women: a guide to the reference literature in the social sciences*. Los Angeles, Cal.: References Services Press, 1977, 349 pp.

S37. Schlachter, Gail, and Donna Belli. "Survival Kit for Term Paper Writers; no. 1: a guide to sources in black studies." *Unabashed Librarian* 19 (Spring 1975), 21–5.

S38. Schneider, Gilbert D. "Daniel Emmett's Negro Sermons and Hymns: an inventory." *Ohio History* 85:1 (1976), 67–83.

S39. Schneider, Joyce B. *A Selected List of Periodicals relating to Negroes, with Holdings in the Libraries of Yale University*. New Haven, Conn.: Yale University, 1970, 26 pp.

S40. Schofield, Edward T., and Irene F. Cypher. *Guide to Films in Human Relations*. Washington, D.C.: National Education Association, Department of Audio-Visual Instruction, 1954(?), 96 pp.

S41. Schomburg, Arthur A. *A Bibliographical Checklist of American Negro Poetry*. New York: Charles P. Heartman, 1916, 57 pp.

S42. Schomburg, Arthur A. "A Selected List of Negro-Americana and Africana: notable early books by Negroes." *In* Alain Locke, ed. *The New Negro: an interpretation*. New York: Albert and Charles Boni, 1925. Reprinted by Arno in 1968 and Atheneum in 1969.

S43. Schomburg, Arthur A., and Robert T. Browne. *Exhibition Catalogue. First Annual Exhibition of Books, Manuscripts, Paintings, Engravings, Sculptures, etc.* By the Negro Library Association at the Carlton Avenue Young Men's Christian Association, 405 Carlton Avenue, Brooklyn, August 7 to 16, 1918. New York: The Pool Press Association Printers, 1917, 23 pp. Reprinted in Betty Kaplan Gubert, *Early Black Bibliographies, 1863–1918*. New York: Garland, 1982, pp. 329–54.

* Schomburg, Arthur A. See also H47.

S44. "The Schomburg Library Opened to Students." *Opportunity* 4 (June 1926), 187.

S45. *School Desegregation*. New York: ERIC Information Retrieval Center on the Disadvantaged, 1973, 142 pp.

S46. *School Desegregation: changing policies and practices*. Washington, D.C.: U.S. Department of Health, Education, and Welfare, 1965.

S47. Schor, Joel, and Cecil Harvey. *A List of References for the History of Black Americans in Agriculture, 1619–1974*. Davis, Cal.: University of California at Davis, Agricultural Historical Center, 1975, 116 pp.

S48. Schroeder, Harry. "Lester Young, 1943–1944." *Micrography* 44 (May 1977), 19.

S49. Schuller, Gunther. "Early [Edward] Duke [Ellington]." *Jazz Review* 2 (Dec. 1959), 6–14; 3:1 (Jan. 1960), 18–22; 3:2 (Feb. 1960), 18–25.

S49A. Schwanniger, A., and A. Gurwitch. *Swing Discographie*. Geneva, Switzerland: Grasset, 1945, 200 pp.

S50. Scott, Nancy, Doris M. Kemler, and Marjorie S. Crisman. *Black American: a selected, classified and partially annotated list of books, periodicals, and audiovisual materials in the Gettysburg College Library*. Gettysburg, Pa.: Gettysburg College, Schmucker Memorial Library, 1970, 106 pp. A supplement was issued in 1971, and in 1972 a second edition of 163 pp.

S51. Scott, Patricia Bell. "Selected Bibliography on Black Feminism." *In* Gloria

T. Hull, Patricia Bell Scott, and Barbara Smith, eds. *But Some of Us Are Brave: black women's studies.* Old Westbury, N.Y.: Feminist Press, 1982, pp. 23–33.

* Scott, Patricia Bell. See also B316, D12, M80, S130, S170, S251, W123, Y2.

S52. Scott, Thelma. *A List of Books by and about the American Negro.* 2nd ed. North Las Vegas, Nev.: North Las Vegas Public Library, 1973, 58 pp.

* Sebillot, Paul. See G2.

S53. *Segregation and Desegregation in American Education.* 2nd ed. Bibliography no. 18. Gainesville, Fla.: University of Florida, College of Education Library, 1956, 14 pp. A third edition in 1960 had 11 pp., and a fourth edition in 1962 had 10 pp.

S54. Seidel, Richard. "[Edward] Duke Ellington Discography." *Rolling Stone* 164 (July 4, 1974), 94.

S55. Seidel, Richard. "[Edward] Duke Ellington: fifty years on record, 1924–1974." *Schwann 1 Record and Tape Guide* 26:4 (Apr. 1974), 34–6.

S56. "Select Books of 1962: a mid-year reappraisal." *Negro Digest* 12 (May 1963), 53–5.

S57. *Select List of References on the Economic History of the South.* Washington, D.C.: Library of Congress, 1907, 33 pp.

S58. *Select List of References on the Ku Klux Klan.* Washington, D.C.: Library of Congress, Division of Bibliography, 1913, 8 pp. Reprinted in Betty Kaplan Gubert. *Early Black Bibliographies, 1863–1918.* New York: Garland, 1982, pp. 253–60.

S59. *Select List of References on the Negro Question.* Washington, D.C.: Library of Congress, 1903, 28 pp. A 2nd edition of 61 pp. was issued in 1906. The 1903 edition is reprinted in Betty Kaplan Gubert. *Early Black Bibliographies, 1863–1918.* New York: Garland, 1982, pp. 203–30.

S60. *Select List of References on Wendell Phillips.* Washington, D.C.: Library of Congress, 1911, 6 pp. A bibliography of 11 pp. was issued by LC in 1931.

S61. *Select Picture List: Negro art from the Harmon Foundation.* Washington, D.C.: General Services Administration, National Archives and Records Service, The National Archives, 6 pp.

S62. *Select References on Housing of Minorities.* Washington, D.C.: U.S. Housing and Home Finance Agency, Office of the Administrator, Racial Relations Service, 1950, 46 pp. An edition of 60 pp. was issued in 1951.

S63. "Selected Annotated Bibliography for Student Reading." *Journal of Education* 147 (Dec. 1964), 103–9.

S64. *A Selected Bibliography by and about Minority Groups.* Frankfort, Ky.: Kentucky Department of Education, Division of Instructional Services, School Library Services, 1966, 7 pp.

S65. *Selected Bibliography for Disadvantaged Youth.* ERIC Document no. ED 002–535. Washington, D.C.: U.S. Department of Health, Education, and Welfare, Office of Education, Programs for the Education of the Disadvantaged, 1964.

S66. *Selected Bibliography for Inter-racial Understanding.* Hartford, Conn.: Connecticut Inter-racial Commission, 1944, 36 pp.

S67. *A Selected Bibliography: Negro-Jewish Relationships.* New York: American Jewish Congress, Commission on Jewish Affairs, 1967, 4 pp.

S68. *A Selected Bibliography of Black Heritage Materials in the James E. Morrow Library.* Huntington, W. Va.: Marshall University, 1980, 21 pp.

S69. *A Selected Bibliography of Books on Race Relations and the Negro.* New York: NAACP, 1960, 2 pp.

S70. *Selected Bibliography of Books, Pamphlets and Articles on Jewish-Negro Relations.* New York: American Jewish Committee, Institute of Human Relations, 1966, 10 pp.

S71. *Selected Bibliography of Books, Pamphlets and Articles on Negro-Jewish Relations.* New York: American Jewish Committee, Institute of Human Relations, 1971, 18 pp.

S72. *A Selected Bibliography of Free and Inexpensive Materials on Negro Education.* WPA Technical Services Educational Circular no. 9. Washington, D.C.: U.S. Works Progress Administration, Division of Educational Projects, 1938, 4 pp.

S73. *Selected Bibliography of Government Publications about the American Negro.* Prepared for Negro History Week 1969. Hyattsville, Md.: Prince George's County Memorial Library, Oxon Hill Branch, Reference Department, 1969, 26 pp. An edition of 50 pp. appeared in 1970.

S74. *A Selected Bibliography of Literature on the Afro-American.* New York: United Presbyterian Church in the U.S.A., Division of Church and Race, 1969.

S75. "Selected Bibliography of Minority Groups." Prepared by Book Review Committee, Los Angeles County Schools. *Negro American Literature Forum* 2 (Winter 1968), 91–104.

S76. "Selected Bibliography of Negro History Material." *Negro Digest* 16 (Feb. 1967), 81–2.

S77. "A Selected Bibliography of Studies of Negro Education." *Journal of Negro Education* 5 (July 1936), 534.

S78. *Selected Bibliography* [on David Driskell]. 1 p.

S79. *Selected Bibliography on Discrimination in Housing.* Sacramento, Cal.: California State Library, Law Library, 1964, 9 pp.

S80. *Selected Bibliography on Human Relations.* Cleveland, Ohio: Cleveland Public Schools, Division of English and Language Arts, and Community Action for Youth, 1964.

S81. *Selected Bibliography on the Negro.* New York: National Urban League,

Department of Research and Community Projects, 1937, 13 pp. A supplement of 13 pp. was issued in 1938 and a revised edition of 47 pp. in 1939. A third edition of 58 pp. appeared in 1940, which was supplemented by 23 pp. in 1942. A fourth edition of 124 pp. was published in 1951; a 48 pp. supplement appeared in 1958; a 36 pp. supplement in 1963; a 51 pp. supplement in 1966; and a 50 pp. supplement in 1968.

S82. "A Selected Bibliography on the Physical and Mental Abilities of the American Negro." *Journal of Negro Education* 3 (1934), 548–64.

S83. *Selected Books for Children with Emphasis on Black History and Culture: an annotated bibliography designed for use by elementary through junior high students, teachers, librarians and parents*. Chicago, Ill.: Illinois Commission on Human Relations. Education Services Department, 1970, 12 pp.

S84. [Selected Cecil Taylor Discography]. *Down Beat* 42 (Apr. 10, 1975), 13.

S85. [Selected Charlie Mingus Discography]. *Down Beat* 42 (Feb. 27, 1975), 13.

S86. *Selected Guide to Materials on Black Studies*. Detroit, Mich.: Wayne State University Library, 1971, 5 pp.

S87. *Selected Items from the George Gershwin Memorial Collection of Music and Music Literature Founded by Carl Van Vechten*. Nashville, Tenn.: Fisk University Library, 1947, 32 pp.

S88. [Selected (Jackie) McLean Discography]. *Down Beat* 42 (Apr. 10, 1975), 32.

S89. *A Selected List of Books by and about the Negro*. Washington, D.C.: Howard University, Carnegie Library, Moorland Foundation, 1940, 11 pp.

S90. *A Selected List of Books by and about the Negro, 1950–1956*. Raleigh, N.C.: Richard B. Harrison Public Library, 1957, 26 pp.

S91. *A Selected List of Books by Black Writers*. Chicago, Ill.: Chicago Public Library.

S92. *A Selected List of Books on American Ethnic Groups for Secondary School Libraries*. Los Angeles, Cal.: Los Angeles City Schools.

S92A. *Selected List of Books, Pamphlets and Articles on Jewish-Negro Relations*. New York: American Jewish Committee, Institute of Human Relations, 1966, 10 pp. An expanded edition of 18 pp. appeared in 1971 with the revised title *Selected List of Books, Pamphlets and Articles on Negro-Jewish Relations*.

S93. *Selected List of References Relating to Desegregation and Integration, 1949 to June 1955*. Tuskegee, Ala.: Tuskegee Institute, Department of Records and Research, 1955, 21 pp.

S94. *Selected List of References Relating to Discrimination and Segregation in Education, 1949 to June 1955*. Tuskegee, Ala.: Tuskegee Institute, Department of Records and Research, 1955, 9 pp.

S95. *A Selected List of References Relating to the Elementary, Secondary, and*

Higher Education of Negroes, 1949 to June 1955. Tuskegee, Ala.: Tuskegee Institute, Department of Records and Research, 1955, 18 pp.

S96. *A Selected List of References Relating to the Negro Teacher, 1949 to June 1955.* Tuskegee, Ala.: Tuskegee Institute, Department of Records and Research, 1955, 3 pp.

S97. *Selected Materials Dealing with the History of the Negro in America for Use in the Two-Year Course in the History of the U.S..* Trenton, N.J.: State Department of Education, Secondary School Bulletin, Division of Curriculum and Instruction, 4 pp.

S98. "Selected Miles [Davis] Discography: recorded Miles as leader with special emphasis on the years 1959–1974." *Down Beat* 41 (July 18, 1974), 20 + .

S99. [Selected Muddy Waters Discography]. *Down Beat* 42 (Feb. 27, 1975), 22.

S100. *Selected Negro Reference Books and Bibliographies: an annotated guide.* Amherst, Mass.: University of Massachusetts Library, Reference Department, 1969, 14 pp.

S101. [Selected Oliver Nelson Discography]. *Down Beat* 42 (Apr. 24, 1975).

S102. "Selected Poems of W.E.B. Du Bois." *Freedomways* 5 (Winter 1965), 88–102.

S103. *Selected Reading List for Adults and Children on Negro History.* Chicago, Ill.: Chicago Public Library, George Cleveland Hall Branch.

S104. *Selected References on Housing for Minorities.* Racial Relations Service Documents. Series F. Bibliographies. No. 1. Washington, D.C.: National Housing Agency, Office of the Administrator, 1946, 4 pp. This is a supplement to Carey and Robinson (C28).

S105. "Selected Resources for Black Studies in Music." *Music Educators Journal* 58:3 (Nov. 1971).

S106. [Selected Sarah Vaughan Discography]. *Down Beat* 44 (May 5, 1977), 17.

S107. *Selected Series of Records Issued by the Commissioner of the Bureau of Refugees, Freedmen, and Abandoned Lands, 1865–1872.* Washington, D.C.: National Archives and Records Service, 1969, 8 pp.

S108. [Selected Sonny Rollins Discography]. *Down Beat* 44 (Apr. 7, 1977), 14.

S108A. *Selected Texts of Afro-American History (U.S.A.).* Santa Barbara, Cal.: University of California at Santa Barbara, Center for Black Studies, 1977.

S109. *Selected Titles on Afro-American and African Collections.* Atlanta, Ga.: Southern Association of Colleges and Schools, Education Improvement Project Staff, 1969, 52 pp.

S110. "Selection discographique." *Jazz Hot* 263 (Summer 1970), 26–7.

S111. *Self-Hatred among Negroes: a selected bibliography.* New York: American Jewish Committee, Institute of Human Relations, 1965, 2 pp.

S112. Sell, Johann Jacob. "Bibliography on the Slave Trade." *Versuch einer*

Geschichte des Negersclavenhandels. Halle: Bei Johann Jacob Geloaner, 1791, pp. 226–44.

S113. Sernett, Milton. *Geographical Literature on Black America: a selected bibliography (including some items of historical interest).* Syracuse, N.Y.: Syracuse University, 1980, 3 pp.

S114. Settle, Elizabeth A., and Thomas A. Settle. *Ishmael Reed: a primary and secondary bibliography.* Boston, Mass.: G.K. Hall, 1982, est. 192 pp.

S115. Settle, Elizabeth A., and Thomas A. Settle. *Ishmael Reed: an annotated checklist.* Carson, Cal.: California State College at Dominquez Hills, 1977.

* Settle, Thomas A. See S114, S115.

S116. *75 Years of Freedom: commemoration of the seventy-fifth anniversary of the proclamation of the Thirteenth Amendment to the Constitution of the United States.* Washington, D.C.: Library of Congress, 1943, 108 pp.

S117. Sewell, Richard H. "Slavery in the Americas: an essay review." *Wisconsin Magazine of History* 51:3 (1968), 238–43.

S118. Sexton, Ira J. *Afro-American Books in the Diablo Valley College Library.* Pleasant Hill, Cal.: Diablo Valley College, 1969, 30 pp.

S119. Shachter, J. "Materials for Young Black and Latino Children." *Drexel Library Quarterly* 12 (Oct. 1976), 54–63.

S120. *Shades of Blackness.* San Francisco, Cal.: San Francisco Public Library, 1971, 2 pp.

* Shambaugh, Cynthia. See Z2.

S121. Shapiro, C. "Hope and Sorrow in the South." *Saturday Review* 48 (Aug. 14, 1965), 31–3.

S122. Sharma, Prakash C. *Slum and Ghetto Studies: a research bibliography.* Exchange Bibliography no. 573. Monticello, Ill.: Council of Planning Librarians, 1974, 11 pp.

S123. Sharpe, Mrs. Johnnie. *Black American Writers.* Orangeburg, S.C.: South Carolina State College, Miller F. Whittaker Library.

S124. Shaw, Arnold J. "The Expanding Jazz Bookshelf." *Saturday Review* 41 (Jan. 25, 1958), 63–5.

S125. Sheatsley, P.B. "A Quarter Century of Jazz Discography." *Record Research* 53 (Feb. 1964), 3–6.

S126. Sheer, Anita, Len Kunstadt, Harrison Smith, and Bob Colton. "Blues Galore: the story of Virginia Spivey." *Record Research* 2:2 (May-June 1956), 3 + . Addenda in 2:4 (Nov.-Dec. 1956), 13.

* Sheppard, Gladys B. See A90.

S127. Shera, Michael G. "Billie Holliday and Lester Young, 1937–1941: a discography." *Jazz Journal* 14 (Aug. 1961), 16.

* Shera, Michael G. See also M142.

S128. Sheridan, Eugene. *Black Books in Greensboro: a report on the current accessibility of Afro-American literature for elementary, junior high and high school students at the Greensboro Public Library (Downtown and Southeast Divisions) and at three publicly supported institutions and an evaluation of some of this literature.* Greensboro, N.C.: Greensboro Public Library and Greensboro Chamber of Commerce (Community Unity Division), 1969, 22 pp.

S129. Sherman, Caroline B. "New Books by and about Negroes." *Rural Sociology* 9:2 (June 1944), 161–9.

S130. Sherman, Joan R. "Afro-American Women Poets of the Nineteenth Century: a guide to research and bio-bibliographies of the poets." *In* Gloria T. Hull, Patricia Bell Scott, and Barbara Smith, eds. *But Some of Us Are Brave: black women's studies.* Old Westbury, N.Y.: Feminist Press, 1982, pp. 245–60.

S131. Sherrill, Perry. *Black Power.* San Francisco, Cal.: San Francisco State College, 1967(?).

S132. Shevory, Joan. *The American Negro: a list of books in the Jamestown Community College Library.* Jamestown, N.Y.: Jamestown Community College Library, 1970.

S133. Shockley, Ann Allen. "American Anti-Slavery Literature: an overview 1693–1859." *Negro History Bulletin* 37:3 (Apr./May 1974), 232–5.

S134. Shockley, Ann Allen. "Black Book Reviewing: a case for library action." *College and Research Libraries* 35 (Jan. 1974), 16–20. Reprinted in W.A. Katz and R. Burgess, eds. *Library Literature 5: the best of 1974.* Metuchen, N.J.: Scarecrow Press, 1975, pp. 407–14.

S135. Shockley, Ann Allen. "Concise Selected Bibliography of Books and Periodicals for an Initial Afro-American Library." *A Handbook for the Administration of Special Negro Collections.* Nashville, Tenn.: Fisk University Library, 1970, pp. 57–63.

S135A. Shockley, Ann Allen. "The Curator of Afro-American Collections." *In* Herman L. Totten, ed. *Bibliographic Control of Afro-American Literature.* Eugene, Ore.: University of Oregon, 1976, pp. 268–92.

S136. Shockley, Ann Allen. "A Descriptive Bibliography of Selected African and Afro-American Periodicals." *Handbook on Black Librarianship.* E.J. Josey and Ann Allen Shockley, eds. Littleton, Col.: Libraries Unlimited, 1977.

S137. Shockley, Ann Allen. *A Selected Bibliography for Black Feminist Reading.* Nashville, Tenn.: Fisk University Library, 1977.

* Shockley, Ann Allen. See also C72, C109, K14, L9.

S138. Shrier, Irene, and David E. Lavin. *Open Admissions: a bibliography for research and application.* ERIC Document no. ED 090–840. New York: City University of New York, Office of Program and Policy Research, 1974.

* Shuler, Eddie. See L34.

* Shuman, R. Baird. See K15.

S139. "[Sidney] Bechet Discography." *Down Beat* 18 (Dec. 14, 1951), 18.

S140. Sieg, Vera. *The Negro Problem: a bibliography*. Madison, Wis.: Wisconsin Library School, 1908, 22 pp. Reprinted in Betty Kaplan Gubert. *Early Black Bibliographies, 1863–1918*. New York: Garland, 1982, pp. 271–92.

S141. Siegel, Judith A. *Racial Discrimination in Housing*. Exchange Bibliography no. 1201. Monticello, Ill.: Council of Planning Librarians, 1977, 14 pp.

S142. Silber, Irwin. "Records: voice from the past [Paul Robeson]." *Guardian* (Apr. 26, 1972), 14.

S143. Silverman, Susan B. *Selected Annotated Bibliography of Research Relevant to Education and Cultural Deprivation*. ERIC Document no. ED 002–240. Minneapolis, Minn.: University of Minnesota, Center for Continuing Studies, 1964.

S144. Simms, H.H. "Abolition Literature, 1830–1840: a critical analysis." *Journal of Southern History* 6 (Aug. 1940), 368–82.

S145. Simon, B. "Charlie Parker: a jazz great." *Billboard* 67 (Mar. 26, 1955), 19.

S146. Simone, R. "[Ferdinand] Jelly Roll Morton Discography." *Matrix* 51 (Feb. 1964), 14–7.

* Simonin, Mary. See R19.

S147. Simons, Sim. "[Theodore] Fats Navarro and Tadd Dameron at the Royal Roost 1948." *Swingtime* 20 (Apr. 1977), 23–4.

S148. Simosko, Vladimir. "John Gilmore Discography." *Coda* 12:7 (June-July 1975), 9–11.

S149. Sims, Janet. *Black Women: a selected bibliography*. Washington, D.C.: Howard University, Moorland-Spingarn Research Center, 1976, 18 pp.

S150. Sims, Janet. *Black Women in the Employment Sector*. Public Administration Series No. 243. Monticello, Ill.: Vance Bibliographies, 1979, 29 pp.

S150A. Sims, Janet. "Jessie Redmon Fauset (1885–1961): a selected annotated bibliography." *Black American Literature Forum* 14, pp. 147–52.

S151. Sims, Janet. *Marion Anderson: an annotated bibliography and discography*. Westport, Conn.: Greenwood Press, 1981, 256 pp.

S152. Sims, Janet. *The Progress of Afro-American Women: a selected bibliography and resource guide*. Westport, Conn.: Greenwood Press, 1980, 378 pp.

* Sims, Janet. See also D62, D63, L56.

S153. Sinclair, Donald A. *The Negro in New Jersey: a checklist of books, pamphlets, official publications, broadsides, and dissertations, 1754–1964, in the Rutgers University Library*. New Brunswick, N.J.: Rutgers University Library, 1965, 56 pp.

S154. Sinclair, Donald A. *New Jersey and the Negro: a bibliography, 1716–1966*. Bibliography Committee of the New Jersey Library Association. Trenton, N.J.: Trenton Free Public Library, 1967, 196 pp.

S155. Sindler, Leon. *Research Bulletin on Intergroup Relations, 1963–1964*. New York: Anti-Defamation League of B'nai B'rith, 1974, 48 pp.

* Singh, Amritjt. Sec F79.

S156. Sitkoff, Harvard. " 'No More Moanin': black rights history in the 1970's." *Prologue* 11 (Summer 1979), 81–9.

S157. Sjolund, James, and Warren Burton. *The American Negro: a selected bibliography of materials including children's books, reference books, collections and anthologies, recordings, films and filmstrips*. Music of Minority Groups, Part 1. Olympia, Wash.: Author, 1969, 9 pp.

S158. Skowronski, JoAnn. *Black Music in America: a bibliography*. Metuchen, N.J.: Scarecrow Press, 1981, 723 pp.

S159. Slaven, Neil. *American R & B/Blues Records, 1964/1965*. New York: Blue Horizon Records, 1965, 24 pp.

* Slaven, Neil. See also L35.

S160. Slevin, Ann D. *A Selection of Holdings on the Afro-American*. Princeton, N.J.: Princeton University, Firestone Memorial Library, 100 pp.

* Sloan, Forrest. See B132.

S161. Sloan, I.J. "The Negro in History." *Saturday Review* 48 (Feb. 20, 1965), 90–2.

S162. Sloan, Irving J. *The Negro in Modern American History Textbooks*. Chicago, Ill.: American Federation of Teachers, AFL-CIO, 1966, 47 pp.

S163. Sloan, Irving J. *The Treatment of Blacks in Current Encyclopedias*. Washington, D.C.: American Federation of Teachers, AFL-CIO, 1970, 32 pp.

S164. Slonaker, John. *The U.S. Army and the Negro*. Carlisle Barracks, Pa.: U.S. Department of Defense, Army, Office of the Chief of Military History, U.S. Army Military Research Collection, 1971, 161 pp. A supplement was issued in 1972.

S165. Smallwood, W. "Tribute to Countee Cullen: memorial collection of contemporary Negro life founded by Harold Jackman." *Opportunity* 25 (July 1947), 168–9.

* Smaw, Darryl M. See M108.

S166. Smith, A.G. "How to Study the South." *Southern Packet* 47 (Sept. 1948), 1–7.

* Smith, Barbara. See B313, D12, M80, S51, S130, S170, S251, W123, Y2.

S167. Smith, Benjamin F. "Integration in Public Education: an annotated bibliography." *In* David W. Beggs and S. Kern Alexander, eds. *Integration and Education*. Chicago, Ill.: Rand McNally, 1969, pp. 164–87.

S168. Smith, Benjamin F. "Public School Integration: an annotated bibliography." *Negro Educational Review* 6 (Jan. 1955), 28–38; 7 (Apr. 1956), 60–78; 10 (Jan. 1959), 32–44; 13 (Jan. 1962), 11–9; 14 (Jan. 1963), 7–16; 15 (Jan. 1964), 4–15; 16 (Jan.-Apr. 1965), 4–18; 17 (Apr. 1966), 52–64; and subsequent issues.

S169. Smith, Benjamin F. "What to Read on Public School Integration." *Integrated Education* 2 (June-July 1964), 40–4.

S170. Smith, Beverly. "Black Women's Health: notes for a course." *In* Gloria T. Hull, Patricia Bell Scott, and Barbara Smith, eds. *But Some of Us Are Brave: black women's studies*. Old Westbury, N.Y.: Feminist Press, 1982, pp. 103–14.

S171. Smith, Bonnie L., and Agnes Hammond. *Afro-American Archives in California and the West*. San Marcos, Cal.: Palomar College, Phil H. Putnam Library.

S172. Smith, Bonnie L., and Agnes Hammond. *The Afro-American: his life and history; a bibliography of works in the Palomar College Library*. San Marcos, Cal.: Palomar College, Phil H. Putnam Library, 1969, 37 pp.

S173. Smith, C. Alphonso. "Dialect Writers." *In* William Peterfield Trent, et al., eds. *The Cambridge History of American Literature*. Vol. 2, pp. 347–66, 611–5. For Booker T. Washington, see pp. 323–5, 605–11, and Vol. 3, Ch. 5. New York: G.P. Putnam's Sons, 1918.

S174. Smith, C.E. "The Name of the Game Was Jazz [historical reissues]." *Jazz & Pop* 7 (Sept. 1968), 51–4.

S175. Smith, C.Y. *Black Newspapers: a preliminary checklist*. Evanston, Ill.: Northwestern University Library, 1973, 5 pp.

S176. Smith, Charles Edward, Frederic Ramsey, Jr., Charles Payne Rogers, and William Russell. *The Jazz Record Book*. New York: Smith and Durrell, 1942, 515 pp. Reprinted by Greenwood, 1978.

S177. Smith, Dwight L. "Afro-American History: a bibliographic survey and suggestions." Paper read at Association for the Study of Afro-American Life and History, New York, 1973, 19 pp.

S178. Smith, Dwight L. *Afro-American History: a bibliography*, Vol. 1. Santa Barbara, Cal.: ABC-CLIO, 1974, 856 pp.

S179. Smith, Dwight L. *Afro-American History: a bibliography*, Vol. 2. Santa Barbara, Cal.: ABC-CLIO, 1981, 394 pp.

* Smith, G. See F64.

S180. Smith, G.R. "Human Crisis in America." *Publishers Weekly* (July 1, 1968), 43–5.

S181. Smith, Gloria L. *A Slice of Black Americana: a regional survey of history, a chronology of publications from 1746–1940, a survey of literary genres for teachers or students of history and literature*. Champaign, Ill.: University of Illinois, 1969, 38 pp.

* Smith, Harrison. See S126.

* Smith, James Ward. See B342.

S181A. Smith, Jessie Carney. "Acquiring Afro-American Literature." *In* Herman L. Totten, ed. *Bibliographic Control of Afro-American Literature*. Eugene, Ore.: University of Oregon, 1976, pp. 69–104.

S182. Smith, Jessie Carney. *Black Academic Libraries and Research Collec-*

tions: an historical survey. Westport, Conn.: Greenwood Press, 1977, 303 pp.

S183. Smith, Jessie Carney. "Developing Collections of Black Literature." *Black World* 20 (June 1971), 18–29.

S184. Smith, Jessie Carney. *A Handbook for the Study of Black Bibliography.* Nashville, Tenn.: Fisk University Library, 1971, 138 pp.

S185. Smith, Jessie Carney. "The Research Collections in Negro Life and Culture at Fisk University." Paper read at the Workshop on Bibliographic and Other Resources for a Study of the American Negro, Howard University, 1968, 26 pp.

S186. Smith, Jessie Carney. "Research Resources in Negro Life and Culture." Paper read at a workshop on Social Science Approaches to the Study of the Negro, Fisk University, 1968.

S187. Smith, Jessie Carney. "Special Collections of Black Literature in the Traditionally Black College." *College and Research Libraries* 35 (Sept. 1974), 322–35. Comment [letter] by Richard Newman, 36 (Jan. 1975), 36.

S188. Smith, Jessie Carney. *Survey of Manuscript and Archival Collections for the Study of Black Culture.* Unpublished paper, 1969(?), 110 pp.

S188A. Smith, John David. *Black Slavery in the Americas: an interdisciplinary bibliography, 1865–1980.* Westport, Conn.: Greenwood Press, 1982, 2 vols.

S189. Smith, Linda. "Literature for the Negro Student." *High Points* 47 (Oct. 1965), 15–26.

* Smith, Nancy. See S6.

S190. Smith, Rebecca W. "Catalogue of the Chief Novels and Short Stories by American Authors Dealing with the Civil War and Its Effects, 1861–1899." *Bulletin of Bibliography* 16:10 (Sept.-Dec. 1939), 193–4; 17:1 (Jan.-Apr. 1940), 10–2; 17:2 (May-Aug. 1940), 33–5; 17:3 (Sept.-Dec. 1940), 53–5; 17:4 (Jan.-Apr. 1941), 72–5.

S191. Smith, Robert M., et al. *Literature of American Minorities Prior to the Civil War: a descriptive bibliography of writings by American "minority group" authors available in the Diablo Valley College Library, Contra Costa County Library System, and some nearby libraries, including literary history, biography, and criticism.* Pleasant Hills, Cal.: Diablo Valley College, 1968, 31 pp.

S192. Smith, Thelma E. "The Communities of the City of New York. Part 13: Harlem." *Municipal Reference Library Notes* 38:7 (Sept. 1963), 213–9.

S193. Smith, Winifred. *The Black Experience.* Douglas, Ga.: South Georgia College Library.

* Smithson, Bruce. See C103.

S194. Smythe, Hugh H., and L. Chase. "Current Research on the Negro: a critique." *Sociology and Social Research* 42 (1958), 199–202.

* Snead, Ernestine. See A38.

S195. Snowden, George. *Negro Political Behavior: a bibliography*. Bloomington, Ind.: Indiana University, Department of Government, 1941, 19 pp.

S196. Snyder, Joann, and Michele Johnson. *Black Studies Bibliography*. St. Mary's City, Md.: St. Mary's College of Maryland.

S197. *The Sociology of the South: a bibliography and critique of unpublished documents, doctoral dissertations and master's theses written on aspects of the South, 1938–1948*. Nashville, Tenn.: Fisk University, Social Science Institute, 1950, 376 pp.

S198. Sodenbergh, Peter A. "Bibliographical Essay: the Negro in juvenile series books, 1899–1930." *Journal of Negro History* 58:2 (Apr. 1973), 179–86.

S199. Sollors, Werner. *Bibliographic Guide to Afro-American Studies (based on the holdings of the Library)*. Berlin, Germany: Free University of Berlin, John F. Kennedy Institute for North American Studies, Library, 1972, 258 pp.

S200. Sollors, Werner. "Black Studies in the U.S.: a bibliography." *Jahrbuch für Amerikastudien* 16 (1971), 213–22.

* Sollors, Werner. See also K13.

S201. *Some Books about the Negro*. Atlanta, Ga.: Atlanta Public Library, Children's Department, 1967, 11 pp.

S202. *Some Books and Pamphlets, Music, Magazines and Newspapers by Negro Writers, Composers and Editors in the Colored Department of the Louisville Free Public Library*. Louisville, Ky.: Louisville Free Public Library, Colored Department, 1921, 11 pp.

S203. "Some 1969 Books for and about Negro Children." *Publishers Weekly* 197 (Jan. 5, 1970), 76.

S204. *Some Recent Books on Negro History and Literature: a bibliography for groups of all ages*. New York: National Federation of Settlements and Neighborhood Centers, 1968, 19 pp.

S205. *Some Significant Books on Afro-American History and Culture*. Philadelphia, Pa.: Free Library of Philadelphia, 1968.

S206. "Some Things to Read on the Race Problem." *Scholastic* 36 (Feb. 12, 1940), 27.

S207. Somerville, M.A. "Language of the Disadvantaged: toward resolution of conflict." *Journal of Negro Education* 43 (Summer 1974), 284–301.

S208. Not used.

S209. Sotendahl, Audrey. *Selected Bibliography of Books on the Negro in America*. Utica, N.Y.: Mohawk Valley Community College, 1969.

S210. *Source Material on the Urban Negro in the US, 1910–1937: a list of selected data*. New York: National Urban League, 1937, 36 pp. Subsequent editions appeared in 1938 and 1939.

S211. *Sources of Educational Information Bearing on Negro Life and Related Subjects*. Washington, D.C.: Federal Security Agency, 1944, 4 pp.

S212. "The South." *Branch Library Book News* [The New York Public Library] 41:3 (Feb. 1964), 27–35.

S213. Southern, Eileen. "William Grant Still: list of major works." *The Black Perspective in Music* 3:2 (May 1975), 235–8.

S214. Southgate, Robert L. *Black Plots and Black Characters: a handbook for Afro-American literature.* Syracuse, N.Y.: Gaylord Professional Publications, 1979, 456 pp.

S215. Sowell, Thomas. *Bibliography of American Ethnic Groups.* ERIC Document no. ED 129–708. Washington, D.C.: Urban Institution, 1976, 2 vols.

S216. Spady, James G. "The Afro-American Historical Society: the nucleus of black bibliophiles (1897–1923)." *Negro History Bulletin* 37:4 (1974), 254–7.

* Spalding, Mary Louise. See P67.

S217. Spangler, Earl. *Bibliography of Negro History: selected and annotated entries, general and Minnesota.* Minneapolis, Minn.: Ross and Haines, 1963, 101 pp.

S218. Spear, Jack B. "Race Relations Through Films." *The Bookmark* (Feb. 1964), 145–7. Updated in the Apr. 1966 issue, pp. 257–60.

S219. Spearman, Marie. *Richard Nathaniel Wright.* CAAS Bibliographies no. 4. Atlanta, Ga.: Atlanta University Center for African and Afro-American Studies, 197?, 19 pp.

S220. *Special Collections in the Erastus Milo Cravath Memorial Library, Fisk University.* Fisk University Library Publication no. 5. Nashville, Tenn.: Fisk University, 1967, 16 pp.

S221. "Special Collections [of Afro-American Material]." *The Ebony Handbook.* Chicago, Ill.: Johnson Publishing Co., 1974, pp. 184–7.

S222. "Special Criteria for Negro Books." *Library Journal* 73 (May 15, 1948), 783–5.

S223. *The Special Negro Collection at the George Cleveland Hall Branch Library.* Chicago, Ill.: Chicago Public Library, George Cleveland Hall Branch, 1968, 6 pp.

S224. "Special Reading Lists: bibliography on the American Negro." *General Theological Library [Boston] Bulletin* 36:1 (Oct. 1943), 5–9.

* Speller, Benjamin F., Jr. See O21.

S225. Spencer, Mary, and Jane Humbertson. *Black Studies: a bibliography.* Hagerstown, Md.: Hagerstown Junior College, 16 pp.

S226. Spencer, R. "Art Tatum: an appreciation." *Jazz Journal* 19 (Aug. 1966), 6–10; (Sept. 1966), 11–16; (Oct. 1966), 13–16.

S227. Spingarn, Arthur B. "Collecting a Library of Negro Literature." *Journal of Negro Education* 7 (Jan. 1938), 12–8.

S228. Spivey, Lydia L. *The Negro in America: a selected bibliography of material in the Public Library of Charlotte and Mecklenburg County.* Charlotte, N.C.: Public Library of Charlotte and Mecklenburg County, 1970, 46 pp.

S229. Spoor, Richard D., Marvin McMickle, and Charlotte Falk. *The Black Experience in America: a selected bibliography of resources in the Union Theological Seminary Library, New York, New York.* New York: Union Theological Seminary, 1975, 105 pp.

S230. Sprague, M.D. "Richard Wright: a bibliography." *Bulletin of Bibliography* 21:2 (Sept.-Dec. 1953), 39.

S231. Sprecher, Daniel. *Guide to Films (16 mm) about Negroes.* Alexandria, Va.: Serina Press, 1970, 87 pp.

S232. Springer, A.B. "Books by Negro Authors in 1959." *Crisis* 67 (Apr. 1960), 237–44.

* Sprinkle, Sylvia. See B138.

S233. Stagg, Tom, and Charlie Crump. *New Orleans, the Revival: a tape and discography of Negro traditional jazz recorded in New Orleans or by New Orleans bands, 1937–1972.* Dublin, Ireland: Bashall Eaves Publications, 1973, 307 pp.

S234. Stagg, Tom, and Charlie Crump. *The Revival Negro Bands and Musicians of New Orleans, 1937–1972.* Chigwell, Essex, England: Storyville Publications, 1974, 340 pp.

* Stalker, John. See J124.

S235. Standifer, James A., and Barbara Reeder. *Source Book of African and Afro-American Materials for Music Educators.* Washington, D.C.: Contemporary Music Project, 1972, 147 pp.

S236. Standley, Fred L. "James Baldwin: a checklist, 1963–1967." *Bulletin of Bibliography* 25:6 (May-Aug. 1968), 135+.

S237. Standley, Fred L., and Nancy V. Standley. *James Baldwin: a reference guide.* Boston, Mass.: G.K. Hall, 1980, 310 pp.

* Standley, Nancy V. See S237.

S238. Stanford, Barbara Dodds, and Karima Amin. *Black Literature for High School Students.* Urbana, Ill.: National Council of Teachers of English, 1978, 273 pp.

* Stanford, Barbara Dodds. See also Dodds, Barbara.

* Stanke, Barbara L. See S240.

S239. Stanke, Michael J. "New York Black Abolitionist Bibliography." *Afro-Americans in New York Life and History* 3:1 (1979), 45–50.

S240. Stanke, Michael J., and Barbara L. Stanke. "Black Abolitionist [Editorial] Project." *The Schomburg Center for Research in Black Culture Journal* 1:2 (Spring 1977), 4–5.

S241. Stanleigh, B. "Jazz [recordings]." *Audio* 54 (Feb. 1970), 76.

S242. States, Marva. *The Negro in the U.S.* Baltimore, Md.: Enoch Pratt Free Library, 1965.

* Steading, Alma D. See D125.

* Stearns, Marshall W. See R68.

S243. Steiner, John. "Jim Europe's Discography." *Jazz Record* (Nov. 1947), 18–20.

S244. Stenbeck, L. "Emile Barnes diskografi." *Orkester Journalen* 21 (Jan. 1963), 34.

S245. Stenbeck, Lennart. "George Lewis Diskografi." *Orkester Journalen* 33 (June 1965), 28; 33 (July-Aug. 1965), 30; 33 (Sept. 1965), 40.

S246. Sterling, Dorothy. "The Soul of Learning." *English Journal* 57 (Feb. 1968), 166–80.

S247. Sterling, Dorothy. "What's Black and White and Read All Over?" *English Journal* 58 (Sept. 1969), 817–32.

S248. Stern, Richard. "The Books in Fred Hampton's Apartment." *The Books in Fred Hampton's Apartment*. New York: E.P. Dutton, 1973, pp. 70–2.

S249. Sterrenburg, F.A.S. *Vijftig jaar jazz op platen [Jazz 1917–1967]*. Amsterdam, Netherlands: I.V.I.O., 1967, 16 pp.

S250. Stetler, Henry G. *Inter-group Relations Bibliography: a selected list of books, periodicals, and resource agencies in inter-group relations, including a special section devoted to Connecticut studies*. Hartford, Conn.: Connecticut State Inter-Racial Commission, 1947, 82 pp. An enlarged edition of 86 pp. was published in 1948. A 1944 edition had 36 pp.

S251. Stetson, Erlene. "Bibliography of Female Slave Narratives." *In* Gloria T. Hull, Patricia Bell Scott, and Barbara Smith, eds. *But Some of Us Are Brave: black women's studies*. Old Westbury, N.Y.: Feminist Press, 1982, pp. 82–4.

S252. Stevens, D.L. "Analysis and Annotated Bibliography of Selected Books for Children about Negro Life." M.A. thesis, Western Michigan University, 1971, 79 pp.

S253. Stevens, Jocelyn E., and Pennie E. Perry. *Bibliography of Master's Theses, 1946–1967, North Carolina College at Durham*. Durham, N.C.: North Carolina Central University, James E. Shepard Memorial Library.

S254. Stevenson, Gordon. "Race Records: victim of benign neglect in libraries." *Wilson Library Bulletin* 50:3 (Nov. 1975), 224–32.

S255. Stevenson, Robert. "The Afro-American Legacy (to 1800)." *Musical Quarterly* 54 (Oct. 1968), 475–502.

S256. Stewart, Ruth Ann. "The Schomburg Center for Research in Black Culture and Its Strengths in the Field of American History Relative to the Bicentennial." *The Bookmark* (Mar.-Apr. 1974), 110–4.

S257. Stewart-Baxter, Derrick. "Blind Lemon Jefferson: a new discography." *Jazz Journal* 7 (May 1954), 15.

S258. Stewart-Baxter, Derrick. "Blues Digest [Arthur Cruddup]." *Record Research* 1 (Apr. 1955), 7–8.

S259. Stewart-Baxter, Derrick. "A Discography of Bunk Johnson." *Melody Maker* 25 (July 30, 1949), 11.

S260. Stewart-Baxter, Derrick. "Lovie Austin Discography." *Playback* 2 (Aug. 1949), 14–8.

* Stewart-Baxter, Derrick. See also P23.

S261. Stiassi, Ruggiero. "Discografia Lester Young." *Musica Jazz* (Jan./Mar. 1975).

S262. Stolper, Darryl M. "Jack Lauderdale, Swing Time Records." *Blues Unlimited* 92 (June 1972).

S263. Stone, Pauline C.T., and Cheryl Luvenia Brown. *The Black American Woman in the Social Science Literature*. Ann Arbor, Mich.: University of Michigan, Women's Studies Program, 1978, 65 pp.

S264. Storen, Helen F. *Readings in Intergroup Relations*. Rev. ed. New York: National Conference of Christians and Jews, 1959, 53 pp. An edition of 48 pp. was published in 1956.

* Story, Lillie. See H27.

S265. Strache, Neil E., Maureen E. Hady, James P. Danky, Susan Bryl, and Erwin K. Welsch. *Black Periodicals and Newspapers: a union list of holdings in the libraries of the University of Wisconsin and the library of the Historical Society of Wisconsin*. 2nd ed. rev. Madison, Wis.: State Historical Society of Wisconsin, 1979, 83 pp.

S266. Strachwitz, Chris. "Cajun Music on LP: a survey." *American Folk Music Occasional* 2 (1970), 25–9.

S267. Strachwitz, Chris A. "[Sam] Lightnin' Hopkins Discography." *Jazz Monthly* 5 (Nov. 1959), 35–6; 5 (Dec. 1959), 13–4.

S268. Strachwitz, Chris. *Texas Blues [Lowell Fulson, Lil Son Jackson, and Andrew "Smokey" Hogg]*. Reprinted from *Jazz Report*, 1966.

* Strateman, Klaus. See E23.

S269. Stroman, Carolyn Alma. "Toward a Sociology of the Black Family: a bibliographical essay." M.A. thesis, Atlanta University, 1973, 60 pp.

S270. Stuart, Alice. *Civil Rights and the Negro: articles appearing in current magazines and journals*. Edison, N.J.: Middlesex County College Library, 1969.

S271. Stuckert, Robert D., and Irwin D. Rinder. "The Negro in Social Science Literature: 1961." *Phylon* 23 (Summer 1962), 111–27.

S272. "Studies in Race and Culture." *Phylon* 24 (Winter 1963), 392–8.

S273. Sturges, Gladys M. *Professional Guide to the Afro-American in Print: a bibliography of current works by and about the black man of America*. Normandy, Mo.: The Afro-American Bibliographic Researcher, 1969.

S274. Stutler, Boyd Blym. *Checklist, John Brown (1800–1859): books, pamphlets, magazine and newspaper articles*. Charleston, Va., 1925, 47 pp.

S275. Suber, Charles. "An Annotated Bibliography of Jazz Study Materials." *Down Beat Music Annual* (1973), 77–8.

S276. *Subject Index to Literature on Negro Art Selected from the Union Catalog of Printed Materials on the Negro in the Chicago Libraries*. Chicago, Ill.: Chicago Public Library Omnibus Project, 1941, 49 pp.

S277. *Suggested Reading*. New Haven, Conn.: Lutheran Women's Missionary League, Atlantic Division, 1968, 2 pp.

S278. Suggs, Susan. *Selected Bibliographies Relating to Black Studies in the Robert W. Woodruff Library.* Atlanta, Ga.: Emory University, Robert W. Woodruff Library.

S279. Sullivan, Lester G., Jr. "List of Selected Books, Pamphlets, and Articles on Blacks and Race Relations in Louisiana." *In* Robert R. MacDonald, John R. Kemp, and Edward F. Haas, eds. *Louisiana's Black Heritage.* New Orleans, La.: Louisiana State Museum, 1979, pp. 231–9.

S280. Sullivan, P.J. "Beating the Squeeze [bargain jazz records]." *Jazz Journal* 20 (Dec. 1967), 43.

S281. Sullivan, P.J. "Beating the Squeeze: a recap on bargain jazz [records]." *Jazz Journal* 21 (Mar. 1968), 25 + .

S282. Sullivan, Patrick. "Charlie Parker on Dial." *Jazz Forum* 6:32 (Dec. 1974), 61 + .

S283. Sumpter, Clyde G. "The Negro in Twentieth Century American Drama: a bibliography." *Theatre Documentation* 3 (Fall 1970-Spring 1971), 3–27.

S284. *Supplementary Catalog of Resources for Inclusion of Negro History and Culture in the Dade County Curriculum Preliminary Edition.* ERIC Document no. 069–559. Miami, Fla.: Dade County Public Schools, Department of Program Planning and Development, 1969.

S285. "Supplementary References of College and University Materials on Rural Education." *Journal of Negro Education* 15 (Winter 1946), 99–102.

S286. Suzuki, Peter T. *Minority Group Aged in America: a comprehensive bibliography of recent publications on Blacks, Mexican Americans, Native Americans, Chinese, and Japanese.* Exchange Bibliography no. 816. Monticello, Ill.: Council of Planning Librarians, 1975.

* Swartout, Ann M. See H94.

S287. Sween, Roger D. *Black Literature and Art Catalog.* Platteville, Wis.: Wisconsin State University at Platteville, Elton S. Karrmann Library.

S288. Sweet, Charles E. *Sociology of the American Negro.* Focus: Black American Bibliography Series. Bloomington, Ind.: Indiana University, 1969, 53 pp.

S289. Sweet, Charles E., and Giovanna R. Jackson. *The Negro and the Establishment: law, politics and the courts/Black Nationalism.* Focus: Black American Bibliography Series. Bloomington, Ind.: Indiana University, 1969, 28 pp.

* Sweet, Charles E. See also S291.

S290. Swisher, Robert, and Jill A. Archer. *Black American Literature and Black American Folklore.* Focus: Black American Bibliography Series. Bloomington, Ind.: Indiana University, 1969, 25 pp.

S291. Swisher, Robert, and Charles E. Sweet. *Psychology of Black Americans/Biological Aspects of Race.* Focus: Black American Bibliography Series. Bloomington, Ind.: Indiana University, 1969, 26 pp.

S292. Swisher, Robert, Carol Tullis, and Richard Hicks. *Black American Biography/Black American Scientists/Black Americans in Public Affairs.* Bloomington, Ind.: Indiana University, 1969, 51 pp.

* Swisher, Robert. See also H65.

S293. Swoboda, Hubert. *The John Coltrane Discographie, 1949–1967.* Stuttgart, Germany: Modern Jazz Series, 1968, 40 pp.

S294. Sykes, Ossie. "The Schomburg Collection: stepchild of learning." *Liberator* 5 (Feb. 1965), 8–9.

S295. "A Symphony of Brotherhood." *Read, See and Hear* 18:4 (Feb. 2, 1970), 4 pp. Issued by the Newark, N.J., Board of Education, Department of Libraries and Audiovisual Education.

S296. Szabo, Andrew. *Afro-American Bibliography: a list of books, documents, and periodicals on black-American culture located in the San Diego State College Library.* San Diego, Cal.: San Diego State College Library, 1970, 327 pp.

S297. Szwed, John F. "The Joyful Noise: the one-foot shelf of the blues." *Jazz* 5:7 (1966), 33.

S298. Szwed, John F. "Ongoing Bibliography of Pennsylvania Folklore and Related Materials: black folk culture in Pennsylvania." *Keystone Folklore* 19 (1974), 113–9.

S299. Szwed, John F., and Roger D. Abrahams. *Afro-American Folk Culture: an annotated bibliography of materials from North, Central and South America and the West Indies.* Bibliographical and Special Series, vols. 31 and 32. Philadelphia, Pa.: American Folklore Society, Institute for the Study of Human Issues, 1978, 2 vols.

T

T1. Tackaberry, M. Liguori, and Anne Bernice Whalen. *Bibliography of Books and Other Material on Negro History and Culture in the Fontbonne College Library.* St. Louis, Mo.: Fontbonne College Library.

* Takle, Cynthia A. See T2.

T2. Takle, John A., and Cynthia A. Takle. *Ethnic and Racial Minorities in North America: a selected bibliography on the geographical literature.* Exchange Bibliography no. 459–460. Monticello, Ill.: Council of Planning Librarians, 1973, 71 pp.

T3. Talbot, William. " 'Uncle Tom's Cabin': first English editions." *American Book Collector* 3:5–6 (May-June 1933), 292–7.

T4. *Tales of Then and Now.* The Black Culture Series for Young Readers. Chicago, Ill.: Chicago Public Library, 1972, 9 pp.

* Tambs, Lewis A. See B135.

T5. Tandy, Jenette R. "Pro-Slavery Propaganda in American Fiction of the [Eighteen-] Fifties." *South Atlantic Quarterly* 21 (1922), 41–50, 170–8.

T6. Tannenbaum, Earl. *Insight: the Negro in the U.S., a selected bibliography*. Terre Haute, Ind.: Indiana State University, Cunningham Memorial Library, 1970, 45 pp.

T7. Tanner, Paul. "A Discography of Teddy Bunn." *Jazz Journal* 23 (Dec. 1971); 24 (Nov. 1972); 25 (Jan. 1973).

T8. Tanneyhill, Ann. *Bibliography on the Negro and National Defense*. New York: National Urban League, Department of Industrial Relations, 1941, 12 pp.

T9. Tanneyhill, Ann. *Vocational Guidance Bibliography*. 9th ed. New York: National Urban League, Department of Industrial Relations, 1940, 45 pp. The 8th ed. in 1939 had 29 pp.

* Tarrant, Don. See M128.

T10. Tate, Allen, and Francis Cheney. "Langston Hughes." *Sixty American Poets, 1896–1944*. Washington, D.C.: Library of Congress, General Reference and Bibliography Division, 1945, pp. 61–2. A revised edition appeared in 1954, in which the Hughes bibliography is on pp. 52–5, and "James Weldon Johnson" on pp. 59–61.

T11. Tate, Binnie. "In House and Out House: authenticity and the black experience in children's books." *Library Journal* (Oct. 15, 1970), 3595–8.

T12. Tate, Binnie. "Integrating Culture: a credo for believers." *Library Journal* 94 (May 15, 1969), 2051–4; *School Library Journal* (May 1969), 39–42.

T13. Taylor, Archie. *Bibliography on Black Art*. San Diego, Cal.: San Diego City Schools, Curriculum Services Division, 196?, 6 pp.

T14. Taylor, Barbara, and Margaret Mattern. *A Guide to Afro-American Resources in University of Rochester Libraries*. Rochester, N.Y.: University of Rochester, Rush Rhees Library and the Center for Afro-American Studies, 1971, 34 pp.

T15. Taylor, Cecil. "John Coltrane." *Jazz Review* 2 (Jan. 1959), 34.

T16. Taylor, David Vassar. *Blacks in Minnesota: a preliminary guide to historical sources*. Minneapolis, Minn.: Minnesota Historical Society, 1976, 33 pp.

* Taylor, F.M. See G52.

T17. Taylor, J.R. "A Horace Silver Discography." *Radio Free Jazz* (Mar. 1977), 21–7.

T18. Taylor, Peter, and Geoffrey Helliwell. "A Discography of Johnny Dodds." *Jazz Journal* 2 (May 1949), 8; 2 (June 1949), 15; 2 (Nov. 1949), 8.

T19. Taylor, R.L. "Professional Development among Black Children and Youth; a reexamination." *American Journal of Orthopsychiatry* 46 (Jan. 1976), 4–19.

T20. *Teaching about Minorities in Classroom Situations*. New York: New York City Board of Education, Office of Publications, 2 pp.

T21. "Teaching about the Negro in U.S. History." *Scholastic Teacher* (Nov. 18, 1967).

T22. *Teaching Black: an evaluation of methods and resources.* Stanford, Cal.: Stanford University, Multi-Ethnic Educational Resource Center, 1971, 83 pp.

T23. "Technical Articles by Members of the Howard Faculty." *Howard Record* 18, p. 143.

T24. *Tell It Like It Is: a creative approach to understanding the inner city.* Baltimore, Md.: Enoch Pratt Free Library, 1968.

T25. Tenot, F. "Au carrefour du blues." *Jazz Magazine* 8 (Dec. 1962), 26–35.

T26. *Tentative Bibliography for Church History 249: the Negro in American church history.* New York: Union Theological Seminary.

T27. Tepperman, Barry. "Budget [Charlie] Bird [Parker]." *Coda* 9:8 (July-Aug. 1970), 10–1.

T28. Tepperman, Barry. "Marion Brown Discography." *Jazz Monthly* 187 (Sept. 1970), 19–21.

T29. Terborg-Penn, Roslyn M. "The Historical Treatment of Afro-Americans in the Women's Suffrage Movement, 1900–1920: a bibliographical essay." *Current Bibliography on African Affairs* 7 (Summer 1974), 245–59.

T30. Terborg-Penn, Roslyn M. "Teaching the History of Black Women: a bibliographical essay." *History Teacher* 13:2 (Feb. 1980), 245–50.

T31. Tercinet, Alain. "Hollywood Hangover: filmographie de [Edward] Duke Ellington." *Jazz Hot* 298 (Oct. 1973), 24–6.

T32. Teubig, Klaus. *Nat "King" Cole Discographie.* Hamburg, Germany: Author, 1964, 16 pp.

T33. Thad Jones Discography." *Swing Journal* 28 (Feb. 1974), 262–9.

T34. Thaden, J.F., and Walter E. Freeman. *A Partial Bibliography on the American Negro: books and their call numbers in the library of Michigan State University as of Sept. 1, 1962.* East Lansing, Mich.: Michigan State University Library, Institute for Community Development and Services, 1962, 12 pp.

T35. *That All Men May Be Free: selected readings on the Negro in America.* Philadelphia, Pa.: Free Library of Philadelphia.

T36. "Thelonious Monk." *Swing Journal* 29 (Nov. 1975), 252–9.

T37. "Thelonious Monk Plattenhinweise." *HiFi Stereophonie* 15:8 (Aug. 1976), 816.

T38. Theobald, Ruth. "Library Services for Negro Children." *ALA Children's Library Yearbook* 4 (1932), 111–22.

T39. Thieme, Darius L. "Negro Folksong Scholarship in the U.S." *African Music* 2:3 (1960), 67–72.

T40. *Think Black!* Baltimore, Md.: Baltimore City Public Schools, 30 pp.

* Thompson, Alma M. See T44.

T41. Thompson, Charles H. "Current Literature on Negro Education: periodicals." *Journal of Negro Education* 7 (Oct. 1938), 576–81.

T42. Thompson, Charles H., and Mildred Jenkins. "Current Literature on Negro Education: periodicals and reference." *Journal of Negro Education* 7 (Apr. 1938), 215–9.

T43. Thompson, Edgar T. *The Plantation: a bibliography*. Washington, D.C.: Pan American Union, Social Science Section, Department of Cultural Affairs, 1957, 93 pp.

T44. Thompson, Edgar T., and Alma Macy Thompson. *Race and Region: a descriptive bibliography compiled with special reference to the relations between whites and Negroes in the U.S.* Chapel Hill, N.C.: University of North Carolina Press, 1949, 194 pp. Reprinted by Kraus in 1971.

T45. Thompson, G.R. "A Second Black Renaissance: black 'New Criticism' and a black aesthetic." *American Literary Scholarship: an annual 1970.* Durham, N.C.: Duke University Press, 1972, pp. 376–401.

T46. Thompson, Judith, and Gloria Woodward. "Black Perspective in Books for Children." *Wilson Library Bulletin* (Dec. 1969), 416–24.

T47. Thompson, Lawrence Sidney. *The Southern Black, Slave and Free: a bibliography of anti- and pro-slavery books and pamphlets, and of social and economic conditions in the Southern states from the beginnings to 1950.* Troy, N.Y.: Whitson Publishing Co., 1970, 576 pp.

T48. Thompson, Lucille Smith, and Alma Smith Jacobs. *The Negro in Montana, 1800–1945: a selected bibliography*. Helena, Mont.: Montana State Library, 1970, 23 pp.

T49. Thompson, Marilyn. *Afro-American Studies*. Downers Grove, Ill.: George Williams College Library.

T50. Thompson, Ralph. "The Liberty Bell and Other Anti-Slavery Gift Books." *New England Quarterly* 7 (1934), 154–68.

* Thompson, Robert. See A108.

T51. Thompson, Vern. "Walter Bishop, Jr." *Different Drummer* 1:13 (Nov. 1974), 10–2.

* Thorne, Barrie. See M118.

T52. Thorne, F. "Microsolco al microscopio [Miles Davis]." *Jazz di ieri e di oggi* 11 (Jan.-Feb. 1960), 48–53.

T53. Thorne, Kathleen, et al. *Minorities in America: a list of books on blacks and Mexican-Americans in the San Jose State College Library.* San Jose, Cal.: San Jose State College Library, 1969, 151 pp.

T54. Thornton, Barbara L. *Bibliography for a Research of the Literature in Non-Verbal Communication, and Its Application, as Related to the Study of Black American Non-Verbal Communication.* ERIC Document no. ED 070–108. Washington, D.C., 1973, 16 pp.

T55. Thorpe, Earl. "Black History and the Organic Perspective: an essay to introduce the Directory and Bibliography no. 870/1/2." Exchange Bibliography no. 869. Monticello, Ill.: Council of Planning Librarians, 1975, 30 pp. See Hudson, Gossie Harold. *Directory of Black Historians . . .* (H112).

T56. Tilghman, Levin. *A Selected List of Reference Sources in Afro-American Studies*. Tampa, Fla.: University of South Florida Library, 1976, 6 pp.

T57. *A Time for Learning*. Seattle, Wash.: King County Library System, 1968.

T58. *A Time to Listen, a Time to Act*. Belmont, Cal.: San Mateo County Library System.

T59. Tinker, Edward L. "Bibliography of French Newspapers and Periodicals of Louisiana [during Reconstruction]." *American Antiquarian Society Proceedings*, Part 1, 42 (1932), 249–82.

T60. Tinker, Edward L. "Gombo: the Creole Dialect of Louisiana, with a bibliography." *Proceedings of the American Antiquarian Society at the Semi-Annual Meeting Held in Boston, April 17, 1935*, pp. 101–42.

T61. Tinker, Edward L. *Les Écrits de la Langue Française en Louisiane au XIXe Siècle; Essais Biographiques et Bibliographiques*. Paris, France: Librairie Ancienne Honoré Champion, 1932, 502 pp.

T61A. Tinney, James S. "Black Pentecostalism: an annotated bibliography." *Spirit: a journal of issues incident to Black Pentecostalism* 3:1 (1979), 64 pp.

T62. Tischler, Alice. *Fifteen Black Composers: a bibliography of their work*. Detroit, Mich.: Information Coordinators, 1981, 328 pp.

T63. Tischler, Nancy. "Ralph Ellison." *In* Louis Rubin. *A Bibliographical Guide to the Study of Southern Literature*. Baton Rouge, La.: Louisiana State University Press, 1969, pp. 191–2.

T64. *To Be a Black Woman*. Pittsburgh, Pa.: Carnegie Library, 1971, 2 pp.

T65. *To Be Black in America: a selected bibliography*. Philadelphia, Pa.: Free Library of Philadelphia, Office of Work with Adults and Young Adults, 1970, 32 pp.

T66. *To Be Equal: a selected list of books about Negroes*. Pittsburgh, Pa.: Carnegie Library, 1965, 7 pp.

T67. *To Have a Dream: a selection of books by and about the Negro for young adults*. Chicago, Ill.: Chicago Public Library, 1967, 9 pp.

T68. Tobias, Richard C. "A Matter of Difference: an interim guide to the study of black American writing." *Literary Research Newsletter* 1, pp. 129–46.

* Tod, Georg-Anna. See K76.

T69. Tollara, Gianni, and Luciano Massagli. "Discografia [(Edward) Duke Ellington's Orchestra, 1939–43]." *Musica Jazz* 18 (June 1962), 42–4.

* Tollo, Pia. See G110.

T70. Tolmachev, Mirjana. *The Contemporary Negro: a selected bibliography of recent material in the Pennsylvania State Library*. Harrisburg, Pa.: Pennsylvania State Library, General Library Bureau, 1970, 24 pp. There are several editions of this list.

T71. Tolson, M.B. "On Building a Black Collection." *Oklahoma Librarian* 27 (Apr. 1977), 8 + .

T72. Tolson, Ruth M. *Hampton Institute Press Publications: a bibliography*. Hampton, Va.: Hampton Institute, 1959, 6 pp.

T73. Tompkins, Dorothy Campbell. *Poverty Studies in the Sixties: a bibliography*. Berkeley, Cal.: University of California at Berkeley, 1970.

T74. Totten, Herman L., ed. *Bibliographical Control of Afro-American Literature*. Papers presented at a conference sponsored by a U.S. Office of Education Library Training Grant under Title II, Part B, Higher Education Act (P.L. 89–329 as amended) July 16–17, 1976, Palmer House Hotel, Chicago, Ill. Eugene, Ore.: University of Oregon, School of Librarianship.

T75. Totten, Herman L., and V.D. Gilchrist. "Systems Approach to Bibliographic Control of Afro-American Literature." *Kentucky Library Association Bulletin* 37 (Spring 1973), 11–5. Revisions appeared in the Fall issue, p. 17.

* Totten, Herman L. See also A29, C52, C103B, J100, J125, M36A, R99, S135A, S181A, W101.

T76. *A Touch of Soul*. New York: The New York Public Library, Countee Cullen Regional Branch, North Manhattan Project, 1970.

* Touchstone, Blake. See B348.

T77. *Toward Integrity in American History*. 3rd ed. Chicago, Ill.: Illinois Commission on Human Relations, Education Services Department, 1969, 11 pp. First issued in 1966.

T78. "Toward the Mountain-Top: a selection of black history books for young people." *Read, See and Hear* 22:6 (Feb. 15, 1974), 7 pp.

T79. Townley, Eric. *Tell Your Story: a dictionary of jazz and blues recordings, 1917–1950*. Chigwell, Essex, England: Storyville Publications, 1976, 416 pp.

T80. Townley, Ray, and Tim Hogan. "Supersax: the genius of Bird X Five [Charlie Parker]." *Down Beat* 31 (Nov. 21, 1974), 15.

T81. "Traditions and Contradictions de Theodore Walter 'Sonny' Rollins." *Jazz Hot* 307 (July/Aug. 1974), 17.

T82. Trager, Helen, and Ethel L. Reiner. *Periodicals Useful in Intercultural Education*. New York: Bureau for Intercultural Education, 1944, 5 pp.

T83. Traill, Sinclair. "Jazz on Brunswick 04516 [Gertrude Malissa Nix Pridgett (Ma) Rainey]." *Melody Maker* 26 (July 15, 1950), 9.

T84. Traill, Sinclair. "[Sidney] Bechet's Recordings with the 'Blind' Englishman." *Melody Maker* 26 (Jan. 28, 1950), 5.

T85. Trainor, Juliette. *A Bibliography of Holdings of the Paterson State College Library relating to Black Studies*. Wayne, N.J.: William Paterson College of New Jersey, Sarah Byrd Askew Library, 1970, 54 pp.

T86. Trappe, Patricia, and Janice Babcock. *Black History Week, Feb. 7–14, 1971: a bibliography by and about black Americans*. Troy, Ohio: Troy-Miami County Public Library, 1971, 14 pp.

T87. Trent, William P., et al. "Paul Laurence Dunbar." In *Cambridge History of American Literature*, Vol. II. New York: G.P. Putnam's Sons, 1917–21, pp. 614–5.

* Trent, William P. See also S173.

T88. Treworgy, Mildred L., and Paul B. Foreman. *Negroes in the U.S.: a bibliography of materials for schools, approvable for purchase in Pennsylvania under NDEA provisions; with a supplement of recent materials on other American minority groups.* University Park, Pa.: Pennsylvania State University Libraries, 1967, 93 pp.

T89. Triche, Charles W. III, et al. *The Sickle Cell Hemoglobinpathies: a comprehensive bibliography, 1910–1972.* Troy, N.Y.: Whitson Publishing Co., 1974, 434 pp. A volume of 144 pp. covering 1973–75 was published in 1976.

T90. *Troublesome Presence: prejudice.* Syracuse, N.Y.: Onondaga County Library System, 1 p.

T91. Truesdell, Marilyn P. *Black Women and Religion: a bibliography.* Cambridge, Mass.: Harvard Divinity School, 1975. Addenda, 1976. See also Marilyn Richardson (R88).

T92. Trumpeter, Margo, and Kathryn Scarich. *The Black Community and Champaign-Urbana [Ill.]: a preliminary subject list.* Urbana, Ill.: University of Illinois Library, 1970, 37 pp.

T93. Tuchman, Helene L. *Negro-Jewish Relations: a bibliography covering materials published from January 1960 through May 1968.* Brookline, Mass.: Hebrew College Library.

T94. Tucker, Veronica E. *An Annotated Bibliography of Fisk University Library's Black Oral History Collection.* Nashville, Tenn.: Fisk University Library, 1974.

T95. Tucker, Veronica E. "A Bibliography of Oral History Interviews, Audiotapes and Films by and about Aaron Douglas in the Fisk University Library." *BANC*: 4:2/5:1 (Sept. 1974/June 1975), 25–6.

T96. Tudor, Dean. "Discography of the Real Blues." *Library Journal* 97:4 (Feb. 15, 1972), 638–40.

T97. Tudor, Dean. "7 Center [Leonard Brackett]." *Coda* 11:4 (Nov.-Dec. 1973), 12–4.

T98. Tudor, Dean, and Nancy Tudor. *Black Music.* Littleton, Col.: Libraries Unlimited, 1979, 262 pp.

T99. Tudor, Dean, and Nancy Tudor. *Jazz.* Littleton, Col.: Libraries Unlimited, 1979, 302 pp.

* Tudor, Nancy. See T98, T99.

* Tullis, Carol. See H65, S292.

T100. Tulloch, H. "But the Cat Himself Knows: slavery in the ante-bellum south, a historiographical survey." *History Today* 30 (May 1980), 57–60.

T101. Tumin, Melvin M. *Research Annual in Intergroup Relations, 1965.* New York: Anti-Defamation League of B'nai B'rith, 1966, 176 pp.

T102. Tumin, Melvin M., and Cathy S. Greenblat. *Research Annual on Intergroup Relations, 1966.* New York: Frederick A. Praeger, 1967, 338 pp.

T103. Tumin, Melvin M., and Robert Rotberg. *Segregation and Desegregation: a digest of recent research*. New York: Anti-Defamation League of B'nai B'rith, 1957, 112. A 32 pp. supplement was issued in 1960.

T104. Turner, Benjamin, and H. Kennicutt. *Afro-American Collection*. Little Rock, Ark.: Philander Smith College Library.

T105. Turner, Darwin T. *Afro-American Writers*. New York: Appleton-Century-Crofts, 1970, 117 pp.

T106. Turner, Darwin T. "Jean Toomer." *In* Louis D. Rubin. *A Bibliographical Guide to the Study of Southern Literature*. Baton Rouge, La.: Louisiana State University Press, 1969, pp. 311–2.

T107. Turner, Gladys. *Black People in the U.S.* Chicago, Ill.: Roosevelt University, Murray Green Library.

* Turner, L.D. See C192.

T108. Turner, Lorenzo Dow. "Anti-Slavery Sentiment in American Literature Prior to 1865." *Journal of Negro History* 14:4 (Oct. 1929), 373–492.

T109. Turner, Lorenzo D. "Linguistic Research and African Survivals." *American Council of Learned Societies Bulletin* 32 (Sept. 1941), 68–89.

T110. Turner, Patricia. *Afro-American Singers: an index and preliminary discography of long-playing recordings of opera, choral music and song*. Minneapolis, Minn.: Challenge Productions, Inc., 1977, 255 pp. A supplement of 8 pp. was issued in 1977 and one of 33 pp. in 1978.

T110A. Turner, W. Burghardt. "The Polemicists: David Walker, Frederick Douglass, Booker T. Washington, and W.E.B. Du Bois." *In* M. Thomas Inge, Jackson R. Brycr, and Maurice Duke, eds. *Black American Writers: bibliographic essays*, Vol. 1. New York: St. Martin's Press, 1978, pp. 47–132.

* Turoff, Sidney. See B280.

T111. Tuttle, William M., Jr. "New Resources in American Studies: black newspapers in Kansas." *American Studies* [Lawrence, Kan.] 13:2 (1972), 119–24.

T112. Tuttle, William M., Jr., and S. Bhana. "Black Newspapers in Kansas: keys to a rich but neglected past." *Books and Libraries* 10 (Dec. 1972), 7–11.

T113. Not used.

T114. Twiggs, Leo. *Black Art Appreciation*. Orangeburg, S.C.: South Carolina State College, Miller F. Whittaker Library.

T115. Twining, Mary Arnold. *Bibliography of the Sea Islands* [Gullah people and Geechee people]. CAAS Bibliography no. 10. Atlanta, Ga.: Atlanta University, 1971, 15 pp. A revised edition was issued in 1974.

T116. Tynes, H.A. "Negro Bibliography." *New York Teacher* 3 (May 1938), 22–3.

T117. *The Tyranny of Poverty*. New York: American Jewish Committee, 1966, 18 pp.

T118. Tyson, Edwin L. *Africa and the Blacks: a bibliography.* San Jose, Cal.: San Jose City College Library. Two supplements were issued, the second by James M. Berg.

U

U1. " 'Uncle Tom's Cabin.' " *Times Literary Supplement* (July 8, 1926), 468.

U2. *"Uncle Tom's Cabin" as Book and Legend: a guide to an exhibition.* Detroit, Mich.: Friends of the Detroit Public Library, 1952, 51 pp.

U3. " 'Uncle Tom's Cabin' 100th Anniversary Exhibit." *Chicago History* 2 (1951), 353–64.

U4. *Undergraduate Library Guide to Finding Materials on Black Topics.* Ann Arbor, Mich.: University of Michigan, Undergraduate Library Staff, 1970, 7 pp.

U5. "Understanding America's Race Problem." *Library Journal* 69 (Sept. 1, 1944), 694–5.

U6. *Understanding Minorities: a multi-ethnic bibliography.* Oklahoma City, Ok.: Oklahoma City Public Schools, School Media Services, 1967/8–1968/9, 40 pp.

U7. Uunila, Edith H. "Black Higher Education: a reading list." *Chronicle of Higher Education* (May 20, 1972).

V

* Vail, R.W.G. See S2.

V1. Van der Raay, Wytze, and Willem Van Eyle. "Thelonious Monk discografie." *Jazz Press* 32 (Feb. 18, 1977), 8–9; 33 (Mar. 4, 1977), 8–9; 43 (Sept. 2, 1977), 6.

V2. Van Eyle, Willem Frederik. *Discography of Albert Ammons.* Zaandam, Netherlands: Author, 1966, 4 pp.

V3. Van Eyle, Willem Frederik. *Discography of Alex Hill.* Zaandam, Netherlands: Author, 1966, 2 pp.

V4. Van Eyle, Willem Frederik. *Discography of Bernard Addison.* Zaandam, Netherlands: Author, 1966, 7 pp.

V5. Van Eyle, Willem Frederik. *Discography of Bessie Smith.* Zaandam, Netherlands: Author, 1966, 7 pp. A revised edition with the same number of pages appeared the same year.

V6. Van Eyle, Willem Frederik. *Discography of Billie Holliday* [*Eleanor Gough McKay*]. Zaandam, Netherlands: Author, 1966, 17 pp.

V7. Van Eyle, Willem Frederik. *Discography of Charlie Christian.* Zaandam, Netherlands: Author, 1966, 7 pp.

V8. Van Eyle, Willem Frederik. *Discography of* [*Clarence Lemont*] *Benny*

Moten. Zaandam, Netherlands: Author, 1966, 3 pp. A revised edition with the same number of pp. appeared the same year.

V9. Van Eyle, Willem Frederik. *Discography of Clifford Brown*. Zaandam, Netherlands: Author, 1966, 6 pp.

V10. Van Eyle, Willem Frederik. *Discography of Coleman Hawkins*. Zaandam, Netherlands: Author, 1966, 46 pp. A revised edition with the same number of pages appeared the same year.

V11. Van Eyle, Willem Frederik. *Discography of [Earl] Bud Powell*. Zaandam, Netherlands: Author, 1966, 10 pp.

V12. Van Eyle, Willem Frederik. *Discography of [Edward] Kid Ory*. Zaandam, Netherlands: Author, 1966, 14 pp.

V13. Van Eyle, Willem Frederik. *Discography of [Ferdinand] Jelly Roll Morton*. Zaandam, Netherlands: Author, 1966, 9 pp. A revised edition with the same number of pages appeared the same year.

V14. Van Eyle, Willem Frederik. *Discography of Freddie Keppard*. Zaandam, Netherlands: Author, 1966, 2 pp.

V15. Van Eyle, Willem Frederik. *Discography of George Mitchell*. Zaandam, Netherlands: Author, 1966, 4 pp.

V16. Van Eyle, Willem Frederik. *Discography of [Gertrude Malissa Nix Pridgett] Ma Rainey*. Zaandam, Netherlands: Author, 1966, 4 pp.

V17. Van Eyle, Willem Frederik. *Discography of Hayes Alvis*. Zaandam, Netherlands: Author, 1966, 11 pp.

V18. Van Eyle, Willem Frederik. *Discography of Henry "Red" Allen*. Zaandam, Netherlands: Author, 1966, 24 pp.

V19. Van Eyle, Willem Frederik. *Discography of Herschel Evans*. Zaandam, Netherlands: Author, 1966, 7 pp.

V20. Van Eyle, Willem Frederik. *Discography of Ivy Anderson*. Zaandam, Netherlands: Author, 1966, 4 pp.

V21. Van Eyle, Willem Frederik. *Discography of [James Osten] Pete Brown*. Zaandam, Netherlands: Author, 1966, 7 pp.

V22. Not used.

V23. Van Eyle, Willem Frederik. *Discography of Jimmy Archey*. Zaandam, Netherlands: Author, 1966, 14 pp.

V24. Van Eyle, Willem Frederik. *Discography of Jimmy Blanton*. Zaandam, Netherlands: Author, 1966, 4 pp.

V25. Van Eyle, Willem Frederik. *Discography of Jimmy Harrison*. Zaandam, Netherlands: Author, 1966, 5 pp.

V26. Van Eyle, Willem Frederik. *Discography of Jimmy Noone*. Zaandam, Netherlands: Author, 1966, 6 pp.

V27. Van Eyle, Willem Frederik. *Discography of Jimmy Yancey*. Zaandam, Netherlands: Author, 1966, 2 pp. A revised edition with the same number of pages appeared the same year.

V28. Van Eyle, Willem Frederik. *Discography of [John Birks] Dizzy Gillespie*. Zaandam, Netherlands: Author, 1966, 28 pp.

V29. Van Eyle, Willem Frederik. *Discography of Johnny Dodds*. Zaandam, Netherlands: Author, 1966, 11 pp. A revised edition with the same number of pages appeared the same year.

V30. Van Eyle, Willem Frederik. *Discography of Johnny Dunn*. Zaandam, Netherlands: Author, 1966, 5 pp.

V31. Van Eyle, Willem Frederik. *Discography of [Joseph] King Oliver*. Zaandam, Netherlands: Author, 1966, 11 pp.

V32. Van Eyle, Willem Frederik. *Discography of Leo Parker*. Zaandam, Netherlands: Author, 1966, 4 pp.

V33. Van Eyle, Willem Frederik. *Discography of [Leon] Chu Berry*. Zaandam, Netherlands: Author, 1966, 12 pp.

V34. Van Eyle, Willem Frederik. *Discography of Louis Armstrong, 1930–1947*. Zaandam, Netherlands: Author, 1966, 13 pp.

V35. Van Eyle, Willem Frederik. *Discography of [Oscar] Papa Celestin*. Zaandam, Netherlands: Author, 1966, 2 pp. A revised edition with the same number of pages appeared the same year.

V35A. Van Eyle, Willem. *Discography of Sidney Bechet*. Zaandam, Netherlands: Author, 1966, 26 pp.

V36. Van Eyle, Willem Frederik. *Discography of [Theodore] Fats Navarro*. Zaandam, Netherlands: Author, 1966, 7 pp.

V37. Van Eyle, Willem Frederik. *Discography of Tommy Ladnier*. Zaandam, Netherlands: Author, 1966, 10 pp.

V38. Van Eyle, Willem Frederik. *Discography of [Warren] Baby Dodds*. Zaandam, Netherlands: Author, 1966, 13 pp. A revised edition with the same number of pp. appeared the same year.

V39. Van Eyle, Willem Frederik. *Discography of [William Geary] Bunk Johnson*. Zaandam, Netherlands: Author, 1966, 6 pp. A revised edition with the same number of pages appeared the same year.

V40. Van Eyle, Willem Frederik. *Discography of [William Henry Joseph Berthol Bonaparte Bertholoff] Willie the Lion Smith*. Zaandam, Netherlands: Author, 1966, 11 pp. A revised edition with the same number of pages appeared the same year.

* Van Eyle, Willem. See also V1.

V41. Van Jackson, Wallace. "The Countee Cullen Memorial Collection at Atlanta University." *Crisis* 54 (May 1947), 140–2.

V42. Van Olderen, Martin. "Albert Ammons." *Boogie Woogie and Blues Collector* 15 (Apr. 1972); and following issue.

V43. Van Vechten, Carl. "How the Theatre is Represented in the Negro Collection at Yale." *The Theatre Annual* (1943), 32–8.

V44. Van Vechten, Carl. "The J. W. Johnson Collection at Yale." *Crisis* 49 (July 1942), 222 + .

* Vance, Mary. See V55.

* Venables, Ralph G.V. See C27.

V45. Vera, Billy. "The Chess Sessions [Chuck Berry]." *Time Barrier Express* 4:1 (Apr./May 1980), 48–9.

V46. Vernon, Harriet. *Bibliography of Books and Periodicals by and about Negroes*. Fayetteville, Ark.: University of Arkansas Library.

V47. Vernon, Harriet, and Georgia Clark. *Reference Notes: aids for Black studies*. Fayetteville, Ark.: University of Arkansas Library, 1970, 2 pp.

V48. "Victor 23028 [William (Count) Basie]." *Record Research* 1:3 (June 1955), 9.

V49. Viet, Jean. *Selected Documentation for the Study of Race Relations*. Paris, France: UNESCO, International Committee for Social Science Documentation, 1958, 81 pp.

V50. *The Visible Man: a selected film list*. Akron, Ohio: Akron Public Library, 1970, 12 pp.

V51. *Vocational Guidance Bibliography*. New York: National Urban League.

V52. Voce, Steve. "The Return of Lonnie Johnson." *Jazz Journal* 16:5 (May 1963), 12–4.

V52A. Vogt, Joseph. *Bibliographie zur antiken sklaverei*. . . . Bochum, Germany: Brockmayer, 1971, 181 pp.

* Voight, Kathleen. See P73.

* Volonte, Giovanni M. See M29, M30.

V53. Von Arx, R. "Johnny Dodds." *Matrix* 72–3 (Sept. 1967), 3 + .

V54. Von Furstenberg, George M., and William S. Cartwright. *Discrimination in Housing: a selected bibliography*. Exchange Bibliography no. 298. Monticello, Ill.: Council of Planning Librarians, 1972, 7 pp.

V55. Von Furstenberg, George M., William S. Cartwright, and Mary Vance. *Discrimination in Employment: a selected bibliography*. Exchange Bibliography no. 297. Monticello, Ill.: Council of Planning Librarians, 1972, 24 pp.

V56. Von Tersch, G. "Records: rhythm 'n' blues." *Rolling Stone* 66 (Sept. 17, 1970), 48.

* Vrande, Louise. See B67.

V57. Vreede, Max E. "A Discography of Georgia Tom [Thomas A. Dorsey] and his Associates." *Matrix* 31 (Oct. 1960), 3–22. See also nos. 38 and 40.

V58. Vreede, Max E. *Paramount 12/13000 Series*. Chigwell, Essex, England: Storyville Publications, 1971, 236 pp.

W

W1. Wade, Jacqueline. *American Racism Bibliography*. Philadelphia, Penn.: University of Pennsylvania, School of Social Work, 1981.

W2. Wade, Mary Pius. *A Bibliography of Books, Pamphlets, Clippings, and Sisters' Theses about the Oblate Sisters of Providence, Oldest Community of Negro Sisters in the U.S*. Baltimore, Md.: Mt. Providence Junior College Library.

W3. Wade, Mary Pius. *A Bibliography of Negro Periodical Publications and*

Some Other Periodicals Containing Articles on the Black Experience.
Baltimore, Md.: Mt. Providence Junior College Library.

W4. Wade, Mary Pius. *Books in Black Studies.* Baltimore, Md.: Mt. Providence Junior College Library.

W5. Waffen, Leslie, et al. *Audiovisual Records in the National Archives Relating to Black History (preliminary draft).* Washington, D.C.: National Archives and Records Service, 1972, 16 pp.

W6. Walker, C.E. "Slavery: our national sin." *Choice* 16 (Sept. 1979), 773 + .

W7. Walker, Cornelia A., and F.F. Greene. *African and African American History and Culture: a comprehensive bibliography.* Frankfort, Ky.: Kentucky State College, Blazer Library.

W8. Not used.

W9. Walker, Malcolm. "Archie Shepp Discography." *Jazz Monthly* 12 (June 1966), 30–1.

W10. Walker, Malcolm. "Charlie Mingus Discography." *Jazz Monthly* 6:3 (May 1960), 24 + .

W11. Walker, Malcolm. "Clark Terry Discography." *Jazz Monthly* 7 (Jan. 1962), 18–9; 7 (Feb. 1962), 28–9; 7 (Mar. 1962), 30–1; 7 (Apr. 1962), 29.

W12. Walker, Malcolm. "Donald Byrd Discography." *Discographical Forum* 30/31, pp. 35–8, and subsequent issues. See also *Swing Journal* 23 (Dec. 1974), 248–55.

W13. Walker, Malcolm. "Jaki Byard Discography." *Jazz Monthly* 14 (May 1968), 29–31.

W14. Walker, Malcolm. "Eric Dolphy Discography." *Jazz Monthly* 11 (Jan. 1966), 30–1; (Feb. 1966), 30–1; (Mar. 1966), 29.

W15. Walker, Malcolm. "Ornette Coleman Discography." *Jazz Monthly* 12 (May 1966), 24–5.

W16. Walker, Malcolm, and Eric Raben. "John Coltrane Discography." *Jazz Monthly* 12 (Aug. 1966), 11–3; 12 (Sept. 1966), 30–1; 12 (Oct. 1966), 23–4; 12 (Nov. 1966), 29–31.

W17. Walker, Robert A. *A Beginning Bookshelf for Teaching Afro-American Culture.* Urbana-Champaign, Ill.: University of Illinois, 5 pp.

W17A. Wall, Bennett H. "African Slavery." *In* Arthur S. Link and Reinhart W. Patrick, eds. *Writing Southern History: essays in honor of Fletcher M. Green.* Baton Rouge, La.: Louisiana State University Press, 1965, pp. 175–97.

W18. Wallace, Patricia, and Helen Lacy. *Black Studies: a bibliography.* Seattle, Wash.: Shoreline Community College, 1969, 79 pp.

W19. Walsh, J. "The First Singer Who Made a Blues Record: Morton Harvey." *Hobbies* 60 (Nov. 1955), 36–8; 60 (Dec. 1955), 30–2.

W20. Walters, Mary Dawson. *Afro-Americana: a comprehensive bibliography of resource materials in the Ohio State University Libraries by or about Black Americans.* Columbus, Ohio: Ohio State University Libraries, Office of Educational Services, 1969, 220 pp.

W21. Walters, Mary Dawson. *Black History Holdings of the Ohio State Libraries: a partial list*. Columbus, Ohio: Ohio State University Libraries, 1969, 36 pp.

W22. Walton, Hanes. *The Study and Analysis of Black Politics: a bibliography*. Metuchen, N.J.: Scarecrow Press, 1973, 161 pp.

W22A. *The War and the Whole People: an exhibition of original manuscripts, books and pamphlets. Open to the public beginning Sept. 25, 1942, at the Schomburg Collection of Negro Literature, The New York Public Library*. New York: The New York Public Library, 1942, 8 pp.

* Ward, Douglas A.M. See H35B.

W23. Washington, Althea H., and Irene E. Dunlap. "Selected 1947 References on Rural Life and Education." *Journal of Negro Education* 17 (Spring 1948), 215–20.

W24. Waterman, Edith F. *Black Americans*. Tacoma Park, Wash.: Montgomery College.

W25. Watkins, Clifford. *Black Music Bibliography*. Orangeburg, S.C.: South Carolina State College, Miller F. Whittaker Library.

W26. Watt, Louis B. *Literature for Disadvantaged Children: a bibliography*. Washington, D.C.: U.S. Department of Health, Education and Welfare, Office of Education, 1968, 16 pp.

W27. Wax, Donald D. "The Negro in Early America." *Social Studies* 60:3 (1969), 109–18.

W28. Waxman, Julia. *Race Relations: a selected list of readings on racial and cultural minorities in the U.S. with special emphasis on Negroes*. Chicago, Ill.: Julius Rosenwald Fund, 1945, 47 pp.

W29. Wayland, Edward M. *Howard A. Kester Papers, 1923–1972*. Glen Rock, N.J.: Microfilming Corporation of America, 1973, 277 pp.

W30. Wayne, J.L. "The History of 'Uncle Tom's Cabin.' " *Hobbies* 50 (Aug. 1945), 106–7.

W31. *We Hold These Truths*. Washington, D.C.: U.S. Veterans Administration, Medical and General Reference Library, 1969, 31 pp.

W32. *We, Too, Made History: a selected resource list on Afro-American history and culture*. Pittsburgh, Pa.: Carnegie Library, 1968, 11 pp.

* Weaver, Alice. See P73.

* Weaver, Constance. See D140.

W32A. Webb, A. "Bibliographies on Social Issues: St. Charles County Library, Missouri, on the Black Manifesto." *Wilson Library Bulletin* 45 (Sept. 1970), 65+.

W33. Webb, Constance. [Bibliography of Richard Wright]. *Negro Digest* 18 (Jan. 1967), 86–92. Reprinted from *Richard Wright: a biography*. New York: G.P. Putnam's Sons, 1968, pp. 423–9.

W34. Webman, Hal. "Stars, Sidemen and Scribes Salute Duke [Ellington] and His Discs." *Down Beat* 19:22 (Nov. 5, 1952), 2+.

W35. Wedgeworth, Robert. "Jazz." *Library Journal* 87 (May 1, 1963), 1830–2.

W36. Weed, Perry L. *Ethnicity and American Group Life: a bibliography*. ERIC Document no. ED 073–208. New York: Institute for Human Relations, 1972.

W37. Wegelin, Oscar. *Jupiter Hammon, American Negro Poet; selections from his writings and a bibliography*. New York: Charles F. Heartman, 1915, pp. 47–51.

W38. Weinberg, Meyer. "De Facto School Segregation: a selected bibliography." *Law and Society Review* 2 (Nov. 1967), 151–65.

W39. Weinberg, Meyer. *Desegregation Research: an appraisal*. 2nd ed. Chicago, Ill.: Integrated Education Associates, 1970.

W40. Weinberg, Meyer. *The Education of the Minority Child: a comprehensive bibliography of 10,000 selected entries*. Chicago, Ill.: Integrated Education Associates, 1970, 530 pp.

W41. Weinberg, Meyer. *The Education of the Poor and Minority Children: a world bibliography*. Westport, Conn.: Greenwood Press, 1981, 2 vols.

W42. Weinberg, Meyer. *School Integration: a comprehensive classified bibliography of 3,100 references*. Chicago, Ill.: Integrated Education Associates, 1967, 137 pp.

* Weiner, Neil Alan. See W149A.

W43. Weinstock, B. "[John] Dizzy Gillespie: a complete discography." *Record Changer* 8 (July 1949), 8.

W44. Weintraub, Irwin. *Black Agriculturists in the U.S. (1865–1973): an annotated bibliography*. University Park, Penn.: Pennsylvania State University Libraries, Office of the Dean, 1976, 317 pp.

W45. Weir, Birdie, et al. *Black Material for the Public Schools: a study guide published by CEMBA, Alabama Center for Higher Education*. Normal, Ala.: Alabama A and M University, Joseph F. Drake Library.

* Weise, Nancy. See Mc39.

W46. Weixlmann, Joe, and Clarence Major. "Toward a Primary Bibliography of Clarence Major." *Black American Literature Forum* 13 (Summer 1979), 70–2.

W47. Weixlmann, Joe, Robert Fikes, Jr., and Ishmael Reed. "Mapping Out the Gumbo Works: an Ishmael Reed bibliography." *Black American Literature Forum* 12:1 (Spring 1978), 24–9.

* Weixlmann, Joe. See also H35B.

W48. Welding, Pete J. "Charlie Parker as Composer." *Hi Fi Stereo Review* 7 (Oct. 1961), 70–1.

W49. Welding, Pete. "Some Recent Piano Blues Collections." *Sing Out* 12 (1962), 55+.

W50. Wells, E.E. "Black Studies: an educational dilemma." *Negro History Bulletin* 36 (Feb. 1973), 29–33.

W51. Wells, Marion. *Materials for Afro-American Studies in Drake Memorial Library*. Brockport, N.Y.: SUNY, College at Brockport, Drake Memorial Library, 1970.

W52. Welsch, Erwin K. *Afro-American Bibliography: a lecture given to the Institute on African and Afro-American Studies.* Madison, Wis.: University of Wisconsin, 1970.

W53. Welsch, Erwin K. *The Negro in the U.S.: a research guide.* Bloomington, Ind.: Indiana University Press, 1965, 142 pp.

* Welsch, Erwin K. See also B327, S265.

W54. Wesley, Charles H. "An Aspect of Bibliography and Research in Negro History." *Negro History Bulletin* 29:3 (Dec. 1965), 51 + .

W55. West, Earle H. *A Bibliography of Doctoral Research on the Negro, 1933–1966.* Ann Arbor, Mich.: University Microfilms, 1969, 134 pp. Supplemented by Joan Peebles.

W56. West, Earle H. "Summary of Research During 1963 Related to the Negro and Negro Education." *Journal of Negro Education* 34:1 (Winter 1965), 30–8. See also 35:1 (Winter 1966), 62–72; 36:1 (Winter 1967), 58–69.

* West, Earle H. See also B100.

W56A. Westlake, Neda M., and Otto E. Albrecht. *Marian Anderson: a catalog of the collection at the University of Pennsylvania Library,* 1981.

W57. Westmoreland, Guy T., Jr. *An Annotated Guide to Basic Reference Books on the Black American Experience.* Wilmington, Del.: Scholarly Resources, 1974, 98 pp.

* Whalen, Anne Bernice. See T1.

W58. Whalum, Wendell. *Afro-American Folklore Songs.* CAAS Bibliographies no. 7. Atlanta, Ga.: Center for African and African-American Studies, 197?, 7 pp.

W59. Whannel, P. *Jazz on Film: a select list of films on jazz.* London, England: British Film Institute, 1966.

* Wharton, Linda F. See D13.

W60. *What Is Black? a booklist of films, biographies and history from the Brooklyn Public Library.* Brooklyn, N.Y.: Brooklyn Public Library, 1970, 4 pp.

W61. Wheat, C. "Selected Bibliography: minority group participation in the legal profession." *University of Toledo Law Review* (Spring 1970), 935–81.

W62. Wheelbarger, Johnny J. "Black Religion: a bibliography of Fisk University Library materials relating to various aspects of black religious life." *Bibliographies of Sources by and about Blacks Compiled by the Interns in the Internship in Black Studies Librarianship Program.* Nashville, Tenn.: Fisk University Library, 1974(?), pp. 70–96.

W63. Whelan, Peter. "Some Items on Black Patti [Sissieretta Jones] and Richtone." *Record Research* 2:4 (Nov.-Dec. 1956), 13.

W64. *Where Do We Go from Here? A Question for Memphis and the Nation: a selected bibliography on the changing role of the Negro.* Memphis, Tenn.: Memphis Public Library, 1968, 14 pp.

W65. *Where It's At: books with a black beat for young people.* Youngstown, Ohio: Public Library of Youngstown and Mahoning County.

W66. Whitburn, Joel. *Top Rhythm and Blues Records, 1949–1971: facts about 4000 recordings listed in "Billboard's" 'Best Selling Rhythm and Blues (Soul) Singles' charts.* Menomonee Falls, Wis.: Record Research, 1973, 184 pp.

W67. White, Andrew N. *The Charlie Parker Collection.* Washington, D.C.: Andrew's Musical Enterprises, 197?, 4 vols.

W68. White, Andrew N. *The Works of John Coltrane.* Washington, D.C.: Andrew's Musical Enterprises, 197?, 10 vols.

W69. White, Anthony. *Discrimination in Housing Loans—Redlining: a selected bibliography.* Exchange bibliography no. 977. Monticello, Ill.: Council of Planning Librarians, 1976, 5 pp.

W70. White, Doris. *Multi-Ethnic Books for Head Start Children. Part 1: black and integrated literature.* Urbana, Ill.: National Laboratory on Early Childhood, ERIC Clearinghouse in Early Childhood Education, 1969, 28 pp.

W71. White, Earnestine Hoffman. "Health and the Black Person." *American Journal of Nursing* 74 (Oct. 1974), 1839–41.

W72. White, Evelyn Davidson. *Selected Bibliography of Published Choral Music by Black Composers.* Washington, D.C.: Howard University Bookstore, 1976, 87 pp.

* White, Kathy. See Mc22.

* White, Patricia. See A38.

W73. Whiteman, Maxwell. *A Century of Fiction by American Negroes, 1853–1952: a descriptive bibliography.* Philadelphia, Pa.: Albert Saifer, 1955, 64 pp. Reprinted in 1974.

W74. Whiting, H.A. "Readings for Unity: curriculum materials." *Journal of Human Relations* 3 (Spring 1955), 118–9.

W74A. Whitney, Philip. *America's Third World: a guide to bibliographic resources in the library of the University of California, Berkeley.* Berkeley, Cal.: University of California, Berkeley, 1970.

W75. Whitlow, Roger. "The Harlem Renaissance and After: a checklist of black literature of the '20's and '30's." *Negro American Literature Forum* 7 (Dec. 1973), 143–6.

W76. Whittlesey, Walter R. *Negro Music: catalog of Negro music actually composed by members of that race.* 1918.

W77. *Who Cares About Human Relations? a selected and critical bibliography deeply concerned with the human relations of family, community, ethnic, and racial groups, religion, education, business, and industry.* Prepared in Committee by the New Jersey Library Association. New York: Scarecrow Press, 1957, 141 pp.

W77A. "Why? [on Watts riot]." Los Angeles, Cal.: Los Angeles Public Library, 1965.

W78. Wiedemann, Erik. "Charlie Parker: an appreciation and addition to Bird's discography." *Melody Maker* 31 (June 25, 1955), 5.

W79. Wiedemann, Erik. "Charlie Parker Discography." *Melody Maker* 27 (Dec. 8, 1951), 4; 27 (Dec. 15, 1951), 4; 27 (Dec. 22, 1951), 4; 27 (Dec. 29, 1952), 4; 28 (Jan. 5, 1952), 4; 28 (Jan. 12, 1952), 4; 28 (Jan. 19, 1952), 4; 28 (Feb. 2, 1952), 4.

W80. Wiedemann, Erik. "Charlie Parker: diskografiskt sedd." *Orkester Journalen* 27 (Jan. 1959), 10–1.

W81. Wiedemann, Erik. "Chords and Discords: discographical disclaimer [Charlie Parker]." *Down Beat* 29 (July 5, 1962), 6.

W82. Wiedemann, Erik. "Corrections and Additions to the Sidney Bechet Discography." *Melody Maker* 28 (Apr. 19, 1952), 9.

W83. Wiedemann, Erik. "Lester Young on Records." *Jazz Review* 2:8 (Sept. 1959), 10–2.

W84. Wiedemann, Erik. "Milt Jackson Diskografi." *Orkester Journalen* 23 (May 1955), 43.

* Wiedemann, Erik. See also S13.

W85. Wiehe, Emma L., Beulah Howison, and Nancy Johnson. *Black Bibliography*. Menomonie, Wis.: Stout State University, Robert L. Pierce Library.

W86. Wiemhoff, Henry. *A Preliminary Bibliography and Resource Guide: race, racism and the gay male community*. New York: Black and White Men Together.

W87. Wilbraham, Roy J. "Bobby Hutcherson [Discography]." *Jazz Monthly* 12 (Feb. 1967), 26–8.

W88. Wilbraham, Roy J. *Charles Mingus: a biography and a discography*. London, England: Author, 1967, 33 pp.

W89. Wilbraham, Roy J. "Charles Mingus: a biography and discography." *Jazz Journal* 20 (May 1967), 18.

W90. Wilbraham, Roy J. [*John Kenwood*] *Jackie McLean: a biography and discography*. London, England: Frognal Bookshop, 1968, 20 pp. See also *Jazz Monthly* 14 (Apr. 1968), 30–1.

W91. Wilcox, Preston. *Bibliography of Significant Educational Statements; dedicated to Congress of African Peoples, Sept. 3–7, 1970*. Atlanta, Ga.: Afram Associates, 1970, 5 pp.

W92. Wilcox, Preston. *Women and Race Bibliography*. New York: Afram Associates, 1969, 4 pp.

* Wilcox, Preston. See also H37.

W93. Wild, David. *The Recordings of John Coltrane: a discography*. 2nd ed. Ann Arbor, Mich.: Wildmusic, 1979, 90 pp.

W94. Wilgus, Donald K. "Negro Music." *Journal of American Folklore* 81 (1967), 105–9; 81 (1968), 88–94.

W95. Wilgus, Donald K. "Record Reviews: Afro-American tradition." *Journal of American Folklore* 84 (1971), 264–71.

W96. Wilkerson, Doxey A. "Bibliography on the Education of Socially Disadvantaged Children and Youth." *Journal of Negro Education* 33:3 (Summer 1964), 358–66.

* Wilkins, Theresa B. See C10.

W97. Wilkins, Walter R., and Robert Mowery. *Subject List of Books on Black Studies*. Bloomington, Ill.: Illinois Wesleyan University, Library.

W98. Wilkinson, Doris Y. "Toward a Positive Frame of Reference for Analysis of Black Families: a selected bibliography." *Journal of Marriage and the Family* 40 (Nov. 1978), 707–8.

W99. [Will Vodery. Piano Roll]. *Record Research* 1:3 (June 1955), 1.

W100. *William Montague Cobb Publications*. Washington, D.C.: Department of Anatomy, School of Medicine, Howard University, 1955, 15 pp. Rev. ed., 1957, 19 pp.

W101. Williams, Daniel T. "Archival and Fugitive Afro-American Literature: the duties of the archivist." *In* Herman L. Totten, ed. *Bibliographical Control of Afro-American Literature*. Papers presented at a conference sponsored by a U.S. Office of Education training grant under Title II, Part B, Higher Education Act (P.L. 89–329 as amended) July 16–17, 1976, Palmer House Hotel, Chicago, Ill. Eugene, Ore.: University of Oregon, School of Librarianship, 1976, Vol. I, pp. 255–67.

W101A. Williams, Daniel T. *Eight Negro Bibliographies*. New York: Kraus Reprint Co., 1970. This is a compilation and photographic reproduction of eight bibliographies issued separately and previously available only at Tuskegee Institute: (1) "The Freedom Rides: a bibliography," 1961, 17 pp.; (2) "The Southern Students' Protest Movement: a bibliography," 1961, 9 pp.; (3) "The University of Mississippi and James H. Meredith: a bibliography," 1963, 9 pp.; (4) (with Carolyn L. Redden) "The Black Muslims in the United States: a selected bibliography," 1964, 19 pp. plus a 1966 supplement of 2 pp.; (5) "Martin Luther King, Jr. 1929–1968: a bibliography," 1968, 22 pp.; (6) "The Awesome Thunder of Booker T. Washington: a bio-bibliographical listing," 1969, 55 pp.; (7) "The Lynching Records at Tuskegee Institute; with Lynching in America: a bibliography," 1969, 39 pp.; (8) (with Cecil S. Belle) "The Perilous Road of Marcus M. Garvey: a bibliography, and some correspondence with Booker T. Washington, Emmett J. Scott, and Robert Russa Moton," 1969, 62 pp.

W102. Williams, Darrell F. *The Political Economy of Black Community Development: a research bibliography*. Exchange Bibliography no. 457. Monticello, Ill.: Council of Planning Librarians, 1973, 43 pp.

W103. Williams, David, and Dave Sax. "Blues Obscurities: a limited edition." *Jazz and Blues* 2:2 (May 1972), 19–20.

* Williams, Deborah. See C172.

W104. Williams, Donald, James Gault, and Allan Covici. *A Preliminary Guide to Ethnic Materials on the Berkeley Campus*. Berkeley, Cal.: University of California, Berkeley, General Library, 1969, 13 pp.

W105. Williams, Edward Christopher. "Negro Americana." *Howard University Record* 16 (Apr. 1922), 346.

W106. Williams, Ethel L., and Clifton L. Brown. *Afro-American Religious Studies: a comprehensive bibliography with locations in American libraries.* Metuchen, N.J.: Scarecrow Press, 1972, 454 pp.

W107. Williams, Ethel L., and Clifton L. Brown. *The Howard University Bibliography of African and Afro-American Religious Studies (with locations in American libraries).* Wilmington, Del.: Scholarly Resources, 1977, 525 pp.

* Williams, Ethel. See also H127.

W108. Williams, Eugene. "[Joseph] King Oliver and His Dixie Syncopators: notes for a discography." *The Record Changer* (Sept. 1944), 49–51.

W109. Williams, Ezekiel, Jr. "Black Fiction Titles, by and about Blacks." *Bibliographies of Sources by and about Blacks compiled by the Interns in the Internship in Black Studies Librarianship Program.* Nashville, Tenn.: Fisk University Library, 1974(?), pp. 70–96.

W110. Williams, Ezekiel, Jr. "Jessie Fauset and Zora Neale Hurston: a selected bibliographical list." *Bibliographies of Sources by and about Blacks Compiled by the Interns in the Internship in Black Studies Librarianship Program.* Nashville, Tenn.: Fisk University Library, 1974(?), pp. 97–101.

W111. Williams, Frederick, and Rita C. Naremore. *Language and Poverty: an annotated bibliography.* Madison, Wis.: University of Wisconsin, Institute for Research on Poverty, 1967.

W112. Williams, J.B. "Some Special Collections in Fisk University Library." *Tennessee Librarian* 16 (Winter 1964), 47–52.

W113. Williams, Martin T. "A Basic LP Jazz Library." *The American Record Guide* 30 (May 1964), 890–1.

W114. Williams, Martin T. "[Ferdinand] Jelly Roll Morton and the Library of Congress Records." *Jazz Monthly* 6 (Mar. 1960), 4–7; 6 (May 1960), 8–9.

W115. Williams, Martin T. "[John Birks (Dizzy)] Gillespie in Concert." *Saturday Review* 45 (Aug. 25, 1962), 41.

W116. Williams, Martin T. "The Listener's Legacy [Charlie Parker]." *Down Beat* 32 (Mar. 11, 1966), 20–1.

W117. Williams, Martin T. "Mostly [Thelonious] Monk." *Saturday Review* 50 (June 10, 1967), 91.

W118. Williams, Martin T. "Tenors' Return [Sonny Rollins]." *Saturday Review* 45 (June 16, 1962), 36–7.

W119. Williams, Ned E. "Reminiscing in Tempo: Ned on early [Edward (Duke)] Ellingtonia." *Down Beat* 19:22 (Nov. 5, 1952), 14.

W120. Williams, Ora. *American Black Women in the Arts and Social Sciences: a bibliographic survey.* Metuchen, N.J.: Scarecrow Press, 1973, 141 pp. A revised edition of 219 pp. was published in 1978.

W121. Williams, Ora. "A Bibliography of Works Written by American Black

Women." *College Language Association Journal* 15:3 (Mar. 1972), 354–77.

W122. Williams, Ora. "Works by Alice Ruth (Moore) Dunbar-Nelson: a bibliography." *College Language Association Journal* 3:19 (Mar. 1976), 322–6.

W123. Williams, Ora, Thelma Williams, Dora Wilson, and Ramona Matthewson. "American Black Women Composers: a selected annotated bibliography." *In* Gloria T. Hull, Patricia Bell Scott, and Barbara Smith, eds. *But Some of Us Are Brave: black women's studies*. Old Westbury, N.Y.: Feminist Press, 1982, pp. 297–306.

* Williams, Thelma. See W123.

W124. Williams, Tony. "Charlie Parker Discography." *Discographical Forum* 8 (1968); 20 (1970).

W125. Williams, Tony. "[Eli] Lucky Thompson Discography and Biography." *Jazz Journal* 20 (Oct. 1977), 14.

W126. Williams, Tony. *[Eli] Lucky Thompson Discography and Biography, Part I (1944–1951)*. London, England: Author, 1967, 31 pp.

W126A. Williamson, Harry A. *An Index to the Literature about Negro Masonry*. New York, 194?, 2 vols.

W126B. Williamson, Harry A. *A List of the Items in the Masonic Collection of Harry A. Williamson, and Now a Part of The New York Public Library (July 1937)*. New York, 194?, 2 vols.

W126C. Williamson, Harry A. *The Negro in Masonic Literature*. Brooklyn, N.Y., Author, 1922, 30 pp.

W127. ["Willie (Big Bill) Broonzy"]. *Record Research* 1:5 (Oct. 1955), 12.

W128. Williford, Doxie Kent. "A Discography of Mississippi Negro Vocal Blues, Gospel, and Folk Music." M.A. thesis, University of Mississippi, 1968.

W129. Willingham, N.L. "Black Artists and Black Art." *Unabashed Librarian* 18 (Winter 1976), 18–9.

W130. Willingham, N.L. "The Black Woman: an annotated bibliography." *Unabashed Librarian* 14 (Winter 1975), 16–7.

W131. Willis, Cecelia A. *Current Bibliography on Literature by and about Blacks [in Farrell Library]*. ERIC Document no. 061–383. Manhattan, Kan.: Kansas State University, Farrell Library, 1972, 121 pp.

W132. Willis, Richard A., and Hilda McElroy. "Published Works by Black Playwrights in the U.S., 1960–1970." *Bulletin of Black Theatre* 1 (Spring 1971), 8–15. Same in *Black World* 21 (Apr. 1972), 92–8.

W133. Wills, Mrs. Gordon. *Racial Minorities: a bibliography*. Marion, Ind.: Marion College Library.

* Wilmore, Gayraud. See E2.

* Wilson, Dora. See W123.

W134. Wilson, John S. "The Best of Jazz! a discography." *New York Times* (Nov. 26, 1967), p. J3.

W135. Wilson, John S. *The Collector's Jazz: modern*. Philadelphia, Pa.: Lippincott, 1959, 318 pp.

W136. Wilson, John S. *The Collector's Jazz: traditional and swing*. Philadelphia, Pa.: Lippincott, 1958, 319 pp.

W137. Wilson, John S. "Early and Current [Edward] Duke Ellington." *New York Times* 108 (Nov. 9, 1958), 14.

W138. Wilson, John S. "[Edward] Duke Ellington Reissues: career of the jazzman from 1928 to 1949." *New York Times* 103 (Aug. 1954), sect. 2, p. 6.

W139. Wilson, Johns. "Jazz from Abroad: a discography of jazz as performed outside the land of its birth." *High Fidelity Discography* 42 (Aug. 1958), 65+

W140. Wilson, John S. "[Jazz] Treasure of the Twenties." *High Fidelity* 14 (Mar. 1964), 207.

W141. Winston, Adelaide. "The Vivian G. Harsh Collection on Afro-American History and Literature." *In* "Special Collections and Services of the Chicago Public Library." *Illinois Libraries* 54:4 (Apr. 1972), 303.

W142. Winston, Michael R. "Writings of E. Franklin Frazier." In [*Program of*] *A Lecture Series in Honor of Edward Franklin Frazier. March 13, 14, 15, 1962, Cramton Auditorium, Howard University, Washington, D.C.* Washington, D.C.: Howard University, 1962, pp. 9–16.

* Winterich, John T. See R25.

W143. Winters, William R., Jr., Thomas A. Klein, and G. Allen Brunner. *Minority Enterprise and Marketing: an annotated bibliography*. Exchange Bibliography no. 185. Monticello, Ill.: Council of Planning Librarians, 1971, 39 pp.

W144. Winther-Rasmussen, Nils. "John Coltrane: private recordings." *Discographical Forum* 28 (Jan. 1972); 29 (Feb. 1973); 30/31 (Mar. 1973).

* Winther-Rasmussen, Nils. See also L145.

W145. Wisdom, Aline Crawley. *Bibliography of Materials on Afro-American Culture in Citrus College Library*. Azusa, Cal.: Citrus College Library.

W146. Wish, Harvey. "Problems of Historical Research." *American Council of Learned Societies Bulletin* 32 (Sept. 1941), 35–45.

* Wittman, Mrs. Walter T. See H4.

W147. Wolf, Edwin II. "Black Americana: a new world of [rare] books." *AB Bookman's Weekly* 58 (Nov. 1, 1976), 2363+.

* Wolf, Janyce. See D139.

W148. Wolfe, Ann G. *About 100 Books: a gateway to better intergroup understanding*. 6th ed. New York: American Jewish Committee, Institute of Human Relations, 1969.

W149. Wolff, Jane, and Eleanor McKay. *The Papers of Daniel Murray: guide to the microfilm edition*. Madison, Wis.: State Historical Society of Wisconsin, 1977.

W149A. Wolfgang, Marvin E., Neil Alan Weiner, and W. Donald Pointer.

Criminal Violence and Race: a selected bibliography. Washington, D.C.: U.S. Department of Justice, National Institute of Justice, 1982, 79 pp.

W150. Wood, Cliff, and Luisa J. Reynolds. *Black American Literature: a bibliography.* Sacramento, Cal.: Sacramento State College Library.

* Wood, Ethel R. See H4.

* Wood, Robert. See Mc6.

W151. Wood, Vivian. *Selected Reference Sources for Afro-American Studies at Kilmer Area Library.* New Brunswick, N.J.: Rutgers University, Livingston College, Kilmer Area Library, 1978, 3 pp.

* Woodard, Gloria. See Mc9A, T46.

W152. Woodfin, Henry A. "Reconsiderations: these foolish things [Lester Young]." *Jazz Review* 2 (July 1959), 30–1.

W153. Woodress, James, et al. "Countee Cullen." *American Literary Scholarship: an annual.* Durham, N.C.: Duke University Press, 1966, pp. 203–4.

W154. Woodress, James, et al. "Harriet Beecher Stowe." *American Literary Scholarship: an annual.* Durham, N.C.: Duke University Press, 1963, pp. 107–9.

W155. Woodress, James, et al. "James Baldwin." *American Literary Scholarship: an annual.* Durham, N.C.: Duke University, 1963, pp. 150–2; 1964, pp. 159–60; 1965, pp. 186–7; 1966, pp. 171–2.

W156. Woods, Alfred I. "An Evaluation of Afro-Americana in Chicago Area Libraries and Agencies." *Illinois Libraries* 57:5 (May 1975), 318–22.

W157. Woods, Hortense. *Bibliography of the Negro History Collection of the Vernon Branch Library.* Los Angeles, Cal.: Los Angeles Public Library, Vernon Branch, 1973.

W158. Woods, Joyce V. *Selected Bibliography on the Black Experience.* Lafayette, Ind.: Purdue University Libraries, 1970, 20 pp.

W159. Woodward, C. Vann. "The Hidden Sources of Negro History." *Saturday Review* 52 (Jan. 18, 1969), 18–22.

W160. Woolfolk, George R. "Sources of the History of the Negro in Texas, with Special Reference to Their Implications for Research in Slavery." *Journal of Negro History* 42:1 (Jan. 1957), 38–47.

W161. Woolfolk, George R. "Sources of the History of the Negro in Texas, with Special Reference to Their Implications for Research in Slavery." *Negro History Bulletin* 20:5 (Feb. 1957), 105 + .

W162. Work, Monroe N. *A Bibliography of the Negro in Africa and America.* New York: H.W. Wilson, 1928, 698 pp. Reprinted in 1965 by Argosy-Antiquarian, and in 1966 by Octagon Books.

W163. Work, Monroe N. "Some Best Books on the American Negro." *Missionary Review of the World* 45 (June 1922), 507–10.

W164. Worrill, Conrad. "Books That Present Theories and Policies Designed to Disrupt and Dismantle the National Black Community." *Black Books Bulletin* 7:1 (1980?), 56–7.

W165. Worsham, John P., Jr. *A Bibliographical Guide to the Black Literature in Planning and Urban Studies Periodicals, 1970–1978*. Public Administration Series no. 299. Monticello, Ill.: Vance Bibliographies, 1979, 26 pp.

W166. Woy, James B. *Helping Minority Business: a list of selected materials*. Chicago, Ill.: American Library Association, Business Service Reference Committee, 1972, 20 pp.

W167. Wright, Dorothy. "Comprehensive Thesaurus of Literature by and on the Negro: H.P. Slaughter Collection." *School and Society* 63 (June 15, 1946), 430–1.

W168. Wright, James E. "Help Change the Pecking Order: a booklist for Negro History Week, Feb. 9–15, 1969." *Library Journal* 94 (Jan. 15, 1969), 153–5.

W169. Wright, Jerome. *Black Background—1966*. Monterey, Cal.: Monterey Peninsula College Library.

W170. Wright, Josephine R.B. "A Checklist of the Published Compositions of Gussie Davis in the Whittlesey File at the Library of Congress." *The Black Perspective in Music* 6:2 (Fall 1978), 194–9.

* Wright, L. See O29.

* Wright, Laurie. See D19.

W171. Wright, Lockwood. *Journal of the Board of Trustees and Minutes of Committees and Inspectors of the Freedman's Saving and Trust Co., 1865–1874*. National Archives Microfilm Publications Pamphlet Describing M874. Washington, D.C.: National Archives and Records Service, 1972, 4 pp.

W172. Wright, Robert Ernest Middleton. *Human Rights: a booklist*. Worthing, Sussex, England: Worthing College of Further Education Library, 1968, 10 pp.

* Wyetch, Pauline. See Mc31.

W173. Wyeth, Ola M. "Negro Spirituals." *Bulletin of the American Library Association* 26 (Aug. 1932), 520–4.

* Wynar, Lubomyr. See B350.

XYZ

* Yagerman, Howard. See R115.

Y1. Yates, E.G. "Annotated Cumulated Index to the 'Journal of Negro History' from January, 1916, through October, 1940." M.S.L.S. thesis, Atlanta University, 1951, 197 pp.

* Yavenditti, Mary Lu. See M90.

Y2. Yellin, Jean Fagan. "Afro-American Women, 1800–1910: excerpts from a working bibliography." *In* Gloria T. Hull, Patricia Bell Scott, and

Barbara Smith, eds. *But Some of Us Are Brave: black women's studies.* Old Westbury, N.Y.: Feminist Press, 1982, pp. 221–44.

Y3. Yellin, Jean Fagan. "An Index to Literary Materials in 'The Crisis,' 1910–1934: articles, belles lettres, and book reviews." *College Language Association Journal* 14:4 (June 1971), 452–65; 15:2 (Dec. 1971), 197–234.

Y4. Yelton, Donald C. *A Survey of the Special Negro Collection and Related Resources of the Vail Memorial Library of Lincoln University.* Lincoln University, Penn.: Lincoln University, 1964, 15 pp.

Y5. Young, Caroline. "The Black Scholar and the Social Sciences." *Black Scholar* 7:7 (Apr. 1976), 18–28.

Y6. Young, Pauline. *The Afro-American: a selected list of books, syllabi, and other sources.* Allentown, Del.: Author(?), 1968(?).

Y7. Young, Pauline. "The American Negro: a bibliography for school libraries." *Wilson Bulletin* 7 (May 1935), 563.

Z1. Zakharova, M.N. "Vtoraia Zhizn' Abolitsionistskoi Knigi" [The Second Life of the Abolitionist Book]. *Novaia i Noveishaia Istoriia* [USSR] (1972), 172–9.

Z2. Zaretsky, Irving I., and Cynthia Shambaugh. *Spirit Possession and Spirit Mediumship in Africa and Afro-America: an annotated bibliography.* New York: Garland, 1978, 443 pp.

* Ziegler, Anette. See B227.

CHRONOLOGICAL INDEX

This index consists of those entries that indicate the inclusive dates of the bibliographies they describe. They have been arranged here in chronological order to facilitate the study of particular periods as well as comparative studies.

1800–1899

1950–1959

1960–1969

SUBJECT INDEX

This index consists essentially of the key words in each title of every bibliography listed in the main body of the book; terms that describe the subjects of the bibliographies—if those terms are not themselves part of the titles, and if it was possible to determine them; the names of the institutions and organizations that sponsored bibliographies, including the institutional libraries from whose collections individual bibliographies were compiled; categories that describe types of material, such as theses, manuscripts, newspapers, and so on.

Public libraries and schools are identified by state, but colleges and universities are not. The locations of special collections are not given unless the name of the collection is a commonplace one. For example, the Benjamin William Arnett Papers are simply listed as such; but, Negro Collection (Hampton Institute).

Nicknames are in parentheses following the person's real names; for example, Ory, Edward (Kid). If the real name is not known, only the nickname is given. People who are best known by their nicknames or assumed names are listed under that name with a "see" reference from the real name to the nickname: McKay, Eleanor Gough. See Holiday, Billie.

Direct action, H82

Disadvantaged, C167, G58, L74, P70, P81, P119, R70, R73, R139, S65, S207, W96

Disadvantaged children, A76, A113, B30, E3, L20, M36, M104, W26, W96

Disciples of Christ Historical Society, D158A, P128

Discographical Society, London, N97

Discographies, A46, A53, C165, M127, P31, R153

Discrimination, B112, B311, C14, D114, D115, D116, D117, D118, L118, M98, R16, S79, S94, S141, V54, V55, W69

Diseases, D50

Dissent, H82

Dissertations. See Theses.

District of Columbia Public Library, A27, B252, N57, P142

Dixie Syncopators, W110

Dixon, Dean, S28

Documents. See also Archives, P102, S197, S296

Dodds, Johnny, J89, T18, V29, V53

Dodds, Warren (Baby), V38

Dodson, Owen, H35B

Dolphy, Eric, K95, R5, W14

Domino, Antoine (Fats), A93, P49

Dorham, Kenny, J37

Dorsey, Thomas A., P61, V57

Douglas, Aaron, C71, H109, T95

Douglass, Frederick, C5, L99, T110A

Dover, Cedric, A87

Drama. See also Playwrights; Theatre, C61, F79, K58, L32, L71, L132, S283

Drew, Benjamin, B141

Drew, Charles R., C123

Driscoll Collection, F48

Driskell, Davis, S78

Dropouts, S7

Drums, C32

Du Bois, William E.B., A94, A95, A96, C72, G73, G74, K25, K93, L43, L121, Mc23, Mc25, P25A, P25B, P25C, P26, P27, P27A, P28, S8, S102, T110A

Duke University, B279, D169, L117

Dunbar, Paul Laurence, B86, B212, B213, B345, J10, K74, L41, M59, M84, T87

Dunbar-Nelson, Alice Ruth (Moore), W122

Dunham, Katherine, K32

Dunn, Johnny, J89A, V30

E. Azalia Hackley Memorial Collection, C61, L71

Earlham College, F10

East Cleveland, Ohio, Public Library, B150

East St. Louis Race Riot, A107A

Eastern Michigan University, A82, B289, B349, K29, R18

Eastern New Mexico University, R89

Eckstein, Billy M162

Ecology, D43

Economics, B29, B297, B320, D25, D149, G1, G55, G59, H25, L97, M66, M101, P25, R62, S57, T47

Edinboro State College, D86

Editors, S202

Education, A47, B118, B156, B234, B235, B267, C6, C7, C8, C9, C10, C38, C42, C99, C159, C160, C168, C197, D107, D115, E3, E4, E48, G52, G59, G92, H28, H53A, J41, J109, J121, K7, K81, K85, L3, L14, L81, L103, Mc5, M92, M101, N28, N101, N114, P15, P15A, P18, P37, P59, P70, P77, P81, P89, P119, P132, R16, R27, R60, R69A, S6, S7, S72, S77, S94, S95, S143, S167, S168, S169, S211, S285, T20, T21, T41, T42, T82, W23, W39, W40, W41, W42, W77, W96

Education, higher. See also Colleges and universities, B67, B131, B298, C70, D47, D145, D153, G58, H24, H117A, H118, S95, S138, U3

Education, in-service, C213

Education, integrated, B88, S167, S168, S169, W42

Education, intergroup, C148, G65, H120, P18, P77

Education, segregated, S53, S94, W39

Educational literature, I20

Educational Testing Service, R73

Educators, B89

El Camino College, A28, D120